Londoners

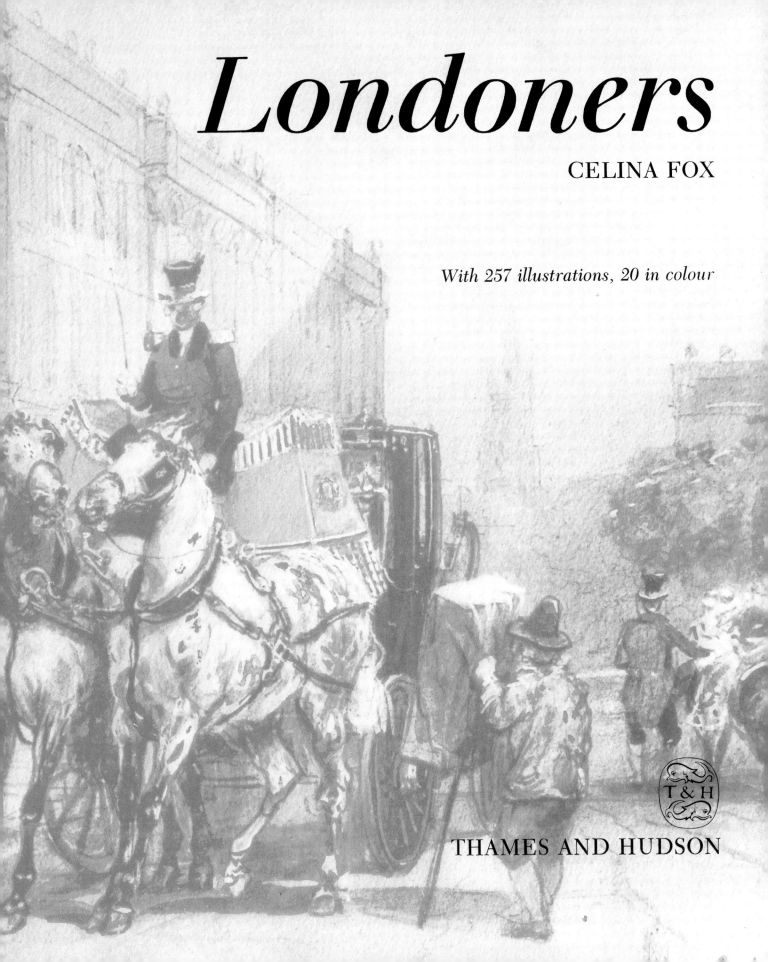

Londoners

CELINA FOX

With 257 illustrations, 20 in colour

THAMES AND HUDSON

For my parents

Printed and bound in Spain by Artes Gráficas Toledo, S.A.
DL.TO: 1860–1986

Contents

ACKNOWLEDGMENTS   6

INTRODUCTION   7

1   *The Crowd*   10

2   *Society*   74

3   *Merchants*   94

4   *Craftsmen*   106

5   *Servants*   126

6   *Markets*   138

7   *Street Traders*   154

8   *Labourers*   168

9   *The Poor*   184

10   *Law and Criminals*   200

11   *Education and the Young*   216

12   *Sickness and Old Age*   232

POSTSCRIPT *Strangers and Foreigners*   244

NOTES ON THE TEXT   249

NOTES ON THE ILLUSTRATIONS   255

SELECT BIBLIOGRAPHY   267

INDEX   269

Acknowledgments

In writing a book that attempts to cover so wide a field, I am deeply indebted to the work of many scholars on specific artists, movements and periods. I have also been greatly assisted by the willingness of curators to think laterally across their collections, formally catalogued using systems from which 'Londoners' are not readily retrievable. The following, in particular, helped to make my research both rewarding and enjoyable: Patricia Allderidge, David Bindman, Brigitte Bötel, Wallace Breem, David Blayney Brown, Frances Carey, Samuel F. Clapp, David Cordingly, Malcolm Cormack, Dr and Mrs J. Th. Semeijns de Vries van Doesburg, William Drummond, Judy Egerton, Elizabeth Einberg, Chris Ellmers, Janet Foster, Philippa Glanville, Antony Griffiths, Susan Hare, John and Eileen Harris, Wesley Harry, Ralph Hyde, Richard Jeffree, Vivien Knight, Comte Henri de Limburg Stirum, Ian Lyle, James Miller, Tessa Murdoch, Marcia Pointon, Roy Porter, Harley Preston, The Hon. Jane Roberts, William Schupbach, David Scrase, James Sewell, Peyton Skipwith, Michael Snodin, Lindsay Stainton, Gillian Sutherland, Anne Sutton, Lavinia Wellicome and Stephen Wildman.

In the Museum of London I received constant encouragement and support from Valerie Cumming and Mireille Galinou. I am also enormously grateful to Shirley Waller for her untiring and uncomplaining efforts to decipher my drafts and type the manuscript. The Museum's photographers, John Edwards and Barrington Gray, played the major role in producing the illustrations. I should also like to thank Thames and Hudson for their time and care in publishing this work. Finally, I owe a personal debt to Elspeth Juda, Arthur Crook and Juliet Wrightson, Marilyn Edelson and Robert Rubin for enabling me to escape from London when the canvas became too crowded.

This work arose out of a sense of irritation that almost every book written on the depiction of London in art and every exhibition to take the city as its theme concerned themselves primarily with the buildings of the metropolis. The millions of inhabitants who provided the *raison d'être* for the physical fabric of London had all but been ignored.

The reasons for their omission are understandable. Buildings are facts: they can be measured, costed, classified, assigned to architects and builders. People cannot be categorized so readily. I hope to restore their presence to the visual history of London.

My guiding principle has been to focus attention on the images themselves, not to indulge in an exercise in parallelism whereby the pictures are used merely to support what we already know. The aim of the artists whose work I have selected was never simply to mirror society, and rarely an attempt at documentary reportage. I want to place the images within the context of the society that surrounded them. In order to recover their meaning, we have to pose the questions which an historian might ask of any document: from whom did it come, to whom was it directed, in what circumstances, and using which conventions. The resulting interaction between the artistic and social conditions offers some fresh and distinct insights into the character of the city, enriching our sense of its past.

My main problem was to decide on the range of visual material to include. 'Urban genre' is a useful modern compound term for paintings of everyday life in the city, but when used retrospectively it blurs the distinctions between artists whose aims were widely differing. The depiction of common life certainly came low in the hierarchy of the arts ordained by academic theory. But Hogarth, for one, sought to invest his 'low' subject matter with the 'high' moral meaning which history painting alone, at the top of the academic hierarchy, was thought to impart. Again, the 'fancy pictures' painted by Mercier, Zoffany, Walton, Morland and Wheatley of urban subjects – porters, maids and street sellers – were not primarily reflections of city life but exercises in poetic allusion, frequently with reference to the Old Masters. Even in the nineteenth century when the academic structure was crumbling, painters of urban life, paying lip-service to Hogarth, still professed to endow their works with generalized moral reflections on the state of modern society. Some of the paintings I have included were commissioned as portraits but, more than being statements about the sitter's personality, they give some indication through setting or symbol of his or her calling – an emblematic style of portraiture first brought to London by Holbein.

There is unfortunately no English equivalent to the extraordinary wealth of pictures depicting scenes from everyday life which were produced in Holland during the seventeenth century. The development of a native school of water-colour artists in the eighteenth century helps to redress the balance, although landscape and topography more frequently supplied the subject matter. Preliminary drawings based on local models by artists working in London occasionally display an immediacy of observed life entirely absent from the finished paintings, and I have noted a number of such examples. Artists have always drawn the life around them but in the early nineteenth century a new emphasis was placed in

ST. PAUL'S FROM LUDGATE HILL

some circles on outdoor sketching as part of an artist's training, and I trace the effect of this development on urban subject matter.

Prints did not suffer overmuch from the academic constraints which affected paintings. Besides using engravings to popularize his art, Hogarth employed the graphic medium as a polemical weapon to convey his feelings on certain issues, such as gin-drinking and cruelty. Prints were also the most important means of spreading visual knowledge about topical events that occurred in London. Many were satirical; some were commemorative; others catered for an interest in the costumes and manners of other nations.

England has always been on the fringes of European artistic life and native talent spluttered into activity only intermittently before the eighteenth century. There were periods of innovation during the Middle Ages, but these were not initiated in the capital. London, unlike Paris, was not a university town and did not enjoy the associated cultural benefits. By the late medieval period, London merchants were acquiring illuminated works from local limners: there are some notable examples of secular illumination produced in London during the fourteenth century, and by the fifteenth century, when London more or less monopolized the country's book trade, some of the works can even be assigned to individual artists, the most famous being William Abell. But it is a poor show compared with the flowering of the arts that was taking place in Italy and the Netherlands during the same period.

The destruction of wall paintings, hangings, sculpture and stained glass during the Reformation, the Interregnum and the Great Fire, necessarily distorts our view of London as an artistic centre. It would nevertheless be almost impossible to imagine how Londoners looked before 1700 without the help of foreign artists, and even in the eighteenth century there are curious lacunae. Depictions of artisans at work in the great period of London craftsmanship are almost non-existent, although such works were being produced at the time in Europe.

There is no butcher's shop like that of Annibale Carracci; no equivalent of the Nuremberg Mendelbuch for a medieval hospice; no portrayal of a civic pageant on the scale of Denis van Alsloot's depiction of the triumph of the Archduchess Isabella in Brussels in 1615; no Copley of a London craftsman to compare with his portrait of Paul Revere; no merchants shown about their business with the empathy of Degas's painting of the New Orleans Cotton Exchange. British art has one major asset in William Hogarth. Hogarth's position is so seminal that some commentators have left him out altogether, overwhelmed by the scale of his innovation and the range of his achievement. One must turn to Ronald Paulson for the detailed cataloguing of his prints and a full-scale biography; a new catalogue of his paintings is being prepared. I have attempted to indicate how the artist broke the mould of convention in virtually every field he touched. He was quite simply unique, even in a European context, and without his example nineteenth-century British art would be immeasurably poorer.

OPPOSITE

St Paul's from Ludgate Hill, 1842
THOMAS SHOTTER BOYS

T o observe a crowd or to be part of its number arouses contradictory reactions. The crowd may be seen to represent the community, or its degeneration, collective solidarity or the break-up of order, just as the physical space which contains it can be viewed as protective shelter or as dangerous territory. To be immersed in the crowd can induce a feeling of sociability or of loneliness; as Boswell observed, 'It was curious to find of how little consequence each individual was in such a crowd.'

This variety of response depends at least in part on the nature of the crowd under discussion. In recent years, historians have viewed the London crowd almost exclusively in terms of social protest. Yet the majority of mass gatherings in the city had little to do with the politics of direct action. Crowds assembled on ceremonial and festive occasions, to honour heads of state, to express pride in civic achievement, to celebrate traditional religious and secular holidays, national victories and peace treaties. Crowds formed to watch or participate in every kind of popular recreation. And many of the streets themselves – with their narrowness, the reckless riders and coachmen, and the hordes of itinerant tradesmen and street sellers – were crowded. It is this broader definition which should be used when considering the depiction of the London crowd in art over the centuries.

There was no uniform method of portraying a crowd. Artists were subject to the social attitudes and constraints of the day – on a basic level, if they hoped to find a market for their work – as well as the stylistic conventions at their disposal. It cannot even be assumed that the crowd was deemed to be appropriate subject matter at all until comparatively recently. In the earliest representations of mass gatherings, the presence of the crowd was recorded merely to reinforce the image of state and civic authority, and not for its own sake; nor was it broken down into constituent members. Such works commemorate royal entries into the city, Lord Mayors' processions and ambassadorial disembarkations at the Tower. They were usually commissioned by the dignitaries involved, who affirmed their own position through the subservient assemblage of citizens. Reproduced in the form of prints for wide circulation, these images could be used as propaganda on behalf of the existing order of society.

Prints also served as advertisements for and souvenirs of traditional, more popular forms of entertainment in London. Paintings of extraordinary events like the Frost Fairs held on the Thames were executed by Dutch artists working in England in the seventeenth century. But again, it is the event itself which commanded the interest of the artist more than the antics of the people who had come to participate. The same may be said of the majority of depictions of the 'shows of London' into the nineteenth century.

William Hogarth (1697–1764) was the first native-born artist to portray the common people massed together, to bring recognizable types, characterized by dress and physiognomy, into focus in the foreground of his works. He diffused the centre of interest away from the procession, fair or execution taking place, and treated the scene as a stage on which the actors up front are turned outwards and engage with the audience. Thus the individual and the mass could be portrayed simultaneously, each counterpointing the other in expressive power.

1
The Crowd

OPPOSITE

Ludgate Hill – A Block in the Street, 1872
after GUSTAVE DORÉ

Doré introduces a hearse threading its way between omnibuses, carts and even a flock of sheep, presumably en route from Smithfield.

Hogarth's example proved to be enormously influential, not only in the field of graphic satire, where Thomas Rowlandson (1756–1827) and Robert Dighton (1752–1814) exploited his compositional forms to full effect, but also for those painters who specialized in the urban genre such as John Collet (1725–80) and William Powell Frith (1819–1909). From the start of the nineteenth century, a new emphasis was placed on outdoor sketching with the result that, at least on an informal basis, the sheer volume of crowds and traffic in the streets was jotted down. But in academic paintings, such mundane subject matter had to undergo a face-lift in order to be rendered sufficiently attractive to a Victorian audience. Frith achieved success by vulgarizing the allusiveness, the open-ended verdict that Hogarth passed on his crowd, into a series of anecdotal tableaux which confirmed the expectations of his audience with regard to urban life and at the same time, possibly, afforded relief from the increasing anonymity and frightening vastness of the city itself.

In the present century, individualization of the person in the crowd has been avoided in favour of the broader abstractions of mass and group identity; this may certainly be seen in terms of changing artistic styles, but also as an attempt to represent the solidarity and power of the people as a whole, uncompromised by individual sentiment.

State and Civic Pageantry

Since the Middle Ages, London and its citizens have acted as a buffer zone between king and country, witnessing the outward show of a complex interchange of mutual obligation. The Mayoralty of London came into existence between 1191 and 1195 during the absence on crusade of Richard the Lionheart, and by the early thirteenth century it was established as annual practice that the newly appointed officer should be presented to the monarch, or his justices who sat at the Palace of Westminster, to swear fealty to him. The journey from the City to Westminster necessitated a procession in state of the Lord Mayor elect, the aldermen, the recorder, sheriffs and other officers. Undertaken on horseback until the 1420s and thereafter by water until 1857, this procession provided the basis for the Lord Mayor's Show. Conversely, from the reign of Richard II, it was customary for the king, on the eve of his coronation, to enter the City in procession. Even before this date, London had celebrated royal victories and alliances, marriages and births with ceremonial pageants. But the royal coronation entry was invested with the greatest significance, symbolizing the dialogue between the monarch and the urban classes, until it was discontinued in the eighteenth century.

These processions and their associated pageants had their origins in folk custom, later modified by the Church into feast-day celebrations. Before the Reformation, midsummer pageants were staged in London on the feast days of St John the Baptist (24 June) and SS Peter and Paul (29 June). The craft guilds organized these festivities, the shows staged for the Mayor, who was chosen from their number, and the royal entries. Municipal government was in their hands; they were accessible to both Court and people; and crucially, they alone had the financial resources. However, pageants also depended on the support of the people for their success. While kings and mayors come and go, it was the crowd that gave their processions the continuity of an institution.

By the end of the fourteenth century, such festivities had a common repertoire. Archways were placed along the route, adorned with castles and fountains bearing allegorical figures representing the virtues as well as biblical and historical characters usually portrayed by children. For a royal entry, a genealogical tree was provided to emphasize the legitimacy of the monarch. The Lord Mayor's procession usually contained references to the patron saint of his guild, its emblems and insignia, and sometimes to an illustrious guild member of the past. There were minstrels and banners to add to the festive spirit. A number of written accounts record the order of procession and the specially commissioned pageants that were enacted at pre-ordained stages on the way. But, compared with continental Europe, few visual commemorations of these public expressions of national and civic government have survived.

There are medieval illuminated manuscripts which depict the entry of the monarch into London some years after the event; for example, that of Edward I in the *Brut*, a popular history of Britain written in French verse around 1338–40 (British Library. Egerton MS.3028.f.62). Richard II is shown being led into London in Creton's *History of Richard, King of England*, begun in 1399 (British Library. Harley MS.1319.f.53v). Although giving no indication of the festivities which accompanied his entry, the latter manuscript at least shows a group of London citizens standing by the city gate to greet him.

However there is no extant illustration of a full-scale royal entry into London until the seventeenth century. Such a dearth is all the more surprising in view of the rich supply of works depicting spectacle and ceremonial in the rest of Europe. There were manuscript drawings illustrating pageants dating back to the fifteenth century, and later engravings or woodcuts in printed books. The entry of Joanna of Castile into Lille in 1496 was commemorated in an illuminated manuscript, as was that of Mary Tudor into Paris in 1415, the Archduke Charles into Bruges in 1515 and Francis I into Lyons in the same year. The Emperor Maximilian I commissioned a whole series of illustrated books to celebrate his life and princely activities, notably Jörg Kölderer's magnificent *Triumphzug*, which depicts his state processions.[1]

The major Continental processions were conceived in the iconographic tradition of the Roman triumph. Ancient precedents were still to be found on Trajan's Column and the Arches of Titus and Constantine to inspire the artists of Renaissance Italy. Mantegna's *The Triumphs of Caesar* was known outside Italy in engravings and was influential in transforming processional arches and chariots into the styles of classical Rome; the monarch was glorified as emperor reborn. The progresses of the rival French and Imperial courts must surely have reached the Tudor court through illustrated as well as ambassadorial accounts; certainly Henry VIII owned a number of portraits of both the Emperor and the French king.[2] But in the first two decades of his reign, at least, the artistic influence of the Renaissance seems to have passed by the English court. The Westminster

Tournament Roll, nearly sixty feet in length, provides a unique record of the great tournament held at Westminster on 12 and 13 February 1511 to celebrate the birth of a son to Catherine of Aragon, recorded in terms of late medieval heraldry.[3] Of the extraordinarily lavish joint entry made by Henry with his nephew the Emperor Charles into London in 1522, although clearly devised as a public spectacle to demonstrate state policy, no visual commemoration would appear to have been made, either as a private token or an instrument of propaganda.[4] Even in the 1530s, Henry's desire to impress his bulky presence on his people does not seem to have extended much beyond Whitehall.[5]

A poignant memento of Edward VI's short reign is provided by the watercolour copy made by Samuel Hieronymous Grimm (1733–94), after a painting which hung in the dining room at Cowdray, Sussex, until it was destroyed by fire in 1793 (*see* col. pl. I). It illustrates the coronation entry of the king into London in 1547, and although it is difficult to be certain of its stylistic origins, given the interpretation of another eye, it would appear to be conceived in the Flemish tradition. There is no trace of the pageantry which is known to have taken place on that occasion, still less any semblance to an Imperial triumph. But the inclusion of the citizens themselves along the route as audience, as well as in the narrow streets and passages of the medieval city, suggests that the artist felt at ease incorporating the humdrum details of everyday life into grandiose themes of religious or political import.

No such record exists of any part of Elizabeth's reign. Contemporary reference was made to a 'Book of Pictures' commissioned to record her coronation procession, but it might simply have been the sketchbook of pen drawings outlining the order of procession made by one of the College of Arms' heralds as a guide to procedure and precedence (British Library. Egerton MS.3320). Despite the Queen's evident concern to perpetuate her memory in a wealth of portraits, no work identifying her specifically with her capital and its citizens has been uncovered. *Eliza Triumphans*, dating from the last years of the Queen's reign and attributed to Robert Peake (*c*.1555–1619), was probably commissioned by Edward Somerset, 4th Earl of Worcester. Surrounded by courtiers and led by six Knights of the Garter in a canopied chair on wheels, the Queen is traditionally thought to be depicted at the marriage of one of her Maids of Honour, Anne Russell, to Worcester's heir, Lord Herbert, which took place at Blackfriars in June 1600. However, the background clearly has nothing to do with London and perhaps alludes instead to Worcester's properties on the Welsh borders, Chepstow and Raglan Castles, the picture simply celebrating his new appointment as Master of the Horse in succession to the Earl of Essex in 1601.[6]

The early-seventeenth-century depictions of pageants in London concentrated in the main on the iconography of the procession, not the impact they had on the spectators. The entry devised for James I in March 1604 was the first to be thoroughly grounded in classical precedent. The complex entertainment, written by Thomas Dekker and John Webster, was accompanied by temporary triumphal arches created by Stephen Harrison, a joiner, and recorded in a series of seven engraved plates by William Kip (fl.1598–1635). From the prints it would appear

The Fishmongers' Pageant on Lord Mayor's Day, 1616

The procession was led by an amphibious 'Fishing Busse' containing three men, 'seriously at labour, drawing up their nets laden with living fish and bestowing them liberally among the people'.

that the arches owed something to those devised for Prince Philip, afterward Philip II of Spain, for his entry into Antwerp in 1549 and known in England through woodcuts.[7] Harrison's arches were not only decorated with emblematic figures but also contained niches for musicians, singers and actors; thus Kip's engravings constitute the first depictions, if only in a formal sense, of the actual participants in a pageant.

The Lord Mayor's Show did not emerge as a separate event until the mid sixteenth century, when it supplanted the midsummer pageants staged by guilds before the Reformation. By the Jacobean period it had become highly elaborate, as is shown in a series of anonymous drawings of a pageant devised by Anthony Munday for Lord Mayor's Day in 1616. That year the Lord Mayor, John Leman, came from the Fishmongers' Company, and the motifs included his personal crest – the lemon tree – boats, crowned dolphins, mermaids, mermen, Sir William Walworth (another Lord Mayor from the Fishmongers' Company who slew Wat Tyler in 1381), besides a pageant devoted to the King of the Moors, which was probably left over from the Goldsmiths' Company procession the previous year. The work was presumably commissioned by the Company to commemorate their pre-eminent role; the drawings focus solely on the pageant and even the protagonists are portrayed with little sense of individuality. They cannot be compared with the splendid set of paintings by the Flemish artist Denis van Alsloot of the *Triumph of the Archduchess Isabella in the Brussels Ommegank* (or Great Procession) of Sunday 31 May 1615, which depicts not only the pageant but also the citizens of Brussels watching and participating in the occasion (Victoria and Albert Museum; Prado, Madrid).

Less grandiose views of state and civic pageantry in London are to be found in
the *alba amicorum* kept by students (particularly those from German Protestant
universities) on their travels, in which the names of friends and acquaintances
were recorded for remembrance sake. Some entries included apt quotations and
dedications; others were decorated not only with the coats of arms of the
signatories but also with small illustrations of the places that had been visited. Men
and women wearing the typical dress of the locality were a favourite subject, as
were leading figures in Society. In London, several students obtained depictions
of James I riding in the city accompanied by train bearers; a view of the Lord
Mayor's procession was usually based on the conventional civic procession
engraved below Norden's London map of 1600.[8]

Charles I's entry into London before his coronation was first cancelled because
of an outbreak of the plague and again the following year, at the King's request;
like his father before him, Charles preferred the comparative security of the court
masque to public displays of civic pageantry.[9] However, the entry of his mother-
in-law, Marie de Médicis, into London in 1637 occasioned a series of anonymous
etchings which were issued in Jean Puget de la Serre's *Histoire de l'Entrée de la
Reyne Mère du Roy Très Chréstien dans la Grande Bretagne* of 1639. The view of
the procession moving along Cheapside is particularly well known, more as a
record of the appearance of pre-Fire London than for the people in it.
Nevertheless, it is the first surviving view – unless one counts the copy of the
Edward VI entry – to convey some impression of the relationship between the
spectacle and the citizens of London at their windows, on balconies and in
specially erected boxes behind the guard lining the route.

The Restoration brought renewed opportunities for commemorating state
occasions which glorified the monarchy, and a number of Dutch artists came to
England eager to supplement native talent. A painting was executed of the entry of
Charles II into London on 29 May 1660 at the head of five regiments of cavalry
proceeding down Whitehall to the Banqueting Hall, watched by crowds of
onlookers (Private Collection). Although attributed to Isaac Fuller (c.1610–72), it
seems too stiff and formal to be the work of the artist who depicted the King's escape
from the Battle of Worcester with such directness and bravura.[10] A more spirited
attempt to convey the brilliance of pageantry was made in the painting attributed to
François du Chastel which records the disembarkation of Claude Lamoral, Prince de
Ligne, at the Tower in 1660, at the start of his mission to convey the felicitations of
Philip IV of Spain to the newly restored monarch (Prince de Ligne, Beloeil). One of
two works commissioned by the Prince to mark the event, it is doubtful whether the
artist was a witness to the scene. More probably he relied on the prints produced
by Wenceslaus Hollar (1607–77) in the 1640s, specifically his view of the Tower
and a series on the dress of London citizens called *Theatrum Mulierum*.[11] Most of
the people lining the wharf are wearing sober Puritan garb which contrasts with
the splash of scarlet and gold of the Prince's entourage and the royal carriage which
the King had thoughtfully sent to meet him.[12]

Charles's splendid entry into London on 22 April 1661, the eve of his
coronation, was deliberately staged to blot out memories of the City's ambivalent

cersidents.   Lordmeijer   scheiffs   Aldermans

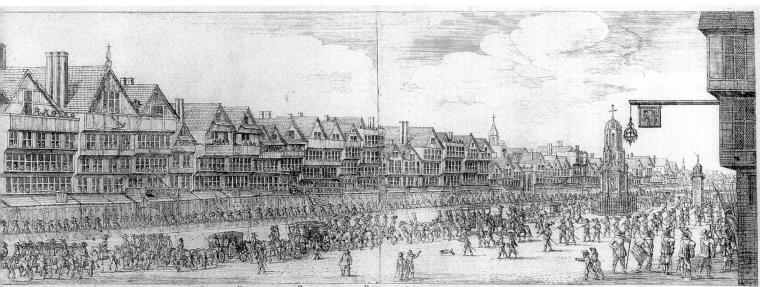

ENTRÉE ROYALLE DE LA REYNE MERE DV ROY TRES-CHRESTIEN DANS LA VILLE DE LONDRES.

loyalties during the Civil War and was recorded in both engravings and paintings. *The Entertainment of Charles II . . .* was published in 1662 by John Ogilby, with engravings by David Loggan from drawings by Sir Balthazar Gerbier of the four huge triumphal arches which lined the processional route, and also with etchings by Hollar of the cavalcade. These were used as the basis for a painting of the royal entry by Dirck Stoop (*c.*1610–83?). As court painter in Lisbon, Stoop created a series of prints depicting Catherine of Braganza's journey to London in 1662, detailing the order of procession and topography of Lisbon with great accuracy.[13] He was certainly not in London to witness the royal entry, but the painting might have been commissioned by the Queen after her arrival. No attempt is made to record either the setting or the spectators, and even the four great arches, presumably based on Loggan's engravings, are rather sketchy. Instead the artist concentrates on the details of the procession itself, which is given an allegorical resonance by the misty no-man's-land of the setting.

The role that art could play in enhancing the position of a monarch was exploited further by William of Orange, first in Holland, then in France and finally in England, with the help of the young Dutch printmaker Romeyn de Hooghe (1645–1708). This artist first rose to prominence with his prints celebrating the victory on the Thames of the Dutch over the English in the Second Anglo-Dutch War and the Peace Treaty of Aachen in 1668. The works were bold in concept, for instead of the coldness and sobriety of most commemorative art, de Hooghe produced a rich panorama of human activity, creating a record which bursts with life. Similarly, the prints which anticipated and accompanied William's arrival in

England convey a sense of vitality and joyous welcome, propagating in visual terms a message of popular support. In fact, for all the topographical backdrops of London and the countryside, de Hooghe did not accompany his patron; the rhetoric and hubris of his compositions carry a conviction which overrides the more mundane considerations of authentic reportage.[14] Few artists could match his daring. In comparison, the painting attributed to Alexander van Gaelen (1670–1728) of the *Entry of William III into London* is lacking in panache: the formal procession in the foreground is static and conventional (Private Collection). In Allard's print of the *Reception of George I at St James's Palace* on 20 September 1714, de Hooghe's sweeping baroque designs are reduced to a tidy formula. It took the Italian artist Luca Carlevaris (1663–1730) to unite de Hooghe's sense of drama with the brilliance of Venetian colouring and produce a gloriously dynamic painting of a state occasion, *The Arrival of the Two Venetian Ambassadors, Nicolo Errero and Celvisi Pisani at the Tower Stairs*, an event which took place on 30 May 1707. Probably commissioned, like the Prince de Ligne's painting, by the ambassador – in this case Pisani – Carlevaris's work has a vibrant sense of movement entirely lacking from the earlier painting. By placing the wharf on a diagonal axis, the artist draws the spectator into the scene as if on board a ship coming into harbour, greeted by the cannon fire, the ships, brilliantly clad royal bargemen, soldiers, citizens and London itself.

After the Restoration, new life was pumped into the Lord Mayor's procession, which had been abandoned in 1639. A painting by an unknown Dutch artist working in England depicts the flotilla of livery company barges being rowed to

The Chariot of the Virgin Queen, Lord Mayor's Day, 1686

According to a contemporary account by Matthew Taubman, the 'Imperial Chariot of Roman Form' used to convey the Virgin Queen was worthy of particular attention: 'the Magnificence of the Structure, the Elegance of the Contrivance, and the Costliness of the Work, has hardly ever yet been parallel'd.'

Westminster on a breezy Lord Mayor's Day in 1683, with the Banqueting House and Whitehall in the distance (Her Majesty the Queen).[15] Marcellus Lauron (1648?–1701) seems to have attended the show several times in the late 1670s and he drew the Lord Mayor going by barge to Westminster, and proceeding on horseback in a cavalcade through the City, along with the sword bearer, standard bearers and musicians.[16] A particularly rare survival is the anonymous fan design which depicts the Lord Mayor's procession of 1686 at the moment when the chariot of the Virgin Queen, emblem of the Mercers' Company, is drawn through the Stocks Market. It is extraordinary to note that this work constitutes the first occasion on which the three elements of pageantry are brought together: the official procession, the pageant itself and the audience, here seen greeting the festivities with some involvement and enthusiasm.

By the late seventeenth century, much of the solemn rhetoric and elaborate symbolism of the pageants had lost their meaning for the audience; Pepys thought them very silly and absurd. Lord Mayor's Day was simply an excuse for festive and riotous behaviour, as numerous accounts testify. Ned Ward, writing in the *London Spy* in 1706, complained, 'I was so close Imprisoned between the Bums and Bellies of the Multitude that I was almost squeez'd as flat as a Napkin in a Press.'[17]

Specially conceived pageants for the procession were abandoned after 1702, and the Hanoverian dynasty did not adopt the tradition of entering the City in state on the eve of a coronation. In fact, to some extent the two traditions merged as it became the custom for the monarch to attend the Lord Mayor's procession in the

first year of the new reign, and for lesser members of the royal family to appear in other years. Thus Frederick Prince of Wales and Princess Augusta are depicted by Hogarth in the scene, *The Industrious 'Prentice Lord Mayor of London* of 1747; indeed, they represent the last bastion of dignity on an occasion which had clearly become dominated by the unruliness of the mob. Hogarth stands the traditional commemorative genre on its head, so that instead of the crowd being subjugated by the procession, they almost overwhelm the carriage. This example of the artist's capacity to undermine the norm, to bring the life of the people to the forefront of a painting, was crucial for the way in which Londoners were depicted. His influence can be seen in a print of 1761, *A View of Cheapside, as it Appeard on Lord Mayor's Day Last* by John June (fl. 1740–70), in which it seems as though the presence of George III scarcely encouraged orderly behaviour. Canaletto stayed aloof from the mêlée, choosing to portray a dignified procession of civic barges on the Thames, rather than grappling with a tortuous journey through narrow City streets.[18]

The formal processional print continued to be issued as a souvenir on occasions such as coronations, Lord Mayor's processions and peace celebrations, with little innovation except in the medium employed. An especially magnificent series of aquatints commemorating the coronation of George IV, with a set of portraits of the leading figures involved, was produced by Whittaker and Nayler from the 1820s.[19] On a humbler level, lively woodcut representations of such events were published by Thompson's of Smithfield, who specialized in cheap topical prints.[20]

London Bridge on the Night of the Marriage of the Prince and Princess of Wales (The Sea-King's Peaceful Triumph on London Bridge, 10th of March, 1863)
WILLIAM HOLMAN HUNT

Hunt himself witnessed the celebrations that took place on London Bridge for the marriage of the Prince and Princess of Wales. The view is from Fishmongers' Hall looking south along the bridge, which was decorated with flags fluttering in the harsh artificial light cast from the braziers.

But something of the lustre of Lord Mayors' processions was lost as the competition from so many other forms of public spectacle grew in the nineteenth century. The Lord Mayor ceased to be transported by water to Westminster in 1857, and from 1883 onwards he only had to travel as far as the Law Courts to swear his oath of loyalty to the monarch.

It took a conscious effort on the part of artists to revive a sense of state and civic spectacle and inject an ancient tradition with new vigour. The most successful paintings worked outward from the vitality supplied by the crowd itself, transmitting the human reaction across the staged formalities. Thus William Holman Hunt (1827–1910), with a self-conscious use of Hogarthian subject matter, portrayed the scene on London Bridge on the night of the marriage of the Prince and Princess of Wales in 1863. So too, William Logsdail (1859–1944) in his painting of the Lord Mayor's Procession of 1887, entitled *The Ninth of November*, from a privileged position at the front of the crowd conveyed the space and dignity accorded to the procession itself while rendering in graphic detail the crush of people around him (*see* col. pl. XVII). And for the first time, one of the obvious features of these glittering occasions is honestly portrayed: the contrast of the gilded coach and brilliant traditional dress with the grey dampness of a typical London November day and the shabby drabness of many of the Londoners watching.

Popular Amusement and Entertainment

Whereas it was to be expected that pictures of state and civic processions should be commissioned by the leading protagonists and that the crowd watching them should only gradually come to be regarded as an essential ingredient when the need for popular support became obvious, the impetus which led to the production of works showing the traditional festivities of the people is less apparent. Certainly, the theme had been represented in Netherlandish art since the sixteenth century when Jan Brueghel the Elder drew on a rich medieval repertoire of folklore, proverbs, morality plays and holy day processions to create a comprehensive cycle of peasant life, albeit with didactic intent. In the seventeenth century, David Vinckboons specialized in painting *kermis*; later, Jan Steen recorded Twelfth Night and Shrovetide customs with anecdotal detail while the *Bamboccianti* artists Jan Miel and Jan Lingelbach depicted festive and carnival scenes set in Rome and the Campagna. It cannot be said that England provided as fertile territory for inspiration, given the discontinuities inflicted by the Reformation and the Puritans on the traditional calendar festivities of Shrove Tuesday, May Day, Ascension Day, Midsummer and St Bartholomew's Day. More to the point, the country simply did not produce artists who had the skills to specialize in the genre, even if there had been sufficient numbers of people wanting to purchase that type of work. The indifferent artistic climate before the eighteenth century is a problem to which we shall repeatedly return.

Yet urban festivities played an essential role in the lives of ordinary citizens, providing them with an excuse for time off work, a brief taste of freedom, even the opportunity to undermine the normal order of society. On May Day, milkmaids danced in garlands made up of customers' silver, pots and pans, accompanied by blackened chimney-sweeps as their beaux. All ranks participated in the fun, the liberation from convention appealing to those whose lives were customarily bound by more rigid codes of behaviour. The capacity of folk gatherings to suggest a pre-urban innocence and picturesque naivety at first explains their presence in pictures of London and its environs. A group of dancers and musicians entertain important guests in the painting executed around 1568 by the Flemish artist, Joris Hoefnagel (1542–1600), *A Fête at Bermondsey* (The Marquis of Salisbury, Hatfield House, Herts.; *see* p.78). A band of mummers performs for a small group of gentrified spectators on the banks of the river in an early-seventeenth-century work by an unknown Flemish artist, *The Thames at Richmond* (Fitzwilliam Museum, Cambridge).[21] The painting executed by Jan Griffier the Elder (1652–1718) of *The Thames at Horseferry* is enlivened with May Day dancers and musicians diverting the company gathered outside a tavern (Galleria Sabauda, Turin). Essentially, the latter two paintings were topographical in intent but, as map-makers had discovered, the introduction of some figures illustrative of the costume and customs of a country provided additional interest.

It took, however, more than a partiality to quaint staffage for anything approximating to a 'merry company' genre to develop. The extraordinary phenomenon of the Frost Fair in London encouraged a closer delineation of the manners of the people. As the Thames was allowed to meander largely at will and its flow was partially dammed by the multi-arched London Bridge, it was a much slower river than it is today. When a hard frost occurred over any length of time, it froze solid. Dutch artists recorded the fairs held on the ice not because, like Avercamp, they were obsessed with skating – even in the late seventeenth century the sport was still something of a novelty in England – but because they thus had a golden opportunity to enliven an orthodox urban scene with a dramatic natural wonder and, moreover, to depict Londoners at their most lively and enterprising, visible altogether in an open space. In the great frost of 1676–77, Abraham Hondius (c.1625–91) painted with great accuracy the state of the ice at Temple Stairs, with children and grown-ups delighting in the massive icicle-laden flows (*see* col. pl. III).

The most memorable seventeenth-century Frost Fair took place in 1683–84, when the river froze for nearly six weeks. By New Year's Day, the Thames watermen had been forced to give up their trade and turned instead to using their oars, sails and blankets to construct stalls on the ice. On 5 January, a coach and six was driven successfully across the river for a wager and the Frost Fair began in earnest. A double row of booths ran across the river from Temple Stairs, conveniently near to warehouse suppliers and to custom from both the City and Westminster. The thoroughfare, known as Blanket Street, Freezeland Street or Temple Street, was lined with taverns, cookhouses and even a printer's shop where cards bearing a customer's name, printed on the ice, could be bought for sixpence as a souvenir. The event inspired the predictable quota of topical ballads, some illustrated with crude woodcuts, at least one of which was also printed on the river. But such was the universal appeal of the occurrence, the 'concourse thereon of people of all qualityes and ages', that a higher grade of publication was also produced in commemoration. The most notable were two large copperplate engravings, *A Wonderfull Fair, or A Fair of Wonders*, looking towards the Temple from the south bank; and, even more impressive, *An Exact and Lively Mapp or Representation of Booths and all the Varieties of Showes and Humours upon the ICE on the River of Thames by London*, which was supposedly commissioned by Charles II. Blanket Street crowded with people sledging, skating and dragging boats across the ice, with improvised rings for bear-baiting and ninepins, may be seen in the drawing by Jan Wyck (1652–1700), inscribed, 'Munday February the 4:/Ao 168¾'.[22] A number of paintings of the scene from a similar viewpoint mid-river, looking towards London Bridge, are also attributed to Wyck while Hondius is credited with another picture, known in several versions, which views the ice from the south bank.[23] The 'concourse and all manner of debauchery' continued until the thaw set in at the beginning of February; stallholders rapidly decamped lest the ice break up beneath them, and by the morning of 5 February all trace of the booths, sideshows and crowds had vanished. Nevertheless, the artists' records remain and the subject continued to inspire painters and printmakers in the eighteenth century, whenever the phenomenon returned. Jan Griffier the Younger (fl.1738–73) painted the row of tents at Whitehall in a bird's-eye view of the *Thames during the Great Frost of 1739–40* (Guildhall Art Gallery).[24]

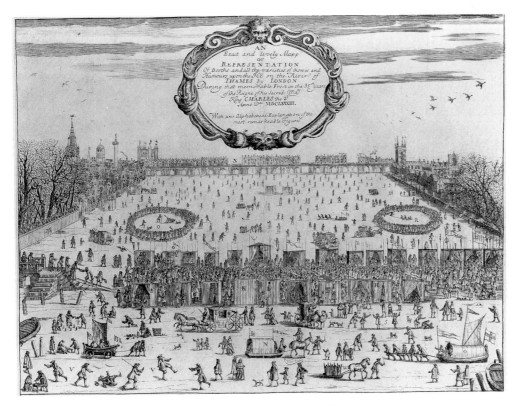

The Frost Fairs were often deemed worthy of comparison with the most famous and ancient of London fairs, St Bartholomew's, which was held annually at Smithfield. Named after the Austin Friars' foundation in a charter granted in 1133 to the prior Rahere, the fair originally took place on 24 and 25 August, but during the reign of Charles II, it was allowed to extend over a fortnight. Its trading function declined and its importance as a centre for all kinds of entertainment increased, despite almost constant complaints about the disorder it encouraged. From the small-scale performances of political squibs and puppet shows, there developed during the course of the eighteenth century more elaborate drolls, ballad operas and pantomimes, performed by some of the leading players of the day who were conveniently taking their summer break from the licensed theatre companies.[25] There were the added attractions of rope-dancers, waxworks, freaks and quacks, bawds and prostitutes. Every variety of refreshment was on offer, particularly the fair's speciality of roast pork. At the height of its popularity, it attracted royalty, leading Society figures, physicians and fellows of the Royal Society interested in seeing the latest freaks. The Fair was celebrated by writers from Shakespeare and Jonson to Wordsworth who, in *The Prelude* Book VII, called it 'This Parliament of Monsters':

> Tents and Booths
> Meanwhile, as if the whole were one vast Mill,
> Are vomiting, receiving, on all sides,
> Men, Women, three-years' Children, Babes in arms.

Yet despite the important place Bartholomew Fair held in the affections of Londoners as a highlight of the social calendar, and its role as the quintessential London experience for many visitors, it does not appear to have received much artistic attention. A souvenir fan design was produced around 1730 showing in naive style the variety of side-shows, booths and refreshment stalls, as well as a range of visitors that included members of the nobility. A number of paintings dating from the same period and attributed to the Spanish artist Balthasar Nebot (fl.1729–c.1762) show the fair in full swing with stalls and shows, puppets, rope-dancers, curds-and-whey sellers being patronized by a mixed crowd of citizens and gentry, and even a visiting Turk.[26]

Surprisingly, in view of the fact that he was born round the corner, Hogarth never seems to have depicted Bartholomew Fair. Instead, in 1733 he painted and engraved a print of Southwark or Lady Fair, possibly because he was spending the summer months on the Surrey side of the Thames. Centred on Borough Street near St George's Church, the Fair had originated with a charter granted by Edward IV in 1462 and ran from 7 to 9 September; by the seventeenth century, like Bartholomew Fair, it extended over a fortnight. According to John Strype, writing in 1720, it was famed chiefly for 'shows, as drolls, puppet-shows, rope-dancing, music booths and tippling houses'. Hogarth includes a comprehensive quota of such wonders but, as in his depiction of the Lord Mayor's procession, attention is really focused on the crowd itself. Everything, from the collapsing stage to the actor being arrested for debt, conspires to bring any elements of magic and fantasy introduced by the shows and spectacles down to an earthy reality.

Efforts to suppress Lady Fair because of the havoc it wreaked on the neighbourhood met with more success than the complaints directed against Bartholomew Fair, for it was finally closed in 1760. May Fair had a much shorter life, despite its fame today, running only from 1688 to 1764, and there seem to be no contemporary depictions of it. However, the semi-rural fairs on the outskirts of London enjoyed a less contentious existence not least because they served a real purpose, combining agricultural business with retailing, as well as providing social entertainment. In a watercolour of 1771, Samuel Grimm depicted *Mortlake Fair* very much in the Dutch manner of a peasant *kermis*. Both John Nixon (fl.c.1781–1818) and Thomas Rowlandson in their watercolours respectively of *Edmonton Statute Fair* and *Brook Green Fair* (Victoria and Albert Museum) used the subject as an opportunity for numerous droll juxtapositions between the well-dressed members of the neighbourhood gentry, the gullible jolly rustics and the cunning show people out to empty their pockets. For the *Microcosm of London*, Rowlandson and Pugin depicted Bartholomew Fair in its final period of brilliance, at night when 'the gaudy glaring lights of various booths' added to the excitement.[27]

Londoners did not have to wait for the annual fairs to seek out their entertainment. Shows of various descriptions were performed throughout the year in the streets, open spaces and pleasure gardens of the capital, indeed, becoming something of a feature of eighteenth-century London. As with the fairs, interest in such amusements transcended the barriers of rank, and wherever they were

The Humours and Diversions of Bartholomew Fair,
c. 1733

Lee and Harper's theatrical booth is next to the main gate of St Bartholomew's Hospital, while 'Pinchbeck's' refers to Christopher Pinchbeck, a skilled clockmaker who specialized in making barrel organs and musical automatons. The crowd is composed of street traders, musicians, showmen, courtesans and a Turkey merchant carrying a coffee pot.

Bartholomew Fair, c. 1730

This fan design provides a comprehensive survey of the Fair's attractions ranging from Lee and Harper's platform stage and the famous conjuror Isaac Fawkes, to gin and roast pork sellers, trinket stalls, a dog cart and even a primitive big wheel.

Southwark Fair, 1733
WILLIAM HOGARTH

Although ostensibly set in front of the old church of St George the Martyr Southwark (demolished the year the print was issued), Hogarth's composition encapsulates the spirit of all London fairs.

Bartholomew Fair, 1811
JOHN NIXON

The shows ranged along the south side of Smithfield include Polito's menagerie, presumably an offshoot of the Exeter Change which he owned from 1810 to 1817.

Punch and Judy Show, 1798
JOHANNES ECKSTEIN

Eckstein's watercolour, exhibited at the Royal Academy in 1799, portrayed a sight which was still relatively novel on the streets of London.

staged small crowds formed to watch. Johannes Eckstein (fl.1770–1802) rendered attractive accounts of two informal gatherings of this kind – a *Punch and Judy Show* and *The Camel at Exeter Change* (*see* col. pl. VIII) – but neither was purely an exercise in the picturesque; both had a more topical appeal.

The English 'Punch' had its roots in a lesser Commedia dell'Arte character, Puncinella, whose role was aggrandized by Italian showmen travelling with marionette puppets through France and coming to London soon after the Restoration. By the eighteenth century, marionette puppet theatres had developed into a fashionable form of entertainment and the character of Punch was grafted onto native traditions of puppet theatre and the long-established role of the clown. But as with all such fashions interest faded, and Punch would have languished in seedy shows at country fairs had it not been adapted as a glove puppet. Marionettes had grown into a comparatively sophisticated art form requiring constant maintenance, elaborate staging and a team of skilled hands; a Punch and Judy show, in contrast, could be set up and staged by one man. The simple booth was easily transported from one street site to another, where it did not have to compete with the noise and alternative attractions of a full-scale fair. First depicted, it would appear, by Rowlandson in the mid 1780s,[28] Punch and Judy shows became a popular subject with artists in the early nineteenth century, notably Benjamin Robert Haydon (1786–1846), who incorporated one in his panorama of London life, *Punch, or May Day* of 1829 (Tate Gallery).

Apart from the Tower, there was no fixed place for the display of menageries in London until the late eighteenth century, when the Exeter Change began to be used for this purpose. The building dated from the last quarter of the seventeenth century and incorporated material from Exeter House, which had stood on the same site in the Strand. On the ground floor there were stalls and toy shops, with a long room above where successful exhibitions of waxworks were held. In the 1770s, Thomas Clarke took over the operation and became a dealer in wild animals and birds. In 1793, his stock was bought by Gilbert Pidcock, who displayed the menagerie alongside human freaks. Evidently, from Eckstein's drawing, some of the animals were allowed into the streets, but Ackermann's *Repository* of 1812 shows the more typical arrangement with the animals caged in.[29]

If Eckstein's watercolours had a contemporaneity, if not exactly a newsworthiness, other shows were being recorded not simply because of their picturesque charm but because they were becoming increasingly rare. None was portrayed being mobbed by crowds; there are only a few onlookers, thus reinforcing the shows' image as survivors from a pre-industrial, almost pastoral age. Charles Cranmer (1780–1841) thus depicted a group of musicians and a street seller of oak leaves in St Margaret Street, Westminster, near his home on *Oak Apple Day*, a festival which took place on 29 May commemorating Charles II's Restoration (Private Collection). May Day festivities survived somewhat longer, but underwent a change in character. In the early 1740s, Francis Hayman (1708–76) had portrayed milkmaids dancing with their attendant chimney-sweeps in a rustic ambience for the decoration of the supper boxes at Vauxhall Gardens, as part of a series devoted to games and pastimes.[30] Hogarth's follower John Collet depicted

May Morning, c. 1760
JOHN COLLET

Collet's motley band of revellers includes a milkmaid with her garland or pyre of silverware and a chimney-sweep fantastically dressed in the full-bottomed wig of a professional man. The music is provided by a hurdy-gurdy player.

May Morning, Upper Lisson Street, Paddington, c. 1840

The folk figure of Jack-in-the-Green is accompanied by a 'lord' and 'lady', in mock court dress, the inevitable little chimney sweeps and a clown dressed in the manner of Grimaldi, first added to the traditional group around 1825.

the merry band with rather less elegance but much liveliness in urban settings, while numerous caricaturists produced versions of the subject in the late eighteenth century for light-hearted squibs on social manners and as a framework for political satires. Following the Napoleonic Wars, however, the antiquarian John Thomas Smith noted that London was gradually losing many of its old street customs, 'particularly that pleasing one of the Milk-maid's garland, so richly decorated with articles of silver, and bunches of cowslips'.[31] Similarly, in his collection of folk customs, *The Every-Day Book* (1827), William Hone referred to the 'lately disused custom of the milkmaid's garland'. The garland was replaced by the more raucous, vulgar character of Jack-in-the-Green accompanied by a 'lord' and 'lady', and lost much of its innocent appeal.[32] May Day continued to be a convenient vehicle for caricaturists and an adornment for illustrated collections of customs, but on the infrequent occasions that it was actually painted in an urban context, such works were clearly intended above all to serve as documentary records of a popular festivity that was dying out.

During the first half of the nineteenth century, the shows and exhibitions that could be sampled in London were more diverse, novel and popular than ever before.[33] There was an extraordinary range of panoramas and dioramas. The Royal Zoological Society opened its gardens in Regent's Park to the public in 1828 and Madame Tussaud's waxworks were established on a permanent basis in Baker Street in 1835. There were innumerable scientific, mechanical and art exhibitions. William Bullock's Egyptian Hall in Piccadilly displayed everything from Napoleon's carriage to Théodore Géricault's painting *The Raft of the 'Medusa'*. The annual exhibitions of the Royal Academy of Arts and the watercolour societies were firmly

established. Moreover, the national monuments and institutions devoted to culture – St Paul's Cathedral and Westminster Abbey, the Tower, the British Museum and the National Gallery – were gradually, if reluctantly, admitting more visitors by introducing longer opening hours and even free admission. In the Select Committee on National Monuments Report of 1841 Allan Cunningham proposed the theory that 'they cease to become a mob, when they get a taste'.[34]

Most of the illustrations of these sights concentrated on the wonders on show, with only a decorous quota of well-dressed members of the public to represent the audience. A more lively impression may be gleaned from the illustrated album kept by Richard Doyle (1824–83) in 1840, when he was only sixteen, detailing the more hazardous aspects of London's tourist attractions – a subject to which he was to return years later in the rather more self-consciously precious and archaicized series for *Punch*, 'Manners and Customes of Ye Englyshe in 1849'. *Punch* in fact

Derby Day, 1856–58
WILLIAM POWELL FRITH

Frith's crowded canvas took fifteen months to complete and was first exhibited at the Royal Academy in 1858 to enormous popular if not critical acclaim. Ruskin described it as 'a kind of cross between John Leech and Wilkie with a dash of daguerreotype here and there and some pretty seasoning with Dickens's sentiment.'

Visit to the Zoo, 1840
RICHARD DOYLE

This illustration from Doyle's manuscript journal is typical of the vignette sketches to be found on almost every page, recording with great fluency and delightful comic wit the sights of London in the year of the Queen's marriage to Prince Albert.

set its face against that greatest of all shows in London, the 1851 Exhibition of All Nations which took place in Hyde Park. In 1850, it attacked the scheme, and particularly Prince Albert, on account of the cost, the threat to tree conservation in the Park and the dangers which would be incurred, only three years after the last Chartist disturbances in England and the revolutions on the Continent, through a vast influx of visitors to the capital. Both Dicky Doyle and George Cruikshank (1792–1878) produced comic prophecies of the streets of London filled with an enormous crush of people.[35] In the event, these fears were not realized and even *Punch* was forced to concede that the Crystal Palace was an unparalleled success, reconciling classes rather than the reverse.[36] However, the official records of the exhibition – its inauguration by Queen Victoria in a painting by Henry Courtney Selous (Victoria and Albert Museum) and the chromolithographs of the interior pavilions published by Dickinson – concentrated on the settings peopled by a sprinkling of well-dressed visitors, not the masses who paid only a shilling entrance fee.[37] It took a little time for the lessons of the Great Exhibition to sink in and for artists to realize that all classes of Londoners could be portrayed in a single crowd without presenting a threat to the social order.

The artist who first made this breakthrough was William Powell Frith (1819–1909) and the subject which first inspired his comprehensive panorama of society was Derby Day, an event which since 1780 had constituted the most popular occasion on which Londoners could escape from the dirt and dreariness of city life. Frith moved cautiously in his attempts to portray modern life. His earliest painting, *Life at the Seaside*, exhibited at the Royal Academy in 1854 and bought by Queen Victoria, depicted a largely middle-class assemblage of holiday-makers at the decorous resort of Ramsgate. *Derby Day*, exhibited four years later at the Academy (where a rail was needed to protect it from the crowds), was again non-urban in setting, and the fact that it represented a traditional holiday, an 'English carnival' as Ruskin expressed it, guaranteed a light-hearted mood. But the race is not the subject of the work: scarcely anyone seems to be watching the course. Rather, within the teeming composition the artist introduces characters and incidents which raise moral questions about the nature of urban life. Derby Day did not have a salubrious reputation. The principal contrast is between the representatives of leisured London Society in the carriages and the straggling band of gypsies and showmen in the centre of the scene. Attempts to bridge the gap are unsuccessful if not positively dangerous: a little boy acrobat is urged by his father to retreat from the picnic being laid out on the grass by a footman; an old woman fortune teller is being studiously ignored by a lady in her carriage, while on the far right a flower-girl is being eyed lasciviously by a cigar-smoking rake. The rake is contrasted most forcefully, however, with his junior replica to the left: a City clerk, a 'gent' aping his betters in dress, but who has just been duped by a thimble-rigging trick into losing all his money, his watch and chain, even his cufflinks. He in turn is compared with a sturdy young countryman in a smock who is being led away from temptation by a worried wife. The painting can be explored endlessly for lessons of this kind which collectively form an indictment of corrupt urban values, yet under the guise of traditional merriment.[38]

I *The Procession of King Edward VI from the Tower of London to Westminster* (detail), 1547
SAMUEL HIERONYMOUS GRIMM

The procession passes the Eleanor Cross watched by goldsmiths standing in their shop doorways on the south (top) side of Cheapside, and guild members lining the north side. Old St Paul's with its spire can be seen in the background.

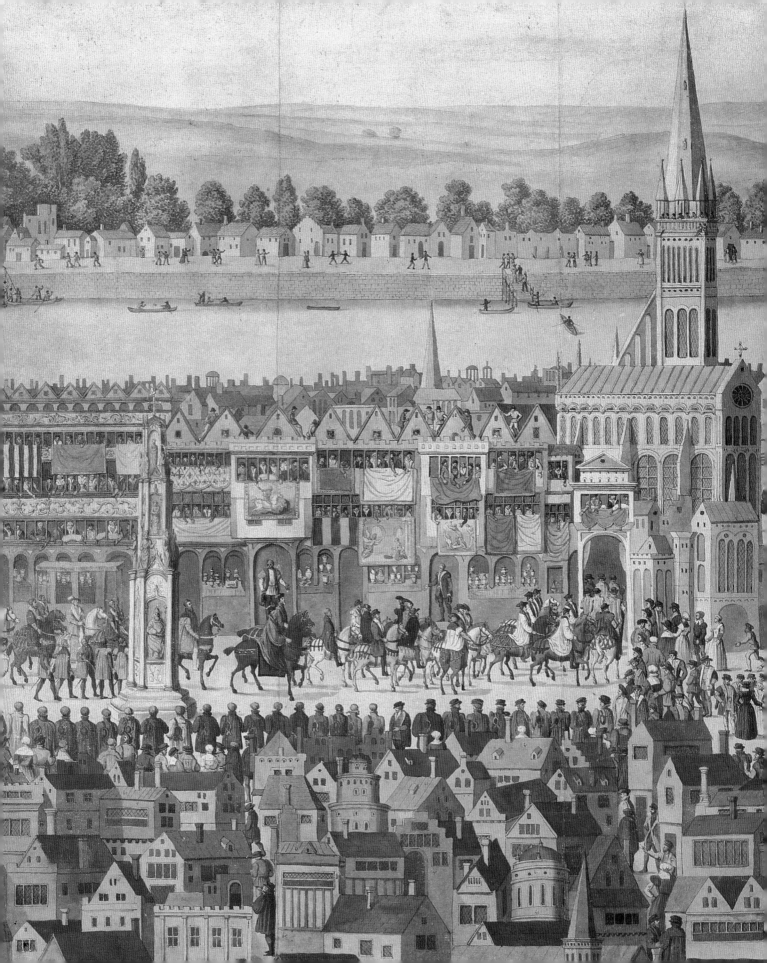

II   III

IV

II *Covent Garden, c.* 1726 PETER ANGELIS

The artist depicts the piazza looking west towards the church of St Paul's and crowded with people of all classes.

III *The Frozen Thames,* 1677 ABRAHAM HONDIUS

Hondius painted the scene as it would have appeared around the New Year, with Old London Bridge, St Saviour's, Southwark, and beyond it part of the tower of St Olave's, Tooley Street, in the background.

IV *Heads of Six of Hogarth's Servants, c.* 1750–55 WILLIAM HOGARTH

The informal composition eludes interpretation but the age range covered serves as yet another illustration of Hogarth's particular interest in physiognomy as a means of expressing character.

VI

V *A Girl Buying a Ballad, c.* 1778 HENRY WALTON

The old sailor is selling prints of naval commanders. The work has a decidedly French character, the self-contained air of the buyer and seller recalling Chardin.

VI *An Optician and his Assistant,* 1772 JOHAN ZOFFANY

The craftsman sits at his workbench in the process of polishing a lens.

VII

VII *The Asylum for the Deaf, c.* 1760
PAUL SANDBY

The image represents a facetious comment on Hogarth's *Enraged Musician*, reversing the point.

VIII *The Camel at Exeter Change,* 1798
JOHANNES ECKSTEIN

The sight of the camel at Exeter Change made Byron 'pine again for Asia Minor'.

IX *The Westminster Election,* 1788
ROBERT DIGHTON

The elegant group formed by the successful Foxite candidate Lord John Townshend, the Duchess of Devonshire and another lady, with their effete Pomeranian dog, contrasts with the rabble around them. John Wilkes to the left is distracted by a pretty ballad-seller while his pocket is robbed.

X *The Strand from the Corner of Villiers Street*, 1824
GEORGE SCHARF

Scharf peoples his scenes with figures who are specific to
the locality: a coal heaver from the Adelphi wharves and
a flower-seller from Covent Garden can be discerned.
Even the fire chief in his distinctive uniform came from
the neighbourhood: the Sun Fire office had a branch in
Craig's Court, Charing Cross.

XI *The Coal Wagon*, 1820–21
THÉODORE GÉRICAULT

Although loosely based on the Adelphi wharf,
Géricault's watercolour is not concerned with
topographical accuracy. The overhanging sky and
expanse of urban wasteland accentuate a feeling of
desolation which reflected not only the artist's
impression of certain aspects of London but also his own
psychological state.

XII   XIII

XII *The Vegetable Seller*, c. 1825
WILLIAM HENRY HUNT

Hunt's vegetable seller wears the strong boots and a silk
neckerchief or kingsman, deemed the most important
articles in a coster's dress.

XIII *The Flower Girl*, 1839
WILLIAM HENRY HUNT

Hunt developed a pointillist stipple technique during
the 1830s, which links him with a later generation of
watercolour artists, but here he retains the freshness of
observation to be found in his earlier reed-pen drawings.

XIV *Billingsgate Fish Market*, 1861 GEORGE ELGAR HICKS

XV

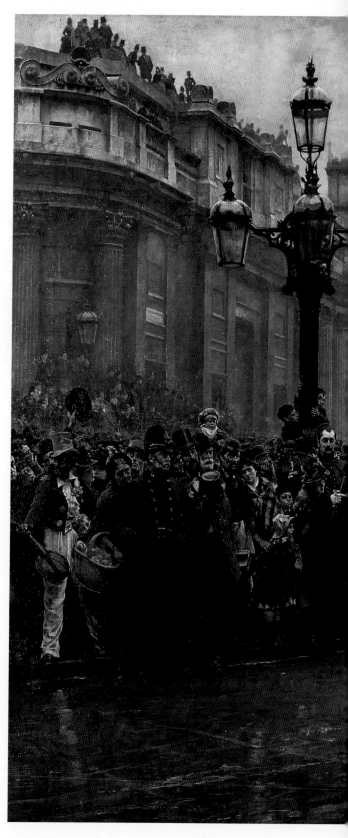

XVI

XV *The Railway Station* (detail), 1862 WILLIAM POWELL FRITH

XVI *Omnibus Life in London*, 1859 WILLIAM MAW EGLEY

XVII *The Ninth of November*, 1887–90 WILLIAM LOGSDAIL

The artist was aware of his subject's historical appeal. The traditions and pageantry associated with the City played a significant role in boosting its importance when reform seemed imminent, following the establishment of the London County Council in 1888.

XVIII *Behind the Bar*, 1882 JOHN HENRY HENSHALL

The scene is set in an archetypal public house in late-Victorian London where the artist has arranged a telling variety of customers. Like the *Graphic* artists, Henshall emphasized the narrative interest but the beautifully observed study of two barmen at work, the broad confident handling and skilful composition, also suggest a familiarity with the masters of French realism.

XIX *Maid Descending Stairs*, 1873 ALBERT GOODWIN

The maid looks over the tea-tray she is carrying to ensure she is not tripped by the cat alongside her, a variation on the familiar juxtaposition of cats and maids which often had sexual overtones.

XX *Women in a Shelter*, 1941
HENRY MOORE

Moore compared the scenes he found in the London underground to 'a huge
city in the bowels of the earth'. It was a city of the dead, the figures draped in
blankets and shawls like shrouds. Colours were used expressively as a
reflection of psychological states.

Derby Day was not the only sporting occasion which brought Londoners together. Regattas had long been held on the Thames, but organized competitive rowing did not commence until the late eighteenth century. In 1792 Robert Cleveley (1747–1809) produced a watercolour of a *Rowing Match at Richmond*, with a well-dressed crowd of onlookers (Laing Art Gallery, Newcastle).[39] The first race between Oxford and Cambridge took place at Henley in 1829; the second from Westminster to Putney in 1836; in 1839 the event became annual and in 1845 it moved to its present course from Putney to Mortlake. Its reputation as an event which united all classes, however, would appear to date from the second half of the nineteenth century when it became established as one of the social events guaranteed to take place year in, year out, and which could therefore be engraved in advance for the illustrated news magazines. Blanchard Jerrold devoted two chapters of *London: A Pilgrimage* (1872) to the Boat Race, duly illustrated by Gustave Doré (1832–83). A more idiosyncratic response was that of the son of a Chelsea boat-builder, a boatman and a friend of Whistler, Walter Greaves (1846–1930). *Hammersmith Bridge on Boat Race Day* is an extraordinary image, painted before the artist's meeting with Whistler, and totally removed from the pastiches of Whistler's work he later produced. The design is dictated by the suspension rungs and ropes over which spectators swarm like brightly coloured ants. It is a masterpiece of primitive art, yet it is more artfully daring in its composition and articulately alive in its mass expressiveness – the lines of dangling legs, waving umbrellas, top hats and boaters – than any aesthetic response to the city.

Greaves's painting is also peculiarly modern in its avoidance of individual expression, to the point of being hard to date; by this means, however, he emphasizes the particular character of the crowd and the atmosphere of excited anticipation. The attempt to distil the essential nature of a crowd despite its anonymity underlies many approaches to the subject in twentieth-century art. The depictions of music-hall audiences by Walter Richard Sickert (1860–1942) are a case in point. It was not as if the theatrical audience had been ignored by artists. Hogarth had produced an engraving of *The Laughing Audience* for a subscription ticket to *Southwark Fair* and *A Rake's Progress* in 1733, showing part of the orchestra, a tightly packed pit and amorous gentlemen in the boxes.[40] Fifty years later, Rowlandson started to produce etchings and watercolours on the same theme, followed by other artists who specialized in visual satire – Johann Ramberg (1763–1840), James Gillray (1756–1815) and the Cruikshank brothers – culminating in the campaign waged to keep prices down at Covent Garden in 1809, known as the Old Price (O.P.) Riots.[41] At the same time, in a more serious vein, no fewer than seven of the aquatints in Ackermann's *Microcosm of London* were devoted to theatres and the delightful drawings produced by Robert Blemmell Schnebbelie (*c*.1790–*c*.1849) in the early decades of the nineteenth century, some for the second volume of Robert Wilkinson's *Londina Illustrata* (1825), ensured that the interior features of both major and minor London theatres in this period were well recorded, along with their audiences.[42] Victorian artists seem largely to have lost interest in the subject; when treated at all, it was merely to characterize in

The Return Home from Epsom, 1848
THOMAS HENRY NICHOLSON

According to the *Illustrated London News*, which reproduced the drawing, 'Here is nearly every phase of visitors, from the gay barouche and drag, the post-chariot, the connubial gig, and overloaded omnibus; interspersed with parties of roadsters and nags.'

BELOW LEFT *Hammersmith Bridge on Boat Race Day*, *c*. 1862
WALTER GREAVES

Hammersmith Bridge, the first suspension bridge in London, dating from 1827, was a convenient vantage point half-way round the course for ordinary people intent on seeing the race. The first boat under the bridge nearly always won. Despite the efforts of the police, spectators swarmed all over the structure but eventually, because of the obvious safety risks, it was closed on Boat Race Day.

OPPOSITE *The Oxford and Cambridge Boat Race*, 1870
GUSTAVE DORÉ

Doré's study shows the race near its completion, the teams having passed under Barnes Railway Bridge (a favourite location for spectators who had travelled by rail) with a flotilla of steamers in their wake.

Edme
1870

At the Hippodrome, 1921
WILLIAM ROBERTS

Roberts's unmistakable style derives primarily from Cubism and later from his membership of the Vorticist group. The Hippodrome was renowned for its run of lavish Albert de Courville revues from 1912 to 1925.

anecdotal terms the class characteristics of an audience in different parts of a theatre.[43]

Such concerns were of no interest to Sickert. Firstly, he turned to a level of theatre which had not been portrayed before. The music hall developed from mid-century into the most popular form of lower-class entertainment, and by the 1880s was beginning to attract artistic bohemia. Secondly, inspired in part by Degas's paintings of theatres and *café-concerts*, he concentrated at first on the relationship between performer and audience, stage and auditorium, later evolving more complex methods of dealing with the spatial problems he deliberately set himself by the introduction of mirror images. Then in the early 1890s, at his favourite music-hall, the Old Bedford, Camden Town, he began to work on a series which concentrated on the audience lurking in the shadow of the gilded balconies, culminating in 'the gods'.[44] Spotlit from below so that the faces attain a generalized cast of feature, the figures piled into the gallery nevertheless express an air of keen attention that was distilled almost to the point of decorative abstract notation in the paintings he made of and from the gallery at the Middlesex Theatre in 1906. Sickert's paintings of theatre audiences retained something of the 'magic and poetry'[45] to which popular entertainment still aspired. For the artists associated with the Vorticist Movement in the immediate aftermath of the First World War, very little of this poetic vision remained. In the paintings and drawings executed by David Bomberg (1890–1957) of the Ghetto Theatre in Whitechapel and *At the Hippodrome* (Leicestershire Museums and Art Galleries) as portrayed by William Roberts (1895–1980) around 1921, the audiences are drained of any sentiment and reduced to schematized cogs in the modern city.

The Play-house, c. 1785
JOHANN HEINRICH RAMBERG

Like Hogarth and Rowlandson, Ramberg satirized the foibles of the genteel audience in the boxes and gallery, conveying something of the intimacy of the London theatres before the 1790s.

Noctes Ambrosianae, 1906
WALTER RICHARD SICKERT

The Middlesex Music Hall in Drury
Lane, known traditionally as the
Mogul Tavern or Old Mo',
rekindled Sickert's enthusiasm for
music-hall subjects on his return
from Dieppe in 1906, following the
destruction of his favourite haunt,
the Old Bedford, Camden Town, in
1899.

The Traffic in the Streets

A crowd did not have to congregate for some fixed event, for civic ceremonies or popular entertainments; it could simply be made up of the mass of people compressed into London and moving from one place to another, on foot, on horseback or by carriage. Their needs drew them into close proximity with one another and no amount of protection by servants or vehicles could entirely insulate any individual once he or she was outside. At the very least the smells or sights of the city obtruded, at worst verbal and physical abuse. The elevation of the theatre of the street into an art genre did not take place until the Victorian period, but the possibilities of the streets as a setting for chance encounters and confrontations, particularly of a comic nature, were being explored in the eighteenth century.

The physical condition of the streets of London scarcely encouraged leisurely perambulations. Each householder had by law to pave and keep in repair the stretch in front of his house, but even so most streets were deep in dirt and arbitrarily dumped rubbish. Overhead the thicket of extended drains and signboards blocked what little air and light remained between the narrow passages and overhanging galleries of the buildings. Some impression of this environment may be gleaned from Hogarth's *The Four Times of Day* of 1738, and in particular *Night*, which shows a narrow street near Charing Cross cast in shadow (National Trust, Upton House, Warwickshire). A fire in the middle of the road has caused a coach to overturn and the distraught passengers look out to find themselves in a warren of brothels and taverns from which drunken lechers emerge.[46]

Louis Philippe Boitard (fl. 1733–65) delighted in drawing crowd scenes of topical humour. In July 1749 he produced a design for a print of the crowds who assembled in the Strand when sailors sacked two brothels and the tarts – some scarcely covered – and their clients fled into the street. A year later, the same artist drew the carriages, coaches and people on foot pressing through Piccadilly to escape out of London, which had been threatened with an earthquake; the universally held belief that such acts of God were punishments for wickedness added piquancy to the motley assembly of harlots, pimps and adulterers with which Boitard populated his sketch.[47]

By the Paving Act of 1762 and its successive amendments, commissioners were appointed to oversee the paving and repair of the streets, to install proper gutters instead of kennels in the middle of the road, to lay Purbeck stone in place of the old road pebbles in the main thoroughfares and to remove the rubbish, the overhanging signboards, the unfenced open cellars and the unprotected coal chutes. Drains were relaid at deeper levels and lighting became less sporadic. But the improvements came about gradually, and besides many of the disturbances were caused by human nature. John Collet made a speciality of painting street affrays, whether provoked by young bloods, by women brawling or by a donkey that stumbled and fell on the cobbles.

Despite appearances to the contrary, the streets of London were not given over to a continual undifferentiated mêlée. As Steele noted in *The Spectator* in 1712:

> the Hours of the Day and Night are taken up in the Cities of *London* and *Westminster* by Peoples as different from each other as those who are Born in different Centuries. Men of Six-a-Clock give way to those of Nine, they of Nine to the Generation of Twelve, and they of Twelve disappear, and make Room for the fashionable World, who have made Two-a-Clock the Noon of the Day.[48]

Hogarth was the first to realize this theme in visual terms, with the *Four Times of Day*. The lady portrayed in *Morning* starting out for St Paul's Church, Covent Garden, meets the revellers left over from the night before; *Noon* is set in Soho where the effetely fashionable members of the congregation from the French Church contrast with the robust earthiness of the natives; *Evening* finds a family of citizens on an outing to Sadler's Wells, and by *Night*, as we have seen, the artist has returned to the heart of the city. Hogarth overlaid the temporal changes with differences in season, in humours and even the ages of man.[49] Other artists took the times of day on a more literal level, Robert Dighton producing a series of four mezzotints in 1795 which follow a rake through his day from breakfast at noon until five in the morning, when he is bundled, drunk and disorderly, into a sedan chair in the Piazza, Covent Garden, by knowing chairmen.

London Street Scene, mid 1770s
JOHN COLLET

In its emphasis on the maltreatment of animals, this drawing forms Collet's version of Hogarth's *The Second Stage of Cruelty* (1750/51), although the sensibilities of at least some of the onlookers appear to be shocked.

The Sailors' Revenge or the Strand in an Uproar, 1749
LOUIS PHILIPPE BOITARD

Boitard's drawing depicts the start of the so-called Penlez Riots in July 1749, which were directed against those – notably brothel keepers – who took advantage of the sailors discharged at the conclusion of the War of Jenkins' Ear.

George Scharf (1788–1860), who arrived in London in 1816, having travelled from Bavaria via the Napoleonic battlefront, was the first to record the different types of crowd to be seen on the streets as the day progressed. An apparently compulsive sketcher of the life he witnessed around him, he made pages of notes showing workmen setting out at six o'clock in the morning; people fetching their breakfasts at eight; bakers' boys taking the first batch of bread to the coffee houses; and people collecting their take-away dinners on Sundays.

This passion for the streets, this observation of the great clock of London, seems to have appealed to all those artists and writers who were essentially reporters of the urban scene. Dickens, following in the footsteps of Steele, devoted two chapters of *Sketches by Boz* (1836) to the streets in the morning and evening. The extraordinary range of individuals to be found every day in London was regarded with some astonishment by foreigners. On a visit in 1820, Théodore Géricault (1791–1824) was fascinated by the streets 'so full of constant movement', and he noted down types who appealed to him in hurried sketches.[50]

The emphasis placed on outdoor sketching by young watercolour artists working in France and England during the early decades of the nineteenth century liberated art from the studied response prescribed by academic theory.[51] They attempted to capture fleeting atmospheric effects, the sparkle of light, the movement of people, and they brought new vigour to the somewhat staid genre of urban topography. Thomas Shotter Boys (1803–72), working in the Bonington circle, was the first artist to introduce this new cosmopolitan breadth of approach to London. The lithographs he produced for *London As It Is* (1842) depict a range of typical sights, as opposed to the calculated 'improvements' that a visitor to the city might have seen. Although mainly concerned with the buildings, his viewpoint is that of the person on the street; and to the generality of top hats and frock coats, bonnets and shawls, he introduced flashes of detail – two Christ's Hospital boys watching a mother guide her children out of harm's way on Ludgate Hill; the paviours and flower sellers round the Bank; removal men blocking the pavement with their cart in Fleet Street.[52] The same elegant bravura of touch may be seen in the watercolour view by Eugène Lami (1800–90) of *Ludgate Circus* in 1850, with the crush of carriages hemming in a coster's donkey-cart. Lami fulfilled those characteristics for which Charles Baudelaire provided the theoretical basis in his essay, 'The Painter of Modern Life', first published in *Figaro* in 1863.[53]

Interior of an Omnibus, late 1870s
CHARLES KEENE

Keene had a penchant for depicting the hazards of public
transport in London, involving large ladies of uncertain years in
encounters with jovial or uncouth drivers and conductors.
Executed in the artist's usual brilliant summary style with a reed
pen, this drawing parodies Egley's picturesque version of the
scene (*see* col. pl. XVI).

Dinner Time Sunday, One O'Clock, 1841
GEORGE SCHARF

The figures scurrying through the streets bear refreshments
ranging from jugs of ale to Sunday roasts and pies.

Baudelaire particularly praised Constantin Guys (1802–92), who worked, like
Lami, in watercolours and who had been employed by the illustrated press, where
a premium was placed on the eye-witness account of a fleeting occurrence. In
England, the *Illustrated London News*, founded in 1842, specialized in such work,
but the skills of the artists they employed were rarely apparent because the
conventional systems of wood-engraving used for reproduction flattened any
individuality of technique to a uniform level of mediocrity. The artists on *Punch*
fared better, for there was not the same urgency to meet deadlines for most of its
visual content. Nevertheless, both magazines accustomed their audiences to the
use of contemporary subject matter. If the *Illustrated London News* took a
somewhat distanced standpoint in the interests of maintaining a tasteful neutrality,
John Leech (1817–64), Charles Keene (1823–91) and others on the *Punch* team

Volunteers Marching Out, 1860
ARTHUR BOYD HOUGHTON

Using a method of lighting the faces reminiscent of the technique employed by Ford Madox Brown – whom he admired – Houghton delineates a cross-section of Victorian street life.

introduced a whole range of urban situations which focused on the individual's predicament in a crowd. Their comic repertoire of cheeky boys, surly cab drivers, over-filled omnibuses and exposure to every type of street obstacle highlights the trials of getting about nineteenth-century London.[54]

It was, however, a different matter to grant such ephemeral subject matter the accolade of more permanent representation in oils. Arthur Boyd Houghton (1836–75), later to achieve fame for his startling series of visual revelations about America in the *Graphic*, painted a number of small-scale oil sketches of London street scenes around 1860. Featuring ragged urchins and model children in their best outfits, wandering entertainers and brisk new recruits to the Volunteer movement that swept through England in the late 1850s, as well as a quota of pretty girls, they recall in their cast of characters and great good humour the work of John Leech, who dominated *Punch* at this date. Similarly, William Maw Egley (1826–1916) painted his *Omnibus Life in London* in 1859 (*see* col. pl. XVI), in which the comic crush usually depicted in *Punch* was softened into a more attractive medley of well-dressed, middle-class passengers; conditioned by the cartoons, the critic of the *Daily Telegraph* found Egley's work 'utterly deficient in humour'.[55]

Baudelaire was unusual for his day in not despising contemporary dress on account of its ugliness; indeed, he was fascinated by women's coquetry and fashion. In contrast, the appearance of the London crowd, completely devoid of aesthetic appeal, was cause for frequent complaint by observers, fuelling the traditional arguments against the introduction of modern dress in art. For Dickens in his essay, 'The Boiled Beef of New England', from the *Uncommercial Traveller* (1860), 'The mass of London people are shabby. The absence of distinctive dress has, no doubt, something to do with it. The porters of the Vintners' Company, the

draymen, and the butchers, are about the only people who wear distinctive dresses; and even these do not wear them on holidays.' In London, as opposed to Paris, the fashions descended, 'and you never fully know how inconvenient or ridiculous a fashion is, until you see it in its last descent.' Similarly, Blanchard Jerrold could assert in *London: A Pilgrimage:* 'An English crowd is almost the ugliest in the world: because the poorer classes are but copyists in costume of the rich. . . . Observe this lemonade vendor. His dress is that of a prosperous middle-class man . . . gone to shreds and patches.'[56]

In *London Labour and the London Poor* (1851) Henry Mayhew provided enough evidence to show that the appearance of the poorer sections of the population, dependent on slop-shop goods and whatever they could get from the second-hand-clothes markets in Petticoat and Rosemary Lanes, was based on necessity rather than choice. But the appearance of the London crowd as a whole made even Frith pause when he embarked on his third large-scale panorama of modern life, *The Railway Station*, in 1860: 'I don't think the station at Paddington can be called picturesque, nor can the clothes of the ordinary traveller be said to offer much attraction to the painter – in short, the difficulties of the subject were great.'[57] Certainly, the artist had behind him two great popular successes in *Ramsgate Sands* and *Derby Day*; the former work even won the royal stamp of approval. But whereas both those paintings had a ready appeal as depictions of high days and holidays, with people in comparatively attractive summer dress, *The Railway Station* was in its very setting making a bold statement about modern urban life and portrayed people at their most unprepossessing, bundled up for a journey. The impressive iron and glass terminus of the Great Western Railway had been completed to the design of Brunel and Wyatt only ten years earlier. The

The Railway Station, 1862
WILLIAM POWELL FRITH

Frith provides a spectrum of contemporary life that was recognized by the *Illustrated London News* at the time as 'comprehensive and epical in the suggestiveness of its range, yet true to literal nature and even the most trivial matter of fact. A more characteristic illustration of the age could not have been selected.' (*See also* col. pl. xv)

railway itself symbolized the restless movement and increasing speed that were a feature of the age, opening up the somewhat frightening possibilities of endless discovery. No wonder Frith packed the platform with a wealth of character and incident to offset these technological feats. A bridal group enlivened the 'clothes of the ordinary traveller'; two well-known policemen staged an arrest. By creating situations which could be correctly interpreted through physiognomic and sartorial clues, Frith achieved a rapport with his audience which ensured the success of his work.

Not all artists were as fortunate as Frith in their critical reception. George Elgar Hicks (1824–1914) was one of a number of painters who sought to depict contemporary themes in the wake of Frith's example. He would appear to have turned for inspiration to a collection of essays which again covered the theme of the times of day in the city, George Augustus Sala's *Twice Round the Clock; or the Hours of Day and Night in London*, first published in 1858 with wood-engraved illustrations by William M'Connell (fl.1850–65). Hicks's *The General Post Office: One Minute to Six*, which related closely to M'Connell's depiction of the same scene, was exhibited at the Royal Academy in 1860 and again is a work calculated to reflect the pace of modern life. Though it was popular with the public, it received generally unfavourable reviews. For the *Athenaeum*, it was 'hopeless and meretricious'; for *Blackwood's* the subject was trivial. But the complaint most commonly voiced was that the newsboys were utterly artificial, 'painted up to the pink of doll-like perfection, and not to the dingy reality of London life'. *The Times* conceded with ironic resignation, 'If we must have a mob of newsboys, let us have them with all their grime and printer's ink, in their threadbare garments and shapeless headgear.'[58] The point was not that the papers were looking for works of uncompromising social realism, but that the artist had failed to introduce the plausible combinations of costume and characters which gave Frith's works their narrative interest.

Hicks's painting of a fixed time of day, however, might have helped to inspire Frith with the subject of his next modern-life proposal: three London street scenes to be called *Morning, Noon* and *Night*, which were commissioned by the print publisher and art dealer, Ernest Gambart in 1862, but never completed. In his autobiography, the artist set forth his plans. Almost inevitably, *Morning* was to be staged in Covent Garden with the familiar mixture of late-night revellers and early-morning workers; 'Regent Street in the full tide of active life' provided the *mise-en-scène* for *Noon*; while *Night* in the Haymarket promised to be the most dramatic work of all,

> the main incident being the exit of the audience from the theatre. . . . This is being observed by an over-dressed and berouged woman, whose general aspect plainly proclaims her unhappy position; and by the expression of her faded though still handsome face, she feels a bitter pang at having lost for ever all claim to manly care or pure affection.[59]

The congregation of hordes of prostitutes on the pavements round the theatres when the curtain fell was not a new phenomenon, as the drawing Ramberg made

The Haymarket at Night, c. 1783
JOHANN HEINRICH RAMBERG

Various classes of prostitute solicit custom from the audience leaving Vanbrugh's Opera House (the King's Theatre).

on his visit to London in the 1780s makes clear. The Haymarket, in particular, had long enjoyed a notorious reputation. With the development of the Victorian cult of domestic values and family life in the privacy of the home, the streets were regarded as representing their antithesis, threatening the social order. Fallen women personified this moral corruption. They undermined the very state of womanhood by exaggerating its charms; their gaudy apparel was a perverse and mocking caricature of fashionable attire. But instead of their presence being noted as a fact of life, or with outright condemnation, for Frith and other Victorian artists prostitutes represented the loss of innocence. By contrasting the young ladies leaving the theatre under the protection of their menfolk with the 'over-dressed and berouged woman' alone and visibly conscious of her fall, Frith reinforced the advantages of conventional Victorian morality. Similarly, the drawings for the unfinished painting *Found* by Dante Gabriel Rossetti (1828–82), of a country drover meeting his former sweetheart in the showy, seedy attire of a prostitute in a street near Blackfriars Bridge, expressed in symbolic terms the corrupting effect of the city.[60] Unlike Hogarth's depiction of *The Harlot's Progress*, in which the woman was seen as a willing partner in her way of life, for Rossetti the woman was a victim.

In the illustrations to *London: A Pilgrimage*, Doré elevated the streets of the city into a metaphor which stood for the commercial hub of the Empire. Crowds press over London Bridge on their way to work, and thread their way between the mountainous loads of cargo, barrows of fish and fruit, cabs and carts in Thames Street, which is seen by Jerrold to 'present such a picture of a thousand errands transacting in one spot, as may not be seen in any other city on the face of the globe'.[61] In one of the most memorable images in the book, the traffic converges with superhuman force on Ludgate Circus; it was not a literal truth but a vision of competitiveness at the heart of the metropolis, blocking the path to St Paul's.

Some fifty years later, the cathedral soars above the painting by Christopher Richard Wynne Nevinson (1889–1946) of Fleet Street crowded with traffic and pedestrians (Museum of London). But the title of the work, *Amongst the Nerves of*

Oxford Street, 1928
CHAS. LABORDE

In his *Rues et Visages de Londres*, Laborde portrays the streets of London with a playful French elegance of line, to be found at the same date in the prints of Segonzac and decorative designs of Dufy.

OPPOSITE

Wet Evening, Oxford Street, 1919
CHRISTOPHER RICHARD WYNNE NEVINSON

In contrast to his jagged Cubist etchings depicting the machine-like movement of the men in the First World War, Nevinson employed the softer medium of lithography to portray the civilian crowd, curved umbrellas and glow from the plate-glass windows of the stores.

the World, does not refer to the human level but to the abstract network of communications created by the criss-cross of telegraph wires in the sky.[62] When Nevinson first visited New York in 1919, it seemed to him to embody the city of the future and buildings dominate his first cityscapes, which are almost devoid of people. London, by comparison, could never deliberately be reduced to a 'soulless city'; the historic monuments and Victorian developments made their presence felt in Nevinson's work of the 1920s. In contrast to the images of men as machines in his paintings and prints of the war period, the artist portrayed a decorative pattern of receding heads and umbrellas against brightly lit shop-fronts in a lithograph of a wet evening in Oxford Street in 1919. During the inter-war period, the streets of London were never seen as an alien zone inhabited by the corrupt society of whores, capitalists and veterans found in the work of Dix, Beckmann and Grosz in Berlin. Chas. Laborde (1886–1941) certainly learned from the linear reductionism of their graphic technique, but for him the streets of London were populated with bright young flappers, dashing subalterns, dignified gentlemen in top hats and boaters, and even a pipe-smoking policeman.

Riotous Assembly

From the Middle Ages Londoners were renowned for their unruliness and lack of deference to authority, while the means of enforcing the law were relatively disorganized compared with other European countries. The common people rioted not simply because of food shortages, but because they felt under pressure from some abuse of power which endangered their traditional rights and customs. Moreover, the threat of mob violence could be exploited by those with real power, so that social protest was often bound up with political factions. These manifestations of turbulent behaviour were depicted, when at all, as propaganda on behalf of at least a section of established authority, who could afford to commission such works, or to provide a retrospective commemoration of the event. Thus Sir John Froissart's *Chroniques de France et d'Angleterre (c.1460)* contains illuminations depicting the Peasants' Revolt of 1381, including the moment when William Walworth the Lord Mayor struck down Wat Tyler at the head of his men in Smithfield (British Library. Royal MS. 18.E.i, ff.165v, 172, 175). A hundred years later, John Foxe's sensational account of the Marian burnings in his *Book of Martyrs* (1563) was accompanied by woodcuts of the victims at the stake in Smithfield encircled by the crowd, which greatly enhanced the work's propaganda value.

The Reformation provoked intense and continued controversy about the nature of religious faith and the pattern of worship, but it was not until the seventeenth century that the plots and popular revolutions which grew out of the bitter antagonisms were reflected in any sustained use of the polemical print. The Gunpowder Plot of 1605–06 aroused sufficient interest abroad for a Dutch or German engraving to be produced which showed Guy Fawkes and his fellow conspirators hatching the plot, in a famous but imaginary group portrait, as well as the manner of their execution before an assembled crowd.[63] The outpouring of tracts during the Civil War was accompanied by engravings which nearly all represented the Parliamentary and Puritan cause. Even Hollar, who had Royalist sympathies and had produced a set of four etchings of Charles's campaign against the Scots of 1639, depicted the trial and execution of the Earl of Strafford in 1641, at least one satire among the many directed against Archbishop Laud and a representation of his trial in the House of Lords in 1644.[64] Given the troubled times and the departure of Hollar's patron, the Earl of Arundel, for Italy in 1642, the artist evidently had to turn to subjects which had a ready market.[65] Composite prints with narrative insets detailing moments of crisis were also issued. *The Malignants Trecherous and Bloody Plot against the Parliament and Citty of London*, published in May 1643, traced in a series of twelve images the abortive plot to hand over the City to the Royalists, while Hollar the same year produced an eight-part propaganda sheet illustrative of the league formed between the English Parliament and the Scots Covenanters.[66] The insets which frame one of his most ambitious and personal works, a comparison of the English and Bohemian Civil Wars, include depictions of the King's seizure of five Members of Parliament in 1641 and the 'Multitudes' protesting against episcopacy and privilege.[67] The

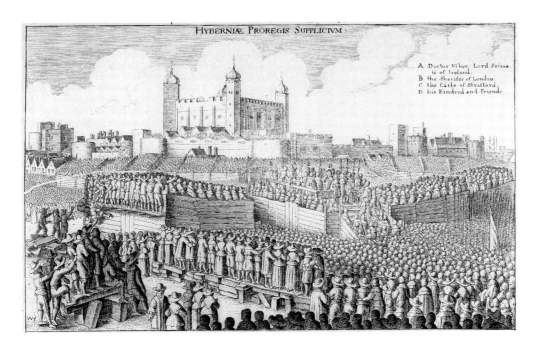

HYBERNIÆ PROREGIS SUPPLICIVM ·

A Doctor VÍher, Lord Prima-
   te of Ireland.
B the Sheriffes of London.
C the Earle of Strafford.
D his Kindred and Friends.

The True Maner of the Execution of Thomas Earle of Strafford, Lord Lieutenant of Ireland, upon Tower Hill, the 12th of May 1641
WENCESLAUS HOLLAR

Hollar depicts the mass of spectators on specially constructed stands – including one which has collapsed – and identifies with letters the main protagonists: Bishop Usher, the Lord Mayor, Strafford, his family and friends.

execution of the monarch was commemorated mainly, it would appear, in prints issued abroad, showing the crowd massed outside an inaccurate rendering of the Banqueting Hall, with a fainting woman and weeping man always prominent in the foreground. The best-known painting of the event, probably by a Dutch artist for Royalists in exile, depicts the scene on a large scale between four medallions which emphasize the pious intent of the work (The Earl of Rosebery).

The Dutch artists who came to England in the wake of the Restoration brought, as we have seen, a new impetus to the country's somewhat stunted artistic growth. It is to one of them that we owe the only painting of the Great Fire that might have been an eyewitness account, viewed from the Tower wharf; the people flee with their possessions in carts and boats, the panic of their exodus muffled in the half light beneath a night sky alive with sparks (Museum of London).[68] But the production of illustrated political broadsheets was curtailed by the Press Licensing Act until events overrode its effects in 1678, when a wave of anti-Catholic propaganda swept the country, provoked by the supposed Popish Plot. The sensational accusations made by Titus Oates were exploited to the full by the Earl of Shaftesbury, leader of the Whig opposition, to attack the pro-French and Catholic tendencies of the King's party. Shaftesbury had a genius for propaganda and from his 'Green Ribbon Club', the first of the political coffee-houses, he conducted the anti-Catholic witch hunt with an armoury of visual propaganda which ranged from Pope-burning processions to Papal-Plot playing cards.

Polemical playing cards were scarcely new, but those issued in 1678–82 were more than emblematic representations of a set of political attitudes. Produced by a number of publishers, they followed the progress of events and, in the case of those designed by the decorative artist and illustrator Francis Barlow (1626?–1704), with a hitherto unprecedented degree of artistic competence which was much copied if not matched.[69] At the same time, again under the patronage of the Whig party, illustrated broadsheets were issued detailing the *Solemn Mock Procession of the POPE, Cardinalls, Jesuits, Fryers, etc* on the anniversary of Queen Elizabeth's accession, 17 November, from 1678 to 1681. They served as a more permanent memento of these mock pageants, fanning the flames of hatred engendered by the processions themselves.

By 1682, however, the backlash was in full swing with the power of the Whigs overturned following the King's dissolution of Parliament and the so-called 'plots' discredited. The Royalist Tory party issued their own pamphlets and playing cards which illustrated the Whigs' travesty of the facts, and accused them of republicanism, recalling 'The Knavery of the Rump'.[70] Oates received some of his own medicine, being brought to trial for perjury in 1685. He was condemned by Judge Jeffreys to imprisonment for life, to stand in the pillory annually at certain specified places, and to be flogged through the city. Astonishingly he survived the latter ordeal and is depicted in a contemporary painting by a Dutch artist in the pillory outside Westminster Hall before a large crowd of spectators.

At the time of Monmouth's rebellion playing cards which depicted the events and the punishment meted out by Jeffreys were again issued. The 'Glorious Revolution' also inspired sets of cards which represented the crimes of James II and his flight. But the cards which most clearly express the burgeoning parties' dependence on popular support come from a pack issued at the time of the trial of the High Church Tory, the Rev. Henry Sacheverell in 1710. Londoners are depicted electing the appropriate political candidates – 'See London Citizens with Heart and Voice,/Chuse Loyal Members that deserve their Choice'; and destroying the property of Dissenters – 'The Clock and Pulpit in the Flames expire,/That help'd Noncon to set the world on Fire'.[71]

In the early years of the Hanoverian dynasty there was a revival of the use of public spectacle to diffuse unrest in the metropolis, together with the calculated inspiration of terror. Sponsored by Whig loyalist societies, Pope-burning processions were resumed with the figures of the Pretenders added to the repertoire; rallies were staged in Hyde Park and vigilante bands attacked the premises of known Tory supporters. But the mass of Londoners remained passively unsympathetic to the new regime, sometimes manifesting their feelings in mocking charivaris. Visual representations of these grass-root reactions have not survived, if they were ever produced. As we have seen, the crowd was represented as an accessory to authority, affirming a course of action. Again in the aftermath of the 1745 Rebellion, the execution of Lords Kilmarnock and Balmerino on Tower Hill in August 1746 occasioned the publication of prints which graphically convey the official viewpoint. The scaffold is surrounded by a heavy guard of troops keeping the crowd well back from the point where they could pose a threat, but at the same time their massed presence legitimized the verdict of high treason.

Hogarth went to St Albans the same month to draw Simon Fraser, Lord Lovat, and published a portrait engraving which enjoyed a massive sale during his trial and execution the following April. In October 1747, the artist produced his series of twelve prints, *Industry and Idleness*, which contrasted the careers of the

e Solemn Mock Procession of the POPE, Cardinalls, Iesuits, Fryers, &c: through ye City of London, Nouember ye 17th 1679

The Solemn Mock Procession of the POPE, Cardinalls, Jesuits, Fryers, etc. through ye City of London. November Ye. 17th. 1679

This depiction of the 'extraordinary triumph . . . to confront the Insolence of the *Romish* faction' was published as a broadside with an accompanying explanation. The procession began at five in the evening setting forth from Moorgate and travelling through the City. The whole route was thronged with people judged 'by a modest Computation' to be not less than 200,000. At Temple Bar there were fireworks and finally the Pope was burnt on a large bonfire.

Titus Oates in the Pillory, c. 1687

Titus Oates stands in New Palace Yard, with Westminster Hall on the left and Palace Gate in the distance. As the latter had been pulled down by 1682, it is probable that the artist based his composition on a Hollar etching of 1647 which had the same viewpoint.

The Idle 'Prentice Executed at Tyburn, 1747
WILLIAM HOGARTH

Plate 11 from *Industry and Idleness* depicts Idle travelling with his coffin in an open cart to the 'triple tree', where an executioner's assistant is making some last-minute adjustments to the rope. A Methodist preacher delivers a pious admonition to the condemned man and soldiers bring up the rear.

The March to Finchley, 1749–50
WILLIAM HOGARTH

The scene is set in Tottenham Court Turnpike at its junction with the New Road, where troops were stationed overnight before proceeding north. Some are already marching in orderly formation towards Hampstead but those in the foreground are trapped by the pleasures and penalties of their nocturnal activities.

London apprentices Goodchild and Idle. The final image for the latter, *The Idle 'Prentice Executed at Tyburn*, can be viewed independently and also as a specific analogy with Goodchild's end. By the eighteenth century, if not earlier, the execution of criminals at Tyburn was far from being the solemn public occasion it was intended to be. Although the event scarcely carried the import of executions for high treason, which signalled the saving of the whole country from betrayal, the underlying function of the public ritual was the same. But the two-mile journey of the open cart carrying the condemned from Newgate to Tyburn clearly did not serve the intended purpose as an awful warning, a dignified exemplum of the supremacy of the law. Francis Place recalled, 'No solemn procession, it was just the contrary; it was a low-lived, black-guard merry-making.' The crowd at Tyburn comprised, 'the whole vagabond population of London, all the thieves, and all the prostitutes, all those who were evil-minded, and some, a comparatively few curious people made up the mob on those brutalizing occasions.'[72] Rather than a state occasion well controlled by the presence of the army, in Hogarth's print the guard is almost swamped by the lurching waves of people. In contrast to the generalized crowd on Tower Hill, Hogarth invests this mob with explicit characterization of feature, dress and behaviour. Furthermore, the print is a pair to Goodchild's procession as Lord Mayor; it casts added doubt on the honours he had achieved, for the mob in both works is roughly the same. Only the manner of transporting the protagonists differs: Goodchild is safely insulated but also trapped inside his coach, while Idle is at one with the masses and, having shared with them the pleasures of freedom, is now suffering from its dangers and consequences. The moral scales are in fact evenly balanced.

Hogarth's view of the tumultuous crowd went even further in undermining the state. *The March to Finchley*, painted in 1749–50, ostensibly sets out to describe the events of September 1745 when the troops recalled from Germany and the Netherlands marched through London, gathered to the north and then marched to Finchley to guard the capital from the forces of the Young Pretender. This patriotic subject could have occasioned orderly troop formations portrayed within the conventional genre of a heroic battle piece. Indeed, such model soldiers can be seen in the far distance. The foreground, however, is full of men turning from the action, unable to move if not precisely deserting, because of their entanglements with women, drink and crime. It is difficult to think of another composition in which the very aspect of the figures in relation to the viewer takes on such significance. As in the artist's depiction of the crowd gathered for Goodchild's inauguration and Idle's execution, we are on ground level, equal to the participants. In *The March to Finchley*, we are also placed in the position of the distractions of London which hold the troops back from their course of duty.

The portrayal of common people by Hogarth had important consequences in the field of political caricature, if it did not loosen the stranglehold of academic theory on painting. Furthermore, the politics of the Wilkite era and the emergence for the first time of something approximating to demotic power inspired depictions of the mob in various artistic forms. Prints recorded the presence of the populace at the Middlesex election of 1768, the riot outside the Mansion House the same year,

The Riot in Broad Street on the Seventh of June 1780
JAMES HEATH after FRANCIS WHEATLEY

The artist was in Dublin at the time of the Riots, but painted this work on his return to London. Unfortunately it was destroyed by fire while on loan to the engraver, but after the print had been completed.

and confrontations between the Wilkites and the court party at Temple Bar and St James's Palace in 1769.[73] The Gordon Riots of 1780 were the worst of the century, lasting six days, involving the destruction of £70,000 worth of private property which belonged to known Catholic sympathizers like Lord Mansfield, and the sack of the main prisons, before the 10,000 troops alerted could restore order. Predictably, the illustrated news broadsheets concentrated on recording the spectacular scenes of violence, notably the attack on Newgate Prison. But the reaction by artists of repute is more complex, emphasizing the strength of the conventions that held them back from the espousal of popular unrest as a theme.

For several months following the riots military encampments were established on open spaces in and around the capital – Hyde Park, St James's Park, Montagu House, Clapham Common. Paul Sandby (1730–1809) was among the many visitors whose curiosity was whetted by this unusual phenomenon, the interest in his particular case possibly being enhanced by his early career as a military draughtsman. He was not inspired to depict precisely enacted manoeuvres, but produced instead a series of what can only be described as picturesque pastorals in which the soldiers recline at ease in and around their tents, gossiping with civilians, or flirting with a pretty laundress or jolly landlady; the only sign of military action is the children imitating soldiers' drill. Produced first as three plates in the *Virtuosi's Magazine* in the autumn of 1780, and then by Sandby himself as two series of ten outline etchings and four large aquatints (the latter in May 1783), they served perhaps to provide reassurance that the capital was, after all, a perfectly safe place.[74]

A rather more heroic account of the events was executed by Francis Wheatley (1747–1821) for the famous London printseller John Boydell, and issued in the year of the latter's Lord Mayoralty in 1790. Wheatley's picture reconstructed the events of 7 June 1780 in Broad Street when troops were called out to stop the mob attacking the Bank of England. Portraits of protagonists leading the well-ordered ranks of the military were included – presumably at the behest of Boydell as a compliment to the civic authorities – while the mob has a somewhat desultory air for all their looting activities, the general disorganization and the presence of women suggesting a certain lack of resolve in the face of the military. Boydell's attempt to found a national school of history painting culminated in the opening of his Shakespeare Gallery in 1789. Unfortunately, the outbreak of the French Revolution curtailed his lucrative trade with France, and possibly he was already looking round for potentially popular national themes. Wheatley's composition was a timely reminder of the damage that London had incurred through mob violence only ten years previously and at the same time it offered reassurance as to the government's capacity to quell disturbance.

Londoners were in a comparatively privileged position in the pre-reform age when it came to expressing their opinions by electoral means rather than direct action. The City had a freeman franchise, meaning that almost half the adult male citizens could vote. The scot and lot franchises in Southwark and Westminster were even wider. Parliamentary elections presented the occasion for the visual representation of political feelings, nowhere more so than at Covent Garden where the open space of the Piazza provided a vast auditorium for massed audiences to observe politicians on the hustings. Robert Dighton made something of a speciality of depicting the successive election campaigns staged there in 1784, 1788 and 1796. The 1784 election in Westminster was the most violent political contest of the Georgian period. Dighton represents the intermingling of aristocrats and citizens in the Piazza, the crush of hats and favours spiced with leading personalities ranging from a bevy of Society belles to the bald-headed Sam House, a Wardour Street publican 'and a republican', who managed Fox's campaign and is seen with a gang of butchers carrying cleavers and marrow bones (Her Majesty the Queen).[75] For the by-election of 1788, the artist introduced an even wider spectrum of personae (*see* col. pl. IX), while in 1796 attention is concentrated on the hustings, with the candidates Gardner, Fox and Horne Tooke being supported by a well-dressed orderly contingent of gentlemen who include the Marquis of Buckingham and the Duke of Norfolk (Museum of London). Significantly, the lower-class characters in the foreground are in the main those who did not count in politics – women and children.

It would be easy to say that Dighton managed to reflect the character of each election: the relative order of the 1796 campaign compared with those of 1784 and 1788. But the artist was not aiming to produce a report of documentary realism. He was making use of the graphic forms at his disposal, given the conventions of political caricature in which he was working. His was a distillation of the character of each campaign certainly, in view of his knowledge of the immediate political context and the audience to whom he was directing his work. But he was nevertheless presenting the crowd as if on an imaginary stage, and he treated major and minor members of the cast according to their rank with a greater or lesser degree of physiognomic or sartorial individuality drawn from a common store of artistic props.

It cannot be said that anything new was added in the nineteenth century to the depiction of the political crowd in London. Rather the reverse: interest in the subject dwindled, possibly because the more colourful methods of registering opinion were gradually eliminated as the political system was reformed. When the vote came to be valued as a human right, it became necessary for those who granted it to give the electoral procedure a certain dignity, as much as it was for those claiming it to show that they were worthy of the responsibility. With the general reform in manners and educational improvement, political gatherings and elections lost much of the 'bread and circuses' element that had marked them in the eighteenth century. Of course there were moments when the government was under threat, but some of the worst outbreaks of violence took place outside London. In 1831, during the build-up to the First Reform Act, the city of Bristol erupted and the action of the military was duly recorded not only in broadsides but also by leading artists of the Bristol School. Dragoons were used to quell election disturbances in Wolverhampton in 1835, again commemorated in cheap broadsides. In 1842, the Chartist disturbances took place in the North of England and in 1848, although the capital was threatened, the government's fears were not fulfilled.

By 1848, the division between news and humorous illustration, which developed with the foundation of *Punch* and the *Illustrated London News*, had been consolidated. The marriage achieved in their work by Hogarth, Dighton and others between identifiable settings and characters was split apart. *Punch* looked after character, the *Illustrated London News* itemized the setting. Hence when the Chartist threat was at its height, *Punch* made fun of the individuals who would be most at risk: the so-called Physical Force Chartists and the special constables enrolled to curb them.[76] The *Illustrated London News*, on the other hand, depicted the mass meeting on Kennington Common, ostensibly the event which provoked all the hysteria, as a generalized mass of top hats. The engraving was based on a daguerreotype. As for the police, they were shown lounging in Bonner's Fields, perfectly at ease in the face of the threat which never materialized, a strange echo of the situation Sandby had portrayed in the royal parks some seventy years earlier.[77] No major artists in the Victorian period ever turned to the politics of the capital for their subject matter. One curiously vivid record of the Manhood Suffrage Riots in Hyde Park in 1866, however, appears in a large canvas by Nathan Hughes. The artist is otherwise unknown and possibly, from the detail of the foreground figures and the waves of crowd movement in the distance, he relied to some extent on photographs. The effect is somewhat obsessive, like the work of Richard Dadd.

The deep-rooted and extensive social crisis of the 1880s, brought about by cyclical trade depression and the decline of some major industries, was given shape and direction by the new forces of socialism, and manifested itself in strikes, street fighting and demonstrations. The artists on the *Graphic* and the *Illustrated London News* portrayed the dramatic events with a pseudo-photographic technique, which they evolved as the increasing use of line and half-tone methods of reproduction began to make their style seem more artificial. The result

The Manhood Suffrage Riots 23 July 1866

NATHAN HUGHES

The riots began by accident rather than design when Hyde Park was closed before a planned meeting of the Reform League. The crowds were so great that disorder broke out and breaches were made in the Park perimeter walls.

carries neither the conviction of documentary reportage nor the individuality of a personal response; the situations and characters singled out for treatment are not simply stereotypes but dull stereotypes with little sense of authenticity.[78]

The artistic potential of massed labour scarcely appealed to English artists before the 1930s. The Artists' International Association was founded in 1933 as a response to the threat of fascism and to express socialist themes. When Clifford Rowe (b.1904) first visited Moscow in 1930, he contributed to a Red Army art exhibition a painting of *Hunger Marchers Entering Trafalgar Square*, based on reports of the event he had read in the *Daily Worker*.[79] The protest march became a staple subject in the exhibitions organized by the Association during the 1930s, generally portrayed in a style approaching realism. Many of the artists who participated earned a living as 'commercial artists' or illustrators, and for them Hogarth had a more profound meaning than the innovations of the international avant-garde. Their emphasis on the experiences of everyday life and the political use of subject matter culminated in the 'Art for the People' exhibition held at the Whitechapel Art Gallery in 1939, but their work continued on a largely unofficial level throughout the Second World War. At the same time, the War Artists' Advisory Committee employed established British artists to record the effects of the conflict on the home front as well as overseas. The suffering endured by Londoners during the Blitz is, perhaps, most profoundly conveyed in the drawings by Henry Moore (1898–1986) of civilians sleeping in the underground (*see* col. pl. XX). Although a development to some extent of his abstracted monumental forms of the late 1930s, the Shelter figures take on a new emotive power from the experience of war; they may be seen as representing a collective stoicism and the will to survive in the face of the assaults on the city from the skies.

That the landed classes should be considered Londoners at all is debatable. The conventional view is of an aristocracy and gentry wedded to their ancestral domains, an image reinforced by the standard country-house portrait with its landscape backdrop. Yet such works only reflected one side of their subjects' lives, feeding a tradition that was designed to bolster not always well-founded aspirations to security of lineage. The fact is that from the sixteenth century onwards the upper classes came to London in ever-increasing numbers for business and for pleasure.

From the reign of Edward IV, the court was almost permanently in London or the Home Counties, as were the meetings of Parliament. The peerage and upper gentry had to travel to London to seek favour and office. They also came to further their property interests, particularly when the amount of land on the market grew dramatically with the sale of church and crown assets following the dissolution of the monasteries and the Civil War. Sales of land were frequently secured in London; disputes and legal business in general could be settled in the courts at Westminster. Lastly, but not least, the upper classes came to London to have fun, to indulge in conspicuous display and every fashionable mode of social intercourse. The observance of an annual Parliamentary term by the 1690s, lasting from November to May, provided an excuse for many in Society to spend half the year resident in London. As Thomas Gisborne wrote in the late eighteenth century,

> London is the centre to which almost all individuals who fill the upper and middle ranks of society are successively attracted. The country pays its tribute to the supreme city. Business, interest, curiosity, the love of pleasure, the desire for knowledge, the thirst for change, ambition to be deemed polite, occasion a continual influx into the metropolis from every corner of the Kingdom.[1]

Until the middle of the eighteenth century it would appear that the great collections of paintings and works of art were kept in London.[2] But their owners did not identify with the capital to the extent of commissioning portraits which actually showed them in a metropolitan setting. Despite the example of the monarch, despite their own extensive property holdings in the city, despite the mundane consideration that sittings for portraits usually took place in London, the upper classes avoided such a background. The portraits painted by Daniel Mytens (c.1590–1647) of the Earl and Countess of Arundel are an exception. The Earl is shown seated on the first floor of Arundel House in the Strand, pointing with his Earl Marshal's baton to his collection of antique marbles in the gallery, with a view of the Thames and the Surrey shore beyond, while his wife sits on the ground floor with the portrait gallery and garden behind her (Arundel Castle, on loan from the National Portrait Gallery).[3] Of all the great palaces along the Strand which were converted from bishops' residences in the sixteenth century, only Somerset House seems to have been similarly recorded, in a group portrait commemorating the signing of the peace treaty with Spain in 1604. The English negotiators sit across a carpeted table from the Spanish representatives in a room hung with tapestries, in front of a large window which appears to open onto a courtyard (National Portrait Gallery).[4]

2
Society

OPPOSITE

A Promenade at Carlisle House, Soho Square, c. 1781
JOHN RAPHAEL SMITH

According to William Hickey, in 1780 'a new species of amusement became quite the rage under the name of the Promenade. Mrs Cornelys' truly magnificent suite of apartments upon the principal floor were opened every Sunday night at seven o'clock for the reception of company. . . . The first people of the kingdom attended it, as did also the whole beauty of the metropolis from the Duchess of Devonshire down to the little milliner's apprentice.'

*The Reception Given by Charles II
for Claude Lamoral, Prince de
Ligne at Banqueting House,
17 September 1660* (detail)
GILLIS VAN TILBORCH

The Prince presents his son, the
Marquis de Roubaix, to the King,
watched by part of his 'innumerable
retinue' to which Evelyn referred.

AVDIANCE QVE DONNE LE ROI D'ANGLETERRE
A SON ALTESSE MONSEIGNEVR
LE PRINCE DE LIGNE
EN QVALITE D'AMBASSADEVR EXTRAORDINAIRE

The portrayal of the upper classes in London arose, first and foremost, because of their proximity to the monarch and their participation in affairs of state. As we have seen, their presence is recorded in royal entries to the capital and in coronation processions. Chapters of the Order of the Garter sometimes took place in London rather than at Windsor. The enhanced prestige of the Order during the reign of Charles I is reflected in the set of designs for tapestries which Sir Anthony van Dyck (1599–1641) commissioned to be hung at Whitehall, illustrating the history and ceremonial of the Garter. The extant oil sketch depicting the grand procession to the chapel, probably at Whitehall, on the feast of St George's Day expresses in the clearest possible terms the alliance between the crown, court and church on the eve of the Civil War (Trustees of Belvoir Estate).[5]

Whitehall provided the setting for the reception given in 1660 by Charles II for Claude Lamoral, Prince de Ligne and ambassador of Philip IV of Spain. The ambassador commissioned the Flemish artist Gillis van Tilborch (c.1625–c.1678) to record the moment when his son was presented to the king in the magnificent surroundings of the Banqueting House. The sumptuous French-inspired fashions of his entourage provide a vivid contrast to the sober attire of the English court, who had been cast into mourning by the death of the Duke of Gloucester from smallpox only four days earlier.

Peter Angelis (1685–1734) painted Queen Anne with the Knights of the Garter at Kensington Palace, where the Chapter was held in 1713 on account of her indisposition (National Portrait Gallery).[6] Around the same time, another Antwerp artist, Peter Tillemans (c.1684–1734), painted the Queen in the House of Lords. The schema dates back to the reign of Henry VIII, when the Blackfriars Parliament of 1523 was depicted in the Wriothesley Garter Book (Her Majesty the Queen); the throne provides the central focus with the Lord Chief Justice and other legal dignitaries seated on the woolsack, clerks at their table and the peers and bishops ranged on three sides. This choice of subject by Angelis and

Queen Anne in the House of Lords,
c.1708–10
PETER TILLEMANS

The Queen is depicted on the
throne, surrounded by her ladies,
Officers of State, Heralds and
pages, in the old House of Lords
which is hung with the Armada
Tapestries.

Tillemans, not long after they had arrived in England, suggests a pragmatic
attempt to win more commissions if not from the monarch then perhaps from the
peerage, which Tillemans at least was subsequently able to secure.[7]

By far the richest source of depictions of London Society relates, however, not
to the intricacies of court or government, but to the pursuit of pleasure. Naturally,
the most important and prestigious forms of entertainment were inspired by the
monarch himself. There are many examples of the elaborate designs made in
advance for the balls and masques enjoyed by the Tudor and early Stuart courts
but unfortunately there appear to be no extant depictions of them actually taking
place.[8]

Outdoor settings provided much greater scope. A tradition developed in the
seventeenth and eighteenth centuries of portraying Society in recognizably
London settings, in particular the semi-private domain of the royal parks.
Originally royal hunting grounds, their proximity to the palaces allowed the easiest
means of escape from the stultifying formalities of court etiquette to the simple
pleasures of strolling, feeding animals and birds, drinking fresh milk and taking up
sports like archery and pall mall. The concept of *rus in urbe* served as a metaphor
in the heart of the city for the ownership of land countrywide. Through a complex
network of walls and fences, the royal parks – initially at least – retained their
exclusivity yet at the same time provided vantage points where members of
Society could be seen by the lower classes.

By the mid seventeenth century there was no lack of precedent for artists to
draw on. The Flemish again provided the initial impetus, the detailed and
naturalistic observation of outdoor life being common in early Netherlandish
painting. More specifically, the compositions and imagery of Pieter Brueghel the
Elder, widely known from the 1560s through prints after his works, provided the
immediate artistic context for a unique record of outdoor festivities in mid-
sixteenth-century London, *A Fête at Bermondsey* by Joris Hoefnagel (1542–1600).

In this painting, which is precocious for its subject matter in the context of Flemish, let alone English art, Hoefnagel intermingled all classes – nobles, citizens, servants, entertainers, rustics – to record a celebration which lies somewhere between the sophisticated Flemish *buitenpartijen* and the informal *kermis*. It appears to be unique for its date, and was probably a specific response to an actual event. But the very duality of the style of celebration has contributed to the difficulty of identifying the event. The occasion might have been the visit of Queen Elizabeth to the home of Thomas Radcliffe, Earl of Sussex, which had formerly been the site of Bermondsey Abbey, but the comparative insignificance of the supposed royal party makes this implausible. It may show the Earl and Countess attending a village celebration. Certainly no other painting for at least another hundred years provides such a rich account of English social life.

Following the departure of Hoefnagel and his Flemish compatriot Anton van der Wyngaerde, the prospects for landscape painting in England were bleak. The more sophisticated genre which developed in France and the Netherlands during the late sixteenth and early seventeenth centuries, combining landscape with scenes from high life, found few parallels in England. But the artistic environment of the court of Charles I brought some innovation to the traditional views of royal palaces. A prospect of Greenwich by Adriaen van Stalbemt (1580–1662), from the hill overlooking the Tudor palace and half-completed Queen's House to the river, was embellished by Jan van Belcamp (d. *c.*1652) with the figures of the King and Henrietta Maria, and with attendant ladies and gentlemen discoursing in elegant groups (Her Majesty the Queen).[9] Presumably the artists and the client were aware of the work of David Vinckboons, Esaias van de Velde and Willem Buytewech, who specialized in compositions of courtly parties feasting, flirting and listening to music in an idealized open-air setting.[10]

Likewise the Continental market for prints of fashionable life by artists such as Abraham Bosse and Jacques Callot must have encouraged the Bohemian artist Wenceslaus Hollar (1607–77) to produce three series of allegorical fashion plates in London during the early 1640s based on the 'Four Seasons'.[11] Each season is represented by a young woman and the settings are, for the most part, distinctively English. For 'Summer' in the second series, a fashionably dressed lady stands in profile cooling the air with her fan before a backdrop of St James's Park, where courtiers stroll and deer graze. It constitutes the first view of the improvements made in the early seventeenth century to what had been a swamp fed by Tyburn stream, until it was enclosed and drained by Henry VIII. A menagerie was established by James I and by 1638, according to Puget de la Serre: 'This Park is full of wild animals [deer?], but as it is the place where ladies of the Court usually take their walk, their kindness has made the animals so tame, that they all submit to the power of their charms rather than to the pursuit of the dogs.'[12]

Hyde Park was sold off, but even during the Commonwealth St James's Park continued to be used by the ladies and gentlemen of Oliver Cromwell's court, although it was not open to the general public. Indeed, more improvements were made: the deer park was restocked and, at the behest of Elizabeth Cromwell, the cows were introduced that were to be a feature in nearly every subsequent depiction of the park.

However, it was during the Restoration that St James's Park flowered into fashion. In 1660, on the orders of Charles II, a canal was cut, young trees were planted in avenues and the park was opened to the public. Following the social patterns adopted by the leisured classes all over Europe but particularly in Paris, the newly designed park quickly became the smartest place for promenading.

LEFT *A Fête at Bermondsey* (detail), *c*. 1568
JORIS HOEFNAGEL

The setting is the south bank of the Thames opposite the Tower, with the church of St Mary Magdalene, Bermondsey, to the right.

RIGHT *Summer*, 1644
WENCESLAUS HOLLAR

The background shows Rosamund's Pond and the Park in a seemingly well-kempt state, the Banqueting House in the distance and old St Paul's beyond.

Its attractions as a subject for artists are not difficult to surmise. In the first place, it was closely connected with the king: he had improved it, he used it and he commissioned artists to depict it. The Dutch painter Hendrik Danckerts (c. 1630– after 1679), lured to England possibly by the potential for patronage in the re-established court, soon managed to win a commission from Charles to paint all the sea-ports and royal palaces. Sycophantic as well as decorative notions no doubt persuaded others to follow the king's lead, judging from the painting Danckerts made for the Earl of Berkeley of *Whitehall Palace and St James's Park*. Incorporating some of the improvements he had carefully noted in his drawings of the park, the artist depicted the king accompanied by courtiers exercising their dogs, as well as other groups of elegantly dressed strollers, deer round the still-young trees and ducks on the canal.[13] That the fashion for such decorative works spread is evident from the fact that Pepys at least contemplated employing Danckerts to decorate his dining room with views of royal palaces, and from the number of versions of the park scene in existence, usually attributed to Thomas Wyck (c.1616–77) or Jan Wyck (1652–1700), and varying only in the maturity of the trees and the scope of the menagerie (one at Hopetoun House features an ostrich).[14] The somewhat repetitive nature of the formula is underlined by a comparison with the delightful drawing made by Jacob Esselens (1626–87), who also travelled from Holland to London in the 1660s, showing people not only promenading but sitting informally in groups on the grass and in the shade of the mature trees near the Banqueting House (Royal Museum of Fine Arts, Copenhagen).[15]

The park continued to enjoy success and by the end of the century was firmly established as a sight to be seen by every foreign visitor. At the same time, the Dutch artists, engravers and publishers who had established themselves in London were well placed to exploit the market for topographical views of improvements to the capital and countryside on an international basis. Operating from a complex network of shared interests, they could offer drawings, engravings and collections of such works equally to the country landowner or to the foreign observer. For example, the production of *Britannia Illustrata* (or 'Views of Several of the Queen's Palaces also of the Principal Seats of the Nobility and Gentry of Great Britain') drew on work executed over a number of years by Jacob Knyff (d. 1681) and Leonard Knyff (1650–1721), who came from Haarlem, Johannes Kip (c.1653–1722), a native of Amsterdam, and various other artists. It was first published in 1707 by David Mortier, who was born in Amsterdam in 1673 and set up shop as a bookseller in the Strand in 1698. Alternatively titled *Nouveau Théâtre de la Grande Bretagne* and with constantly changing contents, it went through at least thirteen editions before 1749.[16]

Amid such burgeoning interest in topographical works, Kip must have been encouraged to publish on his own account in 1720 a magnificent twelve-sheet prospect of the City, Westminster and St James's from Buckingham House, dedicated to Her Royal Highness Wilhelmina Caroline, Princess of Wales. Drawn on such a scale, the staffage is of more than passing interest for it indicates clearly the lines of demarcation in the park. The Mall was the most fashionable walk; Green Walk or Duke Humphrey's (named after the middle aisle of old St Paul's)

The scene shows the eastern end of
the Mall, with Westminster Abbey
and the canal in the distance. The
Mall itself – slightly raised and
boarded in for the game of pall mall
– is crowded with members of
Society, notably Frederick, Prince
of Wales in the foreground
accompanied by three companions,
including possibly the 1st Duke of
Newcastle wearing the Garter.

was nearest the park wall; Close Walk or Jacobite Walk was at the head of
Rosamund's Pond, while the long Lime Walk led to a grove of elms. In the
engraving fashionably dressed ladies and gentlemen stroll in pairs up the Mall
alongside the pall-mall players. The gate in the fence separating St James's from
Green Park is open to allow two royal coaches through, followed by a cavalry troop
on their way to Hyde Park. Troops exercise near Horse Guards. A beggar woman
and her children are kept strictly outside the wall of the park in the lower right-
hand corner, but sweetmeat sellers and milkmaids are allowed to ply their trade
within.[17] The architect John Gwynn recalled, looking back from the 1760s,

> The Mall in a summer's evening was formerly one of the highest entertainments
> that can well be conceived, it was here that the people at a respectable distance
> could behold to advantage some of the greatest personages and most beautiful
> objects in the kingdom, and the order and decorum in which it was kept at that
> time, was sufficient to deter the meaner part of the people from intruding into a
> place which seemed by no means suited to persons of their appearance.[18]

The earliest painted view of the Mall, attributed to Marco Ricci (1676–1730)
around 1710, suggests a similar sense of order, playing on the contrast afforded by
Society enjoying the shade provided by the avenues of trees and the scenes of
pastoral tranquillity on each side.

The production of engraved London views reached a peak around 1750 when
Robert Sayer, in partnership with Henry Overton or John Bowles, produced

elegant prospects of the parks and pleasure gardens of Vauxhall and Ranelagh as well as the streets, squares, churches, public buildings and great houses of the metropolis. Based on paintings by Canaletto, or drawings by John Maurer, Jean-Baptiste-Claude Chatelain, Edward Rooker or Samuel Wale and engraved by Charles Grignion, Johan Sebastian Muller, Thomas Bowles and George Bickham Junior, among others, they give an air of generalized sociability but the figures are, for the most part, small and unimportant.[19]

For a closer look at the meaning and importance of deportment, gesture and manners, books of etiquette translated from the French provide an important source. F. Nivelon's *Rudiments of Genteel Behaviour* (1737), for example, was illustrated with single figures of ladies and gentlemen demonstrating the correct ways to curtsey, bow, carry oneself and so forth. They were executed by Bartholomew Dandridge (1691–*c*.1755) and engraved by Louis Philippe Boitard (fl. *c*.1733–63), both of whom were well acquainted with the French Rococo taste.[20] And it is in this context that an anonymous painting which constitutes the most glorious representation of *St James's Park and the Mall* should be placed. With a sense of movement that recalls Gravelot, the artist enlivens the royal presence and humanizes the topography with a mass of individuals captured in mid-display. The park undoubtedly provided the most advantageous artistic point in London for viewing the dress and manners of polite society.

The titles of two plays – Wycherley's *Love in a Wood; or, St James's Park* (1672) and an anonymous work *The Mall: or the Modish Lovers* (1674) – confirm that from the earliest years of its public existence St James's Park had an ambivalent reputation. César de Saussure's account of 1725 explained:

> the park is so crowded at times that you cannot help touching your neighbour. Some people come to see, some to be seen, and others to seek their fortunes; for many priestesses of Venus are abroad... all on the look-out for adventures.[21]

In his drawing dated 1744, Marcellus Laroon (1679–1772) seems to be indicating the park convention that a gentleman could address a lady unintroduced had its drawbacks. Not so for the ladies of the town who may be seen in two caricatures by Boitard in 1735 and 1745 entitled *Taste à–la–Mode*. Caricature depends for its effect on physical features, expression, carriage, dress, actions – all the mannerisms that make up an individual. Thus it can emphasize nuances which are only hinted at in more formal works. Although Boitard's prints were principally designed to ridicule the fashions of the day – the exaggerated frockcoats of the fops in 1735 and the extraordinary width of the panniered skirts in 1745 – other aspects of park life come to the fore. There is a continuous chain of swivelling eyes across both works as meaningful glances are interchanged. In the 1735 print, footmen with their staffs are present in such numbers as to suggest an uncomfortable familiarity with their betters. Moreover, prostitutes appear to be free to mingle with respectable society and to solicit gentlemen in public with little censure. The come-hither looks and gestures of the ladies and the plebeian appearance of the footmen collectively affirm that the Park was by no means as exclusive as the topographical prospects would have the world believe.

Promenade in the Mall, 1744
MARCELLUS LAROON

Laroon's groups of elegant figures rarely
can be placed topographically but in this
instance, the background is clearly St
James's Palace.

Taste à-la-Mode, 1745
S. F. PATTON after LOUIS PHILIPPE BOITARD

This print is one of a group issued
around 1750 satirizing fashionable
display in the Mall. The width of the
ladies' panniers is the principal
point of ridicule, but Boitard also
makes fun of masculine vanity in the
extravagant array of hats and wigs.

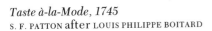

Taste A-La-Mode, 1745
Published According to Act of Parliament Sept 12 1745, Price 6.

This understanding adds a fresh dimension to the appreciation of the painting of *The Mall* by Thomas Gainsborough (*c*.1727–88). It was obviously the subject closest to hand (virtually outside his back door) which could be used for the artist's exploration of poetic landscape. But when it was first exhibited at Schomberg House in 1784, it provoked Bate-Dudley to remark, 'Looks of characteristic significance appear to be mutually exchanged by some of the groups in passing.' As Walpole later commented, the painting is 'all a-flutter like a lady's fan'. It is quintessentially about public display, seeing and being seen in a society where appearances told all. Visiting St James's Park the following year, Madame Roland decoded the scene for her daughter back in France, with a keen nose for social and fashion detail. It was, she found,

> very brilliant on a Sunday evening, and full of well-to-do people and well-dressed women: in general they are all tradespeople and citizens. The men are all dressed with great simplicity in dark cloth, white waistcoats, and always with their hats on their heads. . . . Many of the women wear beautiful white muslin dresses, made exactly like those we have copied from them, but generally tucked up with *cordons* passing under the skirt, which lift the dress to just above the height of the petticoat. They all wear curls under their hats, some large, some small. The hat is also very varied in form, and loaded with ribbons; very few of them are so light and elegant as ours.[22]

Gainsborough's uncharacteristic work represents a brief flirtation with the type of *fêtes galantes* which had been popular in France since the time of Watteau. The dissemination of Watteau's imagery throughout Europe, in engraved form by Jean de Jullienne during the late 1720s, 1730s and 1740s (Gainsborough owned a set of the *Recueil Jullienne*, the volumes of prints after Watteau which Jullienne had gathered together), inspired many imitators and started a fashion for decorative prints illustrating the play of high-life manners. Eighteenth-century France was the arbiter of taste and fashion, setting standards of style, elegance and a sophisticated code of behaviour between the sexes. The prints helped to diffuse these values, and their display indicated perhaps a desire to be considered part of polite society.[23]

By the late eighteenth century, with the added lustre given to the Season by the Prince of Wales, a number of English artists were able to profit from the French example, using their repertoire of subjects, as well as the compositional and rhetorical devices, in an English context. In the same year that Gainsborough painted *The Mall*, Henry Bunbury (1750–1811) engraved *St James's Park. The Fashions of 1783*, and two years later *The Gardens of Carlton House with Neapolitan Ballad Singers at the Fête Given by the Prince of Wales May 18, 1784*. A gentleman amateur who had been on the Grand Tour, Bunbury's gifts as a caricaturist are tempered in these works by a sense of elegant decorum. His career in the army was to lead to his appointment in 1787 as equerry to the Duke of York and certainly there is little sense of mockery in the society he drew. Thomas Rowlandson (1756–1827) would appear to have been familiar with the work of Gabriel de Saint-Aubin, whose etchings *Spectacles des Tuileries* were published in

The Mall, 1784
THOMAS GAINSBOROUGH

Within the rustic landscape complete with
cows, Gainsborough introduces a
sophisticated social interplay of manners.

Vauxhall Gardens, 1784
THOMAS ROWLANDSON

Rowlandson conveys by virtue of the elegance of the setting
and masterly control of the grouping, the superficial
politesse of Society listening to Mrs Weichsel singing from
the Gothic orchestra. But the generalized aura of urbanity is
constantly in danger of toppling over into vulgar excess,
through the calligraphic virtuosity and irrepressible
humour of his line.

The Promenade in St James's Park, 1790
EDWARD DAYES

Besides the usual courteous exchanges,
Dayes records the presence on the right of
chairs, which had been introduced in 1785.
The *St James's Chronicle* reported that the
belles were 'quite delighted with the plan of
being *chaired* and surrounded by the men,
à la mode des Tuileries.'

1760–63. His most famous exhibition watercolour *Vauxhall Gardens* was shown at
the Royal Academy in 1784. Large-scale prints after watercolours by Edward
Dayes (1763–1804) entitled *The Promenade in St James's Park* and *An Airing in
Hyde Park* were published respectively in 1790 and 1793. All these works share
certain characteristics: they are essentially proscenium stages, framed by trees and
sometimes with architectural features. But attention is focused on the interaction
of the players who are, for the most part, fashionable members of Society.
Flirtatious glances are exchanged; exaggerated courtesies are observed. They are
almost static, reinforcing the conscious sense of being on public view.

The variety of fashionable diversions in eighteenth-century London was on the
increase. Around 1710, the Swiss Count Heidegger had introduced the masquerade to England and thereafter throughout the century, with minor intervals,
this form of entertainment proved to be one of the most popular with the upper
ranks of Society. At first, masquerades were held by subscription in the King's
Theatre, Haymarket, and during the summer they came to be staged in the main
public pleasure gardens of Vauxhall and Ranelagh. In the second half of the
century, the most fashionable venues were Carlisle House, Soho Square, presided
over by Mrs Cornelys, and from 1772 Wyatt's magnificent Pantheon in Oxford
Street, 'in point of Ennui and Magnificence the wonder of the XVIIIth Century
and the British Empire', as Edward Gibbon described it.[24] The annual exhibitions
of the Royal Academy of Arts were a highlight of the Season from their inception in
1769, and the opening of Boydell's Gallery in Pall Mall twenty years later provided
another venue for polite society, again safeguarded from the riff-raff by admission
charges. All were added to the repertoire of those artists, like Michel-Vincent

*A Masquerade at the
King's Theatre,
Haymarket, c. 1724*
attributed to
GIUSEPPE GRISONI

Count Heidegger, who
became theatre manager
in 1711, introduced
masquerades at a guinea a
ticket on nights when there
were no performances.
Mist's Weekly Journal
(1718) found the theatre
'beautifully adorned and
illuminated by 500 wax
lights. . . . By the vast
variety of dresses (many of
them very rich) you would
fancy it a congress of the
principal persons of all the
nations of the world.'

The Faro Table, c. 1795
JAMES GILLRAY

Faro was a banker's card game imported from France. Gillray has chosen to depict the moment of highest tension when one dealer calls the three spades, while across the table another house dealer is still raking in the losing stakes from the previous round.

A Gaming Table at Devonshire House, 1791
THOMAS ROWLANDSON

Rowlandson characteristically gives resonance to the overt purpose of the game with punning sexual allusions.

'Charles' Brandoin (1733–1807), Johann Ramberg, John Raphael Smith (1752–1812) and Francis Wheatley (1747–1801), who were not averse to holding up a flattering mirror to the fashionable world and transferring the modes of promenading and greeting to a safer, more circumscribed indoor setting. The associated prints after their work helped to advertise the institutions concerned besides serving as elegant souvenirs of London life, and perhaps even as talismans to be cherished during the dull months of exile in the country.

This was not, of course, the sole image of Society in London purveyed at the time. The caricaturists constantly undermined the dignity of members of the royal family, aristocracy and government. As depicted by Gillray, Rowlandson and a host of lesser talents, the majority of upper-class types were portrayed as reckless and loose-living in the extreme.

In *The Rake's Progress* and *Marriage à la Mode,* Hogarth had underlined the connection between the upper classes and London as a place where money was frittered away on a battery of sycophants and flunkies, on drink, gambling and women. The genre of caricature was more ephemeral and scurrilous in intent than Hogarth's cycles of moral exempla, but it permitted the spectacle of the same range of dissipations. The treatment given by Gillray and Rowlandson to gambling serves as a useful example. Both artists show Society at its most naked and vulnerable, little concerned, for the moment at least, in maintaining a front of sophisticated urbanity. In Rowlandson's finished watercolour, the Duchess of Devonshire is still in the process of emptying her purse when her sister throws the dice. The other gamblers variously express steely concentration, avarice, lust and greed. Gillray's drawing is less individualized, but expresses even more clearly through the vigorous energy of his line an atmosphere of tension and suspense.

If gambling was one of the more private pleasures indulged in by Society, riding in the Row was as public a form of activity as promenading in the Mall. Hyde Park, opened to the public by Charles I, became a rival outdoor attraction as it had the advantage of catering for carriages and horses. Even when it was sold in three lots during the Commonwealth, coaches and horses could still enter for a fee. After the Restoration, it resumed its importance as a fashionable rendezvous, the principal stage for display being provided by the so-called Ring in the centre of the park. The constant complaints about the dust and crowds do not seem to have deterred visitors. In the 1730s, Queen Caroline improved Hyde Park by draining the pools to form the Serpentine and a new road was built to Kensington. The old road then became the most fashionable drive and ride, known as Rotten Row, and was frequented particularly on Sundays. At the same time, some 300 acres were annexed onto Kensington Gardens which was still the exclusive reserve of the royal family except on Saturdays, when they were not in residence. Only those in full dress were admitted and as late as 1795, gentlemen wearing silk neckties or leather breeches without top boots, as well as private soldiers and sailors, were not allowed to enter.[25]

Curiously, no visual record seems to have survived of either the Ring or Rotten Row before the 1780s. Then, with the renewed surge of interest in horsemanship and equipage fostered by the Prince of Wales, the most splendid sights were depicted by sporting artists and, inevitably, by Rowlandson and Gillray. In contrast to Rowlandson's depiction of the dash and daring of fashionable riding in *Showing Off in Rotten Row*, Gillray's panorama of the same scene presented a bathetical mismatch of horses to riders, thus reducing the scene to a farce little designed to inspire respect (New York Public Library).

Showing Off in Rotten Row,
c.1785–90
THOMAS ROWLANDSON

A sketch from Rowlandson's most dynamic period, it encapsulates the fashionable mode of riding in Hyde Park, under the influence of the Prince of Wales.

In the Row, Hyde Park
CONSTANTIN GUYS

The drawing can be traced to the
period in the 1840s, when Guys was
employed as a French tutor in the
family of Dr T. G. Girtin, son of the
watercolourist.

Lady, 1898
WILLIAM NICHOLSON

Although frequently seen in the
context of Toulouse-Lautrec's
poster designs of the 1890s,
Nicholson's bold compositions have
more in common with Joseph
Crawhall's simple reworkings of
chapbook woodcuts, which he much
admired from his youth.

Hyde Park continued to attract artists in the nineteenth century, while St
James's Park became increasingly neglected. Thomas Shotter Boys included a
view of *Hyde Park, near Grosvenor Gate* in *London As It Is.* Building on a
foundation of precise topographical draughtsmanship, Boys had developed during
his years among the Bonington circle in Paris a breadth of composition and
sophisticated handling of colour, enlivened by a sympathy for the human interest
to be found in a location which is quite original.[26] Like many watercolour artists of
his generation, he attempted to augment his meagre income from watercolour
sales through publishing ventures, with varying degrees of success. The critical
acclaim which greeted *Picturesque Architecture in Paris, Ghent, Antwerp, Rouen
. . .* (1839) made *London As It Is* a natural successor. As a sensitive observer of
social mores, Boys must have chosen this particular spot on the edge of the park,
not merely because of the topographical interest with the grand houses on Park
Lane, the trees and open spaces, but because of the contrast between the riders
and people on foot. Society was railed off and insulated by its equipages and
mounts from the bourgeois families out for a walk.

The early nineteenth-century Anglo-French watercolour school left a rich
legacy. It conferred on its subject matter a cosmopolitan vitality which revived the
somewhat faded topographical tradition. The premium it placed on spontaneity of
response enabled its followers to capture the changes of light, atmosphere and

above all, the movement of the people. Constantin Guys and Eugène Lami benefited greatly from their example, frequently all but abandoning an architectural setting. As Baudelaire commented in his essay, 'The Painter of Modern Life', Guys 'delights in fine carriages and proud horses, the dazzling smartness of the grooms, the expertness of the footmen, the sinuous gait of the women, the beauty of the children, happy to be alive and nicely dressed.'[27] Guys's figures in parks require almost no surroundings to be understood.

Similarly, Lami was for Baudelaire 'the poet of official dandyism'[28] and the watercolours he executed in England reveal his sparkling sense of occasion. His view of a presentation to Victoria and Albert at a Restoration costume ball in 1851 provides a glittering contrast to the stiff ceremonial of Claude de Lamoral's reception almost three hundred years earlier (Her Majesty the Queen).[29]

The ready equation of Rotten Row with Society was to last until the Second World War. Blanchard Jerrold extolled its blessings in *London: A Pilgrimage*, accompanied by Doré's depiction of 'Ladies' Mile', using terms which curiously echo Baudelaire's praise of Guys.[30] 'Church Parade' on Sundays was *de rigueur* for the Gibson Girl, over from America in 1897, and the Row was the almost inevitable choice of backdrop for the 'Lady' in the series of woodcuts by William Nicholson (1872–1949) entitled *London Types*, published by Heinemann a year later.[31] Chas. Laborde included the statutory park scene in *Rues et Visages de Londres* of 1928.

Scene in Belgrave Square: Ladies Entering their Carriage, 1850
EUGÈNE LAMI

By 1840, Belgrave Square had become the most fashionable address in London. The ladies emerge in a flurry of shawls and petticoats, well insulated from the horrors of the city by the presence of liveried footmen, the portico, the carpet on the pavement and ultimately the carriage.

The Rake on the Crest of the Wave, 1934
after DAVID LOW

According to Rebecca West, who wrote the accompanying text, George 'tosses notes over his shoulder at the little dancers, since he feels that they too are participants in this gay conjunctive movement which he imagines governs the whole world as well as his own heart.'

The more intimate context of Society 'at home' during the period between the two World Wars was deftly captured in the 'portrait interiors' of Sir John Lavery (1856–1941). The Laverys' own grand way of life gave the artist an entrée to affluent surroundings of relaxed elegance while weekending in the country and, equally, when attending an exclusive soirée like that depicted in *Chamber Music at Wimborne House,* the Arlington Street home of Viscount Wimborne (Private Collection).[32] The illustrators of the *Sphere* and the *Illustrated London News* attempted to create the same aura of being behind the scenes, where the camera was not permitted to enter, but with less success.

Moreover, for those hell-bent on enjoying themselves there were too many competing attractions, better suited to commemoration by flash-bulb and gossip column, for the artistic legacy to survive. The sheer pace of life – fast cars, cocktail parties and nightclubs – to a large extent precluded the dignified portrayal of Society. The politics of the period made the fads and fashions, the extravagance and pretensions of a small group absurdly irrelevant. *The Modern 'Rake's Progress'* as depicted by David Low (1891–1963) in 1934 followed 'George' from his debut as a press celebrity through parties, cabarets, marriage, divorce, racing and gambling before finding his level on the dole queue. T. C. Dugdale's painting of 1936, *The Arrival of the Jarrow Marchers* in London opens the window out of Lavery's world and highlights the decadence within.

3
Merchants

Merchants are, in general terms, those who buy and sell commodities for profit but from medieval times this usage tended to be restricted to wholesale tradesmen, especially those dealing with foreign countries. Thus Chaucer's merchant: 'The sea should be kept free at any cost/(He thought) upon the Harwich Holland range/He was an expert at currency exchange.'

London grew rich through trade both abroad and with the rest of the country. Defoe summarized the role the capital had played for at least two hundred years when he wrote, '*London* consumes all, circulates all, exports all, and at last pays for all, and this greatness and wealth of the City is the Soul of the Commerce to all the Nation.'[1] In his Survey, John Stow allowed that London received great nourishment from the residence of the monarch, from the presence of Parliament and from the Courts of Justice, but he thought that its most important advantage was its situation on the river. London's trading pre-eminence until the sixteenth century was founded on the export of wool and cloth to the Netherlands. However, the loss of Calais in 1558, the outbreak of the Dutch revolt which shook Antwerp's prosperity, the successive severances from the Antwerp market in 1564 and 1569, followed by the sack of the city in 1576 and the closure of its outlet to the sea in 1585, forced the London merchants to diversify their markets. Starting with the Russia Company in 1555, trading companies were founded to secure the monopoly of English trade, and the wealthy London merchants dominated them. The great wholesalers ran extensive financial operations, owned ships, warehouses and granaries, invested in privateering and in land.

Their power base was the leading livery companies, which were in the process of changing from craft guilds to select clubs of traders whose representatives ran Guildhall. Craftsmen were subordinate and, indeed, were largely excluded from membership of the overseas trading companies. The first loyalty of the merchant oligarchy was to the City. Its members had served their apprenticeships within City walls; they usually married the daughters of fellow citizens. Their friendships were formed in the City, through business and civic office, and their success was best understood and appreciated within these circles. In civic government, they were resistant to change and supported order, stability and tradition. Their deep conservatism extended to their private lives. It was usual for them to lease rather than to buy their City residences. On the whole, they avoided ostentatious displays of wealth. They were quite distinct from the more extravagant Court at Westminster.

This context helps to explain the quite different manner in which the merchants of London were depicted from the modes adopted to portray Society. In general, just as they rejected the fopperies of Court dress, so merchants shunned the latest imported fashions in art. And given their reluctance to put down roots in a single property, whether in London or the country, there would not have been the same incentive to accumulate galleries of ancestral portraits. The Great Fire of 1666 probably destroyed much of the evidence, but from that which remains, two characteristics stand out. Firstly, the methods used to depict merchants were highly conservative. Secondly, the purpose of the majority of commissions was institutional rather than individual.

There is some evidence to suggest that by the fifteenth century the richest merchants were buying books illuminated in London.[2] The earliest guild patent of arms to survive, granted by Henry VI to the Drapers' Company in 1439, is a fine example of illumination and heraldic painting. But the portrayal of merchants themselves in the late medieval period is almost non-existent. In the letters patent granted by Henry VI to the Leathersellers' Company in 1444, eighteen members of the mystery are depicted down one margin, kneeling in their blue livery. The same company continued its seemingly unique tradition by illustrating the grant of re-incorporation made by James I in 1604 with pictures of the members grouped in pairs, wearing black robes with red and black hoods, holding documents and involved in earnest discussion. The earliest extant depiction of aldermen, c.1446, is a set of ink and watercolour drawings believed to have been compiled for heraldic purposes by Roger Leigh, Clarenceux King of Arms 1435–60.

The pre-Fire churches that remain give some indication of the wealth of funerary sculpture that might have existed before 1666. St Helen, Bishopsgate, is rich in such monuments, incorporating those of St Martin Outwich, which was demolished in the 1870s. The earliest, dating from around 1400, is the tomb of John de Oteswick and his wife. Near them lie Sir John Crosby (d. 1475) and his first wife, on a tomb which bears the arms of the Grocers' Company and the Staple of Calais. Employed by the crown on many diplomatic missions, he built the sumptuous mansion Crosby Place, which stood south of the church until its demolition and the removal of the hall to Chelsea early this century. More illuminating, perhaps, is the series of wall monuments dating from the second half of the sixteenth to the early seventeenth century. They all depict the deceased kneeling in armour – a sign of gentrification – or wearing sober old-fashioned attire, with their wives and children, piously preparing to meet their Maker. There is only a hint in the inscriptions of the immensely active, even aggressive business lives they led.

Here lies Sir Andrew Judd (d. 1558), Lord Mayor, citizen and skinner, founder of Tonbridge School, who is shown with his first wife, four sons and one daughter; according to the inscription, 'To Russia and Mussova/To Spayne Gynny withoute fable/Traveld he by land and sea/Both Mayre of London and Staple/The Commonwelthe he norished.' There is Alderman William Bond (d. 1576), 'moste famous in his age for his greate adventures by sea and land' and his son Captain Martin Bond (d. 1643), citizen and haberdasher, who was Commander of the City Trained Bands at Tilbury in Armada year, and who is shown in his tent with sentries posted outside and his horse and groom. But the two grandest tombs are in the nave and date from the early seventeenth century. Alderman Richard Staper (d. 1608) was, according to Stow and the inscription on his monument, the greatest merchant of his day, 'the chiefest actor in discoveri of/The trades of Turkey and East/India, a man humble in prosperity.' If anything, this understates his achievements for he was a member of all of the trading companies, imported southern commodities from Seville and Malaga, and had business interests in Morocco and Genoa as well as the Orient. The galleon which surmounts his monument is particularly appropriate since he had shares in the pillaging

Symon Eyer [sic], *c*. 1446

Simon Eyre, originally an upholsterer, was admitted freeman of the Drapers' Company in 1419 and is depicted as alderman for Cornhill Ward. He became Lord Mayor in 1445–46 and was renowned for his acts of charity; he built Leadenhall as a granary for the city.

John Isham

Although John Isham (*c.* 1525–96) was born and died in Northamptonshire, from 1542 to 1572 he had a moderately successful career as a City merchant. As a mercer and Merchant Adventurer, he exported kersey and broadcloth to Antwerp and imported to London luxury textiles of Italian origin until his early retirement, possibly due to the increasing vicissitudes of trade with Antwerp.

expedition of 1598, when five English vessels captured Spanish provisions of grain and arms.[3]

The most magnificent monument is reserved for Sir John Spencer (d. 1609/10), his wife and only daughter. A member of the Clothworkers' Company, he traded with Spain, Turkey and Venice and became extraordinarily rich, according to one seventeenth-century commentator, 'by falsifying and monopolizing of all manner of commodities'.[4] Certainly in 1591 he was accused of appropriating the whole trade with Tripoli but it did not stop him becoming Lord Mayor in 1594–95. In this role he distinguished himself by hunting down Papists with particular zeal, including the Queen's Italian musicians. He restored Crosby Place to its former glory and had a country house at Canonbury, whence his daughter eloped in a baker's basket with Lord Compton. Spencer was against the match and had been gaoled in the Fleet in 1599 for imprisoning his daughter, a well-documented example of the suspicion felt by merchants for the parasitical sloths at Court, which in this instance was to prove well-founded. On Spencer's death a lavish funeral was staged, but true to character he did not leave a single bequest to charity.

A brief resumé of such careers only serves to highlight the discrepancy between the daring exploits and the meagre visual records we have of them. The funeral monuments represent the merchants at their most formal and constrained, giving no indication of the lives they led. The church of St Andrew Undershaft contains a wall monument carved by Gerard Johnson of Sir Thomas Offley (1505?–82), who unlike Spencer was renowned for his charity: 'of merchaunt taylors he was free the staplers chief staye/his dealings just, for whome the poor continually do pray.' Thanks to the survival of his inventory for probate in the Court of Chancery, it is possible to learn a little more about his house in Lime Street. It had a chapel which contained two paintings of the Virgin Mary, and three other paintings or pieces of sculpture of unspecified subjects are listed. The devotional works, perhaps confirming Offley's suspected Catholic sympathies, are unusual for the date, but possibly indifference to art in the City was not as general as is frequently supposed.[5]

The treasures of the guilds comprise above all their gold and silver plate, and they also own some outstanding early textiles in the form of Elizabethan Masters' embroidered garlands or crowns, and rich funeral palls of Italian velvet damask dating back to the fifteenth century.[6] The portraits of the earliest Masters of the companies have largely been repainted. Looking out warily over their starched collars and ruffs, they are clad in rich sober attire or the Lord Mayor's robes and chain of office. They hold at most an embroidered glove or a document, and sometimes a *memento mori* skull rests at their feet. The Merchant Taylors' Company, for example, has a selection dating back to a primitive portrait of Sir Thomas White, Master in 1535, the richest man of his day in London and founder of St John's College, Oxford. The typical standard of City taste is perhaps reflected in the eight paintings which John Vernon, Master in 1609, presented to the Company in 1616; they consisted of his own rather dim portrait, portraits of Henry VIII and Queen Elizabeth, the Arms of England and four miscellaneous portraits, of an equally uninspired nature.[7]

These works represent an institutional equivalent to the ancestral portraits which were commissioned for country seats. The intention was to provide visual evidence of the tradition and continuity of the company in support of its claims to privilege. It is rarely possible to identify the artists. They were not the foreign artists employed in Court circles. Usually, they would have been members of the Painter-Stainers' Company, a fraternity which had existed in the City since at least 1283 and was consequently familiar with the requirements of citizens. Most of the work undertaken by its members was of a decorative variety – external and internal house-painting, wall hangings, shop signs, coach and barge decoration, heraldry – but they also had pretensions to portrait painting. In 1575, they petitioned the Queen, complaining about the 'fraudulent workmanship', 'by such as never have bene brought up in the knowledge of painting as well an conterfeyting of your Majesties picture and the pictures of noblemen and others'.[8] In the early seventeenth century, Inigo Jones was a member and at the St Katherine's Day dinner held by the Company in 1637, the guests also included Sir Anthony van Dyck and his wife. But the presence of these luminaries should not encourage the belief that the majority of members were conversant with Continental artistic practice. On the evidence of the guild portraits, this was palpably not the case.

Sir Lionel Duckett, 1585

Sir Lionel Duckett (1509–87) was one of the richest men of his day and Lord Mayor in 1572–73. His fortune was based on his mining interests in Cumberland and Germany, cloth and wine shipment, piracy and the slave trade.

The degree of their mediocrity, however, can only be assessed in relation to the modes of depicting merchants and their lives which were used at the time in Europe. By the sixteenth century the association of money with the devil had lost much of its force, but both common people and the learned condemned money-lending and usury. It is scarcely surprising, therefore, that there are virtually no portraits of merchants actually handling money. Instead, they were represented in moral exempla, warning of the dangers attendant upon such practices.

The Money Changer and his Wife (The Louvre), painted by Quentin Massys in 1514, does not castigate trade outright. Painting his subjects in half-length close-up, the artist drew on the fifteenth-century Netherlandish tradition of naturalistic observation to render every detail of their appearance and surroundings. The merchant is weighing some money; his wife watches to ensure the accuracy of the balance, her hand resting on a book of illuminated devotions. On the table before them and the shelves behind are objects with connotations of both luxury and piety. The painting is unique in Massys' *oeuvre* for its suspension of judgment. There are none of the grotesque extremes of ugliness to be found in his later treatment of similar subjects, which were taken up by his followers – his son Jan Massys, Jan van Hemessen and Marius van Reymerswael. The work warns against an exclusive adherence to worldly values and gently suggests that behaviour must be righteous in both the spiritual and the temporal spheres.[9]

It is within this context that Hans Holbein's remarkable series of portraits of the merchants of the London Steelyard may be placed.[10] In the Middle Ages, trade in northern Europe was dominated by the merchants who formed the German Hanseatic League, known as the Hanse. They controlled the Baltic trade from Russia to England, including the central European river routes of the Rhine, Elbe and Vistula. In England, they had first obtained privileges from Edward I in 1303,

Georg Gisze, 1532
HANS HOLBEIN THE YOUNGER

None of Holbein's Steelyard
portraits itemized the sitter's
context in such detail; indeed,
Gisze's position on the canvas was
altered by the artist to allow more of
the background to be visible.

Sir Thomas Gresham, 1544

Gresham came from a family who
had been successful merchants in
the City since the fifteenth century.
In 1544 he began trading in the Low
Countries on Henry VIII's behalf,
marking the start of his career as a
brilliant financial agent and
diplomat for the Crown.

which were extended by Edward III and further augmented by Edward IV in 1474. They had warehouses or factories in a number of English coastal towns but their main depot, the Stillyard or Steelyard, was in London. Here they bought houses and land, which gave them the right to participate in City government; they themselves were totally self-governing. The development of the profitable trade in cloth, however, bred resentment of their privileges within the English merchant community, and led to their eventual expulsion at the end of the sixteenth century.

When Holbein arrived in 1532 on his second visit to England, the German merchants were still reasonably secure and by no means unpopular. They imported necessities and charged fair prices for them, while competition with English merchants for the export of English goods drove up prices for home produce. As on his first visit in 1526, Holbein had passed through Antwerp on his journey from Basel and, through the good offices of Erasmus, had met Quentin Massys. He was therefore presumably aware of the secular works Massys was painting and even if he did not share the antipathy towards wealth reflected in many, he might have derived from him the notion of portraying a sitter surrounded by objects of associated meaning.

Holbein's portrait of Georg Gisze of Danzig is life-size and depicts the merchant standing behind a table opening a letter addressed 'To my brother George Gisze in London'. The artist delights in rendering the contrasts in surface textures: the costly Turkey carpet, the glass vase, the delicate carnations picking up the colour of the rich satin sleeves. But most of the accoutrements are distinctly businesslike: letter-writing equipment, scissors, a clock, a metal box filled with change and letters folded behind racks on the wall. With his characteristic linear precision,

Holbein records the wariness of the sitter, as if confirming the worldly-wise motto written on the wall, 'Nulla sine merore voluptas' – 'There is no pleasure without grief'. Beside it the artist painted an unevenly suspended balance, echoing the warning made in *The Money Changer and his Wife*.

As well as painting individual portraits, Holbein executed two large commissions for the Steelyard itself: allegorical paintings representing the Triumph of Poverty and the Triumph of Riches for the hall, and a design for the Parnassus pageant commissioned by the merchants for the entry of Queen Anne into the City in 1533. By 1536 he was firmly established at Court and the merchant portraits ceased. However, his commission from the Barber-Surgeons to paint the granting by Henry VIII of their Charter in 1540, which united the Company of Barbers with the Guild of Surgeons, might have initiated a new phase of work for the City, had not the artist died suddenly of the Plague in 1543.

In view of the cosmopolitan circles in which the London merchants worked, it is perhaps surprising that they did not make better use of artists in the countries where they had closest trading links. Paul Withypoll (*c.* 1480/85–1572), a Bristol merchant taylor, commissioned a triptych from the Venetian artist, Antonio da Solario, and was depicted as the donor in the centre panel, kneeling beside the Virgin and Child (Bristol Museum and Art Gallery).[11] Sir Thomas Gresham (1519?–79), financial agent of the English crown from 1552 to 1574, who divided his time between London and Antwerp, seems to have employed Flemish artists to paint his portrait on a number of occasions. The earliest is full-length and shows him standing with a skull by his right foot; it is dated 1544 and possibly commemorates his marriage to Anne Ferneley that year. The most penetrating, if it be he, is the portrait in the Rijksmuseum by Antonis Mor (1520–76), which is three-quarter length and shows the subject seated in sober merchant dress, all the canniness and weight of experience apparent in his expression.[12] No great London merchant seems to have gone to the daring extremes of Jakob Fugger 'The Rich' who was portrayed by Lorenzo Lotto in 1538 smilingly weighing coins on the scales he is holding – a manner of depiction unique even in Lotto's *oeuvre* (Hungarian National Gallery, Budapest).

During the sixteenth century, London merchants achieved a strong presence abroad. English Merchant Adventurers made their home in Antwerp, supplying an arch for the entry of Philip II in 1549, just as the Hanseatic merchants supported royal entries to London. There was an English Quay for them to the north of the town and a headquarters, the English house, in Prinsstraat. But unfortunately, there seem to be no extant depictions of either location. Instead, the merchant himself came to be portrayed as an identifiable type on the maps, guides and souvenir albums which both reflected and stimulated the curiosity about foreign lands that was growing throughout Europe. Through his international travels, he came to be seen as the quintessential Londoner, his conservative appearance being immediately recognizable, unlike that of the English courtier with his French-inspired fashions and his ambivalent relationship with the capital.

At the foot of the bird's-eye plan of London executed by the Flemish engraver Francis Hogenberg (*c*.1540–*c*.1590) for the first volume of *Civitates Orbis*

Civis Londinensis melioris qualitatis Uxor (Merchant's wife of London), 1643
WENCESLAUS HOLLAR

This miniature plate from Hollar's *Theatrum Mulierum* portrays the sober attire of a citizen's wife, although there are small indications of vanity in her fine lace collar, embroidered petticoat and shoe adorned with a frivolous pompom.

The Lord Mayor and Aldermen, c. 1580
LUCAS DE HEERE

The artist also depicted the citizens' wives, and English noblemen in their parliamentary and Garter robes.

Terrarum in 1572, a London merchant is depicted wearing a long fur-trimmed gown and followed by his servant, who wears a short doublet and carries his master's sword and a small round shield. The figure of the merchant's wife evidently derives from one of the earliest illustrated costume books, François Deserpz's *Recueil de la Diversité des Habits* of 1562. The London citizens found in many costume books produced in Germany and Italy towards the end of the sixteenth century were highly fanciful adaptations of Hogenberg. Only Cesare Vecellio appears to have made a special effort at accuracy: in the second edition of *Habiti Antichi e Moderni* of 1598, the English merchant is shown wearing the serviceable clothing – broad-brimmed hat, short cloak, wide breeches – he would naturally have been seen in when he came on business to Vecellio's native Venice.

In contrast, when travellers came to England they were fascinated by the most distinctive styles of national dress. Lucas de Heere (1535–84), a Protestant refugee from Ghent, drew the Lord Mayor and two aldermen in their liveries for his history *Corte Beschryvinghe van England, Schotland ende Irland*, rather than the merchants going about their business. Similarly, the *alba amicorum* or illustrated autograph albums kept by German students on their tours round Europe are filled with depictions of the Lord Mayor, sheriff and aldermen in procession, not to mention the Lord Mayor's wife with her rich dress and train irresistibly recalling Chaucer: 'To be called "*Madam*" is a glorious thought,/And so is going to church and being seen/Having your mantle carried like a queen.'[13] That the merchant's wife, however, never espoused the fashions of the Court is apparent from the sets of small fashion plates by Hollar, *Ornatus Mulierbris Anglicianus . . .* and *Theatrum Mulierum*, published respectively in 1640 and 1642–44. A clear distinction is made between the dress of ladies of the Court, with their elaborately curled hair, décolleté silk gowns and fans, and that of merchants' wives, who wear felt hats or plain caps and demure dark dresses.[14]

These isolated depictions of individual members of the merchant class scarcely give a comprehensive idea of their lifestyle. For such a view, no image is more instructive than Jost Amman's celebrated woodcut *Allegory of Trade*, published in Nuremberg in 1585. The great merchant sits like a spider at the centre of a web of activity, surrounded by accountants, bankers, brokers, bales of merchandise and barrels of commodities being bought, sold and transported from all over the globe.[15] The heart of this network of intelligence was the bourse or exchange. No town of any size was without one. Merchants had always congregated to hear news, pass on information and do business, but the earliest formal exchange was not set up until 1409, in Bruges; Antwerp followed in 1460 and from there they spread throughout Europe. The exchange in London was built at the expense of Thomas Gresham on land given by the City. It was designed by the Flemish master builder, Henri van Paeschen, who based his plan on that of the Antwerp exchange of Cornelis Floris, constructed in 1518. Gresham also probably commissioned Hogenberg to engrave two views of the building – an exterior and an interior – to commemorate its opening. The latter included a few token groups strolling in the open court, two figures closeted in conversation seated under the colonnade and a couple of dogs.[16] The Royal Exchange, as it became known following the Queen's visit in 1570, quickly established itself as one of the showpieces of London, proof of its cosmopolitan sophistication. It was only three-quarters of a century later, however, that the artistic possibilities of recording the rich diversity of English and foreign merchants pursuing their business within its four walls were realized by Hollar.

We should not expect to find representations of merchants handling the commodities they dealt in: an army of middlemen was employed to get the goods to London, store them and then distribute them round the country. Thus

BELOW LEFT *Byrsa Londinensis vulgo The Royall Exchange of London*, 1644
WENCESLAUS HOLLAR

The exchange is shown at its busiest, swarming with traders. Although no real indication is given of the special areas customarily used by different types of merchant, two Muscovy traders in fur hats can be seen on the left near a woman ballad-seller.

BELOW RIGHT *The Imports of Great Britain from France* (detail), 1757
LOUIS PHILIPPE BOITARD

The scene is set on the legal quays by the Custom House. The French packet disgorges purveyors of French luxury commodities to the delight of fashionable Londoners. On the right, a wine merchant is tasting from a barrel of claret which has been opened for him by two servants.

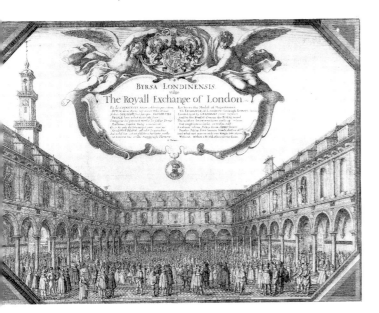

merchants are almost never present in marine paintings of the legal quays which stretched from London Bridge to the Tower, or the wharves and shipyards down river. They were run by the wharfingers aided by watchmen, porters and other labourers. But a vigorous, if imaginary impression of the bustle of the quays is provided by Boitard's satirical print of 1757, *The Imports of Great Britain from France* 'Humbly Address'd to the Laudable Association of Anti-Gallicans, and the generous promoters of the British Arts & Manufactories'. It ridicules the excessive admiration of fashionable London for all things French. The only eighteenth-century portrait showing a merchant on a wharf appears to be that of Thomas Fielder, a fruit-broker, commissioned by the Grocers' Company from Mason Chamberlin (fl. 1763–87) and presented to the sitter in recognition of his service to the Company for forty years.

Part of the difficulty in tracing such works lies in the fact that, by the eighteenth century, the term 'merchant' had ceased to have a precisely defined meaning, even though in general terms it was still used to represent a whole set of attitudes and aspirations which could be taken for granted. Thus Hogarth's *Marriage à la Mode* attacks the marriages that were arranged between Court and City, whereby social position was exchanged for hard cash (National Gallery). In the first painting of the series, *The Marriage Contract*, Lord Squander sits surrounded by Italianate splendour pointing to his family tree while the miserly alderman, in ill-fitting wig and dress, scrutinizes the settlement. In the final scene, his daughter Countess Squanderfield returns to the City to die in her father's unfashionable seventeenth-century house with its dark panelling and casement window open onto a view of old London Bridge.[17]

In reality, many of those who traded on their own behalf in the regulated companies or as agents in the joint-stock companies had scattered to the four winds. One curious survival from the seventeenth century is the portrait of Fabian Smith, who acted as agent for the Russia Company and was appointed ambassador to the court of Tzar Michael Feodorovitch in 1630. In this much-damaged work, he is depicted with a long beard, fur robe and exotic velvet cap, ornamented with a bejewelled clasp (Guildhall Art Gallery).[18] The East India Company merchants fared rather better, artistically speaking, but usually preferred to have themselves painted against a backdrop of the estates they had acquired either in India or England.[19] An exception is the portrait dating from around 1790, attributed to Thomas Hickey (1741–1824), of John Mowbray, who worked for the mercantile firm of Graham, Mowbray and Skirrow in Calcutta (India Office Library). He is portrayed wearing the clothes of a gentleman – black velvet suit, cream silk waistcoat, grey silk stockings, white cravat – but in his office, which is in some disarray. Bundles of papers pile up on his desk: a drawer lies open; ledgers spill out over the floor. An Indian messenger waits for his orders in the background but Mowbray is engaged in quizzing his *banian* or money-agent, who is holding another book of accounts and some keys. Perhaps not surprisingly, the firm went bankrupt in 1790 and Mowbray died of drink in Chinsurah fifteen months later.[20]

Some merchants chose to be painted with the sea as a backdrop, providing an acceptable allegorical reference to their overseas trade in much the same way as it was used for naval commanders in the service of the crown. An early example is the portrait of Sir James Lancaster (1554/5–1618), merchant and seaman who, having commanded the *Edward Buonaventure* in the Armada, went on to make a fortune through trade in the East and West Indies, as well as leading expeditions against Spain and Portugal in South America (National Maritime Museum). As a founder member of the East India Company in 1599, he commanded its first fleet to sail east. He is painted in his best clothes with his sword, his right hand resting on a terrestial globe; in the background is a handsome galleon, possibly the *Edward Buonaventure*. Perhaps the most famous instance of this kind is the portrait painted by Hogarth of Captain Coram in 1740 (Thomas Coram Foundation for Children). The sea in the background serves as a reminder of his trade with the American colonies, and the hat at his feet is a reference to his protection of the London hatters' interests in those lands.[21] Similarly, the group portrait painted by John Francis Rigaud (1742–1810) of the Money Brothers depicts them holding a map of the east with a background of the sea, mountains and a ship (National Maritime Museum). Like their father before them, they all worked for the East India Company, the eldest being a commander before his retirement in 1801 when he became Marine Superintendent of Bombay, a Director of the Company, an Elder Brother of Trinity House and a Member of Parliament; the two younger brothers were in the civil branch.

Of the workings of the institutions that controlled such men from London, there are few visual records. Thomas Malton (1748–1804) executed two watercolours,

Thomas Fielder, 1774
VALENTINE GREEN after
MASON CHAMBERLIN

Thomas Fielder was admitted freeman of the Grocers' Company in 1753 and elected Warden in 1766 and 1772. He was evidently a fruit-broker and is depicted on the quay-side inspecting consignments of dried fruit.

Commemorative Design (detail),
c. 1694

M. LAURENS

This design was presumably created to mark the foundation of the Bank of England in 1694 and emphasizes the dominant role played by merchant finance. It includes the depiction of a room of the Bank (first housed in Mercers' Hall) where merchants are shown depositing money.

possibly on commission, of the appearance of East India House in Leadenhall Street before and after its rebuilding in 1796–99. Small figures of merchants and Orientals round the entrance provide some local colour but give no sense of the transactions that were being negotiated within (India Office Library).[22] When it was decided to rebuild Trinity House, the body which regulated the merchant navy and navigation round Britain, the Merchant Elder Brethren, commissioned a portrait of their number from Gainsborough Dupont (1754–97) (Trinity House). The result, a rare example of eighteenth-century large-scale formal group portrait painting in England, was completed in 1795. It depicts the sitters in full dress uniform against a curtained colonnade; high up in the centre are the allegorical symbols of a lighthouse and the dome of St Paul's, a celestial and terrestrial globe.[23] A more sophisticated form of artistic conceit was adopted by Sir Thomas Lawrence (1769–1830) when called upon by the Court of the West India Dock Company to paint their first chairman, George Hibbert Esq., M.P., in 1811 (Port of London Authority). He is portrayed in the curious hybrid setting of office and classical temple, overlooking the north quay of the new West India Import Dock, in which the old quay-gateway surmounted by a stone model of the West Indiaman Hibbert is a feature.[24]

By this date the merchants themselves had long ceased to congregate in a single location. After the Great Fire, the Royal Exchange was rebuilt to the design of Edward Jarman, the City Surveyor: it was close to the original plan, but never achieved its former success and in fact was something of a millstone round the neck of the Mercers' Company. The shops proved difficult to let and were turned into offices. By the time Ackermann's *Microcosm of London* was published in 1808–09, the Exchange had lost much of its former appeal:

> During the first century after its erection, the appearance of the people of different nations, on their respective walks and their various habits, formed a most attractive and striking spectacle; but that beautiful effect has long since been lost in the present undistinguishing uniformity of dress among the European nations.[25]

The range of businesses which had once been settled at the Royal Exchange – not only commodity transactions, but banking and currency exchange, share-holding and marine insurance – had all developed separate organizations. This world of banking and finance certainly drew on the resources of commerce, but its distinct identity was clear by the end of the seventeenth century. Merchant money played a prominent role in the formation of the Bank of England, as is illustrated in its commemorative design. The overseas trade of the East India Company made it one of the most attractive propositions on the Stock Market, but the new credit institutions gradually took over the financial role that had hitherto been played by merchants.

Increasingly throughout the eighteenth century, merchants were recruited to the moneyed interest: there were larger profits to be made in the manipulation of money than in the exchange of goods. Undoubtedly a few of the greatest financiers invested in land and built on a lavish scale. Many more were content with suburban villas or small estates in the Home Counties within easy reach of the

City, for use by their families in the summer, at weekends and sometimes for their retirement.[26] Beneath the bland surface of many an eighteenth-century country-house portrait no doubt lurks a City dweller partial to the idea of rustic retreat.

The *Microcosm of London* presents a fair round-up of the business world in the early nineteenth century: the Board of Trade meeting in the Treasury, the judicial Court of Excise, the Long Room at the Custom House filled with an assortment of officers and clerks, the Sale Room at East India House where all the goods purchased by the Company in the East were auctioned, the Dividend Hall at South Sea House, the Royal Exchange, the Stock Exchange, the Corn and Coal Exchanges. Commenting on the last of these, William Combe wrote:

> The tall figure with a paper in his hands behind him, appears intended to represent a trader of the old school, and forms an admirable contrast to the buckish *nonchalance* of the more modern merchant leaning against a pillar. The aldermanic figure which appears to be resisting the eloquence of an inferior tradesman, is happily contrasted with the spare and meagre figures which compose that group.[27]

By the early years of the nineteenth century, with the growing uniformity of masculine attire, aldermanic merchants of the old school were something of a picturesque relic. But by exaggerating the features which had long characterized the City merchant – old-fashioned in dress, inelegant in bearing, overweight, given to congregating in groups, straining to read the latest news or hear the latest gossip – the caricaturists had created a prototype which was to represent the City as a whole, long after the original had ceased to exist.

The Bank of England, c. 1785
THOMAS ROWLANDSON

Groups of stockbrokers transact business in the Rotunda of the Bank of England, which was used as the market for government securities from around 1770 until 1838. In the background, one of the Bank beadles holds his staff aloft and with his watchman's rattle endeavours to quieten the noise and control the disorder.

Stock-jobbers Extraordinary, c. 1795
ROBERT DIGHTON

In 1773, brokers moved from Jonathan's Coffee House in Exchange Alley to a building in Threadneedle Street which they called the Stock Exchange. Dighton's caricature suggests that the old coffee-house habits died hard.

U rban craftsmen have been depicted from the medieval period onwards, when the dignity of labour began to be accorded a new respect by the Church. The surviving evidence is scattered across Europe: in the stained glass at Chartres where artisans at work represent the guilds who largely financed the fabric of the cathedral; in the thirteenth-century relief panels in the cathedral at Piacenza showing various crafts; in a carved choir-stall dating from 1284 from the monastery chapel of Pöhlde, north Germany, in which a monk is sitting at his workbench surrounded by a complete range of carver's tools; and perhaps most memorably, in the reliefs on the lower storey of the campanile of Sta Maria del Fiore in Florence, designed and largely executed by Andrea Pisano between 1334 and 1343.

Nothing comparable to these examples remains in London. The great medieval cathedral of St Paul's was destroyed in 1666 but undoubtedly its sculpture and stained glass had been smashed earlier in the waves of iconoclasm unleashed by the Protestant Reformation and Puritan revolution; the same losses had been sustained by every other religious foundation in the city.

Manuscripts have greater chances of survival, but the dispersal of monastic libraries makes it difficult to identify with certainty those produced in London. Secular illustrations are most frequently found in the calendars of Psalters and Books of Hours, where the different times of year are conventionally represented by appropriate seasonal occupations, principally of a rustic character,[1] and in the margins of illuminated manuscripts. Thus the Decretals of Gregory IX dating from the early fourteenth century, written in Italy but illuminated in England and belonging in the late fifteenth century to St Bartholomew's Priory, Smithfield, contain scenes not only from the Bible and lives of the saints, but also from fables and romances and from everyday life (British Library. Roy. MS 10 E.iv).[2]

Furthermore, the temporal callings of saints – St Luke the artist, St Crispin the shoemaker, St Eloi the goldsmith, Joseph the carpenter – were frequently illustrated in works commissioned by the guilds who practised the same trades and adopted these saints as patrons. But again, evidence specifically from London is meagre. It is possible that the majority of such works in England were decorative hangings, which were less durable than Flemish oil paintings.[3] Others could have been frescoes, long destroyed or submerged beneath layers of plaster. In the 1840s, workmen discovered four Scriptural scenes painted on the walls of the old Carpenters' Company hall. The subjects were for the most part appropriately chosen – Noah and the building of the Ark, Josiah rebuilding the Temple, Christ in the Carpenter's Shop, Christ teaching in the Synagogue – and evidently, from the costume of the master carpenter and journeymen depicted, they dated from the extensive refurbishment of the hall in the 1560s.[4]

A second motive for depicting trades was the need to provide information on technical matters. Developing out of the Roman encyclopaedic *omnium gatherum*, specialized treatises with illustrations were prepared on agriculture, the domestic crafts and technological practices. Shops specializing in food and clothing were frequently depicted during the fifteenth century in *tacuina sanitatis*, manuals of health which describe the benefits of particular types of food, drink and clothing, dangers to health and remedies. Guilds also prepared treatises on particular crafts.

4
Craftsmen

OPPOSITE

Painting Room of Mr Baxter, No.1 Goldsmith Street, Gough Square, 1810
THOMAS BAXTER

It was not uncommon for white china to be decorated in studios outside the factory where it was made, and then returned for refiring (or even refired in the painting shops). Baxter evidently specialized in Coalport.

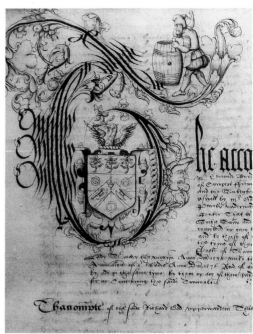

Baker Standing by his Oven and the *Punishment of a Fraudulent Baker*, late thirteenth century

From at least the twelfth century, the Assize of Bread regulated the size of a loaf according to the price of corn and minutely defined the smallest details of the trade, laid down in the *Liber de Assisa Panis*. All infractions were severely punished, the offenders being fined, pilloried, imprisoned or suspended from their trade.

The Master's and Wardens' Accounts of the Coopers' Company (detail), 1575–76

The decorated initial letter T incorporates the arms of the Company and a cooper in the act of trussing a barrel.

A fourteenth-century illustrated account of the workings of the cloth trade at Ypres existed until it was destroyed in the First World War. By the fifteenth century, it was not unusual to decorate copies of guild regulations with scenes of trade activity: examples survive in Paris, Bologna and Cracow. But the most extensive illuminated cycle of craft scenes was compiled in the house book of the hospice for the old, established by the Mendel family of Nuremberg in 1388. Containing almost 340 portraits of craftsmen practising their trades, and extending in date from around 1425 to 1549, it records techniques long lost, the associated tools and equipment being depicted with painstaking care (Stadtbibliothek, Nuremberg).

Very little of this nature survives in England. The earliest London example is a late thirteenth-century *Liber de Assisa Panis*, containing a couple of inconsequential drawings of a baker and the punishment meted out to offenders who broke the prescribed trade rules. Other material is much later in date. There is a set of illuminated ordinances for the Bakers' Company in York composed in the mid sixteenth century (British Library. Add MS 34605). In London, a decorated capital depicting a cooper at work, complete with apron and nails in his mouth, heads the first page of the Master's and Wardens' accounts of the Coopers' Company for 1575–76. Rudimentary drawings were made in 1598 of the meat markets in Eastcheap, St Nicholas Shambles and Grace Church by one Hugh Alley, a plasterer, in his remonstration with the Lord Mayor against the regraters and forestallers of the markets (Folger Shakespeare Library, Washington DC).[5]

In the rest of Europe by the end of the sixteenth century a tradition was developing of painting scenes of everyday life, including work, independent of religious if not always moral connotations. In the Netherlands, both Peter Aertsen and his student Joachim Beuckelaer of Antwerp combined still life and genre in their depictions of kitchens and markets. Beuckelaer's work was acquired for the Farnese collection in Parma where, it is surmised, it influenced Bartolommeo Passerotti and thence the young Annibale Carracci. Carracci's painting of the *Butcher's Shop* (Christ Church, Oxford) was executed in the 1580s and, unlike the coarser representations of the subject by Beuckelaer and Passerotti, is a serious study of the nature of the work, its setting, methods and implements.[6] The painting can be placed in the wider context of the prints designed to spread knowledge in many fields, especially the sciences, geography and ethnography. Braun's *Civitates Orbis Terrarum* (Cologne I–V 1572–82; VI 1618) included not only maps but also entire city vistas and illustrations of local customs and costumes, symptomatic of a new interest in people's lives. Most relevant of all is the *Ständebuch* or *Book of Trades*, produced in Nuremberg in 1567 with woodcut illustrations by Jost Amman and a text by Hans Sachs. With its didactic verse and explanatory pictures, it was aimed at a newly literate artisan class, concentrating on the arts and crafts of manufacture and commerce appropriate to the urban audience. With the increasing sophistication of the print trade by the seventeenth century, other series followed. Around 1600, *Nova Reperta*, a book of plates of new trade inventions, was published in Antwerp with designs by Jan van der Straet (Stradanus) engraved by Adriaen Collaert. Stradanus also made the designs for *Vermis Sericus*, a history and description of the silk trade.

Nothing of this kind was produced in England in the same period, despite the fact that for most of the sixteenth century many of the richest men in London maintained the strongest possible contact with Antwerp, frequently spent some time living there, and had good connections with the major German cities. We do not know whether they liked or bought such paintings or prints; certainly they did not encourage the creation of any home-grown examples. Perhaps they were simply uninterested in painting beyond the narrow sphere of portraiture. The Painter-Stainers' own surviving group effort, a portrait of John Potkyn, Master of the Company in 1631, with the Wardens Carlton and Taylor, is deeply conventional and gives little indication of their calling beyond the miniature Taylor holds in his hand. Despite the fact that the majority of London guilds were craft-based, as we have seen, by the seventeenth century there was a marked division between the merchant oligarchy in charge and the craftsmen members of the company. The most likely reason for the merchants' indifference is that it was considered beneath their dignity to be reminded of humble trade associations.

Furthermore, although London remained the greatest manufacturing centre in England until the nineteenth century, an increasing proportion of that production took place beyond the City walls and outside guild jurisdiction. The latest evidence, based on the burial registers of London parishes, underlines the enormous diversity of London trades and their tendency to localization within particular areas.[7] While production declined in the City, which was dominated by the interests of merchants and financial institutions, manufacturing industries flourished to the north, south and east, secured by the largest concentration of consumers in the country. They ranged from those industries like tanning, glass, oil, soap and starch manufacture, which had always been discouraged if not actually excluded from the City, to weaving and the production of all types of clothing, brewing and victualling in general, metalworking and engineering, shipbuilding and every other variety of building work. But, as with the documentary evidence, illustrations are much more plentiful of merchants than of craftsmen.

Perhaps not surprisingly, when trades were depicted at all they were principally those which catered for the tastes of the Court and the West End, not the heavy industries processing raw materials. By the eighteenth century, London was famous throughout Europe as a centre for the invention and manufacture of scientific instruments. The makers enjoyed the high status accorded to other branches of learning, rather than being considered mere tradesmen. This is reflected in their portraits, where they are shown with their prized creations round them, in much the same way that scholars were often depicted with their books. There were illustrious precedents. In England, the earliest such work is the portrait by Holbein of his friend and fellow-German Nicolas Kratzer (The Louvre), an astronomer, mathematician and designer of instruments. Born in Munich, Kratzer arrived in England around 1516 and became astronomer to the King. He was painted by Holbein in 1528, on the artist's first visit to England, and it is the earliest of his portraits where, as in the Georg Gisze painting, the sitter is shown with the objects that most characterize him. Kratzer holds dividers and a polyhedral dial and is surrounded by other instruments of measurement.[8]

The vital importance of high-quality instruments of navigation for the country's defence as well as for its mercantile power was formally recognized in England when Charles II founded the Mathematical School at Christ's Hospital in 1673. A painting, now at Christ's Hospital, Horsham,[9] was commissioned by the Governors from Marcellus Lauron to depict the monarch 'in a warrlike posture . . . and in it to be Shippes and what may also describe Navigation.' Lauron's work invests the king with suitable dignity and provides the required background of ships; Charles points to a cannon and navigational instruments – a globe, armillary sphere, sextant and dividers – stacked up by his side. The enormous work by Antonio Verrio (c.1639–1707) commemorating the foundation of the School includes a large globe and unrolled map in the foreground, echoing a similar detail in a tapestry cartoon of 1666–67 by Le Brun and Louis Festelin of Louis XIV founding the Académie des Sciences, with which the artist would have been familiar from his stay in Paris.[10] From the time of the Renaissance, it was not uncommon for rulers to be portrayed in a setting which symbolized their patronage of science.[11]

Scientific instrument makers enjoyed a sufficiently high social status to warrant prestige portraits. The watchmaker George Graham (1673–1751) was painted sitting in front of a long-case pendulum; the optician John Dollond (1706–61) holds a lens in his hand; John Bird (1709–76), who was renowned for the delicacy and accuracy of his instruments, points to his design for the Greenwich Brass Mural Quadrant on the table before him; Jesse Ramsden (1731–1800) is painted by Robert Home (1752–1834) with his dividing engine and the altazimuth circle he made for the observatory in Palermo (Royal Society).[12] The inventor extraordinary

John Joseph Merlin (1735–1803) was painted by Gainsborough around 1782 delicately toying with his latest invention, a miniature beam balance (Iveagh Bequest, Kenwood).[13] Merlin definitely considered himself to be a gentleman and is portrayed as such; Graham, Dollond and Ramsden were all admitted to the Royal Society. The reputation of these men was known throughout Europe in enlightened circles, no doubt encouraging the market for mezzotints after their portraits to adorn the libraries of scholars and parsons.

Though the finished instruments were occasionally shown being used,[14] paintings which depicted such craftsmen in a work setting are uncommon. The prevailing prejudices may be gauged from Horace Walpole's reaction to the picture by Johan Zoffany (1733–1810) usually described as representing John Cuff (*c.*1708–77) and an assistant in their workshop (*see* col. pl. VI). It was, he felt, 'Extremely natural, but the characters too common nature and the chiaroscuro destroyed by his servility in imitating the reflections of the glasses.' Like most of his contemporaries, Walpole preferred portraits to depict the genteel in settings which removed them from humdrum reality. Lip-service could thus be paid to the idealizing tenets of high art, even if portraiture as a genre was placed rather low down the artistic hierarchy. Another rarity is the portrait of the watchmaker Benjamin Vulliamy (fl.1775–1820), in which he is shown making designs in an open book, an elegant clock beside him and an unfinished face and movement on the shelf behind, protected by a glass dome.[15]

Goldsmiths enjoyed the same high status as scientific instrument makers and were also rich enough to commission portraits. However, it would appear that there was a much greater reluctance on the part of the London goldsmiths, at least, to be portrayed with any of the products of their skill. Why this should be the case is not at all clear. There were no such inhibitions in Continental Europe. The great sixteenth-century Nuremberg goldsmiths – Jakob Hofmann, Georg Vischer, Wenzel and Christoph Jamnitzer – were all portrayed with works of which they must have been especially proud.[16] In Florence, the workshop of the Medici court goldsmiths was vividly recorded in a painting by Alessandro Fei of 1572 (Palazzo Vecchio). The artistic climate was no doubt much more sophisticated in France and Italy, but the pattern does not change when, in the seventeenth century, artists in England were well acquainted with Continental precedents. Sir Robert Vyner (1636–88), who as one of the City's leading goldsmiths made Charles II's coronation regalia in 1661, was painted by John Michael Wright (c.1617–94) in 1673 with his family on his country estate, Swakelys, Middlesex (Henry Vyner Esq. on loan to Newby Hall).[17] As a very rich man who made a number of considerable – and unfortunate – loans to the government, he presumably considered himself to be first and foremost a great merchant-financier rather than a craftsman. Similarly, in the eighteenth century the London Huguenot goldsmiths, Augustin Courtauld (c.1686–1751), his daughter-in-law Louisa Perina Ogier (1729–1807) and Abraham Portal (1726–1809) are depicted as members of the gentry. Only the portrait of Paul Crespin (1694–1770) gives any indication of his career as one of the greatest Huguenot goldsmiths: he is shown with his sleeves rolled up and he holds a magnificent vase apparently of late-seventeenth-century French design (Victoria and Albert Museum).[18]

It would probably be wrong to suppose that foreign craftsmen who had settled in London made a deliberate point of being depicted in such a way. The commissions no doubt had less to do with self-conscious pride of achievement in a strange country than with the circles in which they moved. When artists came from abroad in the hope of acquiring fame and fortune in London, they naturally gravitated first to fellow countrymen who were, as often as not, fellow craftsmen and from these contacts they gained their initial commissions. Holbein is an obvious example. When Jean-Antoine Watteau (1684–1721) came to London in 1719–20, he made an informal sketch of a fellow Frenchman, presumably one of the engravers employed by Dr Mead whom he had come to consult, working in turban and gown at a garret window. Similarly, Boitard made a drawing of a chaser entertaining two friends in his workroom *cum* bedroom, strongly evocative of the craftsman's world (Yale Center for British Art, Paul Mellon Collection).[19] A portrait of the Swiss harpsichord maker Burkat Tschudi (1702–73) tuning his harpsichord at his home in Meard Street, Soho, with his wife and children around him, has been identified as the work of Carl Marcus Tuscher (1705–51), who was born in Nuremberg. When he arrived in London in 1741, he became friendly with the Swiss ivory carver, Lorenz Spengler, and presumably met Tschudi through him. Tuscher's only other known London work is a portrait of Spengler's friend and fellow-Swiss, George Michael Moser (1704–83), a chaser and enameller, whom he

An Engraver Working at his Table, 1719–20
JEAN-ANTOINE WATTEAU

The engraver, possibly Bernard Baron, worked like all precision craftsmen in the best light, in this instance diffused evenly over the surface of his plate by means of a muslin screen and angled reflecting card.

Burkat Tschudi and his Family, c. 1742
CARL MARCUS TUSCHER

Tschudi came to England in 1718 and from conveniently sited premises in Soho, built up a prosperous business with a fashionable clientèle, including Handel and the Prince of Wales.

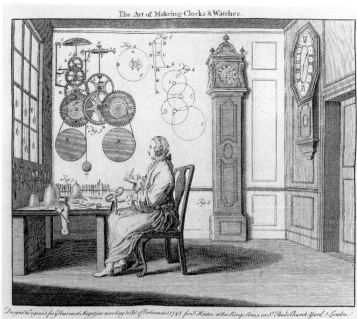

The Art of Making Clocks & Watches.

Designed & engraved for ye Universal Magazine according to Act of Parliament 1748 for J. Hinton at the Kings Arms in St Pauls Church Yard London

Frontispiece to *A Touch-stone for Gold and Silver Wares*, 1677

Badcock's manual described the history of assaying as a protection against fraud. The frontispiece depicts in schematic form the Assay Office with the Assay Master and his assistants at work.

The Art of Making Clocks and Watches, 1748

The engravings of trades in the *Universal Magazine* would appear to be the work of French artists, perhaps those frustrated by the length of time it was taking for the Académie Royale des Sciences to prepare the illustrated *Déscription des Arts et Métiers*.

depicted with his wife in a rustic setting (Geffrye Museum). Further commissions were not forthcoming, perhaps because the artist left in 1743 for the richer artistic pastures of the Danish court.

Nevertheless vast areas of production and manufacture in eighteenth-century London are an artistic *terra incognita*. There would appear to be no portraits of the great London cabinet-makers with their master works, let alone any illustration of their workshops. Yet as the drawings of the carvers Matthias Lock (*c*.1710–65) and Thomas Johnson (1714–*c*.1778) reveal, they could be excellent draughtsmen; John Linnell (1729–96) attended the St Martin's Lane Academy, and the creative powers of Thomas Chippendale (1718–79) were probably developed with the help of a drawing master, possibly Matthew Darly. The engravers who worked on Chippendale's *Director* are known, yet none seems to have considered that, even for a frontispiece, the workshop itself was suitable subject matter.[20] It was also the great age of type-founding in London but again, there are no portraits of printers at work or illustrations of London printers' premises in the eighteenth century. The closest is the anonymous watercolour of Thomas Kirgate, Horace Walpole's printer at Strawberry Hill, shown at the compositor's table (British Museum).[21]

To some degree, the deficiencies can be made up with material from lower down the artistic hierarchy: with frontispieces and illustrations to books and journals, with trade cards and shop signs. A scene in a goldsmith's workshop forms the frontispiece to *A Touch-stone for Gold and Silver Wares* by W.B. (William Badcock), first published in London in 1677, while the allegorical frontispiece to Jean Tijou's *A New Book of Drawings* (1693), designed by his son-in-law Louis Laguerre, appears to include the great ironsmith and his workshop assistants. Leybourn's *The Art of Measuring* (1669) has a frontispiece, divided into four,

showing scenes of the measuring required in building a house; the frontispiece to *The Chimney-Piece-Maker's Daily Assistant* (1766) by the architects Thomas Milton, John Crunden and Placido Columbani, depicts the patron and architect sitting in a room while the journeyman chimneypiece-maker measures up the fireplace and fixes the moulding, his plane and saw beside him. But for the most part, these treatises were illustrated with schematic technical drawings, divorced from the realities of workshop practice.

Similarly, eighteenth-century English encyclopaedias, starting with John Harris's *Lexicon Technicum* (1704), were embellished mainly with technical illustrations of microscopes, hydraulic equipment, electrical experiments, anatomical diagrams and so forth. Occasionally, there is an engraving of a chemical laboratory. The print, issued independently, specifically illustrating Ambrose Godfrey's Golden Phoenix Laboratory in Maiden Lane, is more unusual and was possibly published as some form of advertising. In 1747, however, John Hinton's newly founded *Universal Magazine* 'of Knowledge and Pleasure', which was clearly aimed at a well-educated audience, began to publish engravings of trade processes which were described in the text, as well as the usual quota of technical illustrations and engraved portraits of famous contemporaries. They included depictions of various types of weaving, gold and silver refining, the art of making clocks and watches, glass, coins, wax and tallow candles among others; only occasionally does the subject seem to have been chosen to illustrate technological innovation. But whatever the specific impetus, they certainly anticipated the rather more famous illustrations in Diderot's *Encyclopédie* by a few years.

The need to advertise often provided an incentive for portraying craftsmen in their working environment. In the eighteenth century, London was at the centre

Ambrose Godfrey's Golden Phoenix Laboratory, c. 1728

Ambrose Godfrey (Godfrey Hanckwitz) specialized in preparing phosphorus, invented a successful fire extinguisher and in 1730 was made a fellow of the Royal Society. This engraving shows the east side of the laboratory he built, with doors into Southampton Court (Maiden Lane) on the left.

of a consumer boom. Its massive growth in size provided manufacturers with an unequalled market for goods. Almost one in six of the country's entire population lived in London and the effect of emulative spending was enormous. The need to reach this potential clientèle led to a great increase in advertising. Shop signs were not enough, particularly as they had largely ceased to bear anything but the most tenuous connection to the goods on sale beneath them.[22] Trade cards survive as evidence of the hundreds of shops catering for all sorts of needs. Scarcely in existence before 1700, they reached their peak between 1730 and 1770 and played an important part in shopkeepers' efforts to promote their wares. They were not simply statements about places of sale but unequivocally drew attention to any special qualities or distinctive features that merited patronage.

The styles of engraved decorative embellishment on the cards varied. Some merely made use of the ancient sign over the premises; others were brought up to date with the addition of a fashionable cartouche. Still others incorporated illustrations of the goods on sale: a cutler's stock, all manner of spectacles, gold and silver ware. A few depicted the shop and methods of production. Some of these are clearly fanciful: an alchemist in his laboratory engraved in 1738 by C.N. Cochin after Jacques de Lajoue was adapted by Robert Clee for use as a trade card by the chemist Richard Sidall.[23] The trade card for Jacob Stampe, a calico printer in Houndsditch, c.1680, is an extremely early example. A merchant trading in China and a glass blower's furnace in action provide motifs for Jane Taylor & Son of Pall Mall, glass and china sellers. The card for James Ayscough, an optician at the Great Golden Spectacles in Ludgate Street, incorporated a variety of spectacles in the cartouche and also the small figure of a workman turning a glass in the centre. The card c.1800 for J. Bullwinkle, a bookbinder, stationer and gilder of 61 Leadenhall Street shows men working a press, revealed, as it were, by a lifted curtain, while William and Cluer Dicey's card included small vignettes of the letter press and rolling press within its cartouche border.[24]

Some cards illustrated both the wholesale and retail side of the business, like the design for the goldsmith Peter de la Fontaine, supposedly by Hogarth, which shows the furnace and workshop on the left and a retailer with his assistant selling to customers in the shop on the right; or a drawing by Boitard of a tailor's shop, with the master fitting a client in the foreground and the journeymen tailors behind. Others, as in the case of Watteau's famous shop sign for Gersaint, concentrated on the retail end: the shop of Benjamin Cole, an importer of cambric c.1720; Dorothy Mercier's business as a print seller and stationer in Windmill Street; James Wheeley's paper-hanging warehouse in Little Britain; or the design Hogarth produced in 1730 for his sisters' ready-to-wear clothes shop in the same street.[25]

Hogarth was a Londoner first and foremost, born in the heart of an area that abounded in small workshops. Having been trained as an engraver, he was well-versed in the promotional requirements of shopkeepers and craftsmen. Throughout his life he showed himself to be extremely adept at publicizing his own schemes and print series; he was also sympathetic to native art, to the unpretentious sign painters and coach-panel painters who still made up the bulk of

The Fellow 'Prentices at their Looms, 1747
WILLIAM HOGARTH

Hogarth underlines the contrast between the conduct of the apprentices with emblematic devices: pristine and tattered copies of *The 'Prentice Guide*, appropriate broadsides pinned to the looms' frame and the wall, as well as admonitory extracts from Proverbs forming the captions below.

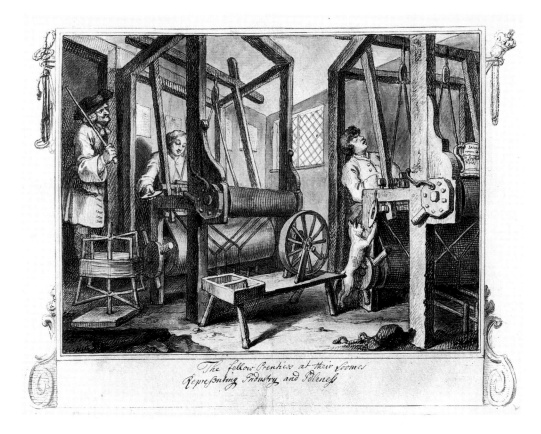

A Tailor's Shop, c. 1749
LOUIS PHILIPPE BOITARD

In the foreground the master tailor, dressed in a gown, slippers and turban carried out a fitting on a customer. Through the window, he can supervise the eleven tailors, sitting in a traditional cross-legged manner on a table lit by the large workshop windows which were typical of most London premises, clearly on an upper floor.

the membership of the Painter-Stainers' Company. Possibly one of his earliest works was a sign for a paviour; and another, *The Carpenter's Yard*, portrays craftsmen at work, unencumbered by any notion of elegant appearance or grandiose composition (Private Collection).[26] When he came to plan his moral series, *Industry and Idleness*, in 1747, he chose to depict the fellow 'prentices Francis Goodchild and Tom Idle working side by side on weaving looms. It scarcely matters that the looms themselves were much simplified for pictorial effect. The main point which Hogarth took for granted, and which would have been understood by his audience, was that only the weaving trade offered such chances for advancement or ruin: the economic fluctuations of the mid-eighteenth century made it the trade with the highest risks in London.[27]

No London artist, however, consistently depicted the different trades in the manner of the Dutch artist Quirijn van Brekelenkam in Leiden during the 1650s. There does not appear to have been a general market for such paintings in England, rather a marked hostility because they did not conform to the tenets of high art. Moreover, the processes of production were largely hidden from public view in small workshops, and were thus unlikely to be the subject of a spur-of-the-moment sketch, let alone a finished work. The trades of London tended to be depicted either because they happened to be part of some larger intention on the part of the artist or because of some specific circumstance pertaining to a particular trade at a particular time; in such cases the artist was frequently an insider or relied heavily on the knowledge of insiders.

Shipbuilding was one of the most important Thames-side industries, employing thousands of workers until its collapse in the 1860s. Like the scientific instrument makers and the goldsmiths, master shipwrights achieved sufficient status and wealth to be commemorated in portraits. They are invariably depicted as gentlemen, but with the sea providing the backcloth on which their finest ship sails. Thus in the painting of Phineas Pett (1570–1647), founder of the famous family of shipwrights, the stern of the almost completed *Prince Royal*, launched in 1610, can be seen through the window (National Portrait Gallery). The ship he built with his son Peter Pett (1610?–70), *Sovereign of the Seas*, launched in 1637, sails in the background of the portrait by Sir Peter Lely (1618–80) of the younger Pett (National Maritime Museum). Jonathan Richardson's portrait of the master shipwright Fisher Harding (d.c.1710) dates from 1710, the year he built the *Royal Sovereign 100* at Woolwich; he is depicted pointing to the ship being launched on the Thames behind him, and holding a pair of dividers in his right hand over a draft of the design (National Maritime Museum).

A closer look at the process of building the ships themselves is unusual: ship paintings concentrated on the moment of launching or the vessel actually at sea. The figures working on her would be tiny in scale. John Cleveley the Elder (c.1712–77), who was himself a former shipwright, painted a *6th Rate on the Stocks*, probably on the morning of her launch, with scaffolding still in place and some last-minute fitting going on (National Maritime Museum). The same artist's view of a *Shipyard on the Thames* (1762) shows carpenters at work on the scaffolding round one half-built hulk (Glasgow Museum and Art Gallery). Samuel

A Thames-side Quay (detail),
c.1760

SAMUEL SCOTT

This has been variously described as
Custom House or Bear Quay, but
the size of the shipping suggests a
wharf further downstream than the
Pool of London. Probably Scott
incorporated elements from a
number of wharves.

Scott (*c.*1702–72) depicted the process of breaming a ship in *A Morning with a View of Cuckold's Point*, *c.*1760 (Tate Gallery). The view of a *Dockyard Scene* by Francis Holman (fl.1767–90) includes a ship launch, timber being unloaded from a barge and the merchantmen *John and William* and *Elizabeth* in dry dock, with repairers on a punt on the river preparing to mend either the dock or the ships; the refit is presumably being discussed by the group of men on the quay (Christie's 22 June 1963, lot 162). In its meticulous delineation of the work undertaken in a yard, the painting serves as the formal equivalent of a trade card. The artist also painted a long panorama of *Blackwall Yard* in 1784, probably at the behest of the yard owner; it shows seven vessels in various stages of construction, surrounded by scaffolding, but with very little sign of activity (National Maritime Museum). The series of large-scale prints of the dockyards at Woolwich, Greenwich and Chatham, published at the time of the French Revolution, concentrated on recording the grandiose sweep of the topography and the ships being built, with only a few figures of carpenters and other workers to add a human dimension to these images of patriotic endeavour.[28] For less hyperbolic statements about Thames-side industry, the quays provided an opportunity to portray a variety of skills at closer range, within the acceptable genre of marine painting. Thus, in his capriccio of a Thames-side quay used by the East India Company, Samuel Scott introduced coopers at work trussing the barrels and the car-men who were privileged to work in the docks, besides the ship master being questioned by a customs official.

Making Tin Cases and Canisters for Shot at the Royal Laboratory Woolwich, c. 1750

This drawing comes from a set of ten depicting the various activities undertaken at the Royal Laboratory. Here the tin cases for grape shot are made from sheet metal and their tops are soldered on.

Driving Fuses, The Royal Laboratory, c. 1750

Royal Artillery gunners wearing surcoats (to protect the saltpetre, sulphur and silt fuse mixture from contamination) sit at elm blocks that hold the fuse cases of well-seasoned beech in copper sockets. A ladle full of fuse composition was put in the case and pushed down by the workers using an iron and brass-tipped drift, struck with a mallet.

It is a truism that London did not play a leading role in that massive growth in manufacturing output during the second half of the eighteenth and early nineteenth centuries, characterized as the Industrial Revolution. But it would be wrong to conclude that London's role was purely parasitical, that it merely lived off the sources of wealth and consumed goods made elsewhere. A great deal of manufacturing continued to take place in the capital, some of which – shipbuilding, brewing – scarcely qualifies as light industry. Nor were forges and furnaces only to be found north of Watford. Following a serious accident in 1716 at John Bagley's foundry in Upper Moorfields, where all guns for government service had hitherto been cast, the Royal Brass Foundry was moved to Woolwich and built to the design of Sir John Vanbrugh. The Woolwich Warren (from 1805, renamed the Royal Arsenal) also housed the Royal Laboratory, where the manufacture, proof and inspection of cannon and shot took place, the barracks of the Royal Regiment of Artillery and numerous storehouses. There exist two series of watercolours which give a vivid picture of the work undertaken in the Laboratory and the Foundry, dating respectively from around 1750 and 1778; in their scope and detail, they present a visual record of eighteenth-century London craftsmanship which is unrivalled.

The tradition of depicting the manufacture of arms and munitions is particularly rich. The possibilities of dramatic lighting effects inherent in the use of forges as subject matter could be exploited by artists either within an allegorical framework – the forge of Vulcan or Venus – or increasingly in genre scenes of blacksmiths' shops. At the same time, the practice of smelting, casting metals and arms manufacture was the subject of many illustrated technical treatises.

However, a more immediate consideration than any of these general precedents is the presence in the Warren of the Royal Military Academy instituted in 1719 and formally established in 1741. On its staff, the Academy had a drawing master, first Gabriel Massiot from 1744, who was joined in 1768 by Paul Sandby (1730–1809). It is more than likely that the two men had a hand in the production of each

series, Massiot for the earlier works relating to the Laboratory, Sandby for the later, much more extensive, set of drawings of the Royal Foundry.

The particular concurrence of circumstances which resulted in these works was not paralleled in any other London trade. However, studies of a handful of London workshops were made on an individual basis, usually initiated through a particular connection or sense of loyalty felt by the artist. Thus John Carter (1748–1817) produced a watercolour of his father Benjamin Carter (d.1766), a maker and carver of marble chimneypieces, after a painting by Richard Pyle, which depicted the craftsman surrounded by examples of his work (British Museum).[29] Michael Angelo Rooker (1745–1800) produced an exceptionally fine watercolour study of the scene-painting studio where he worked at the Haymarket Theatre. The enameller Thomas Baxter (1782–1821) recorded in watercolour the china painters at work in his father's studio at No. 1 Goldsmith Street, Gough Square, and exhibited the work at the Royal Academy in 1811 alongside examples of his enamels. Two years later, John Hill (1770–1850) exhibited his painting of the carpenter's shop he probably owned at Forty Hill, Enfield. Similarly, the McQueen intaglio printing workshop at 184 Tottenham Court Road was depicted in a pen and wash drawing by George Brookes in 1832, more prominence being given to the modern metal printing press and the hydraulic press for flattening prints than to the two printers in the background inking the plates (Thomas Ross and Sons). The drawing was evidently made to commemorate the construction of spacious new premises and perhaps even to impress potential customers with the up-to-date machinery in use.[30] There are also a number of genuinely naive paintings, executed by workers unversed in the use of artistic skills outside their own jobs. The portrait of a Whitefriars glass blower, for instance, which dates from the early nineteenth century, provides a valuable record of working apparel which survives in no other form (Museum of London).[31] Similarly, the interior of George Robinson's pottery at Brentford is depicted in a charming mid-nineteenth-century anonymous work.

The Smithy, The Royal Brass Foundry, Woolwich, c.1778
attributed to PIETER VERBRUGGEN

The collection of fifty drawings traces the successive stages in the manufacture of cannon when the Dutch masters, Jan Verbruggen and his son Pieter ran the Foundry. The smithy prepared the ironwork that would be used in the final preparation of the moulds.

Filling the Moulds in the New Furnace, Royal Brass Foundry, c.1778
attributed to PIETER VERBRUGGEN

The Verbruggens installed the New Furnace, the plaque bearing the cypher of George III and the year 1772 commemorating its completion. In this drawing the furnace has been tapped releasing the molten bronze into the moulds. The pouring was the most critical stage in the manufacture of bronze guns, watched here possibly by Jan Verbruggen and some guests.

Interior of the Carpenter's Shop at Forty Hill, Enfield, 1813?
JOHN HILL

The master carpenter – probably Hill Senior or Junior – is depicted in the background wearing a moleskin hat and dark jacket working with a plane. The two journeymen carpenters in contrast work in their shirt sleeves and wear the traditional paper hats favoured by their trade. Each man has his own green tool-box.

The Interior of George Robinson's Pottery, Brentford, c. 1840

George Robinson specialized in making bricks, tiles, chimneypots and flowerpots. He had premises at Bull Lane, Old Brentford between 1840 and 1861 and also by Potomac Pond in Gunnersbury Park.

OPPOSITE *A Scene Painter in his Studio, c.* 1780
MICHAEL ANGELO ROOKER

The artist, probably Rooker himself wearing protective clothing, is working on a landscape in a scene frame, a system which enabled the work to be moved up or down through a slot in the floor; to reach the upper part of the backcloth, he would stand on the painting bridge, which could also be winched up or down.

The Basket Maker, c. 1820
JOHN THOMAS SMITH

The basket maker, according to
Smith's notes, was a 'journeyman
prickle maker', who worked in a
cellar on the west side of the
Haymarket. He is seated on a
wooden board, raised at one end so
that less cold came up from the
cellar floor. A prickle was a basket
used by wine merchants for empty
bottles.

Manufacturing in nineteenth-century London was still largely confined to small workshops rather than large factories. That the former were not considered showplaces is apparent from Ackermann's *Microcosm of London* where, out of 104 plates only 1 – The Mint – shows craftsmen at work. It depicts the operation of stamping or 'putting the impression' in the print room at the old Mint in the Tower, immediately prior to its removal to Sir Robert Smirke's new building on Little Tower Hill.[32] Of the hundreds of drawings produced by members of the Shepherd family, the vast majority were devoted to 'Metropolitan Improvements', meaning for the most part external building views, not internal workshop conditions. The watercolour by Thomas Hosmer Shepherd (1793–1864) of the interior of a piano factory is a rare illustration of one of the many businesses which, at the time, must have been undergoing a transformation from small workshop spaces to larger, purpose-built semi-factory accommodation. Such subjects were not usually thought worthy of picturesque delineation, any more than the workers who toiled there. Out of all the studies of London characters made by John Thomas Smith (1766–1833) in the early nineteenth century, only two – a basket maker and a potter – can be described as skilled London craftsmen.

The spread of education greatly increased the potential audience for books which described trade activities; many were aimed particularly at the young, guided by their parents or teachers. As the apprenticeship system relaxed and dynastic attitudes to trade weakened, a whole range of possibilities for advancement and self-improvement opened up, which these guides sought to explain. The earliest – Joseph Moxon's *Mechanick Exercises*, first published in 1677–79, and Robert Campbell's *London Tradesman* of 1747 – were unillustrated but the latter's avowed aims give some idea of the purpose of such works. It was

designed for the information of such as are entrusted with the Care and Settlement of Youth ... to afford such Helps to the Guardians and Parents of Youth as might enable them, from a general Knowledge of the Trades of *London*, and the particular Genius of their Child, to chuse an Employment suitable to his Strength and Judgement, and their own Circumstances.

By the early nineteenth century, such works were illustrated with small engravings, as in the case of Phillips's *Book of Trades* of 1805 (probably after drawings by the miniaturist William Marshall Craig), and with woodcuts for Whittaker's *Book of English Trades*, published in 1812–24, which came furnished with a list of 488 questions at the back and a tutor's key which could be obtained separately. Charles Tomlinson's *Cyclopaedia of Useful Arts* (1852–54) and *Illustrations of Trades* made use of wood engravings, although some have a rather jaded air. The author of the latter work, published by the Society for Promoting Christian Knowledge, was apologetic for their inaccuracy. They had originally been made, he wrote in his introduction, 'for a kind of Pictorial Vocabulary for the use of the Deaf and Dumb,' and the artists had not had much technical knowledge.

These works maintained the polite fiction that there was still the possibility of choice, that there were skills to be learned and a standard of living which, through diligent and honest application, could be achieved. In London the reality was

rather different. The distance of the capital from the centres of coal and iron production and the price of metropolitan land were serious drawbacks which prevented its development as an industrial centre processing raw materials. The silk-weaving industry died finally when the Cobden Treaty of 1860 brought about free trade with France. The shipbuilding industry was killed because of the distance from the supplies of iron and steel and high wages. The manufacture of clothing, books, shoes and woodwork was under threat, as Mayhew's first letters in the *Morning Chronicle* in 1849 make clear, through the introduction of machinery and competition from other centres in the Midlands and the North. The only way in which London could compete was to reduce overheads – wages and rent – to a minimum through 'sweating', that is, using cheap labour in cramped conditions.[33] This was not the environment to which any manufacturer wished to draw attention through pictures. It was the subject rather of attack in *Punch*'s engravings, and evangelical reforming magazines like the *British Work-man and Friend of the Sons of Toil* which, in its illustrations, made a clear distinction between the 'honourable' trades and slop work. Victorian fine art had its own conventions, and when craftsmen were portrayed at all, they were usually shown to be kindly old tailors or cobblers in rustic surroundings, as if they had nothing to do with city life.

A Pianoforte Manufactory, c. 1830
THOMAS HOSMER SHEPHERD

Piano-making was one of the major industries of nineteenth-century Camden Town, extending north out of the traditional furniture-making district of Tottenham Court Road. Dozens of small factories were set up to meet the demand for pianos, which symbolized domestic respectability in the ever-growing middle-class Victorian suburbs of the capital.

The most eloquent image of London servants is Hogarth's painting of his own household, executed in the 1750s (*see* col. pl. IV). His motives can only be surmised: perhaps he simply wished to preserve the likeness of six people who were close to him. It is known that in his last years he wanted to keep pictures of his friends around him.[1] At the time, however, the extension of such a desire to servants was highly unusual.

The portrayal of servants in their own right is rare in any age. In Great Britain, a handful are recorded in country houses: at Chirk, Dudmaston, Knole and Drumlanrig. But the most celebrated of all are at Erddig in north Wales, where various members of an eccentric family commissioned portraits of workers on the estate and in the garden, as well as members of the domestic staff. A sentimental wish to commemorate servants of long standing by arranging for their portraits to be painted appears to have extended to the royal family on occasion. John Riley (1646–91) painted Bridget Holmes (1591–1691) when she was ninety-six years old, having been a 'necessary woman' in royal service since the reign of Charles I (Her Majesty the Queen). She is portrayed within the grandiose conventions of the day, a massive vase of flowers behind her and a damask curtain being drawn aside by a Page of the Backstairs. But the image is mock-heroic for she wears a far-from-fashionable cap, cape and tucked-up apron, and with dim eyes but strong hands she wields a broom resignedly as if to shoo the teasing boy away. Riley also painted with Johann Baptist Closterman (1660–1711), to less startling effect, a three-quarter-length portrait of Katherine Elliot (d.1688), nurse to the infant James II when Duke of York, and dresser and woman of the bedchamber to his two Duchesses (Her Majesty the Queen).[2] Perhaps James was inspired to acquire these works because he felt more gratitude to loyal retainers than was usual. Whatever the circumstances of the commission, it is curious that around the same time the artist painted the *Scullion of Christ Church* (Christ Church, Oxford). This famous character worked in the College kitchen and, apart from his menial duties, is said to have been employed to sing satirical and political ballads against the party of James II before the revolution of 1688; it would, however, have been singularly dangerous to the College for such a role to be anything else but unofficial or even Saturnalian.[3]

Equally, Hogarth might have painted his servants for the sheer pleasure of painting, as an exercise in physiognomic variety which could hang in his showroom to display to prospective sitters his skills and his style. He was not the first London artist to use servants as convenient models. As a young man, Charles Beale (1660–1714?) induced the servants of his mother's household in Pall Mall, as well as his family, friends and tradesmen, to sit for a series of chalk drawings he made in sketchbooks. The results are exceptionally lively and spontaneous, free from any formal intent. Similarly, when Paul Sandby visited his brother Thomas at Windsor in the 1750s, he drew a number of domestic scenes, showing maids cooking, washing up and doing the laundry. The fact that Thomas Sandby's second wife Elizabeth Venables, whom he married in 1753, was appointed sempstress and laundress to the Duke of Cumberland from 1757 to 1760, could well explain the milieu in which the younger artist found himself. As an indefatigable observer of

Interior, Portrait of John Sheepshanks, 1832–34
WILLIAM MULREADY

Mulready depicts his patron John Sheepshanks (1787–1833) in the drawing room of his residence at 172 New Bond Street. Unusually for an age when the demarcation line between above and below stairs was tightening, his housekeeper is portrayed in a prominent position, bringing him a tea-tray and the post.

5
Servants

Susan Gill, 1680
CHARLES BEALE

Beale drew a range of female domestics, wearing an interesting variety of caps and kerchieves. The sitter seems to have worked for the Beales from around 1677 to 1681 and she appears in a number of drawings.

his surroundings, he also made several individual sketches of the Duke's servants: a running footman; an Indian footman in livery; Bob Dun, one of the Duke's gardeners; and Voules, the Duke's bailiff who, as an upper servant, was not required to wear his master's livery (Her Majesty the Queen).[4]

Hogarth's group of servants would have been typical for a man of his station in life. They probably comprised a housekeeper and two housemaids, a coachman, a valet and a boy to look after the artist and his wife, his sister, his mother-in-law and his wife's cousin. In its pre-industrial sense, the term servant referred to all the non-family employees of a head of household, who lived under his roof and were subject to his discipline; probably one of the men also assisted Hogarth with his printing or in his studio. By the end of the eighteenth century, one in four Londoners was a servant. They worked not only in private houses but also at inns, lodgings and coffee houses. Although many households included a coachman and a groom, outdoor servants were less important in London than in the country. There is no London equivalent to the whole range of racing, hunt and agricultural servants portrayed by George Stubbs (1724–1806) with a unique combination of sobriety and sympathy.[5] Auxiliary servants – charwomen, laundresses, hairdressers, wigmakers and so forth – came to the house but did not live in.

London was the mecca for servants bent on improving their lot, as the capital expanded and fed the needs of an increasingly affluent society. Tobias Smollett was scarcely exaggerating when Matt Bramble commented in *Humphrey Clinker*, 'At present, every trader in any degree of credit, every broker and attorney, maintains a couple of footmen, a coachman and a postilion.' Servants were necessary, particularly in London where such a premium was placed on appearances, to indicate social position as well as to undertake duties. From the point of view of

Interior of a London Coffee House,
c. 1705

A number of servants attend the
company of men sitting on benches
reading the news-sheets. The
landlady proffers a flute from the
canopied bar. A manservant bends
down to take the clay pipes from a
chest while another pours out the
coffee.

the servant, domestic work offered the chance of some security for little or no
financial outlay. By the time bed and board, clothing and vails were taken into
account, it could even be considered well paid. There were servants who saved
enough to establish themselves as publicans and innkeepers. William Fortnum,
one of Queen Anne's footmen, set up a grocery business supplying the royal
household. It was a commonplace to observe, like Steele, that nowhere in the
world did servants enjoy 'such plentiful Diet, large Wages, or indulgent Liberty'.
It was furthermore often remarked that nowhere else were servants so idle,
dishonest, vicious and wanton. Those who came fresh from the country were much
preferred, having had no chance to be corrupted by London ways.

Almost by definition, servants were most frequently depicted as accessories to
those who employed them. In portraits of fashionable Society, servants –
especially black boys – are dandled at arms' length as exotic but slightly tiresome
trinkets, or are called upon to lead an unseen troop of admirers by gazing upwards
adoringly into the eyes of their owners.[6] As Hogarth and the playwrights of the
period make clear, however, London servants were not loyal family retainers,
mere cyphers for their masters' whims, but were bent on enjoying a life of their
own. They might have acted as pets, accomplices, go-betweens and drudges to the
extent that it suited them, but if the arrangement ceased to be acceptable to them,
they could always remove themselves. In the *Harlot's Progress*, published by
Hogarth in 1732, it is clear that Moll Hackabout was intent on an honorable career
as a maidservant when she stepped off the York coach, had she not been waylaid
by a notorious bawd, Mother Needham. When she is established in her own rooms
as the mistress of a rich London Jew, she is waited on by a neatly dressed maid and
a blackamoor in a smart silver collar and Oriental dress. But when Moll falls on

This fragment represents the right
side of a canvas, described in the
Ambulator (1774) as 'The Wapping
Landlady and the Tars who are just
come ashore'. From the engraving
made after the work, the principal
focus of attention was a sailor
dancing a jig or hornpipe in the
centre, to the music of a violin
player, watched by another sailor
and two maidservants at the bar.

hard times, they disappear and are replaced by a disfigured slatternly servant, who
nevertheless accompanies her mistress to Bridewell, tends her in her last illness
and even sheds a tear when she dies.[7] In the *Harlot's Progress*, Hogarth illustrates
the point that eighteenth-century Londoners measured status not only by dress
and manners, but also by the goods, chattels and servants which London could
provide to embellish the image. In *Marriage à la Mode*, the artist stressed the
ways in which servants could counterpoint as well as be symptomatic of an
ostentatious way of life. As the slovenly young couple slump and stretch their way
through breakfast, one servant with nightcap awry and stockings ungartered
scratches his head and yawns before attempting to tidy up the ravages of the
previous evening's party; the Methodist steward raises his eyes and hand to
heaven and hurries off with a pile of unpaid bills. Morning levées had as licentious
a reputation as masquerades, both being potential rendezvous for illicit assigna-
tions. The Countess makes good use of hers, the fashionable musicians providing
cover for her dalliance with Silvertongue. While the hairdresser is part of the
fripperies of her social life, the two black servants act as negative commentators on
the decadence. The older servant offering chocolate contrasts in his sober virility

with the effeminate castrato, and the black boy pointing to the horns of Actaeon emphasizes the true purpose of the occasion.[8] In his portrayal of servants, Hogarth begs the question as to who is in servitude and who is free. The servants can come and go, while their masters are tied to their property and when that is dissipated they are ruined.

Servants were an agent of social change, an important means by which the dress, habits and customs of the upper classes filtered down to the lower ranks and out of London; those who had migrated from the country returned there each year for a brief respite, taking the latest news back with them. Only male under-servants wore livery. Women servants wore no standard uniform in the eighteenth century and, given the habit of mistresses to hand out clothes to their maids, it was superficially difficult to tell the one from the other, or so foreign observers supposed. To some extent, at least on duty, there would always have been telling differences. As in Hollar's depiction of a London servant from *Theatrum Mulierum* or the Covent Garden paintings of Peter Angelis, the maid would always be carrying the basket when accompanying the mistress shopping;[9] she more ordinarily wore a serviceable apron and had a plainer cap on her head. But it was important for their own self-respect, their prospects of employment and, when employed, the social position of their employer, that servants should look at least clean and neat. When they had time off the much-reported silk dresses probably came out. Being so close to the sources of fashion, they were tempted to try the Mall, to sample the pleasure gardens. It is scarcely surprising that Francis Hayman (1708–76), when commissioned in the 1730s and 1740s by Jonathan Tyers to decorate the supper boxes at Vauxhall, should choose for one of his subjects *The Wapping Landlady*, painting her looking attractive and worldly but by no means a lady, with a male 'lodger' sprawled alongside.

Hayman's figures were clearly French-inspired; Gravelot, in his position as a teacher at the St Martin's Lane Academy and as an illustrator of books, acted as one of the catalysts. Philip Mercier (1689–1760) may fairly lay claim to being the pioneer of 'fancy pictures' in England, as he produced pastiches of Watteau's *fêtes galantes* and etchings after his works in the 1720s. But such works assumed a more clearly English character after the publication of Samuel Richardson's novel *Pamela* in 1740–41. Female servants had hitherto been considered fair game for gentlemen and, as the *Harlot's Progress* clearly shows, many were thought to be all too willing to succumb to temptation. The story of Pamela, related in letters to and from her parents, is of a maid who is left by the death of her mistress to the care of the young master of the house, Mr B. Because of her virtue in repulsing his advances and her generally refined instincts, he eventually ends up marrying her. For the sixth edition of part I and the end of part II, in 1742, Hayman and Gravelot combined to produce twenty-nine illustrations of the work.[10] The following year, Joseph Highmore (1692–1780) advertised that twelve prints would be published after paintings of the novel which could then be seen at his house in Lincoln's Inn Fields.[11] Although they did not overlap in subject matter, both series have something of the same air of dainty elegance. Pamela is a charmingly graceful doll-like figure, well able to carry off the fine silk clothes, cambric aprons, the caps and the Holland linen which Mr B. gives her from her deceased mistress's wardrobe. She is far removed from the earthy substance of Hogarth's servants.

In the early 1740s from his retreat in York, Mercier turned increasingly to fancy pictures. With an eye on the print market, he produced a series of compositions based on single figures or small groups which were of sentimental or anecdotal interest. When engraved in mezzotint by John Faber Junior (1684–after 1756), they proved extremely popular with middle-class buyers. Needless to say, pretty servant girls figure strongly. *The Girl with a Tea-tray*, for example, although identified in an unknown hand as 'Hannah, Mercier's maid' on one mezzotint after the painting, was re-described elsewhere as 'Pamela Bringing Mr B. Tea' (Private Collection). Other prints after Mercier were specifically described as *Pamela* and were unequivocally titillating; in one Pamela emerges provocatively deshabillée from bed, a letter beside her inscribed 'Your dutyful and ever-chaste daughter-Pamela' and in another, she is in the act of removing her stocking.[12] The image of the pretty innocent maid was an ambivalent one and these works echo the reaction to the novel voiced in many quarters, that Pamela's behaviour was a calculated sham.

The market for such works nevertheless lasted until the second half of the century with Henry Robert Morland (1719?–97) producing similar paintings of laundresses and ladies' maids after which prints were made in the 1760s. In both Mercier's and Morland's pictures, the single figure of the maid dominates the composition and usually, by looking out of the picture in a coy but winning way, involves the spectator in a sentimental exchange. In all the works, the girls are neat, pretty and wear dresses which are so seemingly above their station that the myth developed in the nineteenth century that Morland's paintings were in reality portraits of Lady Coventry who had, admittedly, been depicted in relaxed pose *à la Turque* by Jean Etienne Liotard. Similarly, Gainsborough's one excursion into the genre, an unfinished painting entitled *The Housemaid* (Tate Gallery), dating from the mid 1780s, is sometimes thought to be the Hon. Mrs Graham indulging in the simple life inspired by the example of Marie-Antoinette; but the likeness is probably fortuitous as the painting was started some ten years after the lady sat for her portrait.[13]

Nevertheless, these fancy pictures of servant girls mirrored the mistress/maid confusion. In their artful innocence and simplicity, they also appealed to that espousal of refined sensibility which manifested itself in so many other areas of eighteenth-century mores in polite society: a growing repugnance to cruelty, a more openly affectionate relationship with children, the love of nature. But beneath this high-mindedness, the image of the virtuous maid could be invigorated with a touch of naughtiness to tempt those who might wish for something more overtly erotic to peruse in their portfolios.

In France, a more serious approach to the depiction of domestic life was manifest above all in the work of Jean Siméon Chardin.[14] He started to paint figures in the early 1730s, perhaps stung into doing so by those who disparaged his devotion to the lowly genre of still life. Chardin widened the circle round his pantry shelves and kitchen tables, stocked with game, fruit and vegetables,

homely pots and utensils, to include those who habitually used them: women about their household duties and, on one occasion, a tavern-keeper's boy. Instead of the calculated artifice of fancy paintings, Chardin invested his women with a quiet dignity, arising from their graceful acceptance of the inexorable routine. There is something in the hermetic calm of this world reminiscent of Vermeer or de Hooch, and certainly Chardin would have been aware through engravings of the precedents set by seventeenth-century Dutch genre in employing such subject matter, if not of the paintings themselves. But unlike the majority of Dutch painters of low-life scenes, he avoided the anecdotal, even if the enlightening verses added to engravings after his works might occasionally draw out a moralizing point.

These engravings, executed by Charles-Nicolas Cochin père, François-Bernard Lépicié père and others in the late 1730s and 1740s, would have been known to Gravelot, Mercier, Hayman and Highmore. John Faber Junior, who engraved many of Mercier's fancy paintings, re-engraved two of Chardin's subjects in London in 1740 and certainly the tea-tray in Mercier's picture of the maid recalls the still-lifes of Chardin. Yet despite the fact that England seems to have been particularly early in acquiring Chardin's genre scenes, his influence was felt

A Porter with a Hare, 1768
JOHAN ZOFFANY

A Lady's Maid Soaping Linen,
c. 1765
HENRY ROBERT MORLAND

In contrast to the maid's gown of painted silk (a conceit not wholly implausible given the common practice of a mistress to hand her clothes on to her maid), the porter wears rough clothing and a sacking apron, demonstrating that the lowest ranks of servants did not need to be too fastidious about appearances, as they were not employed for show.

A London Potboy, 1759
LOUIS PHILIPPE BOITARD

A Porter at the Hogarth Club,
c. 1860
WILLIAM HOLMAN HUNT

Black formal dress had become the
standard attire for waiters by the
late nineteenth century.

remarkably little. Paul Sandby's sketches at Sandpit Gate, Windsor Park, tackle the same subject matter but they were not formal works intended for public display. Zoffany's painting of a *Porter with a Hare* features a kitchen menial and game but, both in technique and presentation, the work is far removed from Chardin's *oeuvre*. Instead of the velvety atmospheric depths of Chardin's settings, Zoffany's group is spot-lit as if on a stage; furthermore, the acting out of gestures, the humorous liveliness of the boys in contrast to the slow bewilderment of the porter, is essentially anecdotal, harking back to the Dutch masters of low-life scenes. But the scene is also reminiscent of the paintings which Jean-Baptiste Greuze was exhibiting at the Salon from 1755 onwards and with which Zoffany might have been familiar, again through engravings. Closer in mood and composition to Chardin's domestic scenes is the painting by Zoffany's pupil Henry Walton (*c.*1746–1813) entitled *Plucking the Turkey*, exhibited at the Royal Academy in 1776 (Tate Gallery).

The comic treatment of domestics is of course ingrained in English literature and artists likewise found a convenient repertoire of amusing characters in the streets and public places of the capital. Some, like Boitard's memorable rear view of a *London Pot Boy*, were clearly sketches made *en passant*. Others, like the overburdened footman drawn by George Woodward (1760?–1809) or Dighton's leering disreputable-looking sedan-chair men, were part of an army of retainers whose overriding characteristics could be taken for granted. Rowlandson was adept at depicting the tradesmen's-entrance flirtations between maids and street vendors, footmen and pretty street sellers, which suggest that the 'no followers' clause often specified in advertisements was widely flouted. The seedy reputation of the register or intelligence office, where servants could be hired, was likewise endorsed in his drawing where elderly clients ogle the young and attractive men and girls for more than their potential as servants.

The comparatively easygoing relationships between master and servant, family and non-family, gave way to more strict and prescribed forms of service in the nineteenth century. The architecture of country houses, with their increasingly rigid compartmentalization and stratification, reflected these changes.[15] The average narrow London house lacked the space for servants to disappear entirely. They constantly had to fetch and carry from one level to another, as is illustrated in a charming 1873 watercolour by Albert Goodwin (1845–1932) (*see* col. pl. XIX). They were required to insulate households as best they could from the dirt and unpleasantness of the city. At their most visible, they could be observed cleaning windows and scrubbing stairs. They were depicted thus by the graphic artist Auguste André Lançon (1836–87) in Jules Vallès' *La Rue à Londres* (Paris, 1884), wearing, according to the author, lilac-coloured dresses and little crocheted caps. By the end of the century, all traces of sartorial individuality for parlourmaids had given way to formal uniform.[16]

With these growing divisions, however, came a more vocal expression of dissatisfaction from below stairs as well as from the drawing room. The servant problem of the nineteenth century was not new but the scale of the problem was. Furthermore, domestic service was to an increasing extent out of step with

Register Office for the Hiring of Servants, c. 1800–05

THOMAS ROWLANDSON

Privately owned register or intelligence offices for servants filled the recruitment gap left by word of mouth recommendation. Pimps, procuresses and even the press gang were known to frequent them and they were gradually superseded by newspaper advertisements.

Return from Bond Street or Loads of Fashion to Astonish the Vulgar!, c. 1790

GEORGE MURGATROYD WOODWARD

Bond Street's pre-eminence as a luxury shopping street was established soon after its completion in the 1720s. The fashionable pastimes of promenading there, window-gazing and shopping, were also ridiculed by Gillray.

conditions of employment in other fields. There were no specified maximum hours, no set holidays, no free time, no statutory wages and little status; as an occupational group, it was almost entirely ignored in government surveys and reports. Given the lack of official channels of communication, grievances between employers and servants took the form of petty sniping as servants tried to assert themselves and were put down. Nowhere is the expression of these differences more acutely delineated than in the pages of that quintessentially middle-class magazine, *Punch*, almost invariably from the point of view of the employer.

As early as the 1820s, the fear that the 'March of Mind' would give servants pretensions above their station, to the neglect of their duties, was being reflected in the caricatures of William Heath (1795?–1840) which depicted, for example, a coachman reading *The Times*, and a butler and dustman playing chess.[17] George Cruikshank mocked them in *The Greatest Plague of Life: or the Adventures of a Lady in Search of a Good Servant*, edited by the Mayhew brothers and published in 1847. But the most comprehensive mockery of servant aspirations was made by John Leech (1817–64) in the 1850s; the attack, albeit superficially light-hearted, was an expression of the desperation he, along with thousands of other Londoners, had experienced in trying to find good servants and to retain them. 'Servantgal-isms; or What's to Become of the Missuses', which ran in *Punch* during the first half of 1853, are particularly instructive. In the first, the servant girl is saying, 'I tell you what, Cook, with my Beauty and Figger, I a'int a going to stop in sarvice no longer. I shall be orf to Horsetraylier.' Two of the cartoons in the series draw attention to the hierarchy within the servant establishment. The others ridicule servants' pretensions – aping their betters in the way they dress, calling on one

RIGHT *Mrs Mounter at the Breakfast Table*, 1916–17
HAROLD GILMAN

Mrs Mounter confronts her audience across a table, the teapot acting as her vanguard. The face of the sitter, sad, vulnerable yet proud and obstinate, characterizes the ambience of faded gentility and joyless drudgery.

TOP LEFT *Flunkeyiana – a Fact*, 1854 after JOHN LEECH

Flunkey (out of place). 'There's just one question I should like to ask your Ladyship – Ham I engaged for Work, or ham I engaged for Ornament?'

ABOVE *Superior Charlady*, 'I never clean stoves ma'am, it ruins my hands for whist drives,' *c.* 1925
GEORGE BELCHER

Belcher's cartoon is essentially an updated version of the nineteenth-century 'servantgalism', the young flapper wife in the subservient position of her crinolined forebears.

another and going to balls. Some simply abuse their employers because the food is not good enough; because they go to unsuitable seaside resorts in summer; or because the mistress did not knock at the door of the kitchen, which the cook considers to be *her* territory. After Leech had run out of servant-girl jokes, he went on to tackle footmen in the series entitled 'Flunkeyiana'. When the Education Act was being passed in 1870, George du Maurier dreamed up a series entitled 'Culture for the Million, or, Society as It May Be', for the *Punch* almanack, in which servants below stairs sing arias from Italian operas, a butler offers his services to a duchess when she is in need of a dictionary and nursemaids compliment the paintings of their beaux in highly technical language.[18]

These underlying fears proved in the end to be justified, even if it took until the First World War for the number of servants to diminish. In reality, much of the work that had previously been undertaken in the home, particularly food preparation, was transferred to a factory setting. The regular hours, larger wages, fixed conditions of work and greater social freedom of factories attracted girls who would have gone into domestic service in the Victorian period. Furthermore, the

enormous expansion in retailing offered more exciting prospects: it was preferable to work as a lift attendant in Selfridge's or as a 'Nippy' in a Lyons Corner House than to serve in a small dreary household in the suburbs. The pert young maid became the pert young shopgirl working 'up West' but retaining many of the characteristics of her forebears.

This left the women who were too old to go out and get a job but who needed the money because their husbands had died, were unable or unwilling to work. Some, like Mrs Mounter who was landlady to Harold Gilman (1876–1919) in Maple Street, turned their homes over to lodgers. Others went out to work as charwomen. They were not a new phenomenon but had tended in the past to clean mainly for single gentlemen.[19] With the decline of live-in servants and the vast development of office space, they came to represent the archetypal London servant in the twentieth century. As immortalized by George Belcher (1875–1947), they were large, stout-drinking, rugged, righteous and indomitable in their all-enveloping coats and extraordinary bonnets, pillars of the community to be relied upon when so many other aspects of London life were in a state of flux.

The Maid at No. 37, 1926
DAVID JONES

The General Servant, c. 1884
AUGUSTE ANDRÉ LANÇON

In contrast to Lançon's realist depiction of a familiar sight, Jones created a fantasy world out of the suburb where his parents lived at Brockley, Kent. The maid has the air of sitting at the oriel window of a Gothic castle – the romantic aura is enhanced by the delicately curvaceous fronds of the trees reaching out like tendrils, while the beribboned cat echoing the maid's beribboned bottom provides an amusing sexual pun.

'I come next to the markets, which, in such a mass of building, and such a collection of people, and where such business is done, must be great, and very many.' Thus in his *Tour* Defoe introduces his enumeration of the London cattle and flesh markets, the fish, herb, cherry and apple markets, the corn, meal and hay markets, the leather, hide and skin markets, the coal markets, the bay- and broad-cloth market, and finally the 'Bubble market' in Exchange Alley. But from an artistic point of view there was virtually only one market, and that was Covent Garden.[1]

Covent Garden, the convent garden, orchard and burial ground of the monks of Westminster Abbey, was granted to the Russells in 1541 and 1552 following the dissolution of the monasteries. The Church of St Paul, Covent Garden, and houses on three sides of the piazza were built by the enterprising Francis Russell, 4th Earl of Bedford to the designs of Inigo Jones in 1631–39. Groups of traders had evidently already begun by the mid-1640s to gather regularly in the piazza, on the south side in front of Bedford House garden wall. The earliest reference to a booth is noted in 1643/4. Possibly conceding the necessity of drawing retail distribution westward and certainly with a view to tapping the rental value, the 5th Earl obtained a royal charter in 1670 to establish a market for fruit, vegetables and flowers on weekdays within the limits of the piazza. The lease of this market's rights earned £5 for the Earl's family in its first year, £500 in 1705 and £1,200 by 1741. Initially the presence of the market had little effect on the prestige of the quarter, but gradually the gentry moved westwards, lured by new developments which lacked the dubious advantage of a market prospect. In 1700, the 2nd Duke of Bedford gave up Bedford House and about the same time Lord Robert Russell's tenure of a house in the piazza came to an end. The building of Tavistock Row on the south side precipitated the removal of the market into the central railed enclosure in 1705–06. In 1748, the market was placed on a more permanent footing when rebuilding provided for 106 new shops and 229 'stands'.

The homes of the gentry were taken by tradesmen, lodging-house keepers and, more to the point, artists. The miniaturist John Hoskins and the Flemish painter, Remigius van Leemput, were among their first residents. In the 1650s, Samuel Cooper, Francis Clien and Sir Peter Lely moved in, to be followed in 1682 by Kneller and in 1722 by Thornhill. Hogarth, Samuel Scott and Richard Wilson were illustrious eighteenth-century residents. This artistic presence must at least partly explain why Covent Garden market, as opposed to any other market, was so popular a subject for delineation. It was a large space explicitly licensed for use as a market, controlled by one owner; it was not hidden in a jumble of buildings, expanding in higgledy-piggledy fashion through narrow streets and alleys. From a purely aesthetic viewpoint, it was at least in concept an Italianate piazza, framed by fine arcaded buildings whose pleasing architectural rhythm was broken only by the idiosyncratic house built to the design of Thomas Archer for Lord Orford, no. 43 King Street, in the north-west corner, and the stately Tuscan barn of St Paul's. From the practical angle, the artists were close to their colour suppliers and framemakers, who also worked in the neighbourhood, and to their greatest potential source of patronage, in the West End.[2]

6
Markets

OPPOSITE

Covent Garden Market (detail), 1825
GEORGE SCHARF

Scharf concentrates on the activities of the stall-holders and shoppers in the makeshift quarters of the Market, before the construction of Fowler's building.

In the first few decades of the eighteenth century a number of artists living in the district began to paint the market itself. Dubbed the 'Covent Garden Group', they included Peter Angelis (1685–1734), Joseph van Aken (1709–49) and Balthasar Nebot (fl. 1730–after 1765). Angelis, perhaps the most talented, was born in Dunkirk, studied in Flanders and Germany, particularly in Düsseldorf, and became master in the Antwerp Guild in 1715–16. He lived in Covent Garden from 1716 to 1728 and then departed for Rome; he died on the return journey. Van Aken was probably born in Antwerp and came to London around 1720 with (possibly) two brothers, Arnold and Alexander. Nebot is thought to have been of Spanish origin; he certainly married in London in 1729/30, painted views of Covent Garden in the 1730s and, later, country-house landscapes until the 1760s.[3]

The tradition in which all these artists worked was essentially Flemish. In the sixteenth century Pieter Aertsen seems to have initiated the specialized genre of kitchen interiors and market stalls loaded with fish, meat, fruit and vegetables, to be followed by Joachim Beuckelaer. It is clear, however, that the main reason for such works was not social reportage (although the Steen at Antwerp is clearly recognizable in the background to one of Aertsen's paintings), but to impart moral and allegorical messages warning against man's carnality and worldly appetites. In other sixteenth-century paintings, market scenes were related to various times of year, such as the picture of a vegetable market attributed to Lucas van Valkenborch (Kunsthistorisches Museum, Vienna) or the market scene on the Perlachplatz in Augsburg with different activities representing different months (Städtlische Kunstsammlungen, Augsburg). Still others embodied a maxim, like Joachim Wtewael's vegetable market of 1618 (Centraal Museum, Utrecht) which probably illustrates the 'rotten apple' saying. But although Jan van de Velde and Willem Buytewech depicted market scenes, it was not until the middle of the seventeenth century that artists, responding to the fascination with urban topography, turned to the subject with renewed interest.

The reasons for this revival are complex, rooted in an increasingly secular society which no longer disapproved of the depiction of the material side of life. The taste for naturalism helped to promote the importance of still life as a subject in Italy, the Netherlands and Spain at the end of the sixteenth century. There was a growing demand for decorative paintings, and market scenes, with their lavish displays of fruit and vegetables, fish and game, representing the changing months, seasons or senses, were well suited for use in series as part of an interior scheme. In Holland, Hendrick Sorgh specialized in market scenes from the early 1650s, usually adopting a horizontal format with the saleswoman at one side of a stall and streets or docks visible in the distance. Other artists, notably his pupil Adriaen Lucasz. Fontey and Adriaen van Ostade, followed his example.

In England the genre took longer to develop. Hollar's etchings of Covent Garden in 1647 give no indication of a market, but the earliest painted view of the piazza, dating from before 1666–67, does include a few small groups of traders with baskets, trestles and a cart already congregating on the south side outside the wooden rails of the central reservation (The Earl of Pembroke, Wilton House). It was not until the 1720s that the market itself, as opposed to its architectural

setting, became a popular subject. As we have seen, when he first arrived in
England Peter Angelis like Tillemans seems to have been bent on securing
aristocratic patronage. Perhaps, as suggested by Walpole, because he was not as
assiduous in cultivating his connections as he might have been, he turned to
painting the market, possibly inspired by the copies he evidently made of the four
market paintings by Rubens and Snyders which were then at Houghton.[4] With a
style which is usually seen as deriving from Teniers, a certain Rococo elegance in
his delineation of figures and a harmonious use of pretty colours, Angelis recorded
the main elements which were to constitute the distinctive character of the market
in art for another two hundred years (*see* col. pl. II). The principal contrast is
between the traders – mostly old countrywomen wearing distinctive hats, aprons
and cloaks – and the citizens' wives and servants in fashionable London attire. The
porter wheeling a barrow or carrying an enormous pile of baskets on his head is
another recurring theme. But the appeal of Covent Garden was not wholly
business-orientated. As Steele noted in his essay, 'Twenty-four hours in London'
(1712), of the 'ruddy Virgins' walking with their produce to the London markets,
'There was an Air in the Purveyors for *Covent-Garden*, who frequently converse
with Morning Rakes, very unlike the seemly Sobriety of those bound for *Stocks-
Market*.' Young and pretty market girls were singled out for individual attention in
paintings by Angelis and a number of his successors.

Covent Garden Market (and detail, left), 1735

BALTHASAR NEBOT

Nebot's figures are full of individual charm and interest, ranging from the knife-grinder, a young porter with his wheelbarrow, the gentleman greeting the lady with a small bunch of flowers (which perhaps suggests that the area was not completely out of fashion even in the 1730s) to a blind beggar on the right hand side with his dog and staff.

Joseph van Aken painted several views of London markets in the late 1720s which, although they do not give much indication of the skills he was later to acquire as a drapery painter, have the highly distinctive manner apparent in his later works of painting figures and objects at three-quarters angle with over-sharp recession. He was not a skilled topographer, but he chose the more unusual viewpoint in his Covent Garden paintings, looking east instead of west towards the church, perhaps because he lived on the west side of the piazza himself. Van Aken also ventured as far as painting the Old Stocks Market, established in the thirteenth century on the side of the present-day Mansion House. The first building was called the Stokkes after the only fixed pair of stocks in the City. It was rebuilt several times before the Great Fire and in 1668, when St Mary Woolchurch was demolished, it was rebuilt on the site as a general market and flourished, according to Strype, 'surpassing all other markets in London'. Its imminent clearance for the construction of Mansion House might have acted as an incentive for the artist to paint it before it was removed in 1737 to a much less picturesque site in Farringdon Street.

The paintings of Covent Garden by Balthasar Nebot date from the mid 1730s when the market is shown in an even more developed state. Besides the trading activities, the artist included a range of social classes from ladies and gentlemen to beggars, as well as wrestling matches which suggest that the market had some of the qualities of a fair. Nebot continued to paint individual stallholders, in the manner of Sorgh or van Ostade, as late as 1749.[5]

Surprisingly, in view of his attendance at Thornhill's free art academy in Covent Garden and his own residence in the piazza from 1729 to 1733 when newly married to Thornhill's daughter, Hogarth portrayed Covent Garden only once, as the setting for *Morning* from *The Four Times of Day*, painted in 1738 (National Trust, Upton House). Even this work makes use of the Covent Garden setting

principally for its raffish associations – the revellers and lovers brawling outside
Tom King's notorious coffee house – and there is no reference to the market
beyond the odd basket of produce. Nor did Canaletto during his residence in
London deign to depict the market as a fashionable London sight. Nevertheless,
the piazza was included regularly in most of the important series of eighteenth-
century topographical prints of the city: from Overton's *Prospects*, published in
the 1720s, to Sutton Nicholls's famous engraving first listed in the John Bowles
catalogue of 1728 and included in Bowles's *London Described* of 1731, in *London
and its Environs Described* (1761), Rooker's *Views* (1777), Thornton's *History of
London* (1784), De Serres de la Tour's *Londres et ses Environs* (1788), Malton's
Picturesque Tour of 1792 and Ackermann's large view of 1811.[6]

At the same time, if the example of Hogarth and Canaletto was specifically
absent, the influence of both artists can be detected in a number of works by other
painters. Samuel Scott, who lived in Covent Garden until 1758, made two large-
scale overviews of the market around 1750 (Marquess of Tavistock and Trustees of
the Bedford Estates. Museum of London). By this time, the line of sheds on the
south side had been replaced by a row of two-storey buildings, the upper floors of
which were used as bedrooms. The roofs were low-pitched or slightly curved with
projecting chimneys, as can be seen in Scott's views, beyond the grove of trees for
sale and the mass of carts and traders. Some twenty years later, John Collet
produced a painting of similar size and viewpoint. But whereas Scott's treatment of
the subject has something of the breadth of a Canaletto, Collet's picture has a
curious toy-town quality, partly induced by his amateurish grasp of perspective,
and partly because it is bustling with life of a coarser, semi-comic character which
ultimately derives from Hogarth.

Individual vendors were also singled out for depiction in series devoted to the
'Cries' of London. For example, Phillips' *Modern London* of 1804 included thirty-

Covent Garden Market from James Street, 1864
PHOEBUS LEVIN

The seething throng includes handsome Irish women sellers, costermongers and a donkey, countrymen in their smocks, porters, street traders selling hot potatoes and eels, a blind black beggar, ragged children and a sprinkling of gentlemen two of whom are examining a small basket of peaches.

Covent Garden Market, c.1829
FREDERICK CHRISTIAN LEWIS

The north side of the Fowler building appears to be open for business while the south side is still in scaffolding.

one small aquatints of street traders in specific London settings, after watercolours by William Marshall Craig (c.1765?–after 1834). Covent Garden was represented by a strawberry seller, one of the hundreds of women who carried the fragile crop into and around London from Shropshire or even Wales. Around the same time Jacques Laurent Agasse (1767–1849) painted his charming picture of a young flower seller from the market which had become, by the late eighteenth century, the best in England for fruit, herbs and flowers (Private Collection). The herb shops were in the south row and florists on the west side. The coster drawn by

William Henry Hunt (1790–1864) had probably bought his produce wholesale in the market (*see* col. pl. XII). The north side was devoted to root vegetables and kitchen-garden produce except potatoes, which were sold on the south side. Peas, beans, cherries and strawberries in season could be bought on the east, while in the centre there was a free-for-all, with everything from bird sellers to dealers in old iron and crockery, much to the annoyance of residents.

By the early nineteenth century, the market had outgrown its parameters in seeking to serve the needs of the city's increasing population. The large-scale aquatint published by Ackermann in 1811 after Pugin and Rowlandson is an overview from the Hummums *bagnio*, showing the open space of the market covered by a miscellany of sheds, horses, donkeys and carts lining up against the south side of the permanent buildings, while the sellers spill out into the streets with their sacks of vegetables. The sign 'White Painter & Glazier' indicates that there was a variety of trades operating out of the market by this date. George Scharf's watercolour of the sheds on the north side of the piazza clearly conveys the crush of buyers, vendors, porters and baskets, perhaps also hinting at the loose-living characters of the market girls. There were constant disputes about the level of tolls, for which there was no uniform scale. It was becoming increasingly clear that the market had become too large and too complex for the owners simply to lease the rent to the highest bidder and hope for the best.

Accordingly, in 1828–30 a new market building was built to the design of Charles Fowler; it is shown during construction in the painting by Frederick Christian Lewis (1779–1856). This view, the watercolour by William Havell (1782–1857) showing the completed market (Sotheby's 17 November 1983, lot 47), and the painting by Phoebus Levin (fl. 1855–74) of the market from James Street in 1864, all remained on ground level. Instead of entering Fowler's market building, the artists viewed the activity outside – the vegetables spreading over the cobbles, the old women and young beauties selling and carrying, the porters, the odd lady or gentleman, and the 'morning rakes' drawn to the market, as in Steele's day, by the prospect of female company and early breakfasts. The motives for painting Covent Garden did not change. It was a quintessential London location, where a range of characters could be portrayed together in the midst of colourful still-life displays and a distinguished architectural setting.

The Dukes of Bedford waged a losing battle against the overspill, constructing a flower market first in 1862–63, rebuilding it on a large scale in 1871–72 and glassing in the Fowler building in 1874–75. In 1918, after prolonged negotiations, they gave up the market altogether and it passed first into the hands of the Covent Garden Estate Company and then, in 1924, to the Beecham Estate.

Stanley Anderson (1884–1966) was one of the last artists to depict the special character of Covent Garden. In his etchings, the familiar portico of St Paul's provides the backdrop for the baskets heaped on the cobbles, the scrum of now largely motorized carts, the flat-capped porters and here and there the bulky forms of cockney flowerwomen. So far, at least, the new market at Nine Elms has not inspired the same artistic response.

Covent Garden Market, 1922
STANLEY ANDERSON

Beneath the looming portico of St Paul's, symbolic of classical order, the artist depicts the mêlée of the market, with overloaded wagons, porters and old women sellers, who still retain the bonnets and dress of the pre-war years.

No other market was painted with quite such continuity as Covent Garden for none had such a clearly defined social and artistic personality. The pre-eminence of Billingsgate as the free market for fish was confirmed by Act of Parliament in 1698. But perhaps its distance from the artistic quarter and lack of distinguished buildings deterred the Covent Garden Group from portraying it. Only one painting, attributed to Peter Angelis, can possibly be identified as Billingsgate (Christie's 17 June 1983, lot 38). It seems to show the stalls on the west side of the hithe, the tower of St Olave's Southwark in the distance and two matrons viewing a rather paltry supply of fish. Indeed, there are no London equivalents to the still-life displays of the fruits of the sea which frequently occur in Dutch art. A more lively impression of the market was presented, however, in the print *The Humours of Billingsgate* of 1736 by Arnold Vanhaecken (d.1735/36), who was possibly a brother of Joseph van Aken. But the character of Billingsgate was represented above all by the fishwife, so much so in literary terms that Bailey's dictionary of 1736 gives 'Billingsgate' as a synonym for 'scolding, impudent slut'. Hogarth's spirited painting of the *Shrimp Girl* conveys a vivid impression of the charms of some of the sellers. But the more usual visual image was of coarse matronly figures, built on a generous scale as in Rowlandson's drawing. Even Craig's normally picturesque view failed when he portrayed a mackerel seller at Billingsgate: she is a rather woeful figure clutching her basket of wares before her.

LEFT *Billingsgate* (detail), *c*. 1800
THOMAS ROWLANDSON

Rowlandson's fishwives, waiting for the catch to be unloaded, present the typical image of Billingsgate characters.

ABOVE *The Shrimp Girl*, *c*. 1750
WILLIAM HOGARTH

Executed with extraordinary bravura, Hogarth's portrait depicts the girl wearing a broad-brimmed hat to protect her hair, cap and shoulders from the dripping shellfish.

The View and Humours of Billingsgate, 1736
ARNOLD VANHAECKEN

The hithe provides a setting for a mixed range of characters, from those legitimately connected with the coal and fish trades to a quack medicine man with his 'zany', a gentleman sampling oysters and a thief about to steal his hat.

Billingsgate Fish Porters, 1920
FRANK BRANGWYN

As an ex-seaman, Brangwyn was
frequently attracted to Thames-side
subjects and particularly when they
involved the depiction of manual
work, as in his prints of boat
builders and his murals devoted to
dock labour.

Nineteenth-century depictions of Billingsgate come in waves, first inspired by
the building of the new Custom House in 1817 and then, following the
construction in 1849–53 of Bunning's market building by the City Corporation on
the west side of the filled-in hithe. In 1876, this was in its turn replaced by the
present building, designed by Sir Horace Jones and used until 1982 when the fish
market moved to its new premises in Docklands. Samuel Owen (1768/69–1857)
executed a number of views of Billingsgate and the Custom House quay from the
river in the 1820s and 1830s, showing the assemblage of smacks moored alongside
and the crowded market above, in the Romantic marine-watercolour tradition.
However, the only nineteenth-century painting to depict the transactions of the
trade in detail was the interior view of the new building by George Elgar Hicks,
dating from 1861 (*see* col. pl. XIV). It shows the market in full swing at around six
in the morning, crowded with salesmen, porters and buyers, with an impressive
array of cod and flat fish in the foreground. With a typical appeal to Victorian
sentiment, the focus of attention is provided by a pretty fish girl who, according to
the critic of the *Athenaeum,* is 'too proud to carry her own purchases, beset with
offers from ragged fellows to do the job'. But, as at Covent Garden, the prominent
role of market women was being taken over by men by the second half of the
nineteenth century. The fellowship porters, dressed in their distinctive hats and
smocks, who had the privilege of landing fish from the vessels, can be seen in
action in Hicks's work. They rest on the quay in Whistler's etching of 1859, and

carry the trays of fish up from the wharf in the etching made by Frank Brangwyn (1867–1943) in 1920, a bold exercise in heroic realism. Partly, no doubt, because they were immediately recognizable, they came to represent the character of Billingsgate, particularly after the hardy breed of London fishwives had died out.

Apart from Hugh Alley's illustrated appeal to the Lord Mayor of 1598, the depiction of the city's meat markets does not seem to have captured artists' imaginations before the nineteenth century. The reason is fairly obvious. The slaughtered-meat quarter known as the Shambles, running along present-day Newgate Street, and the waste dumped in the Fleet River nearby, were hardly salubrious sights. As Swift and Steele succinctly expressed it in their mock-heroic poem 'The Description of a City Shower' (*The Spectator*, 17 October 1710):

> Sweeping from Butchers Stalls, Dung, Guts, and Blood,
> Drown'd Puppies, stinking Sprats, all drench'd in Mud,
> Dead Cats, and Turnip-Tops come tumbling down the Flood.

Smithfield, immediately outside the City wall, was originally 'smooth field' and had since medieval times been a weekly cattle market. The livestock market grew with London's population, animals being driven from long distances for sale there. The London drovers took over at Islington, and a third set of drovers, who steered the animals to the slaughterhouses after sale, was employed by the butchers. The remaining responsibility rested with the salesmen to whom the cattle-owners consigned their stock; they examined the beasts and decided which should be put up for sale, depending on the demand and the price. By the end of the eighteenth century, Smithfield Market had reached saturation point, despite being held several days a week. In 1810, approximately 140,000 cattle and 1,000,000 sheep were sold every year at Smithfield; by 1828, this had grown to 150,000 cattle and 1,500,000 sheep, and by 1853, to an astonishing 277,000 cattle and 1,600,000 sheep. The accompanying disturbance and debris as the animals were herded through the city streets brought hundreds of complaints and caused constant accidents. As Pip in *Great Expectations* said, Smithfield was 'a shameful place, being all asmear with filth and fat and blood and foam'. Yet absolutely nothing of this squalor is conveyed in the artistic representations of the market at this time: in W. H. Pyne's delicately picturesque portrayals of a city drover, a slaughterer and a butcher in *The Costumes of Great Britain* (1808); in the lively overview of the market by Rowlandson; in Agasse's view of the Friday afternoon horse fair; or in Thomas Hosmer Shepherd's depiction of the market around 1830, for *London in the Nineteenth Century*, with a few cows on the loose outside their pens. Apart from the ever-dominating dome of St Paul's, there is little to distinguish these scenes from the cattle and horse markets of a large county town.

In 1852, the Smithfield Market Removal Act relocated the livestock market to a new site north of Islington in Copenhagen Fields. It was six times larger than Smithfield and could hold fifty thousand animals with ease. It was opened by Prince Albert in 1855 and named the Caledonian Cattle Market. At the same time, licensing controls on slaughterhouses were introduced; the old Shambles was swept away and all the slaughtering was also moved to Copenhagen Fields. The sale of meat, however, continued to take place in central London in a new market building erected to the design of the City architect, Sir Horace Jones, in 1866–68.

Topographical artists recorded the last days of the market in Newgate Street and the new purpose-built markets at Copenhagen Fields and Smithfield. The business being transacted within the latter appealed to artists into the present century, the human activity of buying, selling and carrying being purposefully contrasted with the picturesque nineteenth-century ironwork of the hall, as in Edward Bawden's lithograph series of London markets, published in 1967.

One of the greatest London markets, Leadenhall, which took its name from the Greville family mansion in the fourteenth century which had a lead roof, is barely recorded at all in art. After the Great Fire, it was rebuilt around three large courtyards and possibly this sense of enclosure, added to the fact that it largely dealt in beef, leather, wood and raw hides, might have been discouraging. Most views were confined to the street façade, but in the early nineteenth century a view of the hide market was included in the *Microcosm of London* and described as 'at present the largest or perhaps the best supplied market in Europe'; while another view of the skin market which, typically, focused on the antiquarian

Smithfield Market, c. 1811
THOMAS ROWLANDSON

The open space in front of St Bartholomew's Hospital is filled to capacity with thousands of cattle, sheep and pigs, barely controlled by the stockades. Groups of buyers examine the stock, arguing prices with the salesmen, while the drovers in smocks retain a precarious order.

interest of Leadenhall Chapel, was given in Robert Wilkinson's *Londina Illustrata*, published in 1825. The courtyard structure was replaced by the present market building in 1881, also designed by Sir Horace Jones; its elaborate ironwork was again to be used as a decorative element in Bawden's lithograph.

In the twentieth century, the changing faces of markets have attracted a wide range of artists, some drawn to the subject possibly because of the concentrated human activity in an increasingly impersonal urban environment. Robert Bevan (1865–1925) painted a *Horse Sale at the Barbican* around 1912, in which the crowd of introverted bowler-hatted professionals viewing the horseflesh make a sober contrast with Agasse's cheerful depiction of a similar scene at Smithfield a century earlier. The horse markets were to disappear with the increased use of motorized transport, and the paintings of the Cumberland hay market, executed by Bevan around 1914, give the impression that it was not much-patronized, with the hay hidden beneath tarpaulins and the odd desultory horse and cart.

While some markets disappeared, others have grown more active. London antique markets seem to have been instituted at the Pedlars' or General Market, which took place on Fridays at the Caledonian Market. The general view painted by Clifford Hall (b.1903) in 1933 gives some idea of the atmosphere of this market held among the stockades, where many bargains were to be found. One of the four distinctive Italianate taverns also forms the backdrop to the still-life grouping painted by Harry Morley (1881–1943).

At the same time, the London street markets originally instituted to serve the needs of workers who were paid on Saturdays have retained their buoyancy. Charles Ginner (1878–1952) painted a typical example at King's Cross before the First World War, the canopies of the stalls receding like ships' rigging down the

ABOVE LEFT *Horse Sale at the Barbican*, c. 1912
ROBERT BEVAN

Bevan depicted the horse in far from glamorous surroundings: St John's Wood cabyards and the horse sales held at Tattersall's, Aldridge's and the Barbican. His spare, angular schematic style of draughtsmanship conveys the businesslike atmosphere of his location.

ABOVE RIGHT *A View of Smithfield* (detail), c. 1820
FREDERICK CHRISTIAN LEWIS and GEORGE ROBERT LEWIS (?) after JACQUES LAURENT AGASSE

Agasse excelled at painting thoroughbreds for noble patrons; the Smithfield fair provided him with an opportunity to depict the working horse of various types.

The Caledonian Market, 1936
HARRY MORLEY

The carefully arranged display of bric-à-brac has replaced the piles of fruit and vegetables so lavishly recorded in conventional market paintings.

street (Private Collection). But it is the costermongers themselves who served as an important source of inspiration for modern British artists. When William Rothenstein (1872–1945) exhibited *Coster Girls* at the New English Art Club in 1894, he was undoubtedly in part paying homage to Hogarth's *Shrimp Girl*; yet the bold young woman with her hands on her hips was also recognized as representative 'of the entirely independent girl whose preternaturally sharpened instincts are exercises in a defensive war against society'. Costers symbolized down-to-earth values and a healthy rebellion against stultifying Victorian mores. When he was at the Slade before the First World War, Nevinson led a group of students who called themselves 'The Coster Gang', adopting the dress and manners of the costers. In 1913 Eric Kennington (1888–1960) painted *The Costard Mongers*, investing his figures with monumental dignity (Musée National d'Art Moderne, Paris). In his painting of a *Coster Girl* exhibited at the New English Art Club in 1923, Mark Gertler (1891–1939) – who was born and brought up in Spitalfields – imposed a gypsy brilliance of colour on a classically modelled Madonna form. Ceri Richards (1903–71) first started to draw costers in the early 1930s. They became figures of fantasy, their exuberant displays of pearls and feathers taking on a life of their own; and in the lithographs of their dancing, inspired by the Festival of Britain, they mythologize the indomitable spirit and community feeling of Londoners who had survived the war.

The Caledonian Market, 1933
CLIFFORD HALL

The view is taken from the central clock tower looking south-east towards Pedlar's Way, the White Horse Tavern and the warehouses of Caledonian Road railway station.

ABOVE *Coster Girls*, 1894
WILLIAM ROTHENSTEIN

Like Whistler, Rothenstein uses the Thames as a
flat backdrop for this Japanese-inspired
composition, although the girls' strength of
presence recalls the more earthy traditions of
Billingsgate.

TOP RIGHT *Pearlies Dancing*, 1951
CERI RICHARDS

In response to the Surrealist exhibition of 1936,
the pearl buttons and feathers underwent a
metamorphosis as Richards developed his
theme, so that the individuality of the subjects
was entirely subsumed in a flurry of scribbled
calligraphy, like a Picasso drawing.

CENTRE *Smithfield Market*, 1967
EDWARD BAWDEN

RIGHT *The Common Market*, 1963
WILLIAM ROBERTS

Intended presumably as an ironic comment on
Britain's original failure to join the Common
Market, this carefully ordered composition
skilfully interweaves the formal rhythm of the
poles and awnings with the solid human figures
sampling, buying and selling. The London
Transport roundel on the bus-stop provides the
only indication of location, for the stocky women
in their headscarves could be found in any peasant
market throughout Europe.

William Logsdail /88

Street traders were those members of the urban working population who, lacking the capital investment to trade from a shop or stall, earned a living by plying their wares and services on an individual, itinerant basis. In legal documents, they were described as hawkers, pedlars and petty chapmen.[1] They carried the tools of their trade or the goods they wished to sell and made their presence felt by uttering distinctive cries as they proceeded on their way. Their role was crucial in cities not yet sufficiently sophisticated to have developed permanent shops from which goods and services could be supplied on a regular basis. So their last stronghold was – and still is – the suburbs, where facilities cannot keep pace with the needs of a growing population.[2]

The history of London street traders is encapsulated on a picturesque basis in the *Cries of London*. And as Charles Hindley observed in his *History of the Cries of London* (1881) – published at precisely the time when the tradition which had lasted hundreds of years was drawing to a close – the history of the cries is the history of social changes. But most commentators have been content to examine the street criers purely on an individual basis, noting the appearance and disappearance of particular trades and their associated calls as the market for their services rose and declined. Illustrations in such accounts are merely annexed to rhymes and anecdotes about the cries, and their purpose or their veracity is rarely questioned. True, Hindley doubted whether the Jewish old-clothes sellers really wore three hats at a time, as they are depicted.[3] More significantly, only a dozen years after Wheatley's celebrated *Cries of London* had appeared in 1795, Edward Edwards could observe that the artist's females had a 'meretricious and theatrical air', and singled out the *Cries* 'in which the women are dressed with great smartness, but little propriety, better suited to the fantastic taste of an Italian opera stage than to the streets of London.'[4] The aim here is not to give an illustrated account of London street trades, but to try to discern the reasons why the prints, drawings and even paintings were produced at all.

There have been street traders in London since medieval times: they are mentioned in the prologue to *Piers Plowman* and in an anonymous fifteenth-century poem, the 'London Lyckpenny', quoted in Stow's *Survey* of 1598. Between Westminster Hall and Cheapside, the Kentish protagonist encounters sellers of fine felt hats and spectacles (for the Westminster lawyers), as well as others offering a variety of spices, cooked food, fresh vegetables and commodities. Thereafter, the criers provided a useful fund of reference to the vernacular of the street in verse and song.

Popular prints of itinerant merchants existed in Italy from the fifteenth century and in some quantities by the late sixteenth century. A large sheet of 199 little woodcuts of merchants and itinerant artisans by Ambrogio Brambilla, published in Rome in 1582, expanded and improved on those produced before.[5] In 1589, Francis Hogenberg published a series of *Cries* in Cologne very similar to the Rome series and it was probably Hogenberg who, through his extensive cartographical interests, brought the idea to England. The print he published of Nonsuch Palace after Hoefnagel in *Civitates Orbis Terrarum* (1582) includes not only the nobility, citizens and country women in the border of characters along the

OPPOSITE

St Martin-in-the-Fields (detail), 1888
WILLIAM LOGSDAIL

In his depiction of a damp grey winter's day, Logsdail combines Bastien-Lepage-inspired realism with touches of Victorian narrative interest, contrasting the shabby little flower seller with the well-cared-for child behind.

London Water-Carrier and his Dog, c. 1623–24

In *alba amicorum*, the London water-bearer is usually depicted as old, blind and led by a dog carrying a lantern in his mouth. Until Sir Hugh Middleton brought the New River from Amwell to London in the 1620s, bearers transported the water from the Thames and the conduits in tankards on their backs, and sold it to householders.

Cries of London, c. 1600

This print, one of two companion sheets, would seem to be the earliest extant London series of *Cries*.

bottom, but also a fish seller and a water carrier.[6] So one reason for the popularity of the *Cries* could be that they catered for the general curiosity about the dress and customs of other countries which the spread of learning during the Renaissance had encouraged. The *alba amicorum* are another facet of this same interest. The artists who illustrated these works frequently singled out the Thames water carrier, with his distinctive tankard or horse and cart, to represent the working population of London.

Old shewes or
Bootes will yu buy
some Broome.

I haue Screenes if you Desier
to keepe yᵉ Buter from yᵉ fire

Mussels Lilly
Mussels.   white

The earliest London series of *Cries* appears to date from around 1600 and consists of full-length printed figures, each framed by an arch. Another series dating from around 1640 comprises attractive three-quarter-length woodcuts; something of their decorative quality must have been appreciated from an early stage, for a series of silver counters was produced after them.[7] Presumably designed for use in some game, possibly for children, each counter has a number and a floral design on one side, and on the other the figure of a trader with the words of his or her cry.

Despite their unsophisticated style, the early series of *Cries* were not static; an illustration of the 'Siddan Carriers', for example, was introduced after the sedan chair had been pioneered as a fashionable mode of transport by the Duke of Buckingham.[8] They were specifically urban because the city provided the focus for the greatest variety of types of retailing activity. They fitted into a world view in which everybody had his or her station in life, based on the medieval allegories on the different conditions of man, and were schematic enough to be used as teaching aids for children.

None of the early series was artistically outstanding and none possessed anything more than a generalized typology. Figures were distinguished not so much by their clothes – which were variations on the traditional citizens' dress, with aprons for the women, and sometimes for the men – but by the goods or tools they were carrying. However, the series of depictions of trades which Annibale Carracci drew in his native city Bologna, most probably in the 1580s and early 1590s, revolutionized the genre by emphasizing the real character and occupation of the figures depicted. The *Arti di Bologna* were portrayed on an individual basis and if the urban and rustic settings were sometimes minimal, the action or stance of the figure with his wares seems to have been drawn from life.[9] Although probably intended for publication as prints at the time they were made, they were not in fact engraved for another fifty years, until 1646, when they were issued by Simon Guillain in Rome.

The Cryes of the City of London,
c. 1640
J. OVERTON after ROBERT WHITE

The most sophisticated of the early *Cries of London*, the series comprises thirty-two plates, surviving in two states and three known copies.

TOP *Old Cloaks, Suits or Coats*,
ABOVE *Knives, Combs or Inkhornes*,
c. 1687
MARCELLUS LAURON

These studies come from a volume
which contains the original
drawings for Lauron's famous series
of *Cries*. The engravings, first
published by Pierce Tempest,
exaggerated the formality of the
artist's style.

The first London series to demonstrate some awareness of this new current of realism was the one produced by Marcellus Lauron and first published in 1687. The style of depiction – the heavily shaded and strong outlines of the figures, framed in a bold line border – is close to that of the series executed by Jean-Baptiste Bonnart and published by his brothers in Paris around 1676[10]; but the range of characters and the naming of a number of them suggest that a good portion were based on direct observation. The series first consisted of forty figures but grew eventually to seventy-four. There were successive reprints in 1688, 1689, and the early eighteenth century, besides pirate editions; around 1760 Boitard adjusted the dress and hairstyle of some to bring them up to date. The titles were published in French and Italian as well as English, indicating that the publisher was attempting to capture a foreign sale.

Their appeal was undoubted, but the extraordinary fact is that they were circulated at a time when street traders were most unpopular, for various reasons. From the government's point of view, there was the risk that those who hawked newspapers and pamphlets about the streets were spreading sedition. Consequently, just at the time when the Lauron series was first published, proclamations were issued which attempted to control the trade. In 1686–87, it was resolved to license pedlars to prevent them from dispersing scandalous books, and in 1688 it was forbidden for them to sell any books.[11] James's government was clearly attempting to suppress criticism of his rule rather than to attack street sellers as such; equally clearly, hawkers sold many more goods than cheap publications. Nevertheless, from the City records, it is obvious that the government was not alone in its fears. From the seventeenth century onwards, if not earlier, there was a steady stream of complaints to and directives from the Common Council concerning the hawkers, pedlars and petty chapmen.[12]

The citizens took a self-interested view. By the ancient laws and customs of the City, freemen alone were entitled to take up manual occupations and sell, or display goods for sale. These privileges were being undermined by the activities of the street traders, whose numbers were greatly augmented whenever there was a poor harvest. The events surrounding the revolution of 1688 and the outbreak of war against the French the following year marked the beginning of nearly a decade of economic recession in London, with coal shortages, high bread prices and increased unemployment. In 1694, when the City authorities were hesitating to act, the weavers petitioned Common Council to do something about the 'insolent practices of Hawkers and Pedlars, who daily do increase and take away the trades and subsistence of your petitioners'. The ironmongers and cutlers joined in, attacking the petty chapmen 'who do in a disorderly manner in public inns and other places expose to sale base and deceitful wares', thus bringing down prices.[13] The Court responded by ordering the strict execution of all statutes against offenders who should be found within the City liberties and, as a further remedy, imposed a forty shilling fine. In addition, the Hawkers' Act of 1698 set out the administrative framework for licensing hawkers which was to remain, with various revisions, on the statute book until the present century.[14] However, the act did not cover those who sold official publications, nor sellers of fish, fruit and victuals, and neither makers nor menders of goods. And although they were excluded from cities, an exception was made on fair and market days.

The legislation seems to have caused considerable confusion, with licensed hawkers exploiting their ambiguous position. It proved to be impractical for citizens to proceed by the slow method of civil action against hawkers who were generally 'Foreigners or other Idle Vagabonds', of no fixed abode. Matters came to a head in December 1748 when the citizens petitioned Common Council to cure the evil, concluding with the dramatic warning that unless some speedy and effective action was taken, they would be 'forced to desert this once flourishing Metropolis to the Utter Ruin of the Corporation as well as of the Several landholders and owners of houses within the City and Liberties'.[15] The Court was sufficiently shaken by the threat to set up a committee to produce a remedy, which reported back in January 1749 merely recommending that the laws be strictly enforced.[16] The accounts of a fund, supported by the parish, which rewarded constables with ten shillings for every hawker apprehended, indicate that some fresh initiative was taken, at least for a few years.[17]

As if these grievances were not enough, street traders were also unpopular because of the noise and congestion to which they contributed. In the character of Ralph Crotchett, Addison suggested (*Spectator*, 18 December 1711) that he be appointed Comptroller general of the London cries, to tune and license the instruments used and to

> permit none to lift up their Voices in our Streets, that have not tuneable Throats, and are not only able to overcome the Noise of the Croud, and the rattling of Coaches, but also to vend their respective Merchandizes in apt Phrases, and in the most distinct and agreeable Sounds.

The cries 'so full of Incongruities and Barbarisms, that we appear a distracted City to Foreigners', represented another symptom of that illogical and uncontrolled disorder, which manifested itself in other aspects of city life and was left over from an earlier less sophisticated society. The cries of London, like the shop signs that bore no relation to the businesses they overhung, needed to be tidied up. As the movement to improve the streets of London with lighting, paving and the construction of new wide roads gathered force during the second half of the eighteenth and in the nineteenth centuries, the casual anarchism of the street traders was to seem increasingly out of place.

Hogarth's depiction of the *Enraged Musician* of 1741 includes an itinerant hautboy, an Irish paviour in his distinctive beehive hat, a dustman with a basket, a mounted sow gelder blowing his horn, a yelling fishmonger, a pewterer, a knife grinder, a milkmaid, and a ballad singer with her baby and assorted children. The musician is naturally unable to concentrate amidst the chaos, a lone symbol of order and cultivation in the face of uncontrolled forces of nature. Paul Sandby was to take up the theme some twenty years later, but in *Asylum for the Deaf* the point is reversed, as was frequently the case in Sandby's visual comments on Hogarth's works, with the householders at the open window apparently welcoming the cacophony outside (*see* col. pl. VII). John Collet's street scenes emphasized the

The Curds and Whey Seller, Cheapside, c. 1730

Three young chimney-sweeps buy curds and whey – a popular summer beverage – from a woman seller who appears to be blind. According to J. T. Smith, in 1698 when Cheapside Conduit was no longer used for its original purpose, it became the haunt of chimney-sweeps, who hung their brooms and shovels against it, and waited there for hire.

chaos of a city struggling to cope with the conflicting goals of its inhabitants, whether they were pedlars, hawkers driving their beasts of burden too hard or young bloods spoiling for a fight.

Such scenes do not appear in the eighteenth-century print series of the *Cries of London*, where the sellers are isolated as individuals and removed to a greater or lesser extent from their social context and malodorous reputation. There was, nevertheless, enormous scope for variation within the genre, not least because of the extraordinary variety of street traders in London. Paul Sandby produced at least sixty pen and wash drawings of the *Cries of London* and evidently intended to publish them as etchings in a number of parts, for the designs for the frontispieces of parts two and three survive; in the event, only twelve prints were issued as a set. The drawings are certainly among the finest figure studies ever made by the artist. In the vigour with which they stride across the page, the solidity of their presence and the distinctive backviews of some figures, drawn in movement on a diagonal plane, these drawings recall Carracci's *Arti di Bologna*, but they also seem to be based on close observation and the prints were in fact announced as being 'done from the life'. There are inevitably studies of pretty young women, decked out in the decolleté bodices, short skirts and sprigged prints of the period, but they all wear workmanlike shoes and their sleeves are rolled up to reveal far from delicate forearms. The men on the whole are less picturesque, mainly shown as dirty and dishevelled, with torn clothes and unshaven faces. Some of Sandby's street traders are so odd that it is difficult to believe they could have been dreamed up by the artist: the blind cabbage-net seller, the bagpiper with his dancing dog, a woman selling sieves, another with clothes-horses strung about her person, the fishwife with her hat perched on the back of her head like Britannia's helmet.

Some of the faces have such individual character that they may have been portraits: the wine seller, gimy tarter (whip) seller, the table- and door-mat seller. In one, which depicts a sailor selling stockings, an identifiable background is sketched in – that of the stocks at Charing Cross.

It is unlikely that the buyers of the *Cries of London* suffered directly from the impact of the street traders, as the tradesmen of the City so vigorously professed to have done. However, the profile of a typical customer must remain a matter for conjecture: sophisticated, circulating in West End milieux, visiting from the country or possibly from abroad. Perhaps the *Cries of London* also represented a less ordered form of urban life in which elements of pastoral origins were still visible. As many traders plied their wares or produce only at certain times of the year, they served as a reminder to the city dweller of the passing of the seasons as surely as the calendar of rural activities in a medieval book of hours. 'I am always pleased with that particular Time of the Year which is proper for the pickling of Dill and Cucumbers,' Addison confessed, 'but alas this Cry, like the Song of the Nightingales, is not heard above two Months.' Like the traditional festivities that were still celebrated on the streets of London, the presence of the *Cries* stirred the folk memory. Indeed, on May Day the two strands overlapped, with milkmaids and chimney-sweeps leading the merry-making.

Francis Hayman was the first artist to exploit the picturesque possibilities of this subject matter, including a painting of *May Day* in his decorations of popular customs for Vauxhall Gardens (Marble Hill House). We have seen that Hayman was certainly influenced by the French example in his paintings of servants, and street traders were to provide as fruitful a source of inspiration for painters of fancy pictures in the French style as Richardson's *Pamela*. The novel had given artists a means of tackling contemporary subject matter that still managed to be attractive and, at least superficially, elevating. The pastoral associations of the street traders were depicted by artists in an idealized picturesque way in the latter half of the eighteenth century, with due deference to the sensibilities of their potential clientèle. The known facts about both London servants and London street traders were glossed over.

Henry Robert Morland added street traders to his repertoire of half-length portraits of pretty women; the *Oyster Woman* and the *Letter Woman* (known in a number of versions) are depicted in a flattering Caravaggesque half-light, a technique which was also admirably suited for transfer into mezzotint. Morland's works depend ultimately for their inspiration on the paintings which Mercier executed in the 1740s. But it was the example of Jean-Baptiste Greuze which proved to be the most influential for artists in England working on genre subjects during the second half of the century. Greuze invented scenes from contemporary life in which moralizing sentiments might be expressed. Against simplified settings, the artist's characters portrayed a range of emotions which could be read by an audience as if they were watching a play, a parallel which is also appropriate in terms of the direct, four-square compositional framework he employed. Henry Walton appears to have been the first English artist fully to explore this mode. A gentleman amateur who was sufficiently talented to be a pupil of Zoffany (who, as

Hot Spice Gingerbread, 1796
FRANCIS WHEATLEY

Gingerbread was particularly
popular with London children for it
was made into interesting shapes:
the king on horseback, sheep, dogs
and other animals, in pale and dark
versions. In this design, as the
vendor is a man, Wheatley also
introduces two attractive women
with their charges and a dog, to add
to the interest.

Milk Below Maids, 1793
L. SCHIAVONETTI after FRANCIS
WHEATLEY

Wheatley's picturesque figures are
placed in simplified settings which
nevertheless suggest the elegant
streets and squares of the Georgian
capital.

we have seen, would himself seem to have had some knowledge of Greuze's
oeuvre), he was frequently in Paris and must have seen the paintings of Greuze
which were exhibited at the Salon from 1755 to 1769 and were certainly well
known in prints, as well as the earlier compositions of Chardin. Walton's own
paintings of street traders exhibited at the Royal Academy in the late 1770s, were
composed of a single figure or a small group in a simplified setting; like the work of
the French artists, engravings were made after them (*see col. pl. V*).

The Anglo-French print market played a crucial role by the middle of the
eighteenth century, first in bringing the latest French artistic fashions to the notice
of English painters, and secondly in helping to create and sustain a taste for the
decorative genre in both countries. As an alternative to portraits and town
prospects, picturesque depictions of street traders fitted admirably into the
middle-class home, urban life being tamed and prettified for domestic consumption. It is in this context that the most famous series of *Cries of London*, executed
by Francis Wheatley in the 1790s, may be understood. In his use of small,
carefully composed groups in generalized urban settings, the artist was undoubtedly influenced by Walton and Greuze, evidently being familiar with the work of
the latter through engravings.[18] Wheatley exhibited fourteen small pictures of the
Cries at the Royal Academy between 1792 and 1795. Twelve engraved versions

were published by Colnaghi between 1793 and 1796; a thirteenth appeared in 1797 and the last in 1927. Their titles were given in English and French, suggesting that despite the war the publishers hoped to attract a Continental sale; their universal appeal over 150 years would have exceeded his wildest calculations. The attractions of the series are manifold: they are gracefully composed, and harmoniously balanced between the figures and the setting. Despite their calling, the women sellers are refined, their blandness given more interest by the variety of customers. The background is certainly urban but not intrusively so. The soft stipple engraving is a technique of the appropriate weight for Wheatley's light yet atmospheric touch. For all their hackneyed aura today, it is possible to recover some sense of the potent charm which gave pleasure to so many people, feeding the nostalgia for a more innocent, pre-industrial London.

Needless to say, the divorce between the engravings and reality, noted by Edward Edwards, proved irresistible to the caricaturists who specialized in ridiculing all forms of pretension, and in particular aspirations to elevated moralizing subject matter in art. Gillray produced his acid comment *Sandwich-Carrots! Dainty Sandwich-Carrots* in December 1796,[19] and thereafter the theme of leering old men and pretty young street traders became the staple fodder of satirical prints. Rowlandson exploited the point in his first series of eight *Cries of*

Last Dying Speech and Confession, c. 1798
THOMAS ROWLANDSON

Unlike the arrangements by Walton and Wheatley of attractive figures in the French manner, Rowlandson reduces the genre to the level of bathos. The street sellers are coarse and ragged, and their attentions are largely unwelcome.

Poodles, c. 1805
THOMAS ROWLANDSON

In contrast to Craig's series, Rowlandson's small-scale etchings dwell characteristically on the ambiguous relationship between buyer and seller.

Bellows to Mend/Smithfield 1804
WILLIAM MARSHALL CRAIG

The artist settled in London in 1791 as a drawing master, illustrator and miniaturist, becoming watercolour painter to Queen Charlotte. His series of *Cries*, like his literary illustrations, are small-scale essays in poetic sentiment.

London published as aquatints in 1797. Although his deployment of groups in an architectural setting derived from the Wheatley series, he chose to depict different subjects and, with his grotesque figures, subverted any notion of the picturesque.

Nevertheless, such attempts to undermine the genre do not appear to have spoiled the market. The thirty-one *Cries of London* by William Marshall Craig, dating from 1804, are – as one might expect from a miniaturist – small in scale, dainty and neat; even the little barefooted match-seller looks well fed. Craig identified the locations more precisely than any of his predecessors, itemizing the squares, great houses, porticoed churches and public buildings of the Regency city. W.H. Pyne's *The Costumes of Great Britain* included a number of street traders – a woman selling salop, a milk woman and a rabbit woman – the text remarking on their varied clothing and the different methods they adopted for carrying their wares.[20] In 1820, the bookseller and publisher Samuel Leigh acquired the copyright of fifty-four etchings of London characters drawn by Rowlandson. Advertised as Rowlandson's *Characteristic Sketches of the Lower Orders* and sold in a volume for 7s 0d, the artist followed Craig in working on a small scale and sometimes in identifiable locations but predictably drew the figures with a great deal more humour and liveliness.[21] At the same time, many cheap woodcut series were published, specifically designed to appeal to children and to help them with their alphabet or early reading practice.[22]

Such a development suggests that street sellers were already considered somewhat quaint and out of step with the nineteenth-century metropolis. Certainly, the competition from an ever-growing number of shops placed increasing pressure on irregular forms of trade, limiting their capacity to provide a living. Some *Cries*, as we have seen, had always been more welcome than others and none more so than the flower seller. Henry Mayhew was positively lyrical:

> Perhaps the pleasantest of all cries in early spring is that of 'All a-growing – all a-blowing' heard for the first time in the season. It is that of the 'root-seller' who has stocked his barrow with primroses, violets, and daisies. Their beauty and fragrance gladden the senses; and the first and, perhaps, unexpected sight of them may prompt hopes of the coming year, such as seem proper in the Spring.

Mayhew counted a love of flowers in working people as a sign of civilization; it was, he thought, particularly in evidence among those with punctual and orderly habits like gentlemen's coachmen, or those whose handicraft required taste like Spitalfields silk-weavers, or women, especially those whose callings were indoor and sedentary: 'Flowers are to them a companionship.'[23]

Flower sellers were the most frequently depicted of all the London *Cries* during the nineteenth century. The reasons are ostensibly fairly straightforward. There were plenty of them about, since it was more practical to sell flowers in the open than indoors. They invariably evoked favourable associations, as Mayhew makes clear, with the delights of the countryside, with refined sensibilities and with giving pleasure. Flower sellers offered artists an ideal subject for still lifes. In his version, Jacques Laurent Agasse shows a man with his donkey cart of plants and a satisfied young customer in a street leading off a London square (probably Soho

The Flower Seller, 1822
JACQUES LAURENT AGASSE

The flower seller is thought to be a
self-portrait of the artist, while his
young customers were the family of
his landlord, Booth, in Newman
Street.

Square, as the artist lived at no. 4 Newman Street). It retains an eighteenth-century atmosphere of harmonious calm to be found in the works of Walton, but on a more intimate scale with the domestic detail filled in.

Agasse's subject would have been a reasonably prosperous seller who could afford a donkey and the outlay necessary to buy shrubs and potted plants. By the middle of the nineteenth century, flower sellers were invariably depicted as appealing young girls by artists like William Henry Hunt (*see* col. pl. XIII), Augustus Mulready (fl. 1872–99) and Gustave Doré. They were pretty, bare-footed and dressed in rags. With eyes lifted directly towards the spectator, they fulfilled the role of touching plaintive. But as Mayhew revealed, flower girls were divided into two classes: those who eked out the small gains of their trade with prostitution and those who remained poor but honourable.[24] Thus the real attraction of the flower-seller to the Victorian audience was not merely one of picturesque innocence but the dramatic power of innocence under threat.

The flower seller provides an archetype for the treatment of all London street traders in nineteenth-century art. Essentially, in stark contrast to their lack of pejorative associations in the eighteenth century, at least in art, street traders were increasingly lumped together with the poor, the disreputable and the down-and-out. John Thomas Smith was the first to blur the distinction. *The Cries of London* (1839) was explicitly designed to be a continuation of *Vagabondiana; or, Anecdotes of Mendicant Wanderers through the Streets of London* (1817).[25]

Dancing Dolls, c.1820
JOHN THOMAS SMITH

The boy was one of a dozen involved in this trade from Lucca; the dolls were attached to a board moved by string from his knee.

The Street-Seller of Crockery Ware, c.1851
after RICHARD BEARD

The 'huckster' of crockery-ware bought his goods at a wholesale 'crock swag shop' and bartered them for old clothes, sold for cash at the Clothes Exchange in Houndsditch.

Underlying each work, however, there was clearly a moral code against which individuals were measured. In *Vagabondiana*, Smith singled out two 'industrious beggars' whom he asserted were true objects of compassion, not to be confused with common street beggars. They were Priscilla, an inhabitant of Clerkenwell, who made patchwork quilts and sold them on the streets, and Taylor, a blind shoemaker, who had managed to maintain his whole family through his work.[26] In contrast, *The Cries of London* included Israel Potter, one of the oldest chairmenders in London, who left home early each morning but evidently, 'from the matted mass of dirty rushes' he carried, not with a view to work: 'the fact is that, like many itinerants, he goes his rounds and procures broken meat and subsistence thus early in the morning for his daily wants.' Others, like the spoon seller, William Conway, were singled out by Smith for praise on account of their 'honesty, punctuality, and rigid perseverance'; Conway had never been dependent on parish relief and had never been drunk.[27]

This merging of the identity of street traders with the poor in general was to be taken a stage further by Henry Mayhew in *London Labour and the London Poor*, first published in 1851 and in completed form in 1861–62. Even on Mayhew's own estimate, the London street folk constituted only one fortieth of the working population, yet he chose to devote three out of four volumes to describing their ways. Furthermore, because of the innumerable divisions and subdivisions of classification he created, the frequent brandishing of statistics and the 'real-life' stories with which he fleshed out his narrative, the importance of the street traders was conflated and they came to represent the whole of mid-Victorian London labour and the London poor.[28]

The wood engravings after the daguerreotypes taken by Richard Beard (c.1801–85) helped to fix the image. The subjects would have had to come in from the street to the alien environment of a studio and stand still for thirty seconds. Isolated from their normal surroundings, vulnerable, unsmiling, meanly dressed, the sobriety of their appearance undoubtedly harshened by the contrasts of the engraving, Mayhew's street folk are far removed from the world of Sandby and Wheatley. Beard himself would have had no artistic reasons to make them picturesque; his fortunes were at a low ebb following his bankruptcy and he probably regarded the job as hack work, to be completed as swiftly as possible. Because they were odd, individual and curious, not conforming to any of the traditional artistic modes employed to depict street traders, they seemed to confirm Mayhew's assertion that the wandering tribes were a race apart, physiognomically distinct and of different habits and morals.

As Mayhew's text makes clear, the street folk of London were, for all their endless variety, an endangered species. Their decline was to be slow, varying from trade to trade. The flower sellers are still with us today and certainly have continued to provide a subject for artists – Bastien-Lepage, Logsdail, Wilkinson, Nicholson, Ginner – but gradually they lost the moral connotations they had for the Victorians. Others disappeared because of competition from better organized retail outlets or simply changes in taste. Du Maurier's cartoon in the series *Culture for the Million; or, Society as It Might Be*, which represented as we have

ABOVE *A Coffee Stall, c. 1855*
CHARLES HUNT

Coffee became common on the streets of
London following the large reductions in
the duty payable in 1824 and 1842. The
adulteration of coffee with chicory and other
roots further increased the potential for
profit.

TOP RIGHT *Piccadilly Circus*, 1912
CHARLES GINNER

Ginner's image of the flower-seller hemmed
in by the traffic and ignored by passers-by
helps to explain why the majority of street-
sellers were forced out of Central London.
They could not be heard or seen amidst the
noise and confusion of the modern city.

RIGHT *New Chamber of Horrors at Madame
Tussaud's*, 1870
GEORGE DU MAURIER

seen a fairly patronizing reaction to the 1870 Education Act, anticipated the end.
The scene is entitled *New Chamber of Horrors at Madame Tussaud's* and depicts a
mother reassuring a child who recoils before a dangerous-looking barrel organist.
'Don't be afraid, you little goose!' she says. 'It's only wax-work! Why, I recollect
when people like that were allowed to go loose about the streets!'

The distinction made between an artisan and a labourer in London was based on long tradition, but it was in practice blurred by trades that employed workmen under a skilled foreman instead of journeymen who had served an apprenticeship. Besides, labourers' wages were often as high as those of journeymen, while some of the newer trades employed journeymen on labourers' wages. In times of economic depression, many skilled men took to labouring as a means of earning a living. Indeed, to control such potential instability, the City Corporation instituted a system of licensing porters which guaranteed them the exclusive privilege of work at the same time as binding them as freemen in a fellowship to the City. Watermen (for the carriage of people) and lightermen (for the carriage of goods) served apprenticeships, also formed a fellowship and sometimes even owned their own boats; they were considered skilled labourers. But the car-men who steered the carts carrying goods through the streets, the coal heavers and miscellaneous workers by the waterside, drovers, lay stallmen, scavengers and even stokers in glass manufactories were regarded as labourers. Possibly the most prominent of all were the labourers employed in the building trades, while at the bottom of the heap were the women workers who undertook the most menial jobs like rag-picking and cinder-sifting.

The size and variety of the unskilled labour market in London were enormous, and it is scarcely surprising given its low status and fluid membership that its pictorial possibilities were not instantly recognizable. True, a London carter and meat porter are included in the *album amicorum* of Michael van Meer who visited England in 1614–15. And, as with London craftsmen, the need to advertise proved to be some incentive. Nightmen and rubbish carters at work were frequently depicted on trade cards, perhaps in an effort to convince potential customers of their cleanliness and efficiency. Around 1725, Hogarth evidently painted a sign board for a paviour, of which one side survives; the etching made by Jane Ireland after the picture on the other side shows the bending figures of the labourer and his mate using a rammer, which were re-deployed with some alterations in the background to *Beer Street*.[1]

Paviours were introduced as staffage in topographical works, their presence guaranteeing a continued commitment to improving the quality of metropolitan life which manifested itself on a more permanent level in the fine new buildings thus displayed. They feature quite prominently in the foreground to William Marlow's view of *Whitehall*, looking towards Banqueting House; two figures lay cobbles and a third wheels a barrow away (Yale Center for British Art, Paul Mellon Collection). Porters appear in paintings of Covent Garden market, as we have seen, and drovers in the vicinity of Smithfield. In artistic terms, dray horses were to labour what the thoroughbreds in Rotten Row were to Society: their depiction required the appropriate human accompaniment.

George Stubbs had introduced grooms and jockeys into his paintings without being criticized: the humble figures could easily be dismissed as servants of the noble beasts. But George Garrard (1760–1826) transferred Stubbs's imagery to an urban setting. In his paintings of Whitbread Brewery yard, executed in the 1780s, attention was focused on the sturdy English dray horses (the pose of one derived

OPPOSITE
Navvies Laying a Gas Main (detail), 1834
GEORGE SCHARF

A London Carter and Meat Porter,
1614–15

The carter leads a horse and cart
loaded with bales bearing a
merchant's mark. The meat porter
wears a jerkin and cap with the long
protective flap at the back of the
head favoured by labourers who had
to carry less salubrious products,
notably fish and coal.

Sign for a Paviour, c. 1725
WILLIAM HOGARTH

The paviours work with pick-axes
and shovels at the gates of some
great town house. The foreman
appears to be discussing the job
with a frock-coated man, perhaps
the master or client. The church in
the distance may be intended to
represent St Paul's, Covent
Garden.

directly from Stubbs's *Horse Frightened by a Lion*), but Garrard surrounded them
with car-men and brewery workers rolling barrels across the courtyard and loading
the carts to create a hub of activity within the somewhat bleak confines of the
brewery buildings (Private Collection).[2] Although the paintings were not commissioned by the Whitbread family, and not even acquired by them during the artist's
lifetime, their exhibition at the Royal Academy must have brought Garrard to the
attention of Samuel Whitbread I, if he had not met him earlier when Garrard was
making preliminary studies on Whitbread property. The artist might even have
known that Whitbread had a strong paternalist streak and during the 1780s was
commissioning a series of portraits of his most loyal employees from leading artists:
Gainsborough, Gainsborough Dupont and George Romney (1734–1802) executed
three apiece. Whatever the exact circumstances in which the Whitbread
connection was formed, Garrard certainly found a sympathetic patron. In 1796, he
exhibited at the Academy *A Wharf near London Bridge*, which was commissioned
by the family and probably depicts one of Whitbread's grain carts. Again interest
centres on the dray horses, but Garrard introduced the figures of a car-man
standing by his team and porters unloading the sacks – as in Samuel Scott's
painting of a Thames-side wharf – framed by an open shed with a backcloth of
masts, rigging and City churches. Appropriately, the picture has hung in the
library of the newly acquired family seat, Southill in Bedfordshire, alongside the
nine portraits of members of the family firm.

When Southill was reconstructed by Samuel Whitbread II in the late 1790s,
Garrard sketched the work in progress, and in 1803 he produced a finished
painting for Whitbread in which the labourers unloading and working on the stone
dominate the foreground. Given this unusual viewpoint, it seems probable that
Garrard, if not Whitbread, was aware of the series of three paintings that Stubbs
had executed in 1765–68 for Lord Torrington, who then owned Southill. More
particularly, Torrington had watched some bricklayers at work building a new
lodge and had conceived that they appeared 'like a Flemish subject'. Stubbs
painted a small group of them, disputing how best to put a tail-board on their cart,
in front of the completed lodge.[3]

There are wider implications which arise from Garrard's paintings and his relationship with the Whitbreads. Significantly, mezzotints were published in 1791 and 1792 after the paintings of the Brewery in Chiswell Street. As the lucrative export market in prints dried up because of the Revolutionary Wars, the publishers John and Josiah Boydell turned increasingly to subjects which might appeal to a home market. The image of the solid English horse and honest labour being expended to produce the national drink could scarcely fail to stir the patriotic soul. In dangerous times, English workers were miraculously transformed from being considered idle, profligate and drunk into upright loyal supporters of the country. The possibility of such a change taking place was an article of faith for Samuel Whitbread II. In advancing his case for the reform of the Poor Laws in Parliament in 1807, he explained that his intention was 'to exalt the character of the labouring classes. . . . To give the labourer consequence in his own eyes, and in those of his fellows'; the bill he had introduced was 'for promoting and encouraging industry among the labouring classes'.[4] This makes it easy to understand why Whitbread appreciated Garrard's paintings, with their emphasis on labour, and why, in the posthumous portrait of the brewer commissioned from James Northcote (1746–1831), Garrard's painting of the Brewery Yard should form

A Wharf near London Bridge, 1796
GEORGE GARRARD

The scene is set on the south bank of the Thames facing the Monument and the tower of St Magnus Martyr by London Bridge. The wharf represented is almost certainly Chamberlain's, one of the general sufferance wharves established in the eighteenth century under licence from the Customs to take the overflow trade from the legal quays.

Coal Heavers, c. 1785
PAUL SANDBY

The drawing comes from an album
containing landscapes and studies of
working people, including a
drayman, carter, milkmaid and
laundresses.

the background, rather than the landscape settings in which brewers were usually portrayed.[5]

Jacques Laurent Agasse, who is best known for his outstandingly objective paintings of horses, based like Stubbs on a deep knowledge of anatomy, evidently felt at home in the company of ostlers, horse-jobbers and postilions.[6] His sympathetic attitude towards working people in general we have already seen in his paintings of market and street traders. In 1818 at the Royal Academy, he exhibited *Landing at Westminster Bridge,* in which the watermen are depicted with the same calm, unexaggerated air of men going about their allotted tasks as is found in Garrard's Whitbread paintings (Stiftung Oskar Reinhardt, Winterthur).

Another artist trained in France provided a wholly original perspective on London labour. Théodore Géricault (1791–1824) had first studied under Carle Vernet, who specialized in sporting pictures and horse paintings of the English type. Although drawn to the same subject matter, Géricault soon outclassed Vernet's superficial renderings, and brought a new power and passion to the depiction of horses, inspired by the example of the Old Masters and classical precedents, as well as being founded on a meticulous study of the horse. When he came to England in 1819, he was attracted not simply by the well-groomed racing and cavalry horses, but more especially by the horses of massive strength who ploughed the fields and hauled the coal wagons (*see* col. pl. XI).

The coal from which London derived most of its energy was brought in ships from the north-east to the Thames and unloaded into lighters at Wapping, whence it could be distributed at wharves further upstream in water too shallow to take large boats. Thus the spectacle of coal porters, carters and their teams of horses could be seen at many points along the river. A group of heavers, with their distinctive hats and shovels, were sketched by Paul Sandby and are depicted at work on the foreshore in Pyne's *The Costumes of Great Britain.* A particularly strategic spot for observing the process of transfer was directly below the Adelphi, where the arches built to counteract the slope from the Strand to the river were used for wine cellars and coal wharves. A topographical watercolour of around 1810 shows the coal heavers unloading the lighters and loading the carts which were then drawn by horses through the arches into the Strand, while John Augustus Atkinson (1775–after 1833) depicted the coal being delivered to a London house around the same period. Géricault was clearly fascinated by the teams of horses with their carters as they disappeared into and reappeared out of the Adelphi arches. But instead of making them part of a serene topographical prospect, he dramatized the industrial features of the nineteenth-century city.

It is possible that Géricault was aware of the English artists who, in the early years of the nineteenth century, were practising open-air sketching and studying from life in oil and watercolour. In particular, the pupils of Cornelius Varley (1781–1873) and John Varley (1778–1842) were encouraged to go out on sketching expeditions, especially along the banks of the Thames to the west of London, for John Varley had a country cottage at Twickenham. This younger generation of artists led by William Mulready (1786–1863) was also developing a new approach to the study of the human figure. Mulready had gained entrance to the Academy

*The Adelphi Terrace and Coal Wharf,
c.* 1810

Unusually for a topographical
watercolour, the figures are more than a
token presence. The coal heavers are
unloading the lighters which have
transported the coal from the collier
wharves at Wapping. Illicit scavengers
pick up the loose coal from the
foreshore. Small figures are also at work
in the adjacent stone yard and timber
yard.

A London Coal Cart, c. 1810
JOHN AUGUSTUS ATKINSON

Atkinson's watercolour shows the
carter backing the horse up so that
the cart is as near as possible to the
coal hole, while his companion takes
some refreshment before the thirsty
work of shovelling the coal into the
cellar.

Drayman etc.
WILLIAM MULREADY

Despite the mass of visual and verbal notes on the appearance of working people which Mulready accumulated in his sketchbooks, very few of the artist's paintings are specifically urban in location or content.

Kensington Gravel Pits, 1811–12
JOHN LINNELL

Linnell was characteristically fascinated by the textures of the disturbed ground as much as by the workers. But he carefully delineated their clothing and through the rhythmic movement of the figures across the canvas conveys something of the team effort required to extract the stone.

life school in 1800, but like many of his contemporaries he also had a strong personal interest in pugilism – the human form in action – and was a gifted pupil of one of the leading boxers of the day, Daniel Mendoza. The value placed on pugilism by artists trained in the tradition of high art derived in part from practical considerations: boxers were among the few whose bodies were sufficiently healthy and well developed to be able to serve as models, in any way comparable to the antique.[7] More generally, in the gentlemanly ethos of the day, pugilism epitomized a noble masculinity, uniting all classes of men in pursuit of a sport that was seen to be emphatically British. Mulready provided most of the illustrations to Pierce Egan's *Boxiana: Sketches of Ancient and Modern Pugilism* (1812); Géricault's interest in the English sport is revealed in his lithograph, *Boxeurs* of around 1818, even before his visit to London. Boxing, in fact, helped to liberate the study of the human form from the constraints of antique models, from the grandeur of the ideal to a more vigorous reality.

Both Mulready and his close friend John Linnell (1792–1882) studied from the antique at the Royal Academy schools but they constantly turned to the world around them, filling notebooks with sketches of landscapes and people. Mulready, in particular, gave detailed accounts of the garb, 'combinations of colour seen in passing', the minutiae of a sleeve or leggings worn by ordinary people he saw, making thumb-nail sketches to accompany them. Thus, for example,

Blacksmith and Farrier is distinguished from the working baker by his *Leather* apron and the *colour* of *his dirt*. A shoemaker or cobbler wears a waistcoat and often a night cap. Paviours and their labourers are very like the above in dress but generally if not always without the apron. They carry no very obvious

character about with them except the working dust or road sand. The working Navigator is also the same kind of fellow but his dust is redder – more clayy, damp. The Brick Maker also is like but still redder, and he wears the sackcloth apron. Other fellows are distinguished by the colour of the dirt, the absence or presence of the apron.[8]

As a Londoner, born and bred in the parish of St Giles, and sharing Mulready's commitment to working outdoors, Linnell also made sketches of his surroundings in the early years of the nineteenth century: the somewhat desolate empty stalls of Covent Garden market, the bedraggled fields of St Pancras soon to be obliterated by Gower Street, and workmen laying the foundations of the buildings designed by James Burton in Russell Square; the latter drawings evidently won praise from no less a judge than the President of the Royal Academy, Benjamin West (1738–1820).[9] When Mulready and Linnell moved to Kensington around 1810, this activity did not cease. Kensington was then on the western fringes of London, although convenient for town; it provided services for the city, many of its inhabitants being engaged in market gardening, pig rearing and laundering activities. Gravel digging and brick manufacture were the principal industries. Given the artist's predilections, it is not surprising that Linnell should choose to make Kensington Gravel Pits the subject of a major work, uniting his special interest in landscape with the study of the human form in action, inspired not only by his life classes at the Academy but also by Mulready's example.

By the early nineteenth century, London was expanding at a much faster rate than it had ever done in the past. This building boom accelerated the demand for construction materials to be used in housing and public works, the roads, water

OPPOSITE

The Laying of the Main Water-Main in Tottenham Court Road, 1834

Building the Common Sewers in London, 1845

Building the New Fleet Sewer, 1845
GEORGE SCHARF

Scharf was fascinated by the vast pipes lying like dormant industrial giants beneath the eighteenth-century streets and shops of the capital. In his 'arranged compositions', he introduced more obviously picturesque figures – the schoolboys and woman with her child in Tottenham Court Road – to add a human dimension to the massive feats of engineering in progress.

and sewage supplies and later the railways that served the city. If some artists living in London appear to have spent a great deal of time recording these changes, at least one reason for their bias was that there was a great deal of such labour to be observed.

The March of Bricks and Mortar, Cruikshank's famous etching of 1829, was not simply a caricaturist's fantasy; it was an expression of the feeling many Londoners must have experienced as they watched the semi-rural hinterland where many were wont to spend their free time – the unpretentious little pleasure gardens, muddy tributaries and banks of the Thames, scrubby hedgerows boxing in market gardens and small fields where a few animals grazed – devastated by an inexorable force. If the inhuman face of this invasion was the battery of building materials, then the artillery division was represented by the labourers who swarmed like insects on every site. They can be seen in Edward Rooker's engraving of the building of Blackfriars Bridge in the 1760s, and in much greater detail in the foreground to the aquatint after Augustus Charles Pugin's drawing of Nash's Highgate Archway of 1813.

When George Scharf arrived in London from Bavaria in 1816 he must have been astonished by the scale of activity. As a miniaturist, drawing master and copyist, who had also been trained in the new skill of lithography, Scharf appears at first to have attempted to make a living by issuing prints of political and ceremonial events. But it is clear that even before his arrival in England he was an indefatigable sketcher and that his draughtsmanship was sufficiently accurate to enable him to undertake work for a number of scientific clients. This combination of skills must have recommended him to the New London Bridge Committee in 1830 who commissioned a series of works depicting the demolition of old London Bridge and the construction of the new. Scharf spent three years working on site and in the studio to produce four large oils, a series of watercolours and many pages of notes on the project. Predictably the City jibbed at paying but eventually acquired two of the oils for £30.[10] The surviving watercolours and drawings are fascinating not only for their record of the buildings which were removed, but also as depictions of the gangs of demolition workers, masons measuring and chiselling the stone, the blocks being moved with winches and pulleys, and labourers carrying pieces in a group like coffin-bearers or moving the bricks in hods. On the same pages, Scharf annotated the dress of individual figures – one labourer was wearing a green oilcloth hat, yellow handkerchief, red waistcoat, yellowish-grey jacket and breeches – and he made a detailed watercolour study of 'old Murphy' and 'Starling jaque' his dog.

The notes indicate that he hoped to incorporate the figures into what he called 'arranged compositions'. However, only a few of the thousands of studies he made were ever worked up in this way. Scharf was attracted to every scene which showed the city in motion and, more profoundly, in the process of changing. He drew pavements being laid in Soho Square and outside St Martin-in-the-Fields; he recorded workers digging the foundations for the Royal College of Surgeons in Lincoln's Inn Fields, and laying down gas pipes, the new Fleet Sewer, and the main drains in Tottenham Court Road. He observed the building of Hungerford

Market. He watched carpenters making cases for fossils at the British Museum and securing the Nineveh sculpture to the walls. He penetrated corners where they beat carpets in Maiden Lane, while nearby in Pentonville, he depicted women sifting cinders. And walking with one of his sons in the Hampstead Road in 1836, he saw one of the greatest construction schemes to affect London in the first half of the nineteenth century, the massive cutting being dug for the London and Birmingham Railway; he returned for several months thereafter to chart its progress.

At the same time, John Cooke Bourne (1814–96), a pupil of the engraver John Pye (1782–1874), was also making drawings of the scene and at the suggestion of the journalist and antiquarian John Britton, thirty-six of them were published as lithographs in four parts in 1838–39. The finished wash drawings and lithographs concentrate principally on the massive scale of the enterprise as it made its inexorable progress north-east along the Hampstead Road, driving through Park Village, Mornington Crescent, Camden Town, the Regent Canal, Primrose Hill and onwards into Middlesex with gangs of navigators tending to its needs. But Bourne's more detailed studies carefully describe their individual tasks of digging, carrying, hauling – and occasionally resting – watched by groups of curious onlookers.

The achievements of the navigators – digging cuttings, building embankments, tunnels and bridges – could not but be noticed as Britain led the world in developing the new transport systems associated with the Industrial Revolution. Starting on the canals, sections of navigation had been split up under different contractors who drew their labour from the local agricultural workforce; the relatively high wages encouraged the men to move with the contractor rather than return to the fields, and their alien presence added another dimension to the strange, rather frightening scale of the work. Lithograph series of prints were part of the propaganda drive to reconcile the public to these changes. T.T. Bury's coloured views of the Liverpool and Manchester railway, published in 1831 shortly after the opening of the line, minimized the disruption the railway would cause. The landscape is scarcely ruffled by its presence; livestock graze contentedly; the navvies are unobtrusive, admired by well-dressed onlookers. Bourne focused on the technological feats achieved although he too used rural settings outside London and even in London at the Regent Canal, undisturbed by industrial wharves; the terminus at Euston was shown being built on rough marshland. These touches of the pastoral were to be accentuated in his second great series, *The History and Description of the Great Western Railway*, published in 1846, in which the activity of the navvies is omitted.

Studies of Workmen, 1836
JOHN COOKE BOURNE

Bricklayers are at work on the right constructing possibly a retaining wall on the south side of the bridge under the Hampstead Road.

Work, 1856–63
FORD MADOX BROWN

Work is the most ambitious Pre-Raphaelite painting of city life. Although the navvies provide the central motif, the picture is Hogarthian in moral scope, attacking the fragmentation of Victorian society in an attempt to promote a harmonious social order.

The drawings of labour made by Scharf and Bourne were essentially a private note-taking process, to be used as part of larger compositions. The first formal painting ever to have the navvy as its principal *raison d'être* was *Work*, started by Ford Madox Brown (1821–93) in 1852 and finally completed in 1863. The idea came to the artist from seeing navvies at work on a new sewage system in Hampstead. Like many of his contemporaries, Brown glorified work as the supreme virtue; it was linked to the idea of progress towards civilization in which even the humblest person had an allotted role. The artist was particularly influenced by Carlyle's writings, where labour was seen to have a deeper spiritual value. The labourer took on a heroic, noble quality, becoming the external embodiment of manliness that the boxer had been to an earlier generation. But just as classical precedents had given added authority to the real physicality of the pugilist, so the civilizing end to which the navvy's energies were directed and the all-consuming purity of his labour elevated his stature.

Yet the depiction of urban labour did not acquire the overt political connotations that the portrayal of rural labour was to acquire in France around 1850. The grim, emphatically non-heroic paintings of rural work and life executed by

Courbet, in particular, acquired a resonance of meaning within the complex urban-rural rivalries following the 1848 Revolution. In England, despite the dying remnants of Chartism, the labouring classes were seen as safely contained within the social order.

Work had been financed by the evangelical collector Thomas E. Plint of Leeds, who died before its completion in 1861. The same year, William Bell Scott (1811–90) was commissioned to paint a series of eight murals to decorate the new picture gallery of Sir Walter Trevelyan at Wallington Hall, Northumberland. They represented local industry on Tyneside and included three hammermen in action at the works of Robert Stephenson & Company, locomotive builders. But the labour undertaken in London does not seem to have inspired artists until Frank Brangwyn revitalized the subject for the mural paintings he worked on before the First World War. Brangwyn had depicted some industrial scenes – the Tyne Shipyard, Coal Heavers – while working on the *Graphic* as an illustrator. The opportunity to work on a larger scale first came in 1900 when he was asked to contribute a decorative painting to the panels which filled recesses in the ambulatory of the Royal Exchange. The subjects chosen by the Royal Academicians who had already contributed were mainly historical, relating to scenes from the Royal Exchange's illustrious past or to commerce. Brangwyn finally decided on *Modern Commerce*, using cranes and scaffolding as a background to figures carrying sacks, crates and bundles of fruit. He did not complete the panel until 1906, by which time other large-scale works were under way. He was selected to

Fruit Porters, c. 1903
FRANK BRANGWYN

Brangwyn treated the theme of dock labour, for his commission to decorate the committee luncheon room of Lloyd's Register of Shipping, as an opportunity not only to emphasize the heroic role played by the porters but also to celebrate the Port of London as the centre of world trade. The paintings cannot be read as representative of actual porterage techniques used on the docks. In this study, St Paul's and Cannon Street Station form the backcloth to a superabundance of fruits of the earth.

Brickmakers, 1904
FRANK BRANGWYN

The constant demand for building
materials kept the brickfields round
London stretched to full capacity.
Brangwyn depicted workers at
Wormwood Scrubs, Hammersmith.

decorate the British room at the Venice International Exhibition in 1905 with
subjects specified by the organizing committee; they chose industrial subjects –
Excavators, Steelworkers, Potters and *Blacksmiths* – as an appropriate way of
recording Britain's wealth and might. Following the commission of two large
historical pictures for Lloyd's Register of Shipping, the company decided in
1908 to allow Brangwyn to decorate their newly converted committee luncheon
room with subjects he himself chose. The theme he selected was dockside labour:
he portrayed men carrying fruit, meat, beer, tea and sugar, timber, rugs, pottery
and curios against a backcloth of ships and cranes, St Paul's and Cannon Street
Station.

These works and the historical series commissioned by the Skinners' Company
are suggestive of the desire of the City as a whole not merely to be the hub of the
nation's commerce, but to be seen to be so, both in the present and in the glorious
past. Even if many were dissatisfied with the result, Brangwyn certainly
introduced a heroic dimension into the City's mythology. Mural painting as a
genre recalled the Venetians, whose commercial greatness had been commemorated and enhanced by the works of Titian, Tintoretto and Veronese. Brangwyn's
rich reworkings of historical legends and the monumental stature he gave to
human brawn were little concerned with accuracy; they reassured a City whose
political oligarchy had recently been under threat that it would survive at the heart
of the greatest Empire in the world.

Brangwyn's sympathies for labourers extended beyond their use as fodder for lavish displays of civic pride. He was drawn to depict the rhythms and purposefulness of human toil in the large-scale etchings he made both in England and in Belgium: boat- and barge-builders along the Thames at Brentford and Hammersmith, brickmakers, skinscrapers. But a political commitment to depict workers from the workers' point of view was not made explicit until the formation of the Artists' International Association in 1933. Clifford Rowe, the inspirer and founder of the movement, worked as an illustrator and poster artist for the Communist Party before he went to Russia in 1930, where he stayed for eighteen months. On his return he organized an association which staged exhibitions devoted to the anti-fascist cause, peace and the depiction of social and industrial subjects. To some extent the work produced may be seen in the context of international social realism, but in England at least, the precedents were more quirkily individual, drawing on Sickert and the shabby world of Camden Town, the *Graphic* school of illustrators and even the example set by Hogarth.[11] Rowe continued to depict industrial themes into the 1960s – men cleaning flues at the gas retort station in St Pancras and manufacturing glass at the Whitefriars foundry in Harrow – but most remarkable of all, perhaps, are the studies he made during the war at the round house, Kentish Town: the loading and unloading operations and the cleaning of the engines by women workers, whose labour was once despised as menial, had taken on a vital importance.

The labouring poor were long regarded as synonymous with the lower orders, a largely undifferentiated mass who constituted the major part of London's population. The perception of poverty as a problem, however, referred to more specific groups in society: namely those who could not and those who would not work. People in the former category, largely the aged and infirm, were eligible for relief under the provisions of the Elizabethan poor laws. They constituted the first ever national welfare system, which gave parishes the power to appoint overseers who levied a parish poor rate. England thus gained a reputation for public compassion, and this commitment was supported by a flourishing tradition of private charity.

Nowhere was this charitable initiative more in evidence than in London with its numerous hospitals, schools and other institutions and funds supported by individual and corporate effort. At the same time, these resources attracted the second category of suppliant, variously described as vagrants, sturdy beggars, idle and disorderly persons or incorrigible rogues. The simplest way to elicit charity was by begging on the streets and London with all its wealth offered the richest potential pickings. London also presented the most opportunities for finding casual work. When there was no work about because of trade depressions brought on by poor harvests, currency fluctuations, foreign wars, post-war dislocation and epidemics, vagrancy increased dramatically, the numbers swollen by casual labourers – agricultural workers, navvies, seamen – unable to find a job. The Act of Settlement of 1662 (modified in 1685 and 1693) made birth or residence in a parish a qualification for obtaining parish relief. But the sheer growth of London with its high percentage of migrants ensured that the law was difficult to enforce and expensive to maintain since it involved locking up offenders in bridewells and transporting them to the Middlesex boundary.

The presence of scores of vagrants on the streets was a threat to law and order, and they were seen by the authorities as closely related to the criminal and riotous elements in the populace. To maintain control, *ad hoc* measures included ensuring that supplies of coal and corn reached the poor; on a more permanent if not ultimately successful basis, workhouses were set up to instill, particularly in the young, the discipline of regular work. But the problem remained, and indeed grew at a faster rate than the city's population.

No city was proud of its vagrant population: it provided all too visible evidence that urbanity was only skin deep. The Christian ideal that poverty was blessed, even devoutly to be sought as a passport to heaven, was largely abandoned as society became increasingly secular, although the corresponding responsibility of the rich to undertake charitable works was felt more strongly. However, charity was only to be given to the deserving – the young and unprotected, the old and sick – not to those who would squander resources on a life of idleness and dissipation. It was these acts of charity – the donor thereby gaining power over the recipient – which were most frequently depicted in art, and not the volatile, uncontrollable vagrants themselves.

When beggars were painted at all, they were usually seen in landscape settings, sustaining the myth of the *picaro* – the free-living, devil-may-care rebel. In the

OPPOSITE

Gray's Inn Lane – Robbers' Kitchen, 1869
GUSTAVE DORÉ

According to Blanchard Jerrold, 'We advance into a low, long dark room parted into boxes, in which are packed the most rascally company any great city can show. . . . The place . . . is charged with the unmistakable, overpowering damp and mouldy odour, that is in every thieves' kitchen, in every common lodging house, every ragged hotel.'

A Beggar Boy, c. 1781
THOMAS GAINSBOROUGH

Influenced by Murillo, the artist
developed his own style of rustic
'fancy picture' and yet depended on
the urban models who were readily
available a few steps from his
residence in Pall Mall.

pictures of Pieter van Laer and the *Bamboccianti*, beggars take on a merry camaraderie whether in the *campagna* or Rome itself. The enormous dislocations of life in the seventeenth century – famine, cold, war, disease – do not affect them. Only in the work of Jacques Callot are the poor seen as more than grateful beneficiaries or decorative addenda. *Les Gueux* comprised a series of twenty-five plates etched in Nancy in 1622, based on drawings possibly made in Italy but more probably representing a response to the distress brought about throughout Europe, and most immediately in Lorraine, by the Thirty Years War. The frontispiece entitled *Capitano de Baconi* shows a file of beggars wending their way behind the main figure who may variously be translated as the Leader or Scoundrel. Throughout the series, the faces of the characters are grimly expressive of old age and poverty, with no trace of sentiment.

In contrast, the beggar boys painted by Murillo are in the main happy, lively urchins, enjoying the pleasures of childhood. In creating the genre, the artist was clearly influenced by the painters of the naturalistic school of Seville, but the choice of subject was certainly directed to the Flemish market and might even have been suggested by the Antwerp merchants who traded in Seville. The pictures proved to be an influential source for the fancy pictures that were produced in France and England in the eighteenth century.[1] Gainsborough copied at least one of Murillo's works and acquired the *St John the Baptist* (National Gallery), now thought to be a studio work. He made his own series of studies of beggar children, one of whom with a pitch in St James's Street was metamorphosed into the now lost painting of a *Shepherd*, exhibited at the Royal Academy in 1781. In a witty combination of classical and topical references, Sir Joshua Reynolds (1723–92) portrayed his beggar boy models in the form of *Cupid as Link Boy* and *Mercury as Cut Purse* (respectively, Albright-Knox Art Gallery, Buffalo, New York and the Faringdon Collection Trust, Buscot, Oxfordshire), the sexual and criminal exploits of each little god gaining an added resonance through the contemporary associations.[2] For the most part, artists working in eighteenth-century London took to depicting the indigents they encountered not because of social concern, but because the examples they singled out struck them as appealing and were presumably cheap and available to employ as models; the finished works placed the subjects in a generalized context, based on safe European precedents, not in the streets of the capital. Thus the improbably titled *Beggars on the Road to Stanmore* (Cadland Settled Estate) is a version of the standard group of the Holy Family and St John, with virtually nothing to indicate that according to tradition, the figures are portraits of beggars encountered by Zoffany on the way to visit one of his patrons.[3] Similarly, a mezzotint of the *Brickdust Man* after Nathaniel Hone (1718–84) immediately recalls Old Master paintings of St John the Baptist rather than the beggar who posed for the artist.

For any depiction of the effect of poverty on the urban population it is again to Hogarth that we must turn. Beggary was one aspect of a whole pattern of behaviour that embraced drunkenness, cruelty, gambling, whoring, corruption and crime in settings of appalling dirt and squalor. *Gin Lane* was published in 1751 as part of a campaign against the government's support of the distillers, whose

Gin Lane, c. 1751
WILLIAM HOGARTH

The scene is the slums of St Giles, with the tower of Hawksmoor's church, St George's Bloomsbury, in the distance. Only the pawnbroker, distiller and undertaker thrive amidst the general ruin.

unrestrained production of cheap and powerful spirits had led the poor, in search of short-term alleviation of their lot, into long-term brutalization with often fatal consequences.

In the course of the eighteenth century, it became increasingly difficult to contain the growing number of poor within a system designed for fewer people and a much smaller city. Every riotous disturbance provoked fears for the security of the community at large; every piecemeal reform seemed to uncover more misery and vice than it solved. Furthermore, there was increasing pressure for change,

Vagabondiana: Joseph Johnson,
1815
JOHN THOMAS SMITH

According to Smith, Johnson was a
black who, because he had only
been employed in the merchant
service, was not entitled to a place
at Greenwich Hospital. His wounds
prevented him from going to sea
again and he had no claims to relief
in any parish. He made a living
therefore by singing ballads,
attracting custom with the model he
had made of the ship *Nelson,*
attached to his cap.

encouraged by the writings of Adam Smith and Malthus who, from radically
different standpoints, provided the intellectual basis for the attack on the poor
laws. Malthus in particular redefined the problem of poverty, giving a mathematical basis for the prediction that matters would only get worse. And indeed,
following the Napoleonic Wars, with the attendant problems brought about by
rapid demobilization, cessation of government orders, the fall in urban employment and consequent swelling of the poor rate, this seemed to be the case. In the
face of both practical and theoretical grounds for pessimism, the government
appointed no less than four Parliamentary select committees to investigate the
workings of the poor laws between 1816 and 1820, besides others on the related
subjects of vagrancy and immigration. Their findings, like those of many
subsequent official and unofficial reports into various aspects of the condition of
the poor, were to provoke a visual response, at least on the more immediate level
of graphic illustration, if not in academic painting.

In 1817, following the Select Committee on Vagrancy of 1815–16, the first work
specifically devoted to the representation of mendicants was published by John
Thomas Smith. *Vagabondiana,* subtitled 'Anecdotes of Mendicant Wanderers
through the Streets of London; with Portraits of the Most Remarkable, drawn from
the life by the author', was clearly provoked by the select committee and by the
subsequent tightening up by the authorities which had, according to Smith,
already resulted in a reduction in the number of beggars in the metropolis. Noting
that

> several curious characters would disappear by being either compelled to
> industry, or to partake of the liberal parochial rates, provided for them in their
> respective work-houses, it occurred to the author of the present publication,
> that likenesses of the most remarkable of them, with a few particulars of their
> habits, would not be unamusing to those to whom they have been a pest for
> several years.

Indeed, Smith ventured to hope 'that the interest and curiosity of the present
work are likely to augment in proportion as the characters that have led to its
composition shall decrease in numbers.'[4]

The most obvious visual precedent for Smith's work is Callot's *Les Gueux,*
which he might well have come across in the British Museum, having been
appointed keeper of prints and drawings in 1816. Nor is it the first time that
attention had been brought to the activities of London beggars. Thomas Harman's
Caveat or Warning, for Common Cursetors Vulgarly Called Vagebones (1567) had
enumerated the different types of rogue, notably a 'counterfeit crank' called
Nicholas Jennings, who was spotted by the author pretending to be an epileptic,
covered in blood and dirt from his last fit, and who later emerged considerably
spruced up to beg as an out-of-work hatter; a crude woodcut depicted him in both
guises. Smith mentions this work in his introduction and appears to have been
equally keen to weed out frauds. Of the twenty-five 'vagabonds' selected, seven
were blind, a number were crippled – 'Go-cart, Billies in bowls or sledge-beggars';
some were black, the author noting 'black people, as well as those destitute of

sight, seldom fail to excite compassion'.[5] Among the deserving poor were Joseph Thake and his son who had walked from Watford, finding it impossible to get work, and earned a living by making puzzles which they sold in St Paul's churchyard. Among the imposters were numbered Jack Stuart, Flaxman's model for the blind sailor in the monument to the Misses Yarborough in Campsal Church, and a wooden chain maker who could well afford his tools and therefore did not need to beg.[6]

In 1821, there was yet another select committee on vagrancy, and the same year *Various Subjects Drawn from Life and on Stone by J. Géricault* was published by the firm of Rodwell & Martin. The twelve main plates, printed by Hullmandel, can be divided by subject into four groups of three: elegant equestrian scenes, farriers at work, beasts of burden and, most memorably, aspects of poverty in London. Like many foreigners, Géricault was shocked by the degree of poverty to be found in the capital of what was perhaps the richest country in the world. But it is difficult to see how he could have imagined that the British public wished to be presented with depictions of poverty in a series largely devoted to horses, were it not for the example set by Smith's *Vagabondiana*. Géricault's lithographs of the London poor are devoid of any elements of sentiment in the manner of Wheatley and Morland, of the didacticism to be found in Hogarth or the anecdotal element exploited by Wilkie. His designs, like Smith's etchings, have the air of being grounded in direct observation, but they transcend the merely documentary by their power of expression and the ominous intensity of setting.

Pity the Sorrows of a Poor Old Man whose Trembling Limbs have Born him to your Door, 1821
THÉODORE GÉRICAULT

The title at least in part developed out of the catch-phrase used by all beggars to attract custom. Géricault's beggar has collapsed on the pavement outside a bakery in Southwark, with the dome of St Paul's and Blackfriars Bridge in the distance.

The Piper, 1821
THÉODORE GÉRICAULT

Géricault uses the strong grey tones he could achieve with lithography to create an atmosphere of dingy streets enveloped in the sooty fog that was endemic in London. The air of desolation is further emphasized by the bleak walled-in setting.

Smith was not alone in believing the beggars would soon disappear from the streets of London. In his essay, *A Complaint upon the Decay of Beggars in the Metropolis* of 1820, Charles Lamb announced that 'The all-sweeping besom of societarian reformation . . . is uplift with the many-handed sway to extirpate the last fluttering tatters of the bugbear MENDICITY from the metropolis.' Unlike Smith, however, Lamb did not approve of 'this impertinent crusado or *bellum ad exterminationem,* proclaimed against a species'. The appeals of beggars, he maintained, were to our common nature: 'Theirs were the only rates uninvidious in the levy, ungrudged in the assessment.' They had a dignity springing from the depth of their desolation; their rags were the robes and 'graceful insignia' of their profession:

> The Mendicants of this great city were so many of her sights, her lions. I can no more spare them than I could the Cries of London. No corner of a street is complete without them. They are as indispensable as the Ballad Singer; and in their picturesque attire as ornamental as the Signs of old London. They were the standing morals, emblems, mementos, dial-mottos, the spital sermons, the books for children, the salutary checks and pauses to the high and rushing tide of greasy citizenry.

For Lamb, as for Smith and Géricault, the beggars were singled out for notice because they were the outward, visible sign of poverty. The idea of poverty as part of a complex network of circumstances was barely realized in theory, let alone represented in visual terms. The only solution advanced was to remove vagrants from the streets, to return them to their home parishes, or, following the new Poor Law of 1834, to keep them out of sight in workhouses. As Carlyle observed, 'If paupers are made more miserable, paupers will decline in multitude. It is a secret known to all rat catchers.'

Not only did the Poor Law 'bastilles' shut away the destitute, but with the extraordinary growth of the city from 1 million in 1801 to 2¼ million by 1850, the physical distance between classes increased. To the general public, many working-class districts were *terra incognita;* few had occasion to visit Bethnal Green who did not live there. Some of the worst pockets of poverty were admittedly to be found close to the houses of the rich; as Dickens observed, the brightest lights cast the deepest shadows. Yet even by definition a slum lay hidden from view (slumber in Regency slang meaning a sleepy, unknown, back alley). The routine way of life of the poor was not readily on show.

There were, however, more than social and perceptual difficulties hindering the depiction of the poor. According to academic theory, it was not considered appropriate for artists who wished to aspire to the highest honours to paint the seamier side of life. As Hazlitt expressed it in his *Conversations of James Northcote* (1830), 'What we justly admire and emulate is that which raises human nature, not that which degrades and holds it up to scorn. . . . St Giles's is not the only school of art. It is nature, to be sure, but we must select nature.' Such beliefs even influenced the views held by the first illustrated newspapers; the *Illustrated London News* in its portentous preface of 1842 associated itself with the elevating

The Condition of the Poor, 1846
S. SLY after an anonymous draughtsman

Although the *Pictorial Times* claimed this engraving was drawn from life, the paper's illustrations were often crudely sensationalized and closer to caricature than to a photographic concept of reality.

qualities usually reserved for history painting in the academic hierarchy – the universality, truthfulness and entireness of its instruction. The popular educator Charles Knight saw what this amounted to: 'every scene, in short, where a crowd of great people and respectable people can be got together, but never if possible any exhibition of vulgar poverty.'[7]

Knight's criticism was particularly acute because the 1840s was a decade in which much was being done to expose the problems attendant upon poverty. Official reports, such as those issued annually by the Poor Law Commissioners from 1835 to 1847, Chadwick's Report on the *Sanitary Condition of the Labouring Population*, published by the Poor Law Commission in 1842, and the Reports of the Royal Commission on the Health of Towns in 1845, were fully publicized in the newspapers and reviews. So too were the revelations contained in specialized publications from the Statistical Society of London, the Health of Towns Association and the Metropolitan Sanitary Commission. Even the fiction of the day was preoccupied with the 'condition of England' question. But the impact of these revelations on illustrated journalism in particular and art in general was modest. The *Pictorial Times*, until its demise in 1848 the chief rival of the *Illustrated London News*, was outspoken, virulently attacking the workings of the Poor Law in both article and illustrated form, following the revelations of *The Times* in 1845 concerning conditions in Andover workhouse.[8] To accompany an article on poverty in London in 1846, it led on the front page with a dramatic engraving of a mudlark,

SUBSTANCE AND SHADOW.

supposedly sketched on the banks of the Thames between Lambeth Palace and
Vauxhall Gardens.

Punch, founded in 1841, in its early years also had a more daring policy towards
social problems. It did not have to conform to any basic standard of impartiality,
unlike the illustrated news magazines, nor was it encumbered by any traditional
reverence for high art. In fact the reverse was true. When the cartoons for the
fresco decoration of the new Houses of Parliament were exhibited at Westminster
Hall in 1843, *Punch* published its own series of 'cartoons'. The most famous is John
Leech's ironic comment *Substance and Shadow,* a vignette which depicts a group
of beggars and cripples looking at pictures of the bourgeoisie and their affluent way
of life, exhibited in the Royal Academy. When the *Art-Union* magazine attacked
Punch for containing 'infinitely too much that degrades Art to the purpose of
caricature, and renders personal the satire that should be only universal', the
humorists vigorously counter-attacked:

The *Art-Union* is established as a twelve-penny temple, whereto men are
invited that they may therein ponder on the beautiful; where there are no
politics, no social iniquity, no want, no human suffering to ruffle and distress the
prejudices and sympathies of the reader.[9]

The same could be said for most academic art of the period. However, following
the publication of Thomas Hood's poem 'The Song of the Shirt' in *Punch* in 1843
and encouraged by the success of his picture *The Poor Teacher*, exhibited at the
Royal Academy the same year, Richard Redgrave (1804–88) was inspired to paint
The Sempstress, sitting at work in a mean little garret in the early hours of the
morning. Exhibited at the Academy in 1844, the work was well calculated to
appeal to popular feeling, any disapproval of the low subject matter being allayed
by the wistful prettiness of the girl, who rose above her surroundings like the
Virgin Mary in a painting of the Annunciation. As the *Art-Union* duly observed:

> The story is told in such a way as to approach the best feelings of the human
> heart: she is not a low-born drudge to proclaim her patient endurance to the
> vulgar world; her suffering is read only in the sunken cheek, and the eye
> feverish and dim with watching.[10]

If there were any precedents for an alternative vision of the hierarchy of the arts
in England, one had been set by Hogarth. And increasingly it was to Hogarth that
artists turned whenever they wanted to justify the depiction of vice rather than
virtue, to teach through the illustration of bad rather than good example.[11] What
made Hogarth acceptable was his genius for relating the moral fable through a

series of prints and sealing the fate of the transgressors by the end. It was to the Hogarthian precedent of the Progress that George Cruikshank turned when he wanted to express his own moral message of temperance, and escape the charge of sensationalism.

For the Victorian period, his two series of plates, issued in 1847 and 1848 and entitled respectively *The Bottle* and *The Drunkard's Children* were the drawn-out equivalents of *Gin Lane*. They slowly expose lower-class degradation in the sordid settings of cheap lodgings, gin palaces and dance halls. They move in carefully worked-out stages towards their inexorable conclusion of death, transportation and suicide. The lengthy explanatory captions reinforced the message and, like Hogarth, Cruikshank took care to ensure a wide popular sale – the plates were reproduced cheaply by glyphography and sold at a shilling a set.

Dickens saw the shortcomings of Cruikshank's display of moral teaching. For Cruikshank, drunkenness was the root cause of all other evils; for Dickens, it was merely a symptom of more complex problems. In an article for the *Examiner* in 1848 he wrote:

> Hogarth avoided the Drunkard's Progress, we conceive, precisely because the causes of drunkenness among the poor were so numerous and widely spread, and lurked so sorrowfully deep and far down in all human misery, neglect and despair, that even *his* pencil could not bring them fairly and justly in to the light.[12]

Dickens's comments reveal his more profound understanding of social problems and the ambivalence he felt towards the glib assumptions and solutions adopted by a large section of early Victorian middle-class philanthropists. Moral panaceas rather than economic or political analyses were put forward in an increasing number of cheap, evangelical publications, which boosted their claims by trivializing the Hogarthian model in the wake of Cruikshank's example.[13] Only the *Poor Man's Guardian*, which campaigned on behalf of Poor Law reform, made some effort to investigate the living conditions of the poor in London. In the autumn of 1847, its founder Charles Cochrane visited a number of lodging houses and other places resorted to by the destitute, taking an artist with him. Engraved impressions were published 'some of which especially referred to the evils arising from wretched overcrowded dwellings, and interments in the vaults and churchyards of London, whilst others were illustrative of the economical and social advantages attendant on model lodging houses.' The result was clearly designed to shock, but the very fact that the artist had to cut through sections of buildings to reveal the squalor within, even allowing for the propaganda intent, suggests the degree to which such conditions were hidden from the general public.

Although Cochrane's venture ended in financial disaster,[14] it could have been one of the precedents which spurred Henry Mayhew into making his series of investigations for the *Morning Chronicle* in 1849, following a disastrous outbreak of cholera which gave the reports their urgency. Unlike the evangelical magazines, Mayhew detected many of the underlying causes of poverty in London: the conditions of employment and the seasonal nature of casual work, the degeneracy

and demoralization of skilled craftsmen in the face of increasing mechanization, sweated labour and unrestrained competition. However, Beard's daguerreotypes which accompanied the 1851 edition of *London Labour and the London Poor*, as we have seen, focused attention on individuals who came for the most part from the London street folk, in the manner of Smith's *Vagabondiana* some forty-five years earlier, with only the merest hint of their environment sketched in, usually out of scale and perspective, as a decorative afterthought.

There is some evidence that the manner in which Beard's characters turned out as engravings, with their solid, undramatic but convincing presence, influenced the style of depiction used by artists to portray individual figures for the later edition of the work.[15] But it was at that date still technically impossible to photograph working or living conditions. Consequently, the engraved renderings of 'thieves' kitchens', cheap lodging houses and asylums resorted to the visual clichés used to depict the lower classes in illustrated periodicals, caricaturing their physiognomy and emphasizing the licentious disorder taking place. The drama of such scenes sensationalized the issues and served further to reinforce Mayhew's initial assertion that the 'wandering hordes', the street people of London, were both in looks and habits a separate race.

This style was used to illustrate most of the journalistic investigations undertaken during the 1850s and 1860s, in the wake of Mayhew's example. The finest images were produced by a French artist shocked by the poverty he encountered in London. Hippolyte Chevalier (1806–66), better known as Gavarni, first came to England in 1847 to escape debt in France and stayed to work for the *Illustrated London News* when the French Revolution broke out the following year. In 1849 he published *Gavarni in London,* a compilation of wood engravings

Field Lane Lodging House, 1847

The *Poor Man's Guardian* was the first publication to expose by means of illustrated propaganda the squalid conditions in low lodging houses for the homeless.

Le Gin, 1852
HIPPOLYTE G.S. CHEVALIER (called GAVARNI)

Possibly affected by Cruikshank's moral progresses, Gavarni saw gin as closely related to poverty. His investigation of poverty could have been inspired by Mayhew's example and its visual portrayal by Beard's daguerreotypes; but he invests the images with his own dramatic power and fluency of draughtsmanship.

with a text by Albert Smith.[16] The work was not exceptional; increasingly, however, through his press connections, and perhaps through Mayhew's reports, he turned to the London poor for his subject matter. A number of his 'Types Anglais' appeared in *L'Illustration* in Paris in 1849, including depictions of ragged beggars and street traders. But the most powerful studies were reproduced as a series of twenty lithographs entitled *Les Anglais Chez Eux*, published in the journal *Paris* in 1852–53. Like Géricault, Gavarni used the medium of lithography to infuse his figures with tonal depth for dramatic interest. He contrasted a baby in Grosvenor Square with a baby in Whitechapel, and a middle-class gentleman returning from the market with his shopping being accosted by a ragged woman and her children. But the majority of images depict the destitute poor alone.

Meanwhile in England in 1853, the *Builder,* edited by George Godwin, commenced a wide-ranging survey of the conditions of the poor in London, which was to form a year later the book *London Shadows: A Glance at the 'Homes' of the Thousands*. It was first published at fortnightly intervals, receiving fresh impetus from correspondence, action in Parliament and the cholera epidemic in the autumn. As it stressed the environmental factors which influenced the health, morals and character of the inhabitants, the illustrations by John Brown depict crumbling shanty-towns in which small figures lurk and crouch, like rats in a sewer.[17] Similarly, in 1861 the *Illustrated Times* – edited like the *Pictorial Times* of the 1840s by Henry Vizetelly – accompanied the census enumerator on his rounds, and used the authoritative presence of the officials in their top hats and greatcoats to guarantee the authenticity of their illustrations of a Gray's Inn Lane tenement, a little band of vagrants sleeping rough in St James's Park and another group huddled in the dark arches of the Adelphi. The paper traced a child who had been lost back to a room in Lincoln Court, Drury Lane, and depicted a mother delousing the hair of a bedraggled urchin; in 1863, it visited the dwellings of the poor in Bethnal Green, showing an attic occupied by ten people and exposing the state of the water supply by depicting a queue waiting at a tap.[18]

Such illustrations were artistically primitive compared with Gavarni's work; the figures were doll-like and generalized, as unconvincing as the inhabitants of the workhouse depicted in the *Pictorial Times*. But the specific identification of settings helped to lend a veneer of authenticity, and besides, they echoed the widespread public concern about the state of the poor in London. The attraction of the capital for those seeking work, and the decline in the death rate together with metropolitan improvements in the shape of railways and docks development, street-widening and civic-building schemes, concentrated the problem of over-crowding as never before. During the 1860s London also suffered from harsh winters, the collapse of various staple industries, the expansion of the casual and sweated trades, prolonged unemployment and chronic poverty. If the *Illustrated Times* turned to the subjects of poverty, homelessness, ignorance and crime, it was because there was a good deal of it about and, for the first time, it was being investigated and discussed openly. The mid 1860s saw the first serious legislative attempt to deal with sanitary and housing problems; before then, from an official point of view, they simply did not exist. For all its shortcomings from an aesthetic

point of view, this graphic response helped to prepare the path for the more self-consciously artistic treatment accorded to the condition of the poor in the *Graphic* illustrated magazine, founded by William Luson Thomas in 1869.

The sight of people queuing for casual wards and refuges was well known to Londoners: it was one of the few occasions when they were brought face to face with poverty in the street, as opposed to having to seek it out. *Houseless and Hungry* was drawn by Luke Fildes (1844–1927) from the memory of such a sight one winter's evening, and it appeared in the first number of the new paper in December 1869. The same subject had in fact been drawn two years earlier for the *Illustrated Times* by Matt Morgan (1836–90), an artist who was making his name as a cartoonist for the radical paper *Tomahawk*, with his powerful figure drawings and dramatic political images. However, there are significant differences in the composition and treatment employed by the two artists. Although Morgan's composition was not given the space in the *Illustrated Times* accorded to Fildes by the *Graphic*, it is with its strong diagonals and boldly characterized figures a more forceful statement than the frieze-like static remoteness of Fildes's misty figures. The latter engraving was accompanied by an article which enumerated what amounted to the social service quota of a London parish: the work-shy and out-of-work, the sick and the drunk, the battered wife and gutter children, with of course the good-natured policeman looking on; yet the design remains curiously abstracted. Indeed the article seemed unable to make up its mind as to whether the illustration represented 'portraits of real people' or 'fair types' of a class to be found in such queues.

Houseless and Hungry may also be compared with Doré's depiction of a similar scene two years later in *London: A Pilgrimage*, entitled *Refuge, Applying for*

Admittance. Characteristically, the artist chose the most dramatic moment, when the casuals have to hold up their cards of admission for inspection, while the authorities stand above them on the step. In Fildes's work, the policeman is almost one of the queue, although stoically neutral *vis-à-vis* the applicants. *London: A Pilgrimage* was essentially a continuation of those investigative journeys into unknown territory pioneered by Mayhew and followed by the more radical publications of the 1850s and 1860s. But in this work, Doré's virtuoso draughtsmanship and penchant for chiaroscuro effects heightens the sense of doom to an almost apocalyptic degree. The notorious thieves' kitchen of a common lodging house in Gray's Inn Lane takes on a hallucinatory quality in his compositional drawing, the candlelight throwing into high relief the half-crazed faces of the occupants, gathered round the table, slumped on the floor, lurking in corners of the cavernous space. Doré's was a symbolic vision, a highly personal expression of the idea of poverty, not a realistic description of its effects.

Fildes's work was also distanced from reality, but in a manner which developed out of an entirely different artistic tradition. Its immediate roots were in illustrated magazines, pre-eminently those devoted to literature. Unlike the leading graphic artists of the previous generation – men like Leech, John Gilbert and Kenny Meadows who rarely made rough sketches before tackling the woodblock – the illustrators of the 1860s were strongly influenced by Pre-Raphaelite ideals and took time and care at the preparatory stages. Following the advice given to him by Frederick Sandys (1829–1904), the young George du Maurier, for instance, had 'recourse to nature for everything', so that a drawing that previously had taken him eight to ten hours, now took several days. He did this because he saw a distinct connection between his work and higher artistic goals. 'A day is coming,' he wrote, 'when illustrating for the million (swinish multitude) à la Phiz and à la Gilbert will give place to real art, more expensive to print and engrave and therefore only within the means of more educated classes, who will appreciate more.'[19]

As editor of the *Graphic,* Thomas provided the vehicle for such ambitions and reaped the benefits. His artists were all well versed in the habit of using models as a guarantee of their seriousness of purpose. The Pre-Raphaelites, despite their technical ignorance of the problems of drawing on wood, had set new standards of composition – overall pattern-making, stylized statuesque figures and clear outlining – far removed from the mean little cuts in the early illustrated periodicals. These tendencies were adapted by the *Graphic* artists for real-life rather than fictional subjects.

The romantic and poetic fiction in which the magazines of the 1860s specialized was eminently suited to the literary instincts and feeling for allegory of the Pre-Raphaelites, who underscored its meaning in their illustrations with a resonance of metaphorical allusion. The *Graphic* artists profited from their example, depicting scenes of social suffering in a similar allegorical way. They used types to represent not simply participants in passing events but to stand for pathos and tragedy, and more occasionally humour and hope. They injected an intensity of feeling into their depiction of the poor, which was welcomed by their audience because it awoke in them a feeling of sympathy, rather than presenting a threat.

Our Artist's Christmas Entertainment – Arrival of the Visitors, 1872
after ARTHUR BOYD HOUGHTON

The *Graphic* artists felt no embarrassment at exploiting poverty for artistic effect, provided the charitable intent was made apparent.

It was nevertheless a risk to work such subjects up into exhibition paintings for the Royal Academy and to encounter for the first time criticism based on the traditional view of the role of art. When Fildes exhibited *Applicants for Admission to a Casual Ward* in 1874, many critics praised his honesty and truthfulness, but they also spoke of his originality and daring in tackling the subject at all, and on the scale of a history painting. Yet the work was undeniably well composed, well finished and made serious moral points about modern life. Reluctantly, some accorded him the position of a latter-day Hogarth.

It was as if scenes of social distress could not be tackled without allowing the audience to feel a glow of reassuring emotions: of pathos, sympathy, or charity, which left them feeling munificent rather than guilty. This was, after all, the period when Victorian charitable effort was at its height, five to seven million pounds a year in the metropolis alone going towards the alleviation of distress, in a vast number of disorganized and overlapping efforts. Even the artists participated; Arthur Boyd Houghton invited a party of inmates from Islington workhouse to visit his studio in December 1872, where he sketched them and provided them with an entertainment. 'I was really pleased with our poor acquaintances,' he reported, 'they were so unaffectedly jolly.' The Brueghelesque engraving which was the result showed 'the Cripple Leading the Blind Carrying a Cripple and Leading the Blind', as the subjects themselves expressed it in a thank-you note to the artist.

By isolating a few individuals and investing them with symbolic importance, social problems were brought down to intelligible proportions. And such scenes were usually further alleviated by some additional, recognizably human touch – a fineness of feeling being displayed between the deprived or the presence of another individual representing the human face of charity. The Victorian social realists managed to satisfy many of these needs, providing themselves with a ready path to fame while usually avoiding accusations of vulgarity. If they were required, by dint of having to work for an illustrated newspaper, to abide by some standard of accuracy, clarity and specificity, an underlying moral current of meaning was never far away.

On 19 April 1670, the Court of Aldermen of the City of London ordered that a series of portraits be painted of the judges responsible for settling the property disputes that had arisen in the wake of the Great Fire. The paintings were to be hung 'in some publique place of the citty for a grateful memoriall of this good office'. The 'skillful hand' they finally chose was that of John Michael Wright, and the fourteen full-length portraits he completed were acquired by the City for £36 each (beating down the artist from the £40 he normally charged). The works hung at Guildhall until the mid-eighteenth century, but subsequently suffered from inadequate storage and display conditions and drastic restoration; in the early 1950s, they were dispersed.[1] This was the City's first venture into commissioning and acquiring pictures, and confirms the rise in esteem, at least on an official level, of the legal profession in the late seventeenth and early eighteenth centuries.[2]

The courts of law at Westminster were among the earliest institutions in London to be represented in art. The solemn ritual of the law provided tangible evidence of its majesty, in which both legal officers and the accused or condemned prisoners played their part. The commemoration in visual form of their respective roles helped to ensure that, quite literally, justice was seen to be done. The king's four superior courts – Chancery, King's Bench, Common Pleas and Exchequer – were first illustrated in a manuscript law treatise dating from the reign of Henry VI. The schema adopted emphasizes the legal hierarchy, with the judges at the head and prisoners at the bottom of the sheet. The Court of Wards and Liveries, which was established by Henry VIII to deal with the estates of the king's wards (previously handled by the Court of Exchequer), is depicted with due formality in a picture on vellum dating from around 1585. The setting is a small room in the Palace of Westminster. But the sessions of the Courts of Chancery, King's Bench and Common Pleas were held in the comparatively public domain of Westminster Hall. An early seventeenth-century pen drawing shows the two former courts in session beneath the great window, with groups of lawyers deep in conversation on the main floor and a wooden gallery for spectators to one side.[3] Benjamin Ferrers (fl. 1695–1732) depicted the Court of Chancery still in the same location a hundred years later, while Gravelot opened up the view for an engraving of 1730 to show not only the plaintiffs and lawyers discussing their cases but also the legal bookshops and picture dealers plying their trade along the walls. Pugin and Rowlandson included views of the four courts in the *Microcosm of London*. Eighteenth-century topographical artists – Samuel Scott and John Maurer, among others – painted the elegant surroundings of the Inns of Court with the appropriate staffage. The halls and chambers of the Inns are lined with portraits of illustrious lawyers, the record of their existence providing a visual equivalent to the cumulative authority of their judgments.

It must be admitted, however, that the criminal and his punishment exerted a far greater fascination over the artistic imagination and, indeed, over the population in general. London, with its unrivalled opportunities for crime, its highly developed underworld, its notorious prisons and public executions, hangings and pillories, provided ample stimulus. It was the conscious aim of

10
Law and Criminals

The Court of King's Bench, fifteenth century

A prisoner in fetters stands at the bar, while six others are chained together by the legs in the custody of two gaolers.

authority to instill into the people a due regard for the law through salutary reminders of the horrors of transgression. On hanging days at Tyburn, apprentices were given a holiday, the mourning bells of London churches were buffeted, and the prisoners were drawn – in a sledge if they were traitors, or a cart for ordinary criminals – from Newgate so that the lesson could be apprehended by the maximum number of people, lining the streets. Tyburn itself, as depicted by Marcellus Lauron in the 1680s, comprised three posts ten or twelve feet high held apart by three connecting cross bars. It had stood at the junction of the Edgware and Oxford Roads on the outskirts of the city since Tudor times.[4] John Hamilton's view of 1767 shows the stands and ladders erected for the spectators.

By the eighteenth century, public hangings had become a spectator sport for the masses. In contrast to the solemn abstractions of the law, the speech of the lower classes described the hangings with irreverent humour and even defiance. A Tyburn hanging was 'Paddington Fair'. The cries of hawkers selling last dying speeches filled the streets. Dying confessions had flourished as part of the ballad and chapbook sub-culture since the sixteenth century; they were usually illustrated with crude woodcuts of the scaffold which were endlessly re-deployed. The more sophisticated accounts were written by the Ordinary or prison chaplain of Newgate and formed a substantial part of his income, given the irregularity of his pay from the City. Early collections of such pamphlets were gathered together to form *Lives of the Most Remarkable Criminals* (1735), the *Tyburn Chronicle* (*c.* 1768) and, most extensive of all, *The Malefactors' Register; or the Annals of Newgate* (1776), a four-volume collection edited by John Villette, Newgate Ordinary from 1774 to 1799.[5] Some of these works were illustrated with fine engravings of the sentences being carried out after drawings by artists like Samuel Wale (1721–86), who are better known for their illustrations to literary works.

The confessions were ostensibly intended to uphold justice and provide legitimacy for the courts' decisions, but undoubtedly they appealed also to the general human fascination with all things criminal. Indeed, the criminal could even achieve the status of folk hero. Jack Sheppard gained lasting fame through his extraordinary ability to escape from any gaol, even the condemned cell at Newgate. During his final incarceration, the turnkeys made hundreds of pounds by charging visitors 3s 6d to view him. Plays were composed in his honour; Defoe and later Harrison Ainsworth wrote his life history. Prints were issued describing his methods of escape. On 10 November 1724, six days before his death, it was reported that 'Sir James Thornhill, the King's History Painter, hath taken a draught of Sheppard's face at Newgate'. Two weeks later, on 6 December, a print after the drawing was advertised and published.

Hogarth had accompanied Thornhill on that occasion, and together in 1732/3 they visited Sarah Malcolm, an Irish laundress found guilty of murdering two old women and their maid, two days before she was hanged. The result was a print issued by Hogarth; he was followed by Boitard, who depicted Elizabeth Canning, a domestic servant at the centre of a notorious perjury case in 1753–54 and by Nathaniel Dance (1735–1811), who drew the murderess Mrs Elizabeth Brownrigg, tight-lipped at prayer in the condemned cell in 1767.

FAR LEFT *The Court of Wards and Liveries, c. 1585*

Lord Burghley, who was Master of the Court from 1561 to 1598, presides at the head of the table. On his right sits the Chief Justice of the King's Bench and on the left, the Chief Justice of Common Pleas. Assorted attorneys, surveyors, auditors and a royal messenger make up the rest of the table, with three clerks at the lower end.

LEFT *The Court of Chancery, c. 1725*
BENJAMIN FERRERS

The sessions of the Court of Chancery presided over by the Lord Chancellor, who examined petitions relating to the common law, were held in the south-west corner of Westminster Hall, below the Great Window.

The First Day of Term, c. 1738
HUBERT FRANÇOIS BOURGUIGNON (called GRAVELOT)

The figures are in Gravelot's distinctively elegant, fluent hand and full of incident. Three courts are shown in session – Chancery and King's Bench against the south wall beneath the window and Common Pleas for suits between private persons at the north entrance.

Egan and Salmon, the Thief-Takers, Pilloried at Smithfield, c. 1768
SAMUEL WALE

Egan and Salmon were part of a gang who organized crime and subsequently acted as informers to obtain the reward. In 1750 they were sentenced to seven years imprisonment in Newgate and to be twice pilloried. Egan did not survive the first exposure to the mob, while Salmon died at Newgate.

Back View of Tyburn at an Execution, 1793
JOHN HAMILTON

'A back view or scetch of Tybourn, Taken Oct. the 14th 1767, the day that Guest the Bankers clerk was hanged. It was the custom of Lamplighters . . . to erect their ladders together for persons to mount them at 2d & 3d to see the Execution. Some of their partys frequently pulled down the ladders to get fresh customers to mount.'

LEFT *Sarah Malcolm*, 1732/33
WILLIAM HOGARTH

Malcolm stood trial with remarkable composure, attempting to incriminate accomplices, and her youth (she was twenty-two) and good looks helped to attract considerable attention. According to one source, Hogarth remarked to Thornhill on his visit, 'I see by this woman's features, that she is capable of any wickedness.'

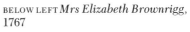

BELOW LEFT *Mrs Elizabeth Brownrigg*, 1767
NATHANIEL DANCE

Elizabeth Brownrigg, a midwife, was hanged at Tyburn for the barbarous murder of a workhouse apprentice, Mary Clifford. Dance's access to the prisoner was no doubt facilitated by his father, George Dance the Elder (1695–1768), who was surveyor of the project to rebuild Newgate Gaol.

LEFT *'Jack' Sheppard*, 1724
SIR JAMES THORNHILL

While awaiting execution at Newgate, Sheppard escaped twice in the most sensational manner, but on each occasion his drunken boasting swiftly brought about his recapture. Finally he was loaded down with three hundred pounds of chains fastened to the floor and guarded day and night.

The Gallows at Tyburn, late
seventeenth century
MARCELLUS LAURON

A confession is being elicited from
one prisoner about to die, while the
chaplain in black reads a prayer.

It would be unfair to dismiss the production of these works simply as a ready
means of making money by exploiting a morbid demand. The curiosity among
artists about the character of the criminal, as revealed in his or her face, arose at
least in part from a more general concern with theories of expression, promoted
above all in Le Brun's *Traité sur les Passions* (1698; English edn 1701). The
attempt by Lavater to elevate physiognomy into a science in the late eighteenth
century provided an added veneer of respectability to what might otherwise have
been seen as merely a prurient interest.[6] In the case of William Mulready's
drawings of John Thurtell during his sensational trial for murder in 1823, the
academic motivation was enhanced by the defendant's involvement in the world of
boxing, for the artist was an *aficionado* of the sport (Victoria and Albert Museum).
His recording of the criminal type extended beyond the fast-living Regency demi-
monde. Frith recalled that Mulready was fond of attending the trials of great
criminals and drew, among others, George and Maria Manning at their trial for the
murder of Mrs Manning's ex-lover in 1849.[7]

The revelations of the Manning case were among the highlights of what Orwell
has described as 'our great period in murder, our Elizabethan period so to speak'.
During the Victorian era, murder mania, fanned by cheap illustrated publications,

Useful Sunday Literature for the Masses; or, Murder Made Familiar, 1849
after JOHN LEECH

Father of a Family (reads). 'The wretched Murderer is supposed to have cut the throats of his three eldest Children, and then to have killed the Baby by beating it repeatedly with a Poker. . . . When at the Station House he expressed himself as being rather "peckish", and said he should like a Black Pudding, which, with a Cup of Coffee, was immediately procured for him.'

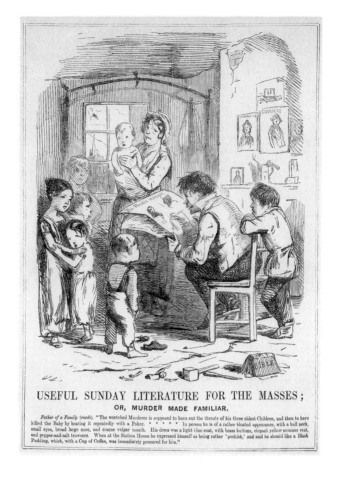

USEFUL SUNDAY LITERATURE FOR THE MASSES;
OR, MURDER MADE FAMILIAR.

Father of a Family (reads). "The wretched Murderer is supposed to have cut the throats of his three eldest Children, and then to have killed the Baby by beating it repeatedly with a Poker. * * * * * In person he is of a rather bloated appearance, with a bull neck, small eyes, broad large nose, and coarse vulgar mouth. His dress was a light blue coat, with brass buttons, elegant yellow summer vest, and pepper-and-salt trowsers. When at the Station House he expressed himself as being rather 'peckish,' and said he should like a Black Pudding, which, with a Cup of Coffee, was immediately procured for him."

gripped the British public to an unparalleled degree. Leech's memorable cartoon, *Useful Sunday Literature; or, Murder Made Familiar*, was published at the height of the Manning furore.[8] Not that the fascination with crime was confined to the uneducated. Archibald Henning (d. 1864) painted a group portrait of the Judge and Jury Society held in the Cyder Cellars, Maiden Lane, from the early 1840s (Christie's 18 April 1986, lot 108). This was a species of community theatre that originated with 'Lord Chief Baron' Renton Nicholson, a fly-by-night character who, in judge's robes, presided over re-enactments of famous murder trials. They were apparently frequented by authentic members of the legal profession, the nobility and literati, among others, in an atmosphere of seedy bohemianism.[9]

The condemned prisoner was invariably depicted in his cell at Newgate with the light filtering through the bars symbolizing his last contact with freedom. Newgate was the main criminal prison for metropolitan London, and despite its splendid exterior, was synonymous in the public mind not only with wickedness and crime, but also with squalor and fever, misery and despair. Every commission of enquiry appointed by Parliament or the City revealed gross mismanagement, overcrowding, extortion from the rich, starvation of the poor and unrestrained vice. Moreover, its population was not made up of prisoners serving sentences, but of

Debtors' Wives and Daughters Attempted to be Raveshed by Gaolers, 1691

The artist highlighted the appalling conditions at Newgate for debtors, who were confined in the same manner as condemned criminals.

those awaiting trial, those on remand pending further action, or those who had been sentenced and were to be transported, pilloried or hanged.

Among the longest-term residents were the debtors who were considered particularly worthy of sympathy, not least because in a country short of specie and heavily dependent on elaborate systems of credit, anybody could become a debtor. The herding together of debtors with common criminals in prison was one of many causes for complaint. A pamphlet entitled *The Cry of the Oppressed*, published *c.* 1691 by Moses Pitt (1641–97), a bookseller who had himself been imprisoned for debt in the Fleet and King's Bench, attacked the system with illustrations depicting torture, starvation, rape and gaol fever, among other dire consequences of imprisonment.

Hogarth had a particular reason to resent the law in this matter for when he was a child, his father had been confined to the Fleet Debtors' Prison for four years. The experience seems to have marked the artist's imaginative world. He was constantly using the prison, both real and metaphorical, as a framework for his characters, on the most fundamental level pitting the deluded and isolated individual against a hostile environment.

One of his earliest paintings, the *Committee of the House of Commons*, depicted the visit to the Fleet Prison of the Committee appointed in 1729 to investigate prisons. Extortion in the Fleet had grown during the wardenship of John Huggins from 1713 to 1728 beyond even the generous levels that were tolerated in the

eighteenth century. But it was the tactlessness of his successor Thomas Bambridge, in antagonizing those with influence, which brought about the enquiry. He had caused the death of Robert Castell, a minor architect, by deliberately exposing him to smallpox; but Castell happened to be a friend of James Oglethorpe, a humanitarian Member of Parliament. Moreover, in January 1729 Bambridge antagonized a baronet, Sir William Rich, who was an inmate at the time and who subsequently stabbed him. The following month, on a motion from Oglethorpe, the Select Committee was appointed and visits to the prison were undertaken. The painting may have been ordered by Sir Archibald Grant, who was on the Committee, as one of a pair to accompany the fictional prison depicted in *The Beggar's Opera,* a version of which he had also commissioned from the artist. The grandeur of the theatrical setting provided a vivid contrast to the dark meanness of the Fleet; Polly Peachum and Lucy Lockit in the role of suppliants could be compared with the ragged prisoner on his knees before the Committee.

Hogarth painted at least six versions of the prison scene from *The Beggar's Opera.* In his moral cycles, the Harlot is depicted beating hemp in Bridewell prison; the Rake is arrested for debt in St James's Street and locked up in the Fleet. Both characters are placed under the control of venal warders. The artist also found a means of expressing the popular aversion to the judiciary.[10] He portrayed the corrupt Bow Street magistrate Sir Thomas de Veil wending his drunken way in Freemason's regalia through the streets near Charing Cross in

The Rt. Hon. John Thomas Thorp, Lord Mayor of London 1820–21

Thorp stands in front of one of the cells in Newgate prison, the ragged petitioners visible behind the bars, and the walls hung with iron manacles. In brilliant contrast, the Lord Mayor wears his robe and chain of office over full court dress, a fossilized style of around 1780.

The Bench, c. 1758
WILLIAM HOGARTH

This oil sketch of the Court of Common Pleas depicts the notoriously immoral Lord Chief Justice, Sir John Willes with Henry Bathurst (afterwards Lord Chancellor) nodding off beside him.

Night. He undermined the whole genre of the legal portrait with his composite view of *The Bench*, which expressed in visual terms the universally held belief that judges fed rapaciously off the miseries of others or that they were slow and delaying and used their arcane knowledge to swindle their victims. The fact that the artist had used a judge in the first plate of the *Analysis of Beauty* to illustrate, albeit ironically, the 'awful dignity' and sagacity imparted by the voluminous robes and full-bottomed wig he wore only threw into focus the hollowness of the disguise. That Hogarth should further issue the design as a print to point the difference between character and caricature reinforced his message as to the impossibility of hiding the true nature of the law despite its trappings.

The campaign for prison reform initiated by John Howard in the late eighteenth century did not inspire any radical new outburst of visual propaganda. Francis Wheatley's painting, *John Howard Visiting and Relieving the Miseries of a Prison* of 1787 (The Earl of Harrowby), was an appeal to sentiment in the manner of Greuze, using every possible emotional chord to elicit sympathy: the old and pathetic, the young and beautiful, the forlorn children, all orchestrated and presented by the figure of Howard himself.[11] The *Microcosm of London* included illustrations of the major London prisons, including Coldbath Fields which had been planned to incorporate Howard's recommended improvements.[12] But the overall view given by the *Microcosm* was sanguine compared with the numerous reports on the conditions of imprisonment that were being published around this date. The courts of both the Fleet and King's Bench prisons, as illustrated by Pugin and Rowlandson, are bathed in sunlight, with games of tennis and skittles in progress, well-dressed people strolling about and pots of flowers on the windowsills. At a time when Newgate was overcrowded by a factor of three and Elizabeth Fry was discovering for herself the chaos and squalor in which women were kept at the prison, the *Microcosm* chose to depict the official view: the chapel at the solemn moment when the condemned sermon was being preached, those about to die sitting round a symbolic coffin in the dock.

Rowlandson was certainly far from squeamish when it came to depicting public executions. But he concentrated his attention on the activities of the crowd: the bun- and ballad-mongers, the pickpockets and massed hordes of spectators outside Newgate, with the church of St Sepulchre, Holborn, in the background. A grimmer view is presented in Géricault's drawing of a hanging in Newgate. Its impact as a close-up is startling – the artist must have arrived at the scene early to have gained such a prominent position – for the psychological intensity of the condemned man's expression and for the matter-of-fact delineation of the hangman and his assistant going about their business adjusting the ropes and hoods, while the Ordinary offers consolation.

The removal of public executions from Tyburn to Newgate in 1783 only reinforced the image of the prison as a place of fear and horror, especially when the suffering was seen as being brought about by a miscarriage of justice. The most unfortunate cases could generate a visual response on the popular commemorative level. The anonymous portrait of the Lord Mayor John Thorp holding a petition

King's Bench Prison, 1808
J.C. STADLER after AUGUSTUS CHARLES PUGIN and THOMAS ROWLANDSON

Wealthy prisoners could purchase the freedom of the Rules – three square miles surrounding the prison – but even within the high walls, there were taverns and gin shops, trading and sporting activities.

from seventeen counterfeiters unjustly condemned in 1820, with the prisoners in the cell behind, is one such peculiarly individual reaction. The obscure artist W. Thomson seems to have made something of a speciality of depicting convicted prisoners at Newgate, including a re-creation some four years after the event of the condemned cell on the morning of the execution of Henry Fauntleroy, who had taken to forgery in an attempt to restore confidence in his bank and for whom there was much public sympathy (Museum of London).[13]

The comparatively free and easy ways of the debtors' prisons were encapsulated at the same time in two paintings executed by the history painter Benjamin Robert Haydon (1786–1846), *The Mock Election* and *Chairing the Member* of 1827–28. The King's Bench, like other unreformed prisons, was largely run and financed by the prisoners, and governed by the Court of King's Bench. The prisoners formed a college which ensured internal order and harmony; by way of light relief public events such as coronations, royal weddings and, in this instance, elections were celebrated.[14] Haydon's motives in bringing to public attention his own plight as a short-term inmate are only in part propaganda for the campaign to abolish imprisonment for debt; he certainly considered himself superior to many of the unfortunate prisoners and that there was little social stigma attached to being arrested on such grounds is further confirmed by the purchase of *The Mock Election* by George IV, who was himself no stranger to the concept of debt. Rather, the artist was drawn by the inherent contradictions in the scene: 'the boisterous merriment of the unfortunate happy', as he expressed it. The scene represented, he believed, the 'finest subject for humour and pathos in the world'.[15]

Haydon's concentration on individual characters and human incident anticipated, like the works of David Wilkie (1785–1841), the Victorian passion for anecdotal genre. But prisoners, as in the case of the poor, were scarcely considered suitable material for academic art. They could of course be portrayed if they were historical figures, bathed in an aura of romance, like the little princes in the Tower, Charles I or even Marie Antoinette; Elizabeth Fry's visits to women prisoners were commemorated in *Newgate 1818*, exhibited by Henrietta Ward (1832–1924) in 1876 to considerable acclaim. But when Frank Holl exhibited *Newgate: Committed for Trial* two years later, the reaction was rather more complex.

The *Art Journal* dismissed it with the comment, 'how an artist, personally so healthy, bright, and manly, can year after year give way to this melancholy habit of mind and brush is beyond our comprehension.' For the *Illustrated London News*, it was a 'most powerful and pathetic but irrepressibly dismal picture'. Few faulted the technical excellence of the work; Holl had trained at the Royal Academy schools and, like all the *Graphic* artists, went to great trouble to obtain authentic models for his subjects. The painting was based on the artist's own experience of visiting the prison, where the Governor was a friend, and he was deeply impressed by the 'scenes of such pathos & agony of mind on both sides' that he witnessed. But in his final composition, he played down the more disturbing sights he had seen and concentrated attention instead on the plight of the women and the prisoners' children. As in Fildes's *Applicants for Admission to the Casual Ward*,

The Mock Election, 1827
BENJAMIN ROBERT HAYDON

The central character is the Lord High Sheriff, Jonas Alexander Murphy, an Irishman, with a chain of curtain-rings. He is surrounded by assorted candidates and election officers, wearing robes improvised out of bedclothes, while the groups on either side in the foreground are more obviously intended to draw sympathy. On the left is 'a good family in affliction'; on the right sits a Major Campbell, who had distinguished himself in the Peninsular War.

Newgate: Committed for Trial, 1878
FRANK HOLL

The scene is set in the part of the prison called the cage, where prisoners could see friends in the presence of a warden. Newgate was regarded with awe and dread; public executions were abolished in 1868 but hangings still took place behind Dance's massive walls.

the painting was saved by the competence of the figure drawing and the elevated moral stance adopted by the artist, which stopped short of being too specific and painful. The *Illustrated London News* conceded:

> although we systematically deprecate the adoption by artists of subjects which are squalid or ignoble, or mawkishly sentimental, or in any way repulsive – it being clearly the mission of art not to repel but to invite and to please – we do not withhold from the painter . . . the very highest praise it is within our power to bestow for the fidelity and assiduity which he displayed.

Prisoners Working at the Tread-Wheel, Coldbath Fields, c. 1862

The nineteenth-century 'reformed' prisons attempted to impose discipline on the inmates through a rigorous programme of forced labour and long periods of solitary confinement.

Yet this emphasis on personal suffering ran counter to the whole tenor of the administration of the law in general and the prison system in particular as it developed in the nineteenth century. Even on the level of the streets the changes were visible with the old parish constables, beadles and much ridiculed watchmen or 'charlies' being replaced by a uniformed professional police force in 1829, largely due to the energies of Sir Robert Peel. In caricature, the image of the aged incompetent watchman was replaced by that of the 'blue devil', an over-zealous thug who was all too eager to use his truncheon.[16] It took time for resentment to fade and for the police to be seen as something more than the impersonal face of authority. Characteristically, Holl humanized the situation by making a stalwart policeman the heroic rescuer of a baby in *Deserted – A Foundling*, first produced as an illustration for the *Graphic* in 1873 and then a painting (now untraced) exhibited at the Royal Academy in 1874.

Compared with the old system, the new prisons – Coldbath Fields, the Penitentiary Millbank, Pentonville, Holloway – were depersonalized, the separate cell and silent systems controlling the prisoners under strictly disciplined regimes. Mayhew's investigation, *The Criminal Prisons of London* (1862), was illustrated not only with artists' impressions but also with engravings after photographs taken by Herbert Watkins, for whom the writer had obtained permission to visit the gaols, provided that the identity of the prisoners was protected.[17] The illustrations expose a dismal world of cage-like cells, treadmills and oakum-picking, in which the prisoners are separated from one another, even to the point of wearing hoods and masks. The advent of photography did not, however, mark the beginning of unrestrained visual coverage of criminals and their world – rather the reverse. The perceived power of photography was to increase further the segregation of the prisoner from the public. On the one hand, photographs could play a vital role in the detection and identification of criminals;[18] on the other, the rights of the accused had to be safeguarded and any tendencies towards sensationalism diminished.

The artist was to meet with the same constraints. In a self-conscious attempt to re-create the Hogarthian moral cycle, Frith produced the *Road to Ruin* and the *Race to Wealth*; the final image in the latter saga, which traced the career of a fraudulent financier, depicted the 'Spider' taking exercise with fellow convicts in the great quadrangle at Millbank Gaol. Frith was given permission to visit the prison, provided that he did not speak to the prisoners – for the first nine months they were condemned to silence. Furthermore, he was only furnished with a convict's suit on the undertaking that he would avoid drawing the slightest resemblance to any of the prisoners whose exercise he had watched. For Frith, working in the Hogarthian mould, most of the point of the work would have been lost if he had not been able to delineate the character of the criminals in their faces: 'I need scarcely say I carefully selected types that may some day take their constitutional at Millbank, but are at present, more or less respectable members of society.' Thus Frith got round the ruling and combined the traditional physiognomy-reading of the deviant within the dehumanized system: he reworked his composition, in the interests of providing an accurate record, by positioning the prisoners so that they would no longer be within speaking distance of one another.

But the most haunting impression of prison life in Victorian London was created by Gustave Doré. His depiction of the *Exercise Yard, Newgate* conveys the historical sense of dread inherent in the very walls of the prison. And in place of, say, the mercurial presence of the condemned Jack Sheppard as drawn by Thornhill, an anonymous chain of prisoners trudge endlessly round as if on a phantom treadmill which fails to produce any degree of human energy.

Exercise Yard, Newgate, c. 1870
GUSTAVE DORÉ

*The Race for Wealth V –
Retribution*, 1880
WILLIAM POWELL FRITH

Frith's cycle of paintings provides a visual parallel to the careers of several prominent Victorian financiers, immortalized by Trollope in *The Way We Live Now* (1875).

From the dissolution of the monasteries, it was the professed intention of those with the welfare of the community at heart to look after children when their parents were unable to do so, and to tame their natural unruliness through education. The authorities provided their charges with clothing as a matter of course and it is this uniform which identified the London child – at least those who were in care – until well into the present century.

The reasons for adopting uniforms are fairly straightforward. Firstly, necessity: many parents were simply too poor to keep their offspring in clean, decent clothing, and foundlings and orphans had nobody to provide them with anything. 'I was naked and ye clothed me' was inscribed above many a charity school entrance. Secondly, distinctive clothing gave a superficial appearance of orderliness and discipline, as well as a ready means of identification should the children misbehave. Thirdly, plain clothing clearly expressed humility and deference to authority on the part of the wearer, reflected in the 'sad' colours adopted by the majority of schools: black, brown and grey for those attached to monastic orders, and blue for apprentices and artisans. Children were also thus freed from the whims of fashion and ornament which might have discriminated between the richer and the poorer. Finally, uniforms tended to give children an *esprit de corps*, particularly when charitable foundations had been in existence for some time. As Charles Lamb observed of the pupil from his own alma mater, Christ's Hospital, 'his very garb, as it is antique and venerable, feeds his self respect'.[1]

The London child can usually be distinguished in art by his uniform and none was more famous than that of Christ's Hospital. The school was one of the three hospitals founded by Edward VI in London – together with St Thomas's Hospital for the Diseased and Bridewell for the Thriftless – and was originally intended to provide food and shelter for destitute children. It took over land in Newgate Street vacated by the Franciscan grey friars at the dissolution of the monasteries, and opened in 1552 with 380 boys and girls. Although a royal charter confirmed the foundation the following year, the funds for its upkeep came mainly from citizens. From its beginnings, it also provided an education, sending a boy to Oxford as early as 1566, and soon it received children from all social backgrounds for schooling. Under increasing financial pressure arising from its irregular income, the very young and crippled were gradually excluded. By the end of the eighteenth century, a junior school and girls' school had been established in Hertford, and in 1902 the rest of the school left Newgate Street for the healthier environment of Horsham. But for 350 years, the distinctively clad Christ's Hospital children were a common sight in the heart of the city.

Their uniform was not established immediately. According to Stow, when the Lord Mayor and Aldermen rode in procession to St Paul's on Christmas Day 1552, the children of Christ's Hospital lined the way in a livery of russet 'cotton' (in fact a coarse woollen cloth with a raised surface), the boys in red caps and the girls with kerchieves on their heads. The following year, however, the children appeared in the familiar blue dress, which resembled the normal wear for very young boys in the mid sixteenth century. Over time certain adaptations were made: breeches were introduced for weak and sickly children in 1736 and by 1760 for everyone;

11
Education and the Young

OPPOSITE

Shaftesbury, or Lost and Found, 1862
WILLIAM MACDUFF

The two shoeblacks point to Lord Shaftesbury's portrait but the artist has introduced other emotive works into Graves' printshop window, notably engravings after Thomas Faed's *Mitherless Bairn,* and in the right-hand corner, Landseer's *Saved.* A notice for a meeting of the Ragged School Union at Exeter Hall lies on the ground.

collar tabs, which were an essential part of Puritan ecclesiastical and scholarly garb, were adopted; and the yellow petticoat was abolished in 1865.

The dress can be observed in two donor paintings which still survive at the school: the first shows the children, both boys and girls, kneeling before their benefactor Edward VI; the second, a massive work by Antonio Verrio, was executed to commemorate the foundation by Charles II in 1673 of the Mathematical School, to equip boys in the art of navigation. They appear to be the only surviving donor pictures relating to a London school and depict the children in the position of suppliants before their monarch, grateful recipients of his charity and bound by his authority. A less solemn view can be seen in the two small watercolours of the children in the Pepys Library;[2] significantly, Samuel Pepys was probably responsible for ensuring that the boys of the Mathematical School obtained funds and clothing for their indentures to masters and commanders of ships.

In one of the Pepys Library drawings the boy wears the large badge of the mathematical scholars; other scholarly benefactions were similarly distinguished, the badge of the boys endowed by Henry Stone in 1688 depicting them at work.[3] The badge was worn as an object of pride, as were the larger white metal buttons sported by the senior boys, the Grecians. Two Grecians are seen in the *Microcosm of London* view of the 'Blue Coat School' delivering two orations in Latin and English in praise of the institution, an annual event which took place on St Matthew's Day, 21 September, in the school hall.

The comparatively rich visual traditions of Christ's Hospital are not to be found in any of the other great London free schools, despite their antiquity and distinction. St Paul's goes back to the early twelfth century but the present foundation dates from 1512 by warrant of Henry VIII. Dr John Colet was made first master under the authority of the Mercers' Company, who took on the care, charge and governance of the school. If any foundation picture was commissioned, it would probably have been destroyed in the Great Fire. Westminster was certainly well established as part of the Benedictine monastery by the mid fourteenth century; it was refounded by Queen Elizabeth and became, with Eton, the most fashionable school in England for the sons of the aristocracy and gentry until the late eighteenth century. Despite its illustrious founder and the fact that its pupils also wore a distinctive dress of 'London russet', no donor painting survives and the pupils were not singled out for notice until William Henry Hunt selected one in his picturesque rowing garb as the subject for a watercolour in the 1820s (Henry E. Huntington Library and Art Gallery).[4] Charterhouse owes its foundation to Thomas Sutton who, having made a fortune exploiting the profitable coal trade while Master of Ordnance in the north, obtained letters patent in 1611 for the foundation of a hospital for poor men and a school in the buildings of the old Carthusian convent, which during the sixteenth century had belonged to the Norfolk family. Although there is a magnificent monument to Sutton by Nicholas Janssen and Nicholas Stone in the chapel at Charterhouse, the schoolboys appear to have been ignored. Neither the boys of Dulwich College, founded by Edward Alleyn in 1616, nor the pupils of Edward Latymer's school, founded in 1624, were commemorated at an early date in art.[5]

Topographical prints did depict the buildings of these venerable foundations. Ackermann produced histories of Westminster, St Paul's and Merchant Taylors in 1816, each comprising twenty-two pages with two coloured aquatints, of which one showed the schoolroom. But the boys were only depicted as token decorative figures, and this applies also to the lithographs executed by C.W. Radclyffe for *Memorials of Charterhouse* in 1844. An early nineteenth-century watercolour of Westminster School Hall includes a few boys in gowns and mortar boards, but more attention is given to the graffiti which, during the school's nadir in the late eighteenth century, extended as far as the Coronation Chair in the Abbey.[6]

From the sixteenth century onwards, most urban parishes had run petty schools to teach basic skills. The Green Coat School of St Margaret's Hospital, Westminster, was founded in 1633 by Charles I to teach reading, writing and book-keeping to poor boys and girls of the parish, in a house donated by the citizens of Westminster. William Shelton founded another Green Coat School in St Giles-in-the-Fields in 1672. A Blue Coat School was started in 1688 in Duck Lane, Westminster. There followed Grey, Black, Brown (Emanuel) and even around 1840 a Drab Coat School in Westminster, not to mention the unprecedented attempt at distinction resorted to by the Governors of St George's School, Hanover Square, of allowing the girls to wear blue and white spotted aprons.[7]

The majority of these charity schools were supported by subscriptions from social groups, under the impetus after 1699 of the Society for the Propagation of

Christian Knowledge, the first Anglican mission. Queen Anne encouraged their work as part of the High Church revival and by 1710, more than sixty schools existed in London with space for nearly 3,000 pupils. Many children wore a complete uniform and others sported a token cap and badge. Great care was taken to ensure that the dress was economical and durable, coarse in material and plain, although with a resemblance to the cut and style worn by contemporary adults. Once established, however, there was a marked resistance to change, partly in deference to the founder's wishes, partly for puritanical reasons and partly to prevent their being used as currency in the pawn shop.[8]

Despite their humble status within the educational pecking order, these children were commemorated in a peculiarly distinctive form. The purpose of the school was proclaimed above the entrance with a carved statuette in wood, stone or lead, or from 1770 to 1790 in Coade stone, depicting a charity boy and girl. Although frequently repainted, they were often preserved and may now be seen in neighbouring churches and museums, one of the few popular art forms in London to survive. Despite their robust and somewhat crude modelling, they provide evidence of the slow evolution of the dress of charity children during the late seventeenth and eighteenth centuries. The boys wore coats and sleeved waistcoats long after the adult fashion for the latter had died; their flat caps with bobbles were a throwback to the Elizabethan period. The dress of the girls reflected the fashions of the day to a greater extent in the position of the waistline and type of head-dress, from the indoor cap with a goffered frill like a miniature fontange head-dress at the beginning of the eighteenth century, to the straw bonnets worn outside in later years. Just as collar bands were indispensable for the boys, so the girls were rarely without tippets, aprons and mittens.[9]

Massed together, charity children presented tangible evidence of the munificence of Londoners. They drew tears from the eyes of Tzar Alexander I at the 1814 peace celebrations. Tickets for attendance at the annual charity school service at St Paul's were always sold out. John Page, vicar choral and conductor of the children, published an illustrated guide for the occasion in 1805. The picturesque appearance of the children in their distinctive dress was more than skin deep; it confirmed that the problem of poor children could be solved. Before the audience lay proof that they were clean, respectable, morally and physically disciplined members of the lower orders. As Combe's text to the *Microcosm* noted, with reference to an illustration of the dining hall of a house of refuge for friendless and deserted girls in Lambeth, the guardians who were present

> seem to contemplate the good order, cheerfulness, innocence, and comforts of their little wards, with all that interest and delight, that luxury of fine feeling, which irradiates the countenance when the heart is glowing with benevolence, animated with the exercise of an important duty, and gratified by the conviction that their virtuous endeavours are crowned with success.[10]

This personification of inner character by outward appearance was taken a stage further for propaganda purposes whenever philanthropists wished to illustrate the effects of their recommended course of action. Thus Jonas Hanway (1712–86)

Frontispiece to Jonas
Hanway, *Three Letters on
the subject of the Marine
Society*, 1758
after GIOVANNI BATTISTA
CIPRIANI

The Marine Society was the most
successful of the London charities
founded in the mid-eighteenth
century, because it combined
humanitarian ideals with practical
benefits, removing a social problem
from the streets and contributing to
Britain's naval strength.

persuaded Giovanni Battista Cipriani (1727–85), Hayman, Wale and others to
illustrate his proposals to found a Marine Society to train destitute boys for the
Navy, donating their services free of charge. With varying degrees of allegorical
embellishment, all the plates produced make the point that the ragged urchins,
once neatly kitted out, could be gainfully employed. Similarly, on a less
professional basis, many indentures for apprenticeships and many fund-raising
dinner tickets issued on behalf of charitable institutions were headed with the
figures of a charity boy and girl in their uniforms on one side, and their wretched
appearance prior to being taken into care on the other.

Given the strength of support it received from artistic quarters during its early
years, Thomas Coram's Foundling Hospital presents a special case, with a more
ambitious iconographic frame of reference.[11] Its first seal of 1739, naturally
enough, depicts the finding of Moses in the bulrushes and was evidently based on
Coram's own design. He himself was portrayed by Balthasar Nebot standing in
front of his foundation with a baby in a Moses basket at his feet. John Michael
Rysbrack (1693–1770), a Governor, executed a marble relief of Charity for the
Court Room chimneypiece. Hogarth and Hayman both produced intriguing
variations on the theme of Moses and Pharaoh's Daughter, while Highmore
painted *Hagar and Ishmael* and James Wills (d.1777) executed a particularly
cloying version of *Suffer the Little Children*. Eight small tondo canvases were
contributed by a number of artists – Gainsborough, Richard Wilson (1713?–82),

The Habits of the Children of the Foundling Hospital, 1747

The drawing was made at a breakfast held on 1 May 1747 to raise money for building the Chapel. The predominant colour of the uniform, designed by Hogarth in 1745–46, was a serviceable brown, trimmed with red.

An Exact Representation of the Form and Manner in which Exposed and Deserted Young Children are Admitted into the Foundling Hospital, 1749
N. PARR after SAMUEL WALE

The print was issued presumably as part of a fund-raising effort, stressing the fairness of the system of admission when the demand for places proved to be too great for the Hospital to handle. The colour of the balls selected by raffle determined the successful candidates.

Edward Haytley (fl. 1746–61) and Samuel Wale – for the decoration of the Court Room. But the work which came closest to describing the actual business of the Hospital was Wale's print of 1749, depicting the moment when the foundlings were admitted by a lottery, with the mothers, officials and a group of petitioning ladies and Governors in attendance. A more poignant, if ephemeral, record is provided by the scrap of paper detailing the uniform of the Hospital, as designed by Hogarth, with a sketch of two of the children appended.[12]

The watercolours executed by John Sanders (1750–1825) in 1773 of the girls massed in the dining-room and chapel of the Hospital provided satisfactory evidence of the uniformity and discipline within the institution, in the same manner as the view of the Lambeth Asylum for destitute girls drawn by Pugin and Rowlandson. The reality was rather different. Even with the help of some of the most eminent physicians in the country, the Foundling Hospital was vulnerable to the many dangers attendant upon children in the eighteenth century: hereditary diseases and handicaps, epidemics, misdiagnoses, incorrect treatment and inadequate nursing, all within primitive hygiene controls. It is scarcely to be expected that any of this should be seen in the depictions of the Hospital which were largely undertaken for fund-raising purposes, to show the charity in the most favourable light.

In the streets the children were vulnerable to other dangers. For a start, their uniform could be greeted with derision. Dickens's Biler in the uniform of the

Charitable Grinders is a case in point. The foundlings were branded by their dress, worn even while serving apprenticeships, as bastards. Nor were charity children insulated from low company, as Hogarth makes clear, as usual undermining the received artistic genre. On one level, he could introduce touches of lively character into his formal paintings of children dressed as fashionable grown-ups, notably his portrait dating from 1742 of *The Graham Children*, whose father was apothecary to the Royal Hospital, Chelsea. Far below them in the social scale are the two charity girls in the background to *Gin Lane* who, ignored by their guardians, toast each other in gin; the babies depicted evidently are not going to survive long enough to enter the Foundling Hospital. In the *First Stage of Cruelty*, published in 1751, the villain of the series Tom Nero wears the metal badge of St Giles's Parish on his arm, showing him to be a charity boy of the parish, possibly attending the Green Coat School. The charity schools were all too often the minimum that a parish could get away with, short of allowing large numbers of children to run loose as vagrants on the streets. Bridewell was the last resort for destitute children, juvenile beggars and delinquents. All the occupants wore blue livery with white hats and stockings; following the construction of new buildings in 1671, a basic form of industrial training was introduced and, much to the dismay of local residents only too aware of their unruliness, the older boys manned a fire brigade. Boitard's drawing of a cross-eyed beggar boy is a unique record of an unreconstituted charity boy, before he had received the Bridewell uniform.

The Graham Children, 1742
WILLIAM HOGARTH

Hogarth underlines the
differences in the children's
characters – from the responsible
elder girl to the carefree boy and
baby – by introducing emblematic
touches which signify the passage
of Time and Innocence.

ABOVE *A Cross-Eyed Beggar Boy*,
c.1747
LOUIS PHILIPPE BOITARD

The inscription suggests that the
child was either destitute or a boy
thief. About a hundred boys were
housed at Bridewell, where they
were apprenticed to resident arts
masters and taught trades, in the
hope that they would not relapse
into vagrancy.

Chimney Sweep and Boys
WILLIAM MULREADY

The artist presents a subtly
ambiguous image. The
schoolboys express both
horror and fascination; at
the same time the sweep's
outstretched hand can be
interpreted as either a
begging or a friendly
gesture. The isolation of the
sweep from the normal
pleasures of childhood and
family life was a recurring
theme in literature.

Despite the efforts of the authorities, gangs of children still roamed the streets begging and thieving, a junior level of *Vagabondiana* who were usually organized by an adult – a Jonathan Wild or a Fagin character. Moreover, many children were put to work legitimately at an extremely early age. The antithesis of the cleaned-up London schoolboy was the chimney-sweep's boy. The appalling conditions under which the climbing boys worked were widely known. They were often sold at an early age by parents desperate for money; they were ill-treated, slept rough or 'black' under soot bags and were frequently forced to climb narrow, decaying chimneys. Despite the introduction of workable cleaning machines in the early nineteenth century, it took over a century of continuous philanthropic effort to get effective legislation passed. But in collusion with householders anxious to safeguard their property from risk of fire, the chimney-sweep lobby was strong. As Sydney Smith remarked, 'What is a toasted child compared with the agonies of the mistress of the house with a deranged dinner?'

There were perhaps deeper reasons for people's reluctance to see them abolished, motives which made their conspicuous presence acceptable on the streets of London when other social abuses were not. At close quarters they might have appeared frightening even to their confrères at school, as Mulready's little sketch suggests. But there was an undertow of fascination to which Blake, Lamb and Dickens succumbed, a prevalent myth that underneath the grime lay a prince who had been a changeling at birth and who would magically be restored to his rightful place one day. The little chimney-sweep was usually depicted in art not as an object to stir the conscience but as a picturesque survival, a quaint example of semi-rural customs which should not be allowed to die. Even when, as part of his prolonged campaign to abolish the practice, Jonas Hanway published a *Sentimental*

The Little Chimney Sweep, 1808
ISAAC CRUIKSHANK

This ballad illustration presents a variation on the usual chimney-sweep myth; a beautiful lady befriends a little sweep she finds huddled in a doorway and later discovers that he is her brother. Cruikshank used the Foundling Hospital for the background.

Frontispiece to Jonas Hanway, *A Sentimental History of Chimney Sweepers in London and Westminster*, 1785

History of Chimney Sweepers in London and Westminster in 1785, he was compelled to enter into the 'sentimental' mythology by using as his frontispiece an illustration of a poor chimney-sweep helping one more unfortunate than himself. It was as if only by those means would people realize the common humanity which bound the boy to his fellows and, it was to be hoped, would they appeal to the consciences of those in a position to alleviate his lot.

The view that children had a fundamental innocence was reflected in art by the late eighteenth century, as the influence of Rousseau's writings spread throughout Europe. But to expect such purity to remain unsullied by the city was perhaps asking too much: as we have seen, Gainsborough tactfully removed his young beggar models to rustic settings, Reynolds to the higher realms of the classics. Throughout the nineteenth century, children were an important source of artistic inspiration, but comparatively few paintings used London as the backdrop and when they did the children were usually insulated from the deleterious effects of the environment with a heavy dose of sentiment.

William Mulready was an exception. A page of notes he compiled giving details of the clothing worn by a child in the Mall, Kensington Gravel Pits testifies to his close observation and, in its matter-of-fact itemization, is a more poignant account of the effects of poverty than any number of urchins clothed in picturesque rags. With four boys of his own to bring up, the artist was also undoubtedly aware of the whole private world of childhood: the primitive laws and codes of honour, the games, fights, friends, enemies, rivalries, which developed uncontrolled unless checked by adult intervention. Even in his paintings of the Mall executed in 1811–12, which are predominantly landscape in character, he introduced small figures lurking at gateways, swinging on posts or purposefully dragging a makeshift cart (Victoria and Albert Museum). The children he painted fighting are tough, uncivilized little specimens who, he clearly indicates, need to be taught a lesson. The main point of *Train up a Child . . .* of 1841 is that the infant has imbibed a rudimentary lesson in charity (Forbes Magazine Collection, New York).[13]

By this date, Mulready had long since abandoned any attempt to locate his works in the suburban environment of Kensington where he lived. Nor did the artists who followed in his wake make much effort to advance beyond the safety of the family parlour or the school, and usually a rural school. The sanctity of the family was uppermost in the Victorian middle-class frame of mind, a belief which was sustained by 'The Art of the Nest', as Ruskin described the domestic character and consequent shallowness of modern art: 'A great part of the Virtue of Home is actually dependent on narrowness of thought. To be quite comfortable in your nest, you must not care too much about what is going on outside.'[14]

Thomas Webster (1800–86) specialized from the 1820s in paintings in the manner of Wilkie and Mulready, of lively children at school and at play, depicted with great charm, humour and well-observed detail, but without the psychological subtlety to be found in the early works of those painters. The artists who joined Webster at Cranbrook, Kent, in the middle decades of the century – Frederick Daniel Hardy (1827–1911), George Bernard O'Neill (1828–1917), John Callcott Horsley (1817–1903) and Augustus Mulready – tended to sweeten their pictures of children to a mawkish degree. Mulready was the only member of the Colony to portray his children in urban surroundings. His flower sellers, crossing sweepers and newsboys are depicted predominantly in mean streets off the more opulent thoroughfares of the late-Victorian capital, their innocence and the pathos of their circumstances underlined with heavy irony in the posters attached to the walls above them, advertising the Gaiety Theatre, meetings of the Foreign Aid Society or, in one instance, a performance of Alfred Lytton's comedy *Money*.

On the whole, however, Victorian artists preferred to suggest a more optimistic future for destitute children. Alexander Blaikley (1816–1903), who worked principally as a portraitist, exhibited at the Royal Academy in 1851 a picture of the first Ragged School, which had been founded in Old Pye Street, Westminster, by Andrew Walker to provide vagrant children with a rudimentary education at the same time as food and shelter. Blaikley appears to have gone to some trouble to introduce authentic portraits of both children and visitors into his work. But he also depicted little girls 'to shew they are not neglected although they were taught in a separate apartment', and undoubtedly to enhance the sentimental appeal of the picture.[15] The Earl of Shaftesbury, who was chairman of the Ragged School Union formed in 1844, was also responsible for helping John MacGregor to organize a Shoeblack Brigade, again in an attempt to inspire some order and pride in the neglected children on the streets of the city. *Shaftesbury, or Lost and Found* painted by William Macduff (fl. 1844–76) commemorates his role with due reverence and affecting pathos as the two little shoeblacks in their uniforms recognize the portrait of their benefactor in the window of Graves's printshop in Pall Mall.

Young Chimney Sweep, c. 1850
HENRY ROBERT HINE

The image is in part nostalgic for the 1834 Act regulated the chimney-sweeps' cries and raised the age of apprenticeship to fourteen.

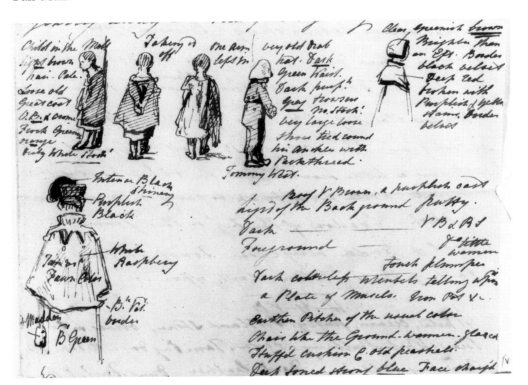

Child in the Mall, Tommy West
WILLIAM MULREADY

According to Mulready's notes, 'Child in the Mall, light brown hair – pale loose old great coat. DB and crome frock green orange, dirty white stock. Taking off. The arm left in. Very old drab hat. Dark green waist. Dark purple. Grey trousers. No stock. Very large loose shoes tied round his ankles with packthread. Tommy West.'

The activities of the Foundling Hospital were also celebrated in a series of three paintings by Emma Brownlow (fl.1852–69), whose father was the Hospital Secretary. Unlike Samuel Wale, she did not concentrate on depicting the highly formalized ritual of the separation of the child from his mother; by the middle of the nineteenth century, the methods employed were increasingly under attack.[16] Nor did she present the children gathered together in the dining hall or chapel in an institutionalized mass. Intead, she chose intimate scenes which highlighted the humane and caring nature of the Hospital, and suggested that the foundlings were part of a large, happy family. In fact, the first picture she painted depicted the reunion of a mother and child in the presence of John Brownlow. Five years later, she selected the moment most likely to give pause to those who criticized the Hospital for rigidly separating parents from children, playing on their Christian conscience: the christening scene, with its poignant substitution of foundling sponsors and siblings for the real family, illustrated by default the abdication of responsibility by the latter for the child's moral welfare. The last painting, dated 1864, portrays a sick room where again all the benefits of the Hospital are made evident, from the kindly medical and nursing staff to the animated brother and sister foundlings gathered round the bed.

With the passing of the 1870 Education Act, it was hoped that the problem of vagrant children running wild on the streets of the city would disappear. As the *Graphic* expressed it on Christmas Eve 1870, with reference to an engraving, entitled *School or Gaol*, of two ragged children crouched together in a dusky half-light before the looming slums: 'The children of the gaol and of the gutter cannot become articulate without the help of school and by the time that has been given to them, we may hope their most painful moments will have passed away.'[17]

But the urchins took rather longer to leave the visual repertoire of London types, even if they were increasingly photographed rather than painted. A mudlark and matchgirl were among the more memorable figures recorded by Beard for Mayhew's *London*. Oscar Rejlander used boys from a children's home in Chalk Farm as models for his photographs of crossing sweepers, shoeblacks and street arabs, some of which were used by charities for fund-raising purposes. From around 1870, Dr Barnardo commissioned a photographer to take 'before' and 'after' pictures of waifs, in the state when they entered his Home and after their supposed transformation into scrubbed, eager trainees in the workshops. The images were sold in packs of twenty, with information about Barnardo's work on the reverse of each card, thus forming a charitable *carte de visite* designed to prick the conscience of recipients. This propaganda intent fed back into art when Barnett Samuel Marks (1827–after 1891) exhibited a painting at the Royal Academy in 1873, *100,000 Neglected and Destitute Children*, representing boys saved by Dr Barnardo.[18]

But on the whole photography freed the artist from the need to practise such didacticism. Certainly the sketches of London street children by 'Phil' May in *Gutter-Snipes* (1896) have something of the pathos of Doré's urchins, with their oversized clothing and stoical little faces, but they owe more in their cheeky cockney humour to John Leech and the *Punch* tradition. George Loraine Stampa

The Foundling Restored to its Mother, 1858
EMMA BROWNLOW

The setting is the Secretary's room of the Foundling Hospital with John Brownlow, the artist's father, standing behind the desk. The original Hospital receipt lies on the floor as well as a box of toys brought for the infant.

The Ragged School, Westminster, 1851
ALEXANDER BLAIKLEY

Watched by visitors who include Lord Ashley, a group of boys in the centre are being taught how to mend shoes, and another group work with a tailor in the background. The blind boy near the shoemaker was evidently a child who could not work but came because he enjoyed the company.

The Brewer's Dray, 1872
GUSTAVE DORÉ

The image shows Doré at
his most emotive, the
massive bulk of the cart
trundling down the
shadowy streets contrasting
with the fragile bundle of
humanity travelling rough
behind.

Charity Children on the Steps of St Paul's, c. 1877
KATE GREENAWAY

The artist adapted the mop cap, fichu and high waist of the charity children for the dress of some of her fictional and allegorical figures.

"ORRIBLE AND RE-VOLTIN' DETAILS, SIR!"

(1875–1919) prolonged the genre into the first decades of the twentieth century; his assortment of youthful characters, *Ragamuffins*, appeared in 1916.

At the same time the typical London child had become something of a tourist sight, as is at least suggested by the purposeful inclusion of two Christ's Hospital boys in Tissot's painting, *London Visitors*, of 1874. As for the charity children, they too had taken on an aura of nostalgia. In 1879, one of the new children's magazines, *Saint Nicholas*, contained an account of the annual service for charity children in St Paul's. The writer extolled the quaint costumes worn by the girls and mourned the passing of knee-breeches for boys; he questioned whether the fashionably dressed 'daughters of dignitaries' in the congregation were 'any prettier than some of the charity girls in their funny mob caps'. The article was illustrated by Kate Greenaway (1846–1901), who certainly found their dress a useful source of inspiration for the aesthetic costume which she fashioned in her drawings of children generally. She was part of an era which romanticized children in literature and art to an unprecedented degree. The real world became a fantasy where a climbing boy could be transformed into a water baby, where Peter Pan could fly into the nursery and where there were fairies in the parks. For the London middle-class child, insulated by nannies whose concept of the great outdoors was limited to Kensington Gardens, the city simply did not exist.

'Orrible and Re-voltin' Details, Sir!', c. 1896
after 'PHIL' MAY

With their ragged clothes and raucous scavenging habits, May's comic repertoire of 'gutter-snipes' suggested nonetheless that poor children still escaped the net of the 1870 Education Act.

The closeness of death was a fact of life in medieval London. Infant mortality was high, life-expectancy low, sickness all-pervasive and disease rampant. Nevertheless, the continuity between life on earth and the hereafter had a tangible and comforting reality, a connection which found expression in charitable works. For rich merchants approaching death, the setting up of hospitals to care for the sick and the old was a particularly appropriate way of serving God and man. It was therefore fitting that the earliest copy in English of the ordinances for the almshouses founded in the early fifteenth century by Richard Whittington should be decorated with an illumination of the benefactor, surrounded by his executors, a priest, a physician and the almsmen and women who benefitted from his will.

There were two major hospitals for the needy sick in London during the medieval period, St Thomas's and St Bartholomew's, both foundations of the Austin Friars dating from the early twelfth century. The mid-thirteenth-century foundation of the Priory of St Mary of Bethlehem had by 1400 become the house and hospital of Bethlem devoted principally to the care of the insane. The Priory of St Bartholomew was dissolved in 1539, but as the hospital had long been in practice a separate foundation, with its own property in the City and country,[1] it escaped closure and was given to the City by letters patent from Henry VIII in 1546, as was Bethlem Hospital. The Priory of St Mary the Virgin south of the river was dissolved by the King in 1540 and its hospital, St Thomas's the Martyr, had to wait until 1553 to be restored by Edward VI. The formal donor painting at Christ's Hospital commemorates the foundation by the king of St Thomas's, Bridewell, and Christ's Hospital. A second foundation painting, depicting the king, which does not include the Christ's Hospital children, probably refers simply to Bridewell, which from 1557 was placed under joint management with Bethlem (Bridewell Royal Hospital, Witley, Surrey).[2]

By the Tudor period, the guilds associated with medicine and sickness were consolidating their position. The College of Physicians, first incorporated during the reign of Henry II, was founded in 1518 by Dr Linacre, physician to Henry VII and Henry VIII. The Barbers' Company, incorporated by Edward IV in 1461, though certainly in existence by the fourteenth century, was united with the Guild of Surgeons in 1540. Holbein's splendid painting, which dates from the last year of the artist's life, of Henry VIII on his throne granting the Charter to representatives from both companies, celebrates the event. Iconic in its static mould, with the monarch portrayed larger than life and the guild members in the role of suppliants, it follows the style of composition developed in miniature decoration for charters and statute books during the last decade of Henry's reign. The work was painted at the behest of the Company, a group of men who were no doubt better acquainted with business documents than with the naturalistic style of portraiture which Holbein had introduced to the Court. At the same time, in its unequivocal affirmation of the King's majesty as Defender of the Realm and of the Faith, Holbein was perpetuating the iconographic form first expressed in his Privy Chamber group at Whitehall.

The third company concerned with the cure of sickness, the Society of Apothecaries, received their charter from James I in 1617, probably through the

OPPOSITE

Greenwich Pensioners Discussing the Merits of the Crimean War, 1861
OCTAVIUS OAKLEY

Given that the news from Crimea deserved less by way of celebration than the victories at Trafalgar and Waterloo, Oakley possibly intended to create an ambiguous image, in which the Pensioners ponder on past glories compared with the most recent war, an elegiac sentiment compounded by their historic uniform.

The Death of Richard Whittington,
1442–43
attributed to WILLIAM ABELL

The scene depicts Whittington on
his deathbed, surrounded by his
three executors – John Coventre,
John Carpenter and William Grove,
a priest – probably John White,
master of St Bartholomew's who was
also an executor, a physician
checking the dying man's urine, and
the thirteen poor almsmen and
women who were going to benefit
from his generosity.

*Henry VIII and the Barber
Surgeons,* c.1540
HANS HOLBEIN

Thirteen people are singled out for
identification including Thomas
Alsop the King's Apothecary on the
extreme left, followed by Sir
William Butts and John Chambre,
the King's personal physicians. On
the right are members of the newly
formed company headed by Thomas
Vicary, Master for 1541, who
receives the royal charter.

efforts of Queen Elizabeth's apothecary, Gideon de Laune, whose portrait is still
owned by the Society.[3] The practice of hanging portraits of distinguished members
of a guild was, as we have seen, an act of piety common to all City companies. A
statute of the Royal College of Physicians of 1596 invited fellows, or even
outsiders, to hoist their portraits or coats of arms in the College hall on payment of
a fee of £10. We shall never know if anyone took up the offer, for the results of
what was possibly a public relations gesture but more probably a fund-raising
initiative would have been destroyed in the Great Fire.[4] The physicians, at the top
of the medical hierarchy, considered themselves gentlemen and viewed manual
work with disdain but, like other men of science and unlike the great merchants,
they did not object to having some form of emblematic reference to their calling –
a bust of Hippocrates or a pile of medical treatises – in their portraits. Holbein
depicted John Chambre, the first in order of the six physicians mentioned in the
letters patent for the foundation of the Royal College of Physicians of London (he
also appears in the Barber-Surgeons' painting), pointing to a book of anatomical
plates in a portfolio (Kunsthistorisches Museum, Vienna).[5]

A more unusual development, however, arose out of the anatomy demonstrations which, somewhat belatedly compared with Continental Europe, were taken
seriously after 1540, the Barber-Surgeons having obtained the right to the bodies
of four malefactors a year. Nearly all those qualified to demonstrate were
physicians and the earliest to be portrayed lecturing in Barber-Surgeons' Hall was
John Banister in 1581. Less expository, perhaps, but equally intriguing in view of
its undermining of a conventional painting genre, was the double portrait of Sir
Charles Scarburgh (1614–94) with his demonstrator Edward Arris, and a dissected
subject in front of them. Commissioned by the Barber-Surgeons' Company from
Richard Greenbury (fl.1626–70), the work confirms that anatomy was an

acceptable, even commendable, part of training by the mid seventeenth century.

The phenomenon of the anatomy portrait can scarcely be said to have developed into a sub-genre, despite the concurrence of interest in the human form on the part of both artists and surgeons. The notable surgeon William Cheseldon (1688–1752) was painted by Charles Philips (1708–47) some time in the 1730s dissecting a cadaver before six gentlemen, in the anatomy theatre built by Inigo Jones for the Barber-Surgeons in 1636–37, based on the famous theatre at Padua. Again, in an unfinished work dating from around 1772, Zoffany painted Dr William Hunter lecturing with a life model, plaster *écorché* figure and skeleton at the Royal Academy, where he had been appointed first Professor of Anatomy in 1768 (Royal College of Physicians).[6]

On a more basic level, surgeons as craftsmen promoted the range of their services on signboards, like the one dated 1623 formerly in the collection of the Royal College of Surgeons and thus possibly once owned by Dr John Hunter. A seventeenth-century wooden stand carved with two phlebotomy scenes, standard medical treatment at that date, was possibly used to rest the arm upon during an operation; a seventeenth-century coconut cup from York was carved with motifs illustrating the skills of barber and surgeon, respectively shaving and blood-letting. Another barber-surgeon's sign was decorated with a phlebotomy scene set in a carved frame of flowers, surmounted by an hour-glass with a skull and crossbones below (Wellcome Museum of the History of Medicine, Science Museum). These items made interesting variations on the more usual striped pole which advertised a surgeon's skills.

Of course practitioners relied on manuscripts and printed books which were illustrated, or which reproduced the illustrations of works printed abroad. The title page of H. Brunschwig, *The Noble Experyence of the Vertuous Handy Warke*

John Banister Lecturing at the Barber-Surgeons' Hall, 1581

John Banister (1533–1610) practised both as physician and surgeon and was much respected for his professional erudition. He is depicted at the head of the corpse, while the two stewards, whose duty it was to undertake the actual dissection are probably the figures at the bottom of the sheet.

Charles Scarburgh and Edward Arris, c. 1650
RICHARD GREENBURY

Sir Charles Scarburgh (1616–94) was one of the most distinguished physicians of his day, succeeding Harvey as Lumleian lecturer at the College of Physicians in 1656 and becoming a founding fellow of the Royal Society. He was physician to Charles II, James II, Queen Mary and Prince George before retiring in 1691.

William Cheseldon Dissecting a Cadaver at the Barber Surgeons' Hall, early 1730s
CHARLES PHILIPS

William Cheseldon (1688–1752) was famed for his anatomy demonstrations and his brilliance as a surgeon, in particular his operation for the stone. He was appointed surgeon to St Thomas's Hospital and in 1727, to Queen Caroline.

of Surgeri (1523), for example, includes a woodcut of trepanning. That such works were written in English is indicative of the fact that surgeons did not have the long liberal arts education which would have enabled them to read Latin easily, unlike the physicians for whom it was still the *lingua franca*. Alternatively, the English books were first-aid manuals like A. Boorde, *The Breviary of Helthe* (1547) or Bullein's *Bulwarke of Defence againste All Sicknes* (1562).[7] Perhaps the most ambitious vernacular medical work published in England in the sixteenth century was *The Herball or a Generall Historie of Plantes* (1597) by John Gerard, a London surgeon; the title page engraved by William Rogers included the depiction of a herb garden which was replaced by an apothecary's shop in some later editions. The first English translation of P. Morellus, *The Doctor's Dispensatory or the Art of Phisick Restored to Practise* (1657), reinforced its message with an engraving showing two scenes of 'The Apothecary's Shop Opened'. The earliest depiction of an official at Bethlem Hospital is given in the frontispiece to *Mikrokosographia* by Dr Hilkiah Crooke, published in 1605. Beneath an emblem of the Divine Eye, the author is portrayed by Martin Droeshout (1601–52?) delivering a lecture on anatomy, as keeper of Bethlem Hospital, to the Barber-Surgeons.[8] But these relics are insignificant compared with the visual riches that were being produced abroad in the field of prints by Goltzius and paintings with depictions of common surgical operations like tooth extraction by Bosch and Pieter Brueghel and, in the seventeenth century, by Jan Steen.

If London lacked the painters of the popular genre who exploited the market for such works in seventeenth-century Holland, it also lacked the Catholic tradition of *ex-voto* paintings which adorned the churches of Italy. Thus whereas there is only one surviving contemporary broadside of the Great Plague which attacked London in 1665 and a few bills of mortality embellished with skulls and shovels, the plague of 1656 in Naples which reduced the 450,000 population by some 60 per cent resulted in a number of church commissions. The paintings invoked divine intervention and protection, depicting the plague victims and *monatti* or corpse bearers, sometimes with the patron saints of the city acting as intermediaries or in identifiable topographical settings.[9]

By the eighteenth century however, with the general rise in the status of scientific enquiry, medicine also developed a more noticeable and distinguished presence in London. Between 1720 and 1745, five new London hospitals were founded: Westminster, Guy's, St George's, the London and Middlesex. Their foundation by private philanthropy was commemorated in portrait form. Thus Thomas Guy's portrait by John Vanderbank (1694–1739) hangs in the hospital which bears his name,[10] unlike the two posthumous paintings by John Theodore Heins (1697–1756) ridiculing his avariciousness, which are now in Norwich Castle Museum. Middlesex Hospital owns perhaps the grandest example, a portrait by Robert Edge Pine (*c*.1730–80) of Hugh, 1st Duke of Northumberland laying its foundation stone in 1755. The Duke apparently considered himself to be the handsomest man in England and was happy for his portraits to hang in public institutions: Middlesex Guildhall owned two, one by Gainsborough and the other by Reynolds.

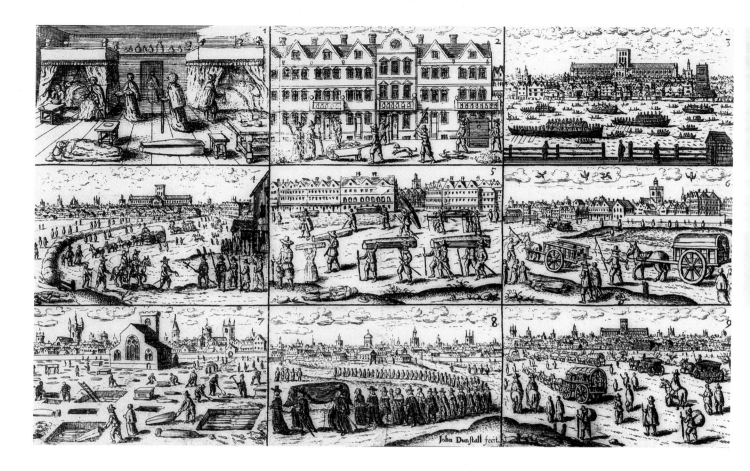

Such works provided an outward gloss of respectability, even a fashionable cachet which was vital if funds were to be maintained on a continuing basis. Similarly, the engravings of the exteriors of London hospitals published by Henry Overton and John Bowles in the 1720s concentrated principally on the architectural distinction of the exteriors rather than the wards within.[11] In the series of roundels presented to the Foundling Hospital, the nearest the artists came to the actual institution was Samuel Wale's depiction of the courtyard of St Thomas's; the rest were for the most part distant prospects with open fields, gardens and even the river in the case of Greenwich Hospital to keep the spectator at a safe distance.[12] Eighteenth-century hospitals were not noted for their record of achievement. They were still primarily charitable institutions for the common people; the rich were nursed at home. Few spectacular advances were made in medicine apart from inoculation for smallpox. Operations were performed without the benefit of antiseptics or anaesthetics, frequently by trainee surgeons. Nurses were untrained and badly paid. Hospitals even discouraged the admission of chronic or highly infectious cases, for which nothing could be done. It is no accident that Hogarth's moral cycles are littered with Londoners going about their lives bearing the marks of disease; those suffering from the effects of sexual, alcoholic or gastronomic excess remained at large. The concept of personal and public hygiene barely existed.

The Great Plague of London, c. 1665
JOHN DUNSTALL

This popular broadside was probably printed when the pestilence was dying down and people took a morbid interest in recalling aspects of its horror – literally a post mortem.

Hogarth contributed generously to the support of the Foundling Hospital, as we have seen, and also to St Bartholomew's, only a stone's throw from where he had been born in Bartholomew Close, Smithfield. Incensed to learn in 1734 that an Italian, Jacopo Amigoni was about to be commissioned to decorate the great staircase of the newly completed wing of St Bartholomew's, he volunteered to undertake the task himself for nothing. The work took three years to complete and the main canvases were devoted to biblical subjects executed in the grand manner, *The Pool of Bethesda* and *The Good Samaritan*; but in the former picture the artist introduced a group of figures modelled on hospital patients. As diagnosed by doctors today, they included a mentally handicapped girl, a woman suffering from anaemia, a blind man with his staff, a woman suffering from jaundice, a man with a bandaged arm, a woman with inflammation of the breast and, in the centre middle distance, a woman with a child suffering from hereditary syphilis.[13]

This allegorical representation of the divine gift of healing cannot be taken as evidence that Hogarth held a favourable view of doctors, medicine and hospitals in general; from many of his works it is apparent he felt quite the opposite. For a start, he poured scorn on the quack-doctors who undermined any standards that serious practitioners wished to uphold by claiming the cures they sold had miraculous healing properties. In practice the divide was not always clearly drawn, for if many eminent physicians used methods which were highly unorthodox, outright charlatans were not only tolerated but licensed by the authorities. During the seventeenth century, the College of Physicians tried to suppress medical practitioners not licensed by their body but some quacks still managed to obtain a licence from the king and even achieved respectability.[14] Travelling quacks, who usually came from abroad, set up stages and employed a 'zany' or 'Merry Andrew' to perform tricks and draw an audience to listen to his master's patter; in London their favourite haunts were Moorfields and Tower Hill. Sixteenth-century treatises had singled out charlatans for notice in woodcut illustrations.[15] A late-seventeenth-century engraving shows a quack on stage with his zany, thought to be Hans Buling, a Dutch mountebank who travelled all over England at that date. In the *Harlot's Progress*, Hogarth depicted two well-known quacks, Dr Richard Rock and Dr Jean Misaubin, quarrelling over the merits of their respective cures for venereal disease in front of the patient, who is clearly dying. His print, the *Company of Undertakers*, published in 1737, the year he completed the decoration in St Bartholomew's, presents the artist's views even more explicitly, playing on the three characteristics which distinguished a physician: gravity, a cane head and (like the judges) a periwig.[16]

Hogarth produced a horrifying drawing of a hospital ward in which the elegant stances adopted by the assembled practitioners as they undertake their duties only serve to highlight the ghastliness of the operation about to be performed. He reserved the full battery of his attack for the depiction of the interior of 'Bedlam' at the end of the *Rake's Progress* (Sir John Soane's Museum). Rakewell is shown semi-naked in the posture of the statues of Melancholy and Raving Madness executed by Caius Gabriel Cibber (1630–1700) in 1675 for the portal of Bethlem Hospital. An attendant fastens manacles to his ankles and he is surrounded by

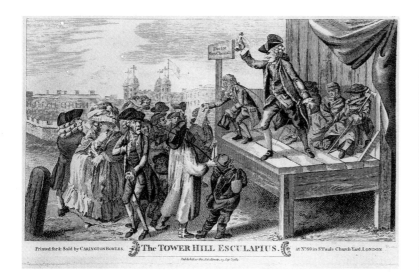

lunatics – a tailor, musicians, a melancholy lover – and two young women who have come, as was the fashion, to view the entertainment.[17]

The callous temper of the age was epitomized in Hogarth's *The Reward of Cruelty*, published in 1751 as a woodcut by John Bell. It depicts a public dissection of a criminal, an appropriate fate for Tom Nero who was the perpetrator of the pain inflicted in the earlier stages of the series. The setting is probably intended as a loose amalgam of the old Barber-Surgeons' theatre, which the Surgeons had been forced to quit following their separation from the Barbers in 1745, and the Cutlerian theatre of the College of Physicians in Warwick Lane. The Surgeons' new theatre in nearby Newgate did not open until a few months after the print was issued. But despite the justice of Nero's fate and Hogarth's friendship with the President of the College of Surgeons, John Freke, surgeon at St Bartholomew's from 1729 to 1755, the image is far from complimentary to the medical profession. Rather it appeals most obviously to the antipathy that was commonly felt in London towards surgeons, who were seen to conspire to deprive the malefactors on whom they performed their anatomies of the chance of at least a Christian burial or even, given the possibility of an unsuccessful hanging, of resurrection. The demand for corpses increased to such an extent in the early eighteenth century, with changing methods of teaching anatomy and the creation of the new London hospitals, that the authorized quota for the Royal College of Physicians and Company of Barber-Surgeons was supplemented through the illegal and much-hated activities of body-snatchers.[18]

Physicians did not escape this opprobrium. They were most frequently condemned in caricatures for their excessive fees, the images of the benevolent and the rapacious practitioner being contrasted in pairs of prints. Moreover, the Royal College of Physicians was attacked from within the medical world as an oligarchic monopoly. Although they were the body responsible for licensing practitioners in and around London, licentiates were not eligible for membership of the College as of right, and besides, the College excluded not only Catholics and

The Tower Hill Esculapius, 1782
after ROBERT DIGHTON

A quack accompanied by his zany sells patent medicine from a makeshift stage to a small crowd of citizens. The most famous quack doctors of the day were James Graham (1745–94), best remembered for the 'celestial bed' he created as a cure for sterility, and Katterfelto who travelled about the country in a large caravan accompanied by a great number of black cats.

An Operation Scene in a Hospital, c.1747
WILLIAM HOGARTH

The scene is a cutting ward in a hospital. The agonized patient looks on as the surgeon, wearing over-sleeves to protect his frockcoat, cauterizes a leg wound. The physician holds a urinal up to the light, while a servant in the foreground appears to be setting his full bottomed wig on fire with a candle.

The March of the Medical Militants to the Siege of Warwick-Lane-Castle in the year 1767
JOHN JUNE after an anonymous draughtsman

The distinctive octagonal domed Cutlerian Theatre of the College of Physicians (known as the 'pill box' because of the gold ball on its pinnacle) forms the background to the march of the disaffected licentiates led by William Hunter on horseback.

dissenters from its ranks but also those trained at universities other than Oxford and Cambridge. Matters came to a head in 1767 when a group of licentiates led by Sir William Duncan and William Hunter, who had trained in Scotland, and fronted by a hooligan element recruited on an *ad hoc* basis from the neighbourhood, stormed the College premises in Warwick Lane, an event recorded in contemporary prints. It was to no avail.[19] The College maintained its closed-shop policy with regard to fellowships until well into the nineteenth century, even if it appeared to move with the times in other directions. According to William Combe's commentary which accompanied the illustration after Pugin and Rowlandson in the *Microcosm of London*, depicting the College hall with candidates being examined by an elderly group of fellows, 'The solemn mummery of the profession is considerably abridged and the mysteries of physic, like the mysteries of religion, have almost disappeared in an age more liberal and enlightened.'[20] The old-fashioned tie-wig, the author maintained, had become an object of ridicule rather than respect. Significantly, the *Microcosm* chose to depict the more modern hospitals in London rather than the ancient foundations. It was part of the publication's general tendency to emphasize select attractions and improvements to the capital rather than its long-standing problems. And when foundations were ancient, as in the case of St Bartholomew's, its antiquities were selected for delineation rather than its contemporary role. Thus *An Historical Sketch of the Priory and Royal Hospital of St Bartholomew* (1844), illustrated by the hospital librarian, W. A. Delamotte, concentrated principally on the medieval remains of the priory; and whereas a large lithograph was devoted to the great hall on prize day, only a small token wood engraving was included of 'Rahere's Ward' which scarcely gave an impression of conditions for patients.

Sickness was usually depicted by Victorian artists bathed in sentiment, sombre questions of life and death mediated by the reassuring presence of the doctor and loved ones within the comforting setting of the family home. This privatization of illness was possibly a partial reaction to the growing body of knowledge about the causes and spread of disease. It cannot be said that London became any healthier with the massive increase in population during the first half of the nineteenth century. Lack of adequate housing, overcrowding, the absence of sanitation, polluted water supplies, adulterated food and malnutrition all contributed to the increased risk of infections and fatal disease. Cholera first arrived in England in 1831–32, returning to London in 1848–49, 1853 and 1866. As we have seen, its appalling toll acted as a catalyst for the investigation undertaken by Henry Mayhew into why the poor were the main victims, and by George Godwin into their housing in the 1850s. But there was almost no way of portraying the waves of fever that hit the country other than by symbolic means: the figure of death or a filthy Father Thames as depicted in *Punch*. Leech's design, *A Court for King Cholera*, published in 1852, showing a slum court heaped with refuse and dead rats and crowded with stunted inhabitants, was the nearest *Punch* got to a Hogarthian view of sickness as a fact of life.[21] For artists without a polemical axe to grind, the victims of such conditions, the young men or women dying of consumption, the children overcome by fever, were removed to a tasteful private domain where the causes of their sickness could not be seen as a generalized comment on the state of public health and the slowness of sanitary reform.

Like the Christ's Hospital boys and the charity children, the pensioners of the royal hospitals founded at Chelsea and Greenwich in the seventeenth century, respectively for soldiers and sailors, became objects of public sentiment in the nineteenth century. To be sure, individuals had been singled out before this for depiction as curiosities on account of their length of service and extreme age, in the manner of Riley's portrait of the ancient royal retainer Bridget Holmes. In the Royal Hospital, Chelsea, there is a portrait of William Hiseland, painted two years before his death in 1732 at the age of 112, by George Alsop. He had served for over eighty years, fighting at Edgehill as a royalist, in the wars in Ireland under William and for the Duke of Marlborough in Flanders; he had married at over 100 years of age.[22] But in fact the general reputation of ex-servicemen was low, principally because even when housed in the royal hospitals in comparative comfort, they begged on the streets and swiftly turned to brutal abuse if those propositioned were unwilling to comply. Their behaviour was singled out for condemnation by the Select Committees on Vagrancy immediately following the Napoleonic Wars, when many had been demobilized and were in the situation of contributing to the economic depression as well as being its victims.[23]

Within this context, therefore, David Wilkie's famous painting of *Chelsea Pensioners Reading the Waterloo Dispatch* can be interpreted as something of a rehabilitation exercise. The Duke of Wellington's first ideas for the commission were voiced to the artist in August 1816 when distress was widespread throughout the country. He emphasized the comfortable impression he wanted the picture to convey: 'the subject should be a parcel of old soldiers assembled together on their seats at the door of a public house, chewing tobacco and talking over their old stories.' By its completion in 1822, Wilkie had transformed this germ of an idea

into an example of contemporary history painting, with the dramatic interest focused on the reading of the *Gazette*, a compliment to the Duke which further served the purpose of emphasizing the patriotic feelings of the old men, rather than any looser moral connotations that the setting of a public house might suggest.

The painting was extraordinarily influential, not only as a successful marriage between modern life and the requirements of high art, but because of the entirely new image it gave to a previously despised section of London street life. John Burnet (1784–1868) was encouraged to produce an equivalent picture of the naval hospital's residents, *Greenwich Pensioners Commemorating Trafalgar* in picnic fashion with the famous view of the river and London as a backdrop; this was duly acquired by the Duke in 1841.[24] Octavius Oakley (1800–67) singled out two figures in his watercolour of 1861, *Greenwich Pensioners Discussing the Merits of the Crimean War*; and while in search of a subject for the *Graphic*, Hubert Herkomer (1849–1914) visited the Chapel of the Royal Hospital, Chelsea when the pensioners were attending a service: 'What grand old heads! *here* was a subject of the first water! . . . After the service I lingered on, got into conversation with one or two of the veterans, and soon found there would be no difficulty in getting them to sit – for a consideration.'[25] The result, *Sunday in Chelsea Hospital*, when it appeared in the *Graphic* in 1871, made the artist's name as an illustrator. He reworked the composition in oil and exhibited it at the Royal Academy in 1875 under the title *The Last Muster: Sunday at the Royal Hospital, Chelsea* (Lady Lever Art Gallery). The elegiac sentiment was not lost on the reviewer from the *Illustrated London News*: 'the pathos of the deep marks of time and service and hardship in the rows of aged heads, telling the life-story of each man; and the force

and truth of the painting of those heads are worthy of the highest praise.'[26] The figure of the old soldier personified patriotic and religious sentiment on a human scale, which could be appreciated. But without such traditional associations critics were less happy with Herkomer's brand of realism. When the artist exhibited what could be seen as the female version of *The Last Muster*, a depiction of the women's ward of Westminster workhouse in 1878, entitled *Eventide*, the *Illustrated London News* commented rather sourly that, 'although noticeable as a most vigorous impression of a crowd of ancient female paupers supping their afternoon tea, and although replete with expression, it is broad well nigh to the verge of coarseness.' The subject was too disturbing. With its dark tones and huddled groups, it suggested grimness and hardship rather than the poetic qualities of the assembled pensioners. It did not arouse tender feelings. The artist was, the critic asserted, 'deficient in refinement'.

Herkomer had first tackled the subject for the Christmas number of the *Graphic* in 1876. In an engraving entitled *Christmas in a Workhouse*, he had depicted an attractive nurse in the guise of ministering angel helping one of the old women receive her present of a small packet of tea from a lady visitor. The seasonal spirit was reinforced by the mottoes 'Merry Christmas' and 'God Bless our Master and Matron' framed in holly on the walls and a few lines of verse printed below the picture.[27] As in the case of destitute children and the poor in general, old age could only be depicted if it was romanticized, softened by personal acts of charity and kindness. *Eventide* presented too great a threat, raised too many questions about the way the old were treated in the workhouse and cast doubt upon the very concept of picturesque and contented old age, a role so ably and so publicly espoused in London by the Chelsea and Greenwich pensioners.

W ho, after all, are Londoners? Those born within the sound of Bow Bells, within the area governed by the L.C.C., the G.L.C., the inauspiciously named London Residuary Body? Does the mere chance of birth have much to do with the feeling of belonging to a city? As far as London is concerned, many thought and think not. London has always been characterized by its extraordinarily high level of immigration. In the past, these immigrants more than made up for the mortality levels, which high fertility did not entirely counter, since the married population was relatively small. London exerted an enormous pull; it was the centre of the country's economic and political life as well as being – unusually for a capital city – a major port. Migrants flocked to London from all over Britain as well as from abroad.

If so many people were migrants how quickly did they become assimilated? How did they stand out, remain visible as foreigners; how did they register their 'themness' against the massive 'usness' that constituted Londoners? Obviously, their speech betrayed them: accent, dialect, a slowness to understand metropolitan colloquialisms and street patter. More to the point, as artists make clear, they were rendered conspicuous by their dress, their deportment, their whole pattern of behaviour and even the areas where they were to be found, clustered in colonies. The degree to which they maintained a separate identity depended, of course, on their own cultural traditions and the circumstances surrounding their arrival in London, the length of their stay, the roots they put down. And the manner in which they were depicted by artists reflects these points.

At the top of the social scale were the foreign ambassadors who sometimes sought to commemorate their posting to London with a portrait souvenir executed in the capital. The French ambassador Jean de Dinteville was both extremely discerning and peculiarly fortunate when he chose to mark the visit of a friend, Georges de Selve, Bishop of Lavour, with the commission of a double portrait of them both from Holbein in 1533. Presumably from his residence in Bridewell, Dinteville had learned of and seen the portraits painted by the artist of German merchants trading out of the nearby Hansa Steelyard. The magnificent result of his commission, *The Ambassadors* (National Gallery), scarcely portrays them as aliens, but as Renaissance men whose interests transcended national boundaries and whose worldly calling was but a stage on a longer spiritual journey, at that moment fraught with difficulties.[1] No other artist working in England achieved such profound insight into the diplomat, although Sir Godfrey Kneller (1646– 1723) became quite adept at portraying sympathetically some of the exotic ambassadors to the Stuart court: *Mohammed Ohadu*, the Moroccan ambassador in 1684 (Department of the Environment, Chiswick House), and *Ahmed iben Ahmed, Qadran-Nasir* in 1707 (Duke of Buccleuch, Drumlanrig).[2] Those who were in London on short missions like Claude Lamoral, Prince de Ligne, in 1660 and the Venetian ambassadors Nicolo Errero and Celvisi Pisani in 1707, preferred to save until their return home the commissioning of more extensive testimonies to their moments of glory.

There were also those foreigners who were brought to London not to assimilate into the community but because of their very differences from the local

OPPOSITE

London Visitors (detail), 1874
JAMES TISSOT

The American visitors are portrayed by Tissot as distanced from even though surrounded by London, its historical and cultural attractions epitomized by the figure of the Christ's Hospital schoolboy and the setting of the portico of the National Gallery.

A Red Indian in St James's Park,
1615–16

Unusually for an *alba amicorum* drawing, the study was apparently made from life and the Indian possibly came from the entourage of Princess Pocahontas.

The Savoyards, c. 1825
JOHN AUGUSTUS ATKINSON

Savoyards played a particular type of hurdy-gurdy with several strings, which made a droning noise. French, Italian and German musicians came to London in the hope of earning a living.

inhabitants. Such is the lone Red Indian recorded in St James's Park around 1615 from Michel van Meer's *album amicorum*. He was one of a number imported as trophies by explorers returning from voyages of discovery, who fed a natural curiosity and, increasingly, a philosophical interest in the significance of racial differences which developed after the Restoration into the ideal of the noble savage. Possibly the theory was best illustrated by the visit in 1774 of the celebrated Omai, the first Polynesian to come to England. He was not brought over for exhibition purposes but came at the invitation of Captain Furneaux, Cook's second-in-command, in the hope of eliciting help for the recovery of ancestral lands lost in island warfare. During his two-year stay, he was received by the King and was portrayed by Reynolds (Castle Howard Collection) and Nathaniel Dance, among others.[3]

American Indians could also be treated with respect. Reynolds depicted the visit of a member of the Cherokee Embassy from South Carolina to the court of George III in 1762 (Thomas Gilcrease Institute of American History and Art, Tulsa, Oklahoma). The famous surgeon and physiologist John Hunter (1728-93) commissioned from William Hodges (1744-97) two portraits of the Cherokee Indians who visited London in 1790-91; they had fought during the American War of Independence on the side of the British and were taken up in London by Sir Joseph Banks's circle. It is clear from Hunter's collection of portraits that his interest in differing racial types was more clinical than philosophical. Alongside his paintings of Omai and the Cherokees, a Labrador woman, a Malay woman and a Chinese Mandarin (probably Quang at Tong who visited the Royal Society in 1775) were depictions of the dwarf Joseph Boruwlaski, commissioned by Hunter from Philip Reinagle (1749-1833), Maria Teresia, the so-called 'Corsican fairy', and Carolina Crachami, the Sicilian dwarf (Royal College of Surgeons).[4] Around 1788,

Hunter employed Zoffany to paint an albino Negro woman with her family (a picture destroyed by bombing in 1941). This fascination with freaks was common in the medical profession and physicians visited the great London fairs for the purpose of examining the latest batch of specimens.[5]

Such unfortunate victims stood little chance of assimilation even if they survived long enough to make it possible. More problematic were the waves of immigrants who came to London as a result of economic or political circumstances in their countries of origin. Although Britain ostensibly adopted an open-door policy towards the Huguenot refugees from Louis XIV's France, when they arrived in London they encountered the general contempt in which foreigners were held. Any well-dressed stranger was liable to abuse as a 'French dog' and an exaggerated espousal of fashion – be it in clothes or behaviour – characterized the depiction of the French in London even when, as in the case of Laroon or Boitard, the artists themselves were barely eligible for naturalization. However, through their craft skills and commercial acumen, their loyalty and commitment to a country which had offered them a haven, Huguenots could scarcely be depicted as a race apart after a couple of generations. The view of the French as foppish degenerates scarcely accorded with a community renowned for its sober industry, as Hogarth noted in his depiction of the congregation leaving L'Eglise des Grecs in Hog Lane, Soho, in *Noon* from the *Four Times of Day*.[6]

The Huguenots were in a position to have themselves portrayed by fellow Huguenot artists in a manner which rarely drew attention to their foreign origins, but the Irish and Jewish immigrants who came to London in far greater numbers over a longer period were hardly able to scrape a living. They are subsumed in art under the general class of the poor in London, only to emerge as individuals in particular roles, hallowed by custom. Thus, from the enormous pool of unskilled labour employed on the 'metropolitan improvements' in the early nineteenth century, George Scharf isolated one Irish navvy working on the new London Bridge. The majority of his workmates would have been Irish too, and so were the chairmen, porters, coal heavers, milk sellers and a fair proportion of the hawkers who serviced the city. The Jews were depicted as sellers of second-hand goods, particularly clothes. Less well known perhaps is their connection with the trade in slippers, spices and rhubarb.

If the poorer class of immigrant is portrayed at all, therefore, it is within the tradition of depicting London street cries. Indeed, we may pause to consider whether those figures often singled out as quintessential Londoners can be thought to belong to the city. Certainly some of the pretty girls carrying loads of fruit and vegetables in Wheatley's *Cries* would have been part of the seasonal migration of women who travelled on foot from as far afield as Shropshire and North Wales to work in the market gardens round London, carrying their produce to Covent Garden each day. There were Italian sellers of images, toys and artificial flowers as recorded by Collet, Smith and others; there were Savoyard and German bands seen in a picturesque light by John Augustus Atkinson, or as the bane of the capital by Hogarth and virtually every comic artist to tackle the streets of London as a subject in his wake.

The Indian Crossing Sweeper, 1848
CARL HARTMANN

Crossing-sweeping was taken up as an occupation by the London poor because it required no more than a broom to start, served as an excuse for begging, and could achieve a certain stability of income from neighbouring householders if a regular crossing was obtained.

The Nabob of Surat in the Mineral Room of the British Museum, 1844
GEORGE SCHARF

Britain's commercial and colonial power ensured that the streets of London were always enlivened by foreigners wearing exotic forms of dress.

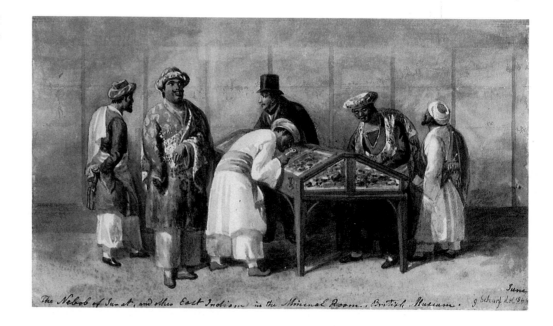

Moreover, there were sufficient numbers of Blacks to draw comment from both foreign visitors and native commentators by the early eighteenth century. Most frequently they were portrayed in paintings as servants, to be dandled as playthings by a master or mistress; occasionally, they were depicted with some sympathy, as in Reynolds's portrait of a young Black.[7] But in eighteenth-century graphic art, their occupational roles are much more varied, taking in a range of street trades, and seemingly undifferentiated from others on the grounds of race or colour. Indeed, if Smith is to be believed, when it came to outright begging, it was a positive advantage to be Black.[8] Worst off of all were the Lascars brought over as crew on East India Company ships, discharged on arrival in London and abandoned for months before being shipped back. They barely appear to have surfaced artistically,[9] although Carl Hartmann (1818-57), who kept a sketchbook on his visit to London in 1848, jotted down an Indian crossing sweeper who might have been attempting to earn a living on a temporary or permanent basis.

If anything is indicated by this brief survey it is that London has always been and still is a cosmopolitan city; its capacity to absorb newcomers has been a part of its very nature, intrinsic to its fundamental appeal. We may accompany Hollar to the Royal Exchange, Boitard to the Custom House. We can travel the streets with George Scharf and build up a collection of prize visitors of varying residential status: a spectrum of street sellers of every nationality – Indians in Leadenhall Street, a Russian in Piccadilly, a Greek in Tottenham Court Road, an Abyssinian Princess. And is that the first depiction of a tourist: the Nabob of Surat and other East Indians spotted in the Mineral Room of the British Museum in 1844? Perhaps, as Tissot's painting of London visitors may suggest, it is only with the advent of the entirely disconnected tourist that an identity can properly begin to develop, a feeling of belonging, of being at least in their eyes Londoners.

248 · STRANGERS AND FOREIGNERS

Notes on the Text

Abbreviations

B.M. British Drawings = Edward Croft-Murray and Paul Hulton, *British Museum Catalogue of British Drawings*, i (1960).

B.M. Satires = F.G. Stephens and M.D. George, *British Museum Catalogue of Political and Personal Satires* (1870–1954).

CLRO = Corporation of London Records Office.

Journals = Journals of the Court of Common Council CLRO.

THE CROWD

1   *The Great Tournament Roll of Westminster* (Oxford, 1968), introd. Sydney Anglo, pp. 7–9, 77. Sydney Anglo, *Spectacle, Pageantry and Early Tudor Policy* (Oxford, 1969), pp. 6–7. Roy Strong, *Art and Power* (1984 edn), pp. 7–11.
2   Edward E. Shaw, 'Three Inventories of the Years 1542, 1547 and 1549–50 of Pictures in the Collections of Henry VIII and Edward VI', *Courtauld Institute Texts for the Study of Art History*, no. 1 (1937).
3   Anglo, *The Great Tournament Roll*, pp. 74–82.
4   Sydney Anglo, 'The Imperial Alliance and the Entry of the Emperor Charles V into London: June 1522', *Guildhall Miscellany*, ii, no. 4 (1962), pp. 131–55. Anglo, *Spectacle*, pp. 170–206.
5   Edward Croft-Murray, *Decorative Painting in England*, i (1962), p. 163. Oliver Millar, *Tudor, Stuart and Early Georgian Pictures in the Collection of Her Majesty the Queen* (1963), nos 22–25, pp. 54–56. Roy Strong, *Holbein and Henry VIII* (1967), pp. 9–10, 24–25.
6   Roy Strong, *Artists of the Tudor Court* (Victoria and Albert Museum exhibition catalogue, 1983), no. 204, pp. 127–28.
7   David M. Bergeron, 'Harrison, Jonson and Dekker: The Magnificent Entertainment for King James (1604)', *Journal of the Warburg and Courtauld Institutes*, xxxi (1968), pp. 445–48.
8   Ralph Hyde, *Gilded Scenes and Shining Prospects. Panoramic Views of British Towns 1575–1900* (Yale Center for British Art, New Haven exhibition catalogue, 1985), no. 4,

pp. 42–43.
9   David M. Bergeron, 'Charles I's Royal Entries into London', *Guildhall Miscellany*, iii, no. 2 (1970), pp. 91–97.
10   Malcolm Rogers, 'Isaac Fuller and Charles II's Escape from the Battle of Worcester', *Connoisseur*, cci (1979), pp. 164–69.
11   Richard Pennington, *A Descriptive Catalogue of the Etched Work of Wenceslaus Hollar 1607–1677* (Cambridge, 1982), nos 908, 1778–1898, pp. 149, 292–306. The source of the artist's impression of the fortifications to the west of the White Tower is unclear. Certainly as depicted, they bear only a loose relationship to what is known from historical and archaeological sources and have little connection with the drawing made by Hollar of the river front at this point. *B.M. British Drawings*, i, no. 4, p. 349.
12   Félicien Leuridant, *Une Ambassade du Prince de Ligne en Angleterre 1660* (Brussels, 1923?).
13   Bernard Adams, *London Illustrated 1604–1851* (1983), no. 10, p. 19.
14   F.W.H. Hollstein, *Dutch and Flemish Etchings Engravings and Drawings* (Amsterdam), ix, no. 143. *The Quiet Conquest. The Huguenots 1585–1985*, compiled by Tessa Murdoch (Museum of London exhibition catalogue, 1985), no. 129, p. 100.
15   Millar, *Tudor, Stuart and Early Georgian Pictures in the Royal Collection*, no. 441, p. 160.
16   Robert Raines, 'Drawings by Marcellus Lauron – "Old Laroon" – in the Pepysian Library', *Apollo*, lxxxii (1965), suppl. pp. 2–4. *Catalogue of the Pepys Library at Magdalene College, Cambridge*, iii, part i, compiled by A.W. Aspital (Woodbridge, 1980), nos 276a–81b, p. 25.
17   Ned Ward, *The London-Spy Compleat* (1706), i, pt 2, pp. 293–98, quoted in Sheila Williams, 'The Lord Mayor's Show in Tudor and Stuart Times', *Guildhall Miscellany*, i, no. 10 (1959), pp. 16–17.
18   W.G. Constable, *Canaletto* (Oxford, 1962), ii, no. 435, pp. 392–93.
19   J.R. Abbey, *Scenery of Great Britain and Ireland in Aquatint and Lithography 1770–1860* (1952), nos 258–60, pp. 171–77.
20   Ian Maxted, *The London Book Trades 1775–1800* (Folkestone, 1977), p. 224.
21   H. Gerson, J.W. Goodison, Denys Sutton, *Fitzwilliam Museum Catalogue of Paintings*, i (Cambridge, 1960), no. 61, p. 44.
22   *B.M. British Drawings*, i, no. 2, pp. 552–53.
23   John Hayes, *Catalogue of the Oil Paintings in the London Museum* (1970), no. 57, pp. 110–12.
24   *The City's Pictures* (Barbican Art Gallery exhibition catalogue, 1984), no. 6, p. 27. *The Works of Art of the Corporation of London*, compiled by Vivien Knight (Cambridge, 1986), p. 123. Griffier the Elder painted a

view of a Frost Fair, this time at ground level, from Westminster looking across to Lambeth, which from the costume would seem to be *c*. 1700 in date. It was exhibited in the Christmas exhibition of the Prinsenhof Museum, Delft, in 1952–53.
25   Sybil Rosenfeld, *The Theatres of the London Fairs in the 18th Century* (Cambridge, 1960), pp. 1–43.
26   A painting by Nebot entitled *Powell's Puppet Show, Covent Garden* but appearing to show the main gateway of St Bartholomew's Hospital in the background was in the Alexander sale at Christie's, 26 July 1935, lot 142. Another painting, less certainly the work of Nebot, showing the stages erected in Smithfield looking south, is in a private collection in London.
27   *Microcosm of London* (1808), i, p. 52.
28   George Speaight, *Punch and Judy* (1970), p. 74.
29   Ackermann's *Repository*, viii (1812), no. 43, pl. 2.
30   Lawrence Gowing, 'Hogarth, Hayman and the Vauxhall Decorations', *Burlington Magazine*, xcv (1953), pp. 4–19.
31   John Thomas Smith, *Vagabondiana* (1817), p. 28.
32   Roy Judge, *The Jack in the Green* (Cambridge, 1979), pp. 15–27.
33   For the most comprehensive account see Richard D. Altick, *The Shows of London* (1978), pp. 221-34 and *passim*.
34   Cited in the *Report from The Select Committee on National Monuments*, HC. 1841 (416), p. vii, qu. 1849.
35   *Punch*, xix (1850), p. 132. Henry Mayhew, *The Adventures of Mr. and Mrs Sandboys* (1851).
36   See particularly, 'The Pound and the Shilling. Whoever thought of meeting you here?' *Punch*, xx (1851), p. 247. Also, *Illustrated London News*, xix (1851), pp. 100–02, which contrasted the crowds to be seen on 'The Shilling Day' – Saturdays – which were patronized, according to the accompanying article by Angus Reach, by 'the great folks', as opposed to the 'little folks' on other days.
37   Abbey, no. 251, pp. 166–68.
38   For other depictions of the race see Patricia Connor and Lionel Lambourne, *Derby Day 200* (Royal Academy of Arts exhibition catalogue, 1979), pp. 71–80, 107–22.
39   Another version is in the Victoria and Albert Museum, dated 1793.
40   Ronald Paulson, *Hogarth's Graphic Works*, i (1970 edn), no. 130, pp. 153–54.
41   Iain Mackintosh and Geoffrey Ashton, *The Georgian Playhouse* (Arts Council of Great Britain exhibition catalogue, 1975), nos 260–64. Geoffrey Ashton and Iain Mackintosh, *Royal Opera House Retrospective 1732–1982* (Royal Academy of Arts exhibition catalogue, 1982–83), nos 169–73, pp. 108–11.

42 Mackintosh and Ashton, *The Georgian Playhouse*, nos 328–55.

43 Christopher Wood, *Victorian Panorama* (1976), pp. 195–98.

44 Wendy Baron, *Sickert* (1973), pp. 22–33, 39–45.

45 Sickert's words in the catalogue preface for an exhibition of 'London Impressionists' which took place at the Goupil Gallery in December 1889. Quoted in D.S. MacColl, *The Life Work and Setting of Philip Wilson Steer* (1945), Appendix C, pp. 175–76.

46 Paulson, *Hogarth's Graphic Works*, i, no. 155, pp. 181–82. Paulson, *Hogarth: His Life, Art and Times* (1971), i, pp. 398–403.

47 *B.M. Satires*, no. 3076.

48 *Spectator*, Monday, 11 August 1712.

49 Paulson, *Hogarth's Graphic Works*, i, nos. 152–55, pp. 178–82. Paulson, *Hogarth: His Life, Art and Times*, i, pp. 398–404.

50 Lorenz E.A. Eitner, *Géricault His Life and Work* (1982), pp. 222–23.

51 Marcia Pointon, *The Bonington Circle* (Brighton, 1985), pp. 15, 59–66.

52 Adams, no. 196/23, 24, pp. 468–71.

53 Charles Baudelaire, *The Painter of Modern Life and Other Essays*, trans. and ed. Jonathan Mayne (1964), p. 9.

54 Michael Wolff and Celina Fox, 'Pictures from the Magazines', *The Victorian City*, ed. H.J. Dyos and Michael Wolff (1973), ii, pp. 559–82.

55 Quoted in Wood, *Victorian Panorama*, p. 217.

56 Gustave Doré and Blanchard Jerrold, *London: A Pilgrimage* (1872), pp. 35–36.

57 W.P. Frith, *My Autobiography and Reminiscences* (1888), i, p. 327.

58 Quoted in Rosamond Allwood, *George Elgar Hicks* (Geffrye Museum exhibition catalogue, 1983), no. 22, pp. 25–27.

59 Frith, i, pp. 336–37.

60 *The Pre-Raphaelites* (Tate Gallery catalogue, 1984), nos 63, 196, pp. 126, 264–65.

61 Jerrold, *London: A Pilgrimage*, p. 23.

62 Hayes, *London Museum Paintings*, no. 79, pp. 144–46.

63 A.M. Hind, *Engraving in England in the Sixteenth and Seventeenth Centuries* (Cambridge, 1952–55), ii, no. 64, pp. 391–93 for the group portrait which is attributed to the workshop of Crispin van der Passe I of Utrecht.

64 Pennington, nos 482, 544–555, pp. 72, 85–88. See also no. 491A, pp. 74–76.

65 Alexander Globe, *Peter Stent London Printseller circa 1642–1665* (Vancouver, 1985), pp. 5–6.

66 *B.M. Satires*, no. 374. Pennington, nos. 469–76, pp. 69–71.

67 *B.M. Satires*, no. 144. Pennington, no. 543, p. 85.

68 Hayes, *London Museum Paintings*, no. 40, pp. 74–80.

69 An album containing sixty-one satirical drawings for illustrated playing cards of the 1678 Popish Plot, the so-called Meal-Tub Plot of 1680 and the Rump Parliament is in the British Museum. *B.M. British Drawings*, i, no. 137, pp. 135–48.

70 *B.M. Satires*, nos 1092, 1093.

71 Freeman M. O'Donoghue, *British Museum Catalogue of the Collection of Playing Cards, bequeathed . . . by . . . Lady Charlotte Schreiber* (1901), i, pp. 39–42. *B.M. Satires*, no. 1546. *Catalogue of the Collection of Playing Cards of Various Ages and Countries formed by Henry D. Phillips* (1903), no. 241, p. 78.

72 British Library Add. MSS.27826 (Place Collection 'Grossness'), f.107, quoted in Peter Linebaugh, 'The Tyburn Riots against the Surgeons', *Albion's Fatal Tree*, Douglas Hay *et al.* (1975), p. 68.

73 *B.M. Satires*, nos 4190, 4223, 4281.

74 Adams, no. 59/3–5, pp. 139–40. *The Art of Paul Sandby* (Yale Center for British Art, New Haven exhibition catalogue, 1985), no. 112, pp. 84–86.

75 Anon., *History of the Westminster Election* (1784) illustrated with etchings relating to the course of the election by Rowlandson, *passim*.

76 *Punch*, xiv (1848), pp. 124, 157, 167, 172, 175; xv (1848), p. 101.

77 *Illustrated London News*, xii (1848), pp. 242, 391.

78 See particularly the reaction of the *Graphic* to the riots in the West End on 8 February 1886 and to 'Bloody Sunday', 13 November 1887, xxxiii (1886); pp. 176–77, xxxvi (1887), pp. 573–77.

79 Lynda Morris and Robert Radford, *The Story of AIA Artists International Association 1933–1953* (Museum of Modern Art, Oxford exhibition catalogue, 1983), p. 8.

SOCIETY

1 Quoted in Lawrence Stone and Jean C. Fawtier Stone, *An Open Elite? England 1540–1880* (Oxford, 1984), p. 35.

2 Francis Haskell, 'The British as Collectors', *The Treasure Houses of Great Britain*, ed. Gervase Jackson-Stops (National Gallery of Art, Washington D.C. exhibition catalogue, 1985–86), pp. 50–51.

3 *The Treasure Houses of Great Britain* provides the most recent summary of the literature, nos 49 and 50, pp. 126–27. Nicholas Hilliard depicted George Clifford, 3rd Earl of Cumberland *c.* 1590, dressed as Champion of the Tilt for the fancy-dress tournament held annually on Queen Elizabeth's Accession Day, with a panorama of the Thames looking across from the south bank to Westminster and Whitehall (National Maritime Museum). Strong, *Artists of the Tudor Court*, no. 216, pp. 134–35.

Jacob Esselens portrayed Viscount and Viscountess Campden *c.* 1665 standing in front of Campden House, Kensington, but Kensington was scarcely considered part of London at that date. John Harris, *The Artist and the Country House* (1979), no. 42, pp. 55.

C.R. Leslie's painting of *The Family of the 1st Marquess of Westminster*, which depicts them in the new gallery at Grosvenor House in 1831 and commemorates the recently conferred marquisate, and the same artist's portrayal of *The Library at Holland House*, with Lord and Lady Holland, Dr Allen, William Doggett and a portrait of Addison on the floor, painted to mark Lady Holland's birthday in 1838, are two rare nineteenth-century works showing members of the upper classes in London settings. Sacheverell Sitwell, *Conversation Pieces* (1936), p. 82. Lord Ilchester, *The Home of the Hollands 1605–1820* (1937), p. 365. Christopher Simon Sykes, *Life in the Great London Houses* (1985), pp. 249–51.

4 Roy Strong, *National Portrait Gallery Tudor & Jacobean Portraits* (1969), no. 665, pp. 351–53.

5 Oliver Millar, 'Charles I, Honthurst and Van Dyck', *Burlington Magazine*, xcvi (1954), pp. 39–42. Oliver Millar, *Van Dyck in England* (National Portrait Gallery exhibition catalogue, 1982–83), no. 43, pp. 86–87.

6 David Piper, *Catalogue of the Seventeenth-Century Portraits in the National Portrait Gallery 1625–1714* (Cambridge, 1963), no. 624, p. 392.

7 Harris, *Country House*, pp. 224–25.

8 Hieronymus Janssens's depiction of Charles II dancing at a ball at The Hague on the eve of his return to England, of which there are a number of versions, is the most approximate.

9 Millar, *Tudor, Stuart and Early Georgian Pictures in the Royal Collection*, no. 197, pp. 111–12.

10 Elise Goodman, 'Rubens's *Conversatie à la Mode*: Gardens of Leisure, Fashion, and Gallantry', *Art Bulletin*, lxiv (1982), pp. 247–59.

11 Pennington, nos 606–13, pp. 96–101.

12 Quoted in Jacob Larwood, *The Story of London Parks* (1877), pp. 75–76.

13 *B.M. British Drawings*, i, pp. 296–97. There is also a panoramic sketch *c.* 1674–75 by Danckerts of Whitehall from the Park in the Museum of London.

14 *Pepys's Diary*, ed. Robert Latham and William Mathews, ix (1983), pp. 421, 423, 438, 445, 504.

15 Henry Reitlinger, 'Two Seventeenth-century Views of London', *Burlington Magazine*, lxviii (1936), p. 294.

16 Harris, *Country House*, pp. 91–95. Adams, no. 22, pp. 36–45.

17 Hyde, *Gilded Scenes*, no. 27, pp. 76–77.

18 John Gwynn, *London and Westminster Improved* (1766), p. 88.

19 Usefully assembled and republished in Laurie's *Views of the City of London* (*c.* 1840) by Richard Holmes Laurie who inherited the Sayer stock. Adams, no. 191, pp. 448–54.

20 *The French Taste in English Painting during the First Half of the Eighteenth Century* (Iveagh Bequest, Kenwood exhibition catalogue, 1968), no. 85, p. 37. Compare with similar figures drawn or engraved by Gravelot, nos 67, 68, pp. 31, 32.
21 *A Foreign View of England in the Reigns of George I & George II*, ed. Mdme van Muyden (1902), pp. 47–48, quoted in Millar, *Tudor, Stuart and Early Georgian Pictures in the Royal Collection*, p. 196.
22 Quoted in Larwood, *London Parks*, p. 249.
23 Jean-Richard Pierrette, *Graveurs Français de la Seconde Moitié du XVIIIe Siècle* (Musée du Louvre exhibition catalogue, Paris 1985), pp. 7–8.
24 Celina Fox and Aileen Ribeiro, *Masquerade* (Museum of London exhibition catalogue, 1983).
25 Larwood, *London Parks*, p. 130.
26 Pointon, *The Bonington Circle*, pp. 137–39.
27 Baudelaire, *The Painter of Modern Life*, p. 11.
28 Charles Baudelaire, 'The Salon of 1846. On the Heroism of Modern Life', *Art in Paris 1842–1862*, trans. and ed. Jonathan Mayne (1965), p. 118.
29 Anthony Blunt, *The French Pictures in the Collection of His Majesty the King at Windsor Castle* (1945), no. 474, p. 75.
30 Jerrold, *London: A Pilgrimage*, pp. 87–88.
31 Charles Dana Gibson, 'Church Parade', *London* (New York, 1897).
32 Kenneth McConkey, *Sir John Lavery R.A. 1856–1941* (Ulster Museum, Belfast and the Fine Art Society exhibition catalogue, 1984–85), pp. 89–93. Sykes, *Great London Houses*, pp. 331–33.

MERCHANTS

1 *The Complete English Tradesman* (London, 1727), II, ii, p. 142, quoted in Max Byrd, *London Transformed* (New Haven, 1978), p. 17.
2 Kathleen L. Scott, 'A Mid-Fifteenth-Century English Illuminating Shop and its Customers', *Journal of the Warburg and Courtauld Institutes*, xxxi (1968), pp. 170–96.
3 Hendryk Zins, *England and the Baltic* (Manchester, 1972), p. 98.
4 Quoted from D. Papillon, *Vanity of the Lives and Passions of Men* (1651), p. 48 in the *Dictionary of National Biography*, xviii, pp. 765–66.
5 Susan Foister, 'Paintings and Other Works of Art in Sixteenth-century English Inventories', *Burlington Magazine*, cxxiii (1981), pp. 273–81.
6 *Works of Art Belonging to the Livery Companies of the City of London* (Victoria and Albert Museum exhibition catalogue, 1927).

7 Frederick M. Fry, *The Pictures of the Merchant Taylors' Company* (1907), no. 31, pp. 67–71.
8 W.A.D. Englefield, *The History of the Painter-Stainers' Company of London* (1923), p. 56.
9 Larry Silver, *The Paintings of Quinten Massys* (Oxford, 1984), pp. 136–38, no. 16, pp. 211–12.
10 Kurt Löcher, 'Der Londoner Stahlhof und Hans Holbein', *Stadt im Wandel* (Braunschweigisches Landesmuseum exhibition catalogue, 1985), iii, pp. 667–86.
11 Raimond van Marle, 'Two Carpaccesque Panels in the National Gallery', Shirley Falcke, 'A Triptych by Antonio da Solario', *Burlington Magazine*, lxix (1936), pp. 130–31, 229–30.
12 The identity of the sitter is doubted by Strong, *National Portrait Gallery Tudor & Jacobean Portraits*, no. 352, p. 130.
13 John Nevinson, 'The Dress of the Citizens of London 1540–1640', *Collectanea Londiniensia* (London & Middlesex Archaeological Society, special paper no. 2), 1978, pp. 265–80.
14 Pennington, nos 1778–1907, pp. 292–307.
15 Kurt Pilz, 'Die Allegorie des Handels aus der Werkstatt des Jost Amman. Ein Holzschnitt von 1585', *Scripta Mercaturae*, 1/2 (1974), pp. 25–60.
16 Hind, i, pp. 64–66, nos 5 and 6, pp. 69–70.
17 Paulson, *Hogarth: His Life, Art and Times*, i, pp. 465–97.
18 William Samuel Page, *The Russia Company from 1553 to 1660* (1911), pp. 178–93. *Works of Art of the Corporation of London*, p. 300.
19 Mildred Archer, *India and British Portraiture 1770–1825* (1979), passim. Ole Feldbeck, 'A Danish Portrait of an East India Captain', *Burlington Magazine*, cviii (1966), pp. 193–94.
20 Archer, *India and British Portraiture*, pp. 216–17.
21 Paulson, *Hogarth: His Life, Art and Times*, i, pp. 436–39.
22 Mildred Archer, *British Drawings in the India Office Library*, ii (1969), nos 2459, 2460, p. 621.
23 John Hayes, 'The Trinity House Portrait', *Burlington Magazine*, cvi (1964), pp. 309–16.
24 Bertram Stewart, *The Library and Picture Collection of the Port of London Authority* (1955), pp. 24–25.
25 *Microcosm*, iii, p. 20.
26 Stone, *Open Elite*, pp. 218, 254, 390.
27 *Microcosm*, i, p. 119.

CRAFTSMEN

1 Nigel Morgan, *Early Gothic Manuscripts (1) 1190–1250* (1982), nos 35–37, 50–53, 68, pp. 84–87, 96–101, 113–14.

2 Otto Pächt, 'A Giottesque Episode in English Mediaeval Art', *Journal of the Warburg and Courtauld Institutes*, vi (1943), p. 55.
3 Foister, '16th-Century English Inventories', p. 274.
4 B.W.E. Alford and T.C. Barker, *History of the Carpenters' Company* (1968), pp. 225–28. The frescoes still remain in the Company's possession and have recently been restored.
5 Hugh Alley, *A Caveatt for the Citty of London or a Forewarninge of Offences against Penall Lawes* (1598).
6 James Byam Shaw, *Paintings by Old Masters at Christ Church Oxford* (1967), no. 181, pp. 100–01. Donald Posner, *Annibale Carracci* (1971), i, pp. 12–16; ii, no. 4, pp. 3–4.
7 A.L. Beier, 'Engine of Manufacture: the Trades of London', *London 1500–1700*, ed. A.L. Beier and Roger Finlay (1986), pp. 141–67.
8 Otto Pächt, 'Holbein and Kratzer as Collaborators', *Burlington Magazine*, lxxxiv (1954), pp. 134–39. John Rowlands, *Holbein* (Oxford, 1985), p. 73, no. 30, pp. 134–35.
9 Robert Raines, *Marcellus Laroon* (1966), pp. 9–10.
10 Croft-Murray, *Decorative Painting*, i, pp. 56–57, no. 17, pp. 238–39.
11 Early Continental precedents include the portrait of Landgraf William IV of Hesse and his wife Sabina, Princess of Würtemburg, with astronomical instruments, the astronomer Tycho Brahe and master builder Eberhard Baldewein behind them and the Kassel Observatory in the background, dating from 1577 (Hessisches Landesmuseum, Kassel). Van Dyck painted Thomas Howard, 2nd Earl of Arundel, with Aletheia, Countess of Arundel, the Earl pointing to Madagascar on a large globe and the Countess holding an astrolabe in her lap and pointing with dividers to the same spot. The work commemorates the revival of the Madagascar Scheme in 1639. Millar, *Van Dyck in England*, no. 59, p. 99.
12 Maurice Daumas, *Scientific Instruments of the Seventeenth and Eighteenth Centuries and their Makers* (1972), passim. Roy Porter et al., *Science and Profit in Eighteenth-Century London* (Whipple Museum of the History of Science, Cambridge exhibition catalogue, 1985). Norman H. Robinson, *The Royal Society Catalogue of Portraits* (1980), pp. 250–51. The tradition continued into the nineteenth century: see particularly the portraits of Sir Marc Isambard Brunel (1769–1849) by James Northcote (1812) and Samuel Drummond (c. 1835). Richard Walker, *National Portrait Gallery Regency Portraits* (1985), i, nos 978, 89, pp. 70–71.
13 Anne French, *John Joseph Merlin The Ingenious Mechanick* (The Iveagh Bequest, Kenwood exhibition catalogue, 1985), no. A1, pp. 33–34.
14 The earliest depiction of a quadrant and

telescope being used in London would appear to be the etching, *Prospectus Intra Cameram Stellatam*, showing the Octagon Room of the newly built Flamsteed House, the home of Charles II's Royal Observatory. It comes from a series devoted to the Observatory by Francis Place (1647–1728) after drawings by Robert Thacker, which might have been commissioned to celebrate the Observatory's opening in 1678, or as illustrations for *Historiae Coelestis Britannicae* by the Astronomer Royal, John Flamsteed, posthumously published in 1712 but containing only one plate. *Catalogue of the Pepys Library*, iii,i, nos 261–69, pp. 23–24. Eric G. Forbes, *Greenwich Observatory*, i (1975), pp. 22–24.

15 A large unattributed painting *c*. 1740–50 of the interior of a clock- and watch-maker's shop with two journeymen at the workbench and the master showing an elaborate clock to a group of customers in Turkish dress is in the Musée des Beaux Arts, Besançon. Although traditionally thought to represent the premises of a London maker, both the tools being used and the view from the windows rather suggest a Continental workshop.

16 Kurt Löcher, 'Nürnberger Goldschmiede in Bildissen', *Wenzel Jamnitzer und die Nürnberger Goldschmedekunst* (Germanisches National Museum, Nuremberg exhibition catalogue, 1985), pp. 167–90.

17 Sara Stevenson and Duncan Thomson, *John Michael Wright The King's Painter* (Scottish National Portrait Gallery, Edinburgh exhibition catalogue, 1982), no. 27, pp. 79–80.

18 *The Quiet Conquest*, no. 344, p. 238. Tessa Murdoch, 'Harpies and Hunting Scenes', *Country Life*, clxxviii (1985), pp. 556–58.

19 *Rococo, Art and Design in Hogarth's England*, ed. Michael Snodin (Victoria and Albert Museum exhibition catalogue, 1984), no. Hl, p. 129.

20 Christopher Gilbert, *The Life and Work of Thomas Chippendale* (1978), i, pp. 5–7, 93–107. Helena Hayward and Pat Kirkham, *William and John Linnell: Eighteenth-Century London Furniture Makers* (1980), i, p. 2.

21 *Horace Walpole and Strawberry Hill* (Orleans House Gallery, Twickenham exhibition catalogue, 1980), no. 223, p. 48.

22 Celina Fox, 'Introduction', *Specimens of Genius Truly English* (Galdy Galleries, New York exhibition catalogue, 1984).

23 *Rococo*, no. Cl4, p. 46.

24 Ambrose Heal, *London Tradesmen's Cards of the XVIIIth Century* (1925) and the collection of the Museum of London.

25 Paulson, *Hogarth's Graphic Works*, i, no. 46, p. 111.

26 Sidney Sabin has suggested in correspondence that the yard in question might have belonged to William Wood, a prosperous timber merchant at Chertsey, possibly a relation of Hogarth's friend Thomas Wood. Hogarth's house at Chiswick was on the Great Chertsey Road.

27 M. Dorothy George, *London Life in the Eighteenth Century* (Peregrine edn, 1966), pp. 180–96.

28 Boydell probably commissioned Ralph Dodd (fl.1779–1817) to paint the series depicting the Royal Dockyard, Woolwich, the Royal Dockyard, Deptford, and the Launch of the *Bombey Castle* at Blackwell from which prints were published in 1789. The engravings published by B.B. Evans in 1793 were after paintings of Deptford and Chatham by Richard Paton (1717–91) with figures by John Hamilton Mortimer (1740–99) exhibited at the Royal Academy respectively in 1776 and 1778.

29 *Portrait Drawings XV-XX Centuries*, introd. J.A. Gere (British Museum exhibition catalogue, 1974), no. 157, p. 44. Only the figure was copied: the setting was the work of the draughtsman. Robert Gunnis, *Dictionary of British Sculptors 1660–1851* (1951), p. 84.

30 Iain Bain, 'Thomas Ross & Son. Copper- and Steel-Plate Printers since 1833', *Journal of the Printing Historical Society*, no. 2 (1966), frontispiece. Anthony Dyson, *Pictures to Print* (1984), pp. 85–87.

31 The working practices of the Whitefriars Glass factory were recorded by Edgar Schligmann during the 1920s and in the late 1950s and 1960s, after the company had moved to Harrow, by Clifford Rowe (Museum of London).

32 *Microcosm*, ii, pp. 202–05.

33 E.P. Thompson and Eileen Yeo, *The Unknown Mayhew* (1971), pp. 51–95 *et passim*. Gareth Stedman Jones, *Outcast London* (Oxford, 1971), pp. 19–32.

SERVANTS

1 Paulson, *Hogarth: His Life, Art and Times*, ii, pp. 244–46.

2 Millar, *Tudor, Stuart and Early Georgian Pictures in the Royal Collection*, nos 330, 331 p. 140.

3 Byam Shaw, *Christ Church Paintings*, no. 263, pp. 132–33.

4 A.P. Oppé, *The Drawings of Paul and Thomas Sandby in the Collection of His Majesty the King at Windsor Castle* (1947), nos 245–56, 345–54, pp. 63–65, 76.

5 Judy Egerton, *George Stubbs 1724–1806* (Tate Gallery exhibition catalogue, 1984–85), p. 17 *et passim*, but particularly the three paintings commissioned by Lord Torrington to show the outdoor servants and workmen of Southill, nos 46–48. See Francis Russell, 'Lord Torrington and Stubbs: a footnote', *Burlington Magazine*, cxxii (1980), pp. 250–53.

6 David Dabydeen, *Hogarth's Blacks* (Kingston-upon-Thames, 1985), pp. 21–27.

7 Paulson, *Hogarth's Graphic Works*, i, nos 121–26, pp. 141–49.

8 *Ibid.*, nos 228–33, pp. 267–75, for a full commentary on the prints made after Hogarth's paintings by G. Scotin.

9 Pennington, no. 1891, p. 305.

10 *The French Taste in English Painting*, no. 64, pp. 29–30.

11 Elizabeth Johnston, *Paintings by Joseph Highmore 1692–1780* (The Iveagh Bequest, Kenwood exhibition catalogue, 1963), nos 15–26, pp. 21–23.

12 John Ingamells and Robert Raines, 'A Catalogue of the Paintings, Drawings and Etchings of Philip Mercier', *The Walpole Society*, xlvi (1976–78), nos 168, 174–75, 205–08, pp. 44, 45, 49–50.

13 Waterhouse, *Gainsborough*, no. 811, p. 104. John Hayes, *The Drawings of Thomas Gainsborough* (1970), i, no. 837, pp. 303–04.

14 Pierre Rosenberg, *Chardin 1699–1779* (Cleveland Museum of Art exhibition catalogue, 1979), pp. 187–293.

15 Mark Girouard, *The Victorian Country House* (1979 edn), pp. 27–30.

16 Phillis Cunnington and Catherine Lucas, *Occupational Costume in England* (1967), pp. 210–13. Phillis Cunnington, *Costume of Household Servants* (1974), p. 125.

17 *B.M. Satires*, nos15604, 15604†, 15779, 15779†.

18 *Punch*, xxiv (1853), pp. 98, 104, 118, 130, 134, 144, 160, 170, 204; xxvi (1854), p. 44; xxxvi (1859), p. 194; lviii (1870), Almanack. See also George Orwell's essay on Charles Dickens (1939) in which he notes the number of jokes in nineteenth-century comic papers dealing with the uppishness of servants. He maintains that when Dickens wanted to draw a sympathetic picture of a servant, he created what is recognizably a feudal type.

19 John Thomas Smith, *The Cries of London*, ed. J.B. Nichols (1839), pp. 81–82.

MARKETS

1 The markets of the City of London were however fully surveyed following the Great Fire. For a useful account of these markets and the survey, see Betty R. Masters, *The Public Markets of the City of London Surveyed by William Leybourn in 1677* (London Topographical Society Publication no. 117, 1974).

2 For the fullest account of the development of the area in general and the piazza in particular, see *Survey of London xxxvi The Parish of St Paul Covent Garden* (1970), pp. 1–15, 77–97. For Covent Garden as an artists' quarter, also, William T. Whitley, *Artists and their Friends in England 1700–99* (1928), i, pp. 330–36. Louise Lippincott, *Selling Art in Georgian London The Rise of Arthur Pond* (1983), pp. 32–33.

3 There has been little recent research published on the group. 'Vertue Note Books, vol iii', *Walpole Society*, xxii (Oxford, 1933–34). C.H. Collins Baker, 'Nebot and

Boitard', *Connoisseur*, lxxv (1926), pp. 3–6.
Hilda F. Finberg, 'Nebot and Pictures of
Covent Garden', *Connoisseur*, lxxvi (1926),
pp. 36–38. Ralph Edwards, 'The
Conversation Pictures of Joseph van Aken',
Apollo, xxiii (1936), pp. 79–85. Harris,
Country House, pp. 158–62. The Viennese
artist Franz de Paula Ferg (1689–1740) is
sometimes considered part of the group, but
the Covent Garden painting attributed to him
by Finberg, 'Pictures of Covent Garden in the
Duke of Bedford's Collection', *Country Life*,
l (1921), pp. 327–29, is certainly by Angelis
and he seems principally to have painted
Italianate landscapes and seascapes of a
general idealized variety, not specific
topographical works.
4 Horace Walpole, *Anecdotes of Painting in
England*, ed. Ralph N. Wornum (1849), ii,
p. 650. According to Walpole's catalogue of
the collection at Houghton Hall, however,
there would appear only to have been four
paintings of markets by Snyders. They hung
in the Gallery and represented Fowl, Fish,
Fruit and Herb markets; two more in Munich
were of Horse and Flesh markets. Horace
Walpole, *Ædes Walpolianæ or, a Description
of the Collection of Pictures at Houghton Hall
in Norfolk* (1747), p. 71.
5 Two such works were in the collection of
Lord Woolavington. 'Curious Crowe', 'Four
Pictures at Lavington Park', *Country Life*, lix
(1926), pp. 949–51.
6 Adams, nos 26/23, 29/26, 41/26, 58/6,
61/67, 65/5, 72/35, pp. 57, 72, 108, 139, 146,
155, 174.

STREET TRADERS

1 Little distinction was made in common
usage between hawker and pedlar although
Mayhew connected the former more
specifically in historic terms with the sale of
textile fabrics. Henry Mayhew, *London
Labour and the London Poor* (1861-62), i,
p. 376. The Hawkers Act of 1888 made the
distinction that the hawker travelled with a
horse or other beast of burden while the
pedlar travelled on foot.
2 Charles Hindley, *History of the Cries of
London* (1881), pp. 23, 101.
3 *Ibid.* p. 27.
4 Edward Edwards, *Anecdotes of Painters*
(1808), p. 269, quoted in Mary Webster,
Francis Wheatley (1970), p. 83.
5 Karen F. Beall, *Kaufrufe und
Strassenhändler. Cries and Itinerant Trades.
A Bibliography* (Hamburg, 1975), no. 125,
p. 354.
6 Hind, i, no. 8, p. 72.
7 F.P. Wilson, 'Illustrations of Social Life
III: Street Cries', *Shakespeare Survey*, xiii
(Cambridge, 1960), pp. 108–09.
8 *Ibid.* p. 110. Margery Corbett and
Michael Norton, *Engraving in England in the
Sixteenth and Seventeenth Centuries*
(Cambridge, 1964), iii, no. 84, p. 369.

9 Beall, no. Il, pp. 323–24. Posner, i. pp.
17–19.
10 Beall, no. F8, pp. 224–26.
11 Sir William Holdsworth, *A History of
English Law*, vi (1924), p. 311.
12 CLRO, P.D.10.126.
13 *Journals*, li, fols 307b, 311.
14 9–10 Gul. III c. 27. Amended in 25
George III c. 28, 29 George III c. 26,
repealed in 35 George III c. 91 and
reintroduced in 50 George III c. 41.
15 *Journals*, lix, fols 170b–171.
16 *Ibid.*, fol. 174b.
17 CLRO, Misc. MSS 210.6. A high
proportion of those arrested appear from the
names to have been Jewish. Some like Jacob
Ephraeim and Sarah Chapman were repeated
offenders. The scheme petered out by 1765
but the account was not closed until 1793.
18 Webster, *Wheatley*, pp. 82-83, who
reproduces two line engravings by J.F.
Beauvarlet of *La Marchande des Marrons*
(after a drawing exhibited at the Salon in 1761)
and *La Marchande de Pommes Cuites*. Also,
Anita Brookner, *Greuze* (1972), pp. 150–53.
19 *B.M. Satires*, no. 8886.
20 W.H. Pyne, *The Costume of Great
Britain* (1808), pl. ii and the text for the
'Rabbit-Woman'.
21 Adams, no. 126, pp. 290–94.
22 Beall, p. 115.
23 Mayhew, i, p. 132.
24 *Ibid.*, i, p. 13.
25 Smith, *The Cries of London*, p. xiii. The
same indiscriminate mixture of beggars and
street sellers was used as staffage in Smith's
drawings for *Antient Topography of London*
(1815), identified by J.B. Nichols in an
appendix to *The Cries of London*, pp. 96–99.
26 Smith, *Vagabondiana*, p. 22.
27 Smith, *The Cries of London*, pp. 53,
63–64.
28 The process is best described in
Gertrude Himmelfarb, *The Idea of Poverty*
(1984), pp. 312–54.

LABOURERS

1 Paulson, *Hogarth's Graphic Works*, i, no.
185, pp. 207–09.
2 Stephen Deuchar, *Paintings, Politics and
Porter, Samuel Whitbread and British Art*
(Museum of London exhibition catalogue,
1984) nos. 5, 20, 21, pp. 38–39, 46–47.
3 *Ibid.* no. 53, pp. 66–68. Egerton, *Stubbs*,
nos 47–48, pp. 74–77.
4 Samuel Whitbread, *Substance of a Speech
on the Poor Laws* (1807), pp. 21, 97, quoted in
Deuchar, *Whitbread*, pp. 15–16.
5 *Ibid.* no. 8, pp. 40–41. Sir Benjamin
Truman, Mark Beaufroy and Whitbread
himself as a young man were all portrayed by
Gainsborough against landscape backgrounds.
Waterhouse, *Gainsborough*, nos 52, 674, 720,
pp. 54, 93, 96. The Whitbreads actually came
from the minor gentry. Dean Rapp, 'Social
Mobility in the Eighteenth Century: the

Whitbreads of Bedfordshire 1720–1815',
Economic History Review, xxvii (1974),
pp. 380–94.
6 C.F. Hardy. 'The Life and Work of
Jacques Laurent Agasse', *Connoisseur*, xlv
(1916), pp. 193–94, 197.
7 Marcia Pointon, 'Painters and Pugilism in
Early Nineteenth-Century England', *Gazette
des Beaux-Arts*, 6ième période xcii (1978), pp.
130–40. Jonathan Richardson I (1665–1745)
made a powerful half-length portrait drawing
in chalk of James Figg, dated 1714, five years
before he became English champion pugilist
(Ashmolean Museum, Oxford). He is thought
to have been included in several works by
Hogarth, notably *Southwark Fair*, where
Figg kept a booth for display fights.
8 Mulready sketchbook, Whitworth Art
Gallery, D. 121 (i) 1895 recto.
9 Katharine Crouan, *John Linnell, A
Centennial Exhibition* (Fitzwilliam Museum,
Cambridge, exhibition catalogue, 1982),
pp. xi, nos 6–12, pp. 3–5.
10 F.S. Schwarzbach, 'George Scharf and
Early Victorian London', *Victorian Artists
and the City*, ed. Ira Bruce Nadel and F.S.
Schwarzbach (1980), pp. 97–98. They were
destroyed by enemy action in the war.
11 Morris and Radford, *The Story of the
AIA Artists*, pp. 14–15.

THE POOR

1 Ellis Waterhouse, 'Murillo and
Eighteenth-Century Painting outside Spain',
Bartolomé Murillo (Royal Academy of Arts
exhibition catalogue, 1983), pp. 70–71.
2 *Reynolds*, ed. Nicholas Penny (Royal
Academy of Arts exhibition catalogue, 1986),
nos 92, 93, pp. 264–65. Smith,
Vagabondiana, p. vi.
3 Mary Webster, *Johan Zoffany, 1733–1810*
(National Portrait Gallery exhibition
catalogue, 1976), no. 55, p. 49.
4 Smith, *Vagabondiana*, p. 18.
5 Reprinted in *The Elizabethan
Underworld*, ed. and introd. A.V. Judges
(1930), pp. 85–90. Smith, *Vagabondiana*,
pp. 15–16, 26.
6 *Ibid.* pp. 19–20, 22–24.
7 Charles Knight, *Passages of a Working
Life During Half a Century* (1864–65), iii,
pp. 246–47.
8 *Pictorial Times*, viii (1846), pp. 136–37.
9 *Art-Union*, vii (1845), pp. 165–67. *Punch*,
viii (1845), p. 256.
10 *Art-Union*, v (1844), p. 158.
11 See particularly Charles Lamb's
laudatory essay, *On the Genius and
Character of Hogarth* (1811). For Hogarth's
influence on nineteenth-century literature
see J.R. Harvey, *Victorian Novelists and their
Illustrators* (1970), pp. 44–75.
12 [Charles Dickens], 'Cruikshank's "The
Drunkard's Children"', *Examiner*, 8 July
1848.
13 Celina Fox, 'The Development of Social

Reportage in English Periodical Illustration during the 1840s and 1850s', *Past & Present* no. 74 (Oxford, 1977), pp. 106–07.

14 *Ibid.* pp. 108–09.

15 Compare, for example, the *Vagrant from the Refuge in Playhouse Yard, Cripplegate* (from a photograph) with *Vagrants in the Casual Ward of Workhouse* (from a sketch). Mayhew, iii, facing pp. 384 and 402.

16 Republished in Paris in 1862 as Em. de Labedollière, *London et les Anglais*. Proof states of eight of the wood engravings by Henry Vizetelly are in the Victoria and Albert Museum.

17 George Godwin, *Town Swamps and Social Bridges* (Leicester, 1972 edn), introd. A.D. King, pp. 8–18.

18 Illustrated in Michael Wolff and Celina Fox, 'Pictures from the Magazines', *The Victorian City*, ed. H.J. Dyos and Michael Wolff (1973), ii. pl. 389, 393, 394, 398–400.

19 *The Young George du Maurier*, ed. Daphne du Maurier (1951), pp. 36, 86.

LAW AND CRIMINALS

1 James L. Howgego, 'The Guildhall Fire Judges', *Guildhall Miscellany*, no. 2 (1953), pp. 20–30. Stevenson and Thomson, *John Michael Wright*, p. 22.

2 Geoffrey Holmes, *Augustan England* (1982), pp. 115–65.

3 *B.M. British Drawings*, i, pp. 6–7.

4 *Catalogue of the Pepys Library*, iii, i, nos 316a–c, p. 26.

5 P. Linebaugh, 'The Ordinary of Newgate and his Account', *Crime in England 1550–1800*, ed. J.S. Cockburn (1977), pp. 246–69.

6 Mary C. Cowling, 'The Artist as Anthropologist in Mid-Victorian England: Frith's *Derby Day*, the *Railway Station* and the new Science of Mankind', i, *Art History*, vi, no. 4 (1983), pp. 470–71. See also *Illustrated London News*, i (1842), p. 30 for the publication of a feeble engraving of the murderer Daniel Good justified on the grounds that it might appeal to disciples of Lavater.

7 Frith, i, p. 179, quoted in Pointon, 'Painters and Pugilism', pp. 138–39. Kathryn Moore Heleniak, *William Mulready* (1980), pp. 21–22. It is worth noting that Mulready's teacher John Varley was deeply interested in physiognomy, albeit from a rather rarified viewpoint; he published a *Treatise on Zodiacal Physiognomy* in 1828. C.M. Kauffmann, *John Varley 1778–1842* (1984), pp. 40–45.

8 For the best account of the Victorian passion for sensational murders, see Richard D. Altick, *Victorian Studies in Scarlet* (1970).

9 Renton Nicholson, *An Autobiography* (1860), pp. 168–72.

10 J.A. Sharpe, *Crime and the Law in English Satirical Prints 1600–1832* (Cambridge, 1986), pp. 25–29.

11 Webster, *Wheatley*, pp. 68–69.

12 *Microcosm*, i, pp. 126–27.

13 Hayes, *London Museum Paintings*, no. 103, pp. 182–84.

14 Joanna Innes, 'The King's Bench Prison in the Later Eighteenth Century: Law, Authority and Order in a Debtor's Prison', *An Ungovernable People*, ed. John Brewer and John Styles (1980), pp. 281–86, 385.

15 *The Autobiography and Memoirs of Benjamin Robert Haydon*, ed. Tom Taylor (1926 edn) i, pp. 414–27; ii, pp. 431–40.

16 Sharpe, *Crime and the Law*, pp. 36–38.

17 Part of a letter is reproduced in Thompson and Yeo, *The Unknown Mayhew*, plate III, from Mayhew to an official of Tothill Fields Prison. He asks permission to photograph dinner in the boys' oakum room giving assurances that in the finished engravings, the identity of the prisoners would be unrecognizable.

18 Valerie Lloyd, 'The Camera and Dr. Barnardo', *The Camera and Dr. Barnardo* (1974), pp. 14–15. For an artistic impression of photographing prisoners, see *The Bashful Model* after Luke Fildes in the *Graphic*, viii, (1873), p. 440.

EDUCATION AND THE YOUNG

1 Charles Lamb, 'On Christ's Hospital and the Character of Christ's Hospital Boys', *Gentleman's Magazine*, lxxxiii (1813), p. 542.

2 *Catalogue of the Pepys Library*, iii, i, no. 406, p. 33. The drawings might have been made at a marriage ceremony arranged between a boy and girl at the Hospital, who had inherited the estate of two wealthy citizens. Their public wedding took place at Guildhall Chapel in 1695 and was witnessed by Pepys.

3 *See also* R.C. Carrington, *Two Schools* (1971), pp. 32–33, 91.

4 John Witt, *William Henry Hunt* (1982) no. 401, p. 180.

5 Alleyn left his pictures to his foundation, including a portrait of himself and his wife, but most were decorative works. In 1686 William Cartwright left a large miscellaneous collection to the College for which the inventory still exists, but few works can now be traced. The Dulwich Gallery collection of course principally comprises the Desenfans-Bourgeois Bequest of 1811. Peter Murray, *Dulwich Picture Gallery a Catalogue* (1980), p. 17.

6 Reproduced in Lawrence E. Tanner, *Westminster School* (1934), pl. 6. The School also has a number of portraits of masters and king's scholars, but the latter do not appear to have been acquired as part of a conscious policy as at Eton.

7 Phillis Cunnington and Catherine Lucas, *Charity Costumes* (1978), pp. 119–55.

8 *Ibid.* pp. 20–64.

9 Gregory Holyoake, 'Survivors of the First Free Schools, London's Charity Children Statues', *Country Life*, clxviii (1980), pp. 1787–91.

10 *Microcosm*, i, p. 25.

11 Paulson, *Hogarth: His Life and Times*, ii, pp. 37–50. Benedict Nicolson, *The Treasures of the Foundling Hospital* (Oxford, 1972), pp. 1–31.

12 Hogarth had also designed the heading of a document giving the Hospital a power of attorney, the drawing for which is in the Mellon Collection. Brian Allen, 'Engravings for Charity' (Jonas Hanway symposium), *Royal Society of Arts Journal*, cxxxiv (1986), pp. 646–50.

13 Heleniak, *Mulready*, p. 100. Marcia Pointon, *Mulready* (Victoria and Albert Museum exhibition catalogue, 1986), pp. 121–26, no. 112, p. 129.

14 John Ruskin, 'On the Present State of Modern Art . . . ' (Lecture delivered at the British Institution, 7 June 1867), reprinted in *The Works of Ruskin*, ed. E.T. Cook and Alexander Wedderburn, xix (1905), pp. 200–01.

15 See Wood, *Victorian Panorama*, p. 75 for a coarser representation of a ragged school in Portsmouth by John Barker, dated 1857.

16 Bernd Weisbrod, 'How to Become a Good Foundling in Early Victorian London', *Social History*, x (1985), pp. 193–209.

17 *Graphic*, ii (1870), p. 617.

18 Lloyd, 'The Camera and Dr Barnardo', pp. 11–16.

SICKNESS AND OLD AGE

1 *Cartulary of St Bartholomew's Hospital*. A calendar prepared by Nellie J.M Kerling (1973), pp. 1–15.

2 Edward Geoffrey O'Donoghue, *Bridewell Hospital. Palace, Prison, Schools* (1923) i, pp. 165–82.

3 Cecil Wall, H. Charles Cameron and E. Ashworth Underwood, *A History of the Worshipful Company of Apothecaries of London 1617–1815* (1963), pl. IV.

4 David Piper, *Royal College of Physicians of London Portraits*, ed. Gordon Wolstenholme (1964), p. 77.

5 Rowlands, *Holbein*, no. 82, p. 149.

6 Piper, *Royal College of Physicians Portraits*, pp. 232–33. Webster, *Zoffany*, no. 75, p. 58.

7 Eric Sangwine, 'The Private Libraries of Tudor Doctors', *Journal of the History of Medicine and Allied Sciences*, xxxiii (1978), p. 172. Paul Slack, 'Mirrors of Health and Treasures of Poor Men: The Uses of the Vernacular Medical Literature of Tudor England', *Health, Medicine and Mortality in the Sixteenth Century*, ed. Charles Webster (Cambridge, 1979), pp. 237–73.

8 Edward Geoffrey O'Donoghue, *The Story of Bethlehem Hospital from its Foundation in 1247* (1914), pp. 156–63. Hind, ii, no. 13, p. 360.

9 *Painting in Naples 1606–1705 from Caravaggio to Giordano*, ed. Clovis Whitfield and Jane Martineau (Royal

Academy of Arts exhibition catalogue, 1982), p. 30, nos 66, 100, 101, 150, pp. 175, 209–10, 252–53.

10 H.C. Cameron, *Mr Guy's Hospital 1726–1948* (1954), frontispiece and p. 65.

11 An exception was the engraving of *Guy's Hospital for Incurables* surrounded by eight small supplementary views by Thomas Bowles, four each of exteriors and interiors, including an extremely neat ward. It was published as part of John Bowles, *London Described* (1731). Adams, no. 29/43, p. 73.

12 Nicolson, *Foundling Hospital Treasures*, pp. 54–61.

13 Paulson, *Hogarth: His Life, Art and Times*, i, pp. 378–86, who, however, diagnoses the child as suffering from rickets. Meningitis and Crohn's disease have also been suggested.

14 Leslie G. Matthews, 'Licensed Mountebacks in Britain', *Journal of the History of Medicine and Related Sciences*, xix (1964), pp. 30–45.

15 For example, the woodcut of two quack surgeons treating a chest wound in T. Gale, *An Enchiridion of Chirurgerie* (1567) and a charlatan at work in William Clowes, *A Brief and Necessary Treatise Touching . . . Morbus Gallicus* (1585), p. 9.

16 Paulson, *Hogarth's Graphic Works*, i, nos 125, 144, pp. 147–48, 172–74. Paulson, *Hogarth: His Life, Art and Times*, i, pp. 254–55.

17 Paulson, *Hogarth's Graphic Works*, i, no. 139, pp. 169–70. Paulson, *Hogarth: His Life, Art and Times*, i, pp. 326–27.

18 William Brockbank and Jessie Dobson, 'Hogarth's Anatomical Theatre', *Journal of the History of Medicine*, xiv (1959), pp. 351–53. Paulson, *Hogarth's Graphic Works*, i, no. 190, pp. 214–15. Paulson, *Hogarth: His Life, Art and Times*, ii, pp. 103–09. Linebaugh, 'The Tyburn Riot Against the Surgeons', *Albion's Fatal Tree*, pp. 65–117.

19 Lloyd G. Stevenson, 'The Siege of Warwick Lane', *Journal of the History of Medicine*, vii (1952), pp. 105–21. Ivan Waddington, 'The Struggle to Reform the Royal College of Physicians 1767–71. A Sociological Analysis', *Medical History*, xvii (1973), pp. 107–26.

20 *Microcosm*, i, pp. 152–53.

21 *Punch*, xxiii (1852), p. 139.

22 C.G.T. Dean, *The Royal Hospital Chelsea* (1950), pp. 138, 222.

23 *2nd Report of the Select Committee on Mendicity and Vagrancy in the Metropolis* (1816), pp. 12–14, which cited a number of examples, recommended that measures should be taken to stop such practices 'as they are not only inconvenient to the public, but bring disgrace on the Government, which is reproached for permitting those to be in destitute situations who have suffered in the service of their country.'

24 C.M. Kauffmann, *Catalogue of Paintings in the Wellington Museum* (1982), no. 24, pp. 39–40.

25 Hubert von Herkomer, *The Herkomers* (1910), pp. 82–83, 107–11.

26 *Illustrated London News*, lxvi (1875), p. 446.

27 *Graphic*, xiv (1876), Christmas number, p. 30.

POSTSCRIPT: STRANGERS AND FOREIGNERS

1 Rowlands, *Holbein*, no. 47, pp. 139–40.

2 J. Douglas Stewart, *Sir Godfrey Kneller and the English Baroque Portrait* (Oxford, 1983), nos 26, 536, pp. 90, 121.

3 Penny, *Reynolds*, no. 100, pp. 271–72. See also Christie's sale of Tribal Art, 23 June 1986, lots 137–42, material relating to Omai consigned for sale by a descendant of Tobias Furneaux.

4 William LeFanu, *A Catalogue of the Portraits and other Paintings, Drawings and Sculpture in the Royal College of Surgeons of England* (1960), nos 241–52, pp. 81–84.

5 For one of the best accounts of the visits made to London by noble savages, freaks and exotica in general, see Altick, *The Shows of London*, pp. 24–49, 253–87 and *passim*.

6 Paulson, *Hogarth's Graphic Works*, i, no. 153, pp. 179–80. Paulson, *Hogarth: His Life, Art and Times*, i, p. 404. For an extensive survey of the impact of the Huguenots on London see Murdoch, *The Quiet Conquest*.

7 Penny, *Reynolds*, no. 77, pp. 245–46.

8 Smith, *Vagabondiana*, pp. 24–25.

9 For interpretations of Mulready's curious work depicting lascars, *Train up a Child . . .* (1841), see Heleniak, *Mulready*, pp. 98–103, no. 154, pp. 215–16 and Pointon, *Mulready*, pp. 121–26, no. 112, p. 129.

Notes on the Illustrations

Locations of pictures mentioned in the text are all in London unless otherwise stated.

ABBREVIATIONS

T = top, B = bottom, C = centre, L = left, R = right
B.M. Satires = F.G. Stephens and M.D. George, *British Museum Catalogue of Political and Personal Satires* (1870–1954).

p. 8 Lithograph. 245 × 463 mm. The Museum of London. *London As It Is*. (Not in Museum edition)

p. 10 Wood engraving. 235 × 189 mm. Jerrold, *London: A Pilgrimage*, p. 118.

p. 15 Pen and ink and wash with gilding. 425 × 6350 mm (in its entirety). The Worshipful Company of Fishmongers.

The design of the pageants themselves was for the most part traditional, but some inspiration might have come from the particularly grand set of etchings by Remignio Cantagallina after designs by Giulio Parigi for the wedding of Cosimo de'Medici to Maria Magdalena of Austria in Florence in 1608.

The Fishmongers' Pageant on Lord Mayor's Day 1616, Chrysanaleia, or the Golden Fishing, introd. John Gough Nichols (1859).

p. 17T Watercolour and bodycolour. 130 × 180 mm. Edinburgh University Library. MS La.III.283, f.90.

J.L. Nevinson, 'Sketches of 17th-Century London, A Student's Album', *Country Life*, cxlii, (1967), pp. 1256–57. J.L. Nevinson, 'Illustrations of Costume in the Alba Amicorum', *Archaeologia*, cvi (1975), pp. 167–76.

p. 17C Etching. 273 × 775 mm overall from two sheets. The Museum of London.
Adams, no. 3/9, pp. 6–7.

p. 17B Oil on canvas. 635 × 2007 mm. The Museum of London.

The principal personalities, the King and the Duke of Albemarle, are clearly recognizable. Stoop corrects Hollar in one respect, showing the Gentlemen Pensioners surrounding the King with pole-axes, as opposed to the partisans carried by the Yeomen of the Household: Hollar had depicted both sets of personal bodyguards to the King armed with partisans. He also correctly records the colours of the military plumes, armour and horse trappings, as specified by Sir Edward Walker, Garter Principal King at Arms, in his *Circumstantial Account of the Preparations . . .* (1660).

Eric Halfpenny, 'The Citie's Loyalty Display'd', *Guildhall Miscellany*, i, no. 10 (1959), pp. 19–35. Pennington, no. 570–75, pp. 91–92.

p. 18 Oil on canvas. 1359 × 2520 mm. Alte Pinakothek, Munich (Schloss Schleissheim).

Neither the buildings of the Tower nor the distribution and profile of the post-Fire City churches, including St Paul's, conform to the architectural facts, although Wren's classical Custom House, completed in 1686, is portrayed with considerable accuracy. The subject can be connected with the painting of almost identical size of the *Entry of the British Ambassador, the Earl of Manchester* into the *Ducal Palace, Venice* (City of Birmingham Museum and Art Gallery). The Earl's arrival took place in July 1707 and represented a further stage in the diplomatic negotiations to involve the Republic in the alliance against Louis XIV.

p. 19 Pen and ink and wash. 173 × 485 mm. The Museum of London.

The topography is comparatively accurate. For the Lord Mayor's pageant that year, the procession did not turn off at Cheapside to attend the traditional Guildhall banquet, but continued on down Poultry to the Grocers' Hall. The artist depicts the pageant at the end of its route before turning north to Grocers' Hall, with the barely completed Wren church of St Stephen Walbrook in the background.

Tessa Murdoch, 'The Lord Mayor's Procession of 1686: the Chariot of the Virgin Queen', *Transactions of the London and Middlesex Archaeological Society*, xxxiv (1983), pp. 207–12.

p. 20 Etching and engraving, 3rd state. 279 × 400 mm. The Museum of London.

Paulson, *Hogarth's Graphic Works*, i, no. 179, pp. 201–02.

p. 21 Engraving. 242 × 342 mm. Trustees of the British Museum.

Lord Mayor's Day in 1761 was particularly unruly for the visit paid by George III in the first year of his reign to dine with the new mayor, Sir Samuel Fludyer, was turned into a political occasion by the presence of William Pitt and Lord Temple, who hogged all the honours, and riots ensued.

B.M. Satires, no. 3819.

p. 22 Oil on canvas. 650 × 980 mm. Visitors of the Ashmolean Museum, Oxford.

The Pre-Raphaelites, no. 124, pp. 200–02.

p. 25 Engraving. 373 × 425 mm. Guildhall Library, Corporation of London.

The print was first published by William Warter, a Fleet Street stationer, but was pressed into further service with some minor changes for the Frost Fair of 1715.

Robert A. Beddard, 'The London Frost Fair of 1683–84', *Guildhall Miscellany*, iv (1972), pp. 70–72.

p. 27T Engraving. 438 × 540 mm. The Museum of London.

The precise relationship of this work to Hogarth's *Southwark Fair* is problematical, as neither work appears to relate specifically to a particular year. William Dicey, the publisher, certainly produced a plagiarized version of *Southwark Fair* entitled *The Humours and Diversions of Southwark Fair*, which reverses Hogarth's design and was doubtless intended to form a pair with the present engraving. But there is no stylistic and very little compositional similarity between the two works. It is tempting to speculate whether Hogarth, having seen this print, decided to produce his own vastly superior version of the theme; it might also explain why he chose Southwark instead of the more obvious Fair close to home.

p. 27C Bodycolour on vellum. 165 × 530 mm. Trustees of the British Museum.

The design was presumably made as the basis for a souvenir to be sold at the Fair, although no contemporary prints appear to have survived. The figure wearing a Garter ribbon is identified in the aquatint version, published by J.F. Setchel in 1824, as Sir Robert Walpole, the Prime Minister.

Rosenfeld, *London Fairs*, p. 26.

p. 27B Etching and engraving. 365 × 473 mm. The Museum of London.

Paulson, *Hogarth's Graphic Works*, i, no. 131, pp. 154–58.

p. 28T Pen and ink and watercolour. 460 × 695 mm. The Museum of London.

p. 28B Pen and ink and watercolour. 360 × 448 mm. Her Majesty the Queen.

The present work and colour plate VIII were exhibited at the Royal Academy in 1799 with the titles *Punch* and *The Camel*. Both drawings were purchased by the Prince of Wales from Colnaghi for £88s on 16 April 1800. They were engraved in reverse by Eckstein with aquatint by C.F. Stadler.

A.P. Oppé, *English Drawings, Stuart and Georgian Periods, in the Collection of His Majesty the King* (1950), nos 193–94, p. 45.

p. 30L Oil on canvas. 430 × 530 mm. The Museum of London.

The location has not been identified but the ambience is decidedly risqué (possibly the Strand), with a house of ill-repute on the left. Collet also painted a group of May Day characters dancing in front of Temple Bar. (*ex. coll.* Earl of Jersey).

p. 30R Oil on canvas. 375 × 456 mm. The Museum of London.

The scene is set in one of the streets constructed to the north of the New Road in the late eighteenth century and work can be dated not only from the costume of the figures but also from the shops, which the artist has described in some detail.

Hayes, *London Museum Paintings*, no. 26, pp. 54–55.

p. 31T Oil on canvas. 1016 × 2235 mm. Trustees of the Tate Gallery.

Frith, i, pp. 268–303. Connor and Lambourne, *Derby Day*, nos 8.1–8, pp. 71–78.

p. 31B Pen and ink. 184 × 241 mm (volume open). Trustees of the British Museum.

The journal also contains scenes of home life in the Doyle family, depictions of crowds – pressing to see the Queen, the Prince, the royal wedding cake and the illuminations on the night of the wedding – visits to the Royal Academy to admire Maclise's *Macbeth* and make fun of Landseer, to the National Gallery, the Opera, to concerts to hear Liszt and Eliason play Beethoven, and to the Tower.

Lawrence Binyon, *British Museum Catalogue of Drawings by British Artists*, ii (1900), no. 44, pp. 104–11.

p. 50T Pencil and watercolour with white

heightening. 192 × 237 mm. The Museum of London.

Illustrated London News, xii (1848), p. 350.

p. 50B Oil on canvas. 914 × 1397 mm. Trustees of the Tate Gallery.

The painting first achieved fame when exhibited by William Marchant at the Goupil Gallery in 1911 as part of a show devoted to the forgotten artist's work. It was in a poor state, having been neglected for years, and was much over-painted. Greaves's confused recollections of when he painted it add to the difficulties in dating.

Tom Pocock, *Chelsea Reach* (1970), pp. 46–47, 159, 169, 178.

p. 51 Pen and wash with white heightening. 436 × 338 mm. Visitors of the Ashmolean Museum, Oxford.

Doré and Jerrold viewed the race from the terrace of The Limes, Mortlake, so the present work (not used in Jerrold's book) was drawn from the artist's imagination. Certainly the bridge in the distance did not then exist.

Jerrold, *London: A Pilgrimage*, pp. 49–64.

p. 52T Oil on canvas. 978 × 926 mm. Leicestershire Museum and Art Gallery.

p. 52B Pen and ink and watercolour. 262 × 378 mm. Niedersächsisches Landesmuseum, Landesgalerie, Hanover.

F. Forster-Hahn, *Ramberg as a Caricaturist & Satirist* (Kestner Museum, Hanover exhibition catalogue, 1963) no. 32.

p. 53 Oil on canvas. 635 × 762 mm. Nottingham Castle Museum and City Art Gallery.

A number of studies survive, including a full pastel drawing and another less detailed version in oil (City of Birmingham Museum and Art Gallery). Sickert also produced an etching of the same composition at this date and two years later, a version based on the left side of the gallery.

Baron, *Sickert*, no. 230, pp. 340–41.

p. 55T Pen and ink and watercolour. 305 × 445 mm. Leeds City Art Galleries.

p. 55B Pen and wash. 202 × 307 mm. The Museum of London.

From the text of the engraved version of the work, it would appear that Boitard issued the print to coincide with the hanging of the unfortunate civilian Bosavern Penlez, who was caught up in the riots, and this drawing is probably an imaginary reconstruction of the event.

B.M. Satires, no. 3035.

p. 56 Watercolour with white heightening. 140 × 242 mm. Trustees of the Victoria and Albert Museum.

The artist executed a number of London street scenes published as lithographs with those of Henry Monnier in an album entitled *Voyage en Angleterre*, published by Firmin-Didot in Paris and Colnaghi in London in 1829.

p. 57L Pen and ink. 140 × 201 mm. Yale Center for British Art, Yale University Art Gallery, The Edwin Austin Abbey Memorial Collection.

p. 57R Pencil. 222 × 134 mm. Trustees of the British Museum.

p. 58 Oil on canvas. 254 × 355 mm. The Iveagh Bequest, Kenwood (English Heritage).

Houghton introduced a portrait of Charles Keene, an enthusiastic supporter of the Volunteers, escorting the artist's future wife, Susan.

Paul Hogarth, *Arthur Boyd Houghton, 1836–75* (Victoria and Albert Museum exhibition catalogue, 1975–76) no. 26, p. 21. Paul Hogarth, *Arthur Boyd Houghton* (1981), pp. 15–19.

p. 59 Oil on canvas. 1167 × 2564 mm. Royal Holloway College, University of London.

The character in the distance talking to the engine driver is, appropriately enough, Louis Victor Flatow, the flamboyant dealer who had commissioned the painting on the basis of being shown a trial sketch. He paid the artist £4,500 and an extra £750 for the exclusive rights of exhibition. Unlike *Ramsgate Sands* and *Derby Day*, therefore, the picture was not first exhibited at the Royal Academy but on its own at the Haymarket Gallery from April to September 1862, where Flatow was able to inveigle people into subscribing to the engraving.

Great Victorian Paintings (Arts Council of Great Britain exhibition catalogue, 1978), no. 15, pp. 36–37. Chapel, *Victorian Taste*, no. 23, pp. 87–92.

p. 61 Pen and ink and watercolour. 248 × 397 mm. Niedersächsiches Landesmuseum, Landesgalerie, Hanover.

Forster-Hahn, *Ramberg*, no. 31 as *Drury Lane*.

p. 62 Etching. 282 × 232 mm. The Museum of London.

Rues et Visages de Londres was the second in the artist's series of prints of street life in various capital cities. Paris was the first (1927) and there followed Berlin (1930) and New York (1932).

Guy Laborde, 'Chas. Laborde', *Nouvelles de l'Estampe*, nos 6–7 (Paris, 1970).

p. 63 Lithograph. 740 × 480 mm. Private Collection.

Celina Fox, *C.R.W. Nevinson. The Great War and After* (Maclean Gallery exhibition catalogue, 1980), no. 24.

p. 65 Etching. 184 × 256 mm. The Museum of London.

The second state, from volume 4 of the *Theatrum Europaeum* of J.P. Abelin and others was published in Frankfurt in 1643 with a German title and key. The present third state is from *Rerum Germanicorum ... libri 55*, of J.P. Lotichius, published in Frankfurt in 1650.

Pennington, no. 552, p. 87.

p. 67T Engraving. 460 × 503 mm. Guildhall Library, Corporation of London.

B.M. Satires, nos 1072, 1084, 1085. Sheila Williams, 'The Pope-Burning Processions of 1679, 1680 and 1681', *Journal of the Warburg and Courtauld Institutes*, xxi (1958), pp. 104–18. O.W. Furley, 'The Pope-Burning Processions of the Late Seventeenth Century', *History*, xliv (1959), pp. 16–23.

p. 67B Oil on canvas. 625 × 747 mm. The Museum of London.

Hayes, *London Museum Paintings*, no. 112, pp. 194–95.

p. 68T Etching and engraving. 257 × 400 mm. The Museum of London.

Paulson, *Hogarth's Graphic Works*, i, no. 178, pp. 200–01.

p. 68B Oil on canvas. 1003 × 1333 mm. Thomas Coram Foundation for Children.

The painting was offered as a prize in a lottery by Hogarth to those who subscribed to the engraving. When the issue closed, the artist gave the remaining 167 chances to the Foundling Hospital who drew the lucky number.

Paulson, *Hogarth's Graphic Works*, i, no. 237, pp. 277–80. Paulson, *Hogarth: Life, Art and Times*, ii, pp. 86–96. Nicolson, *Treasures of the Foundling Hospital*, no. 41, pp. 69–70.

p. 70 Engraving. 479 × 629 mm. The Museum of London.

The print was dedicated 'To the Gentlemen of the London Light Horse Volunteers, and Military Foot Association, This Memorial of their Patriotic Conduct, is Inscribed by their obliged Servants – John & Josiah Boydell.'

Webster, *Wheatley*, pp. 52–55, no. E69, p. 169.

p. 73 Oil on canvas. 1575 × 2286 mm. Private Collection.

The police resisted when the demonstrators entered, as shown in Hughes' work, using their truncheons in retaliation against the stone-throwing. The arrival of a detachment of life guards, pictured left, and a body of mounted police restored order; the crowds dispersed of their own accord, but not before the speeches had been made.

p. 74 Crayon. Oval 313 × 389 mm. Trustees of the Victoria & Albert Museum.

As a highly skilled exponent of mezzotint, Smith published a print after the drawing on 1 December 1781, no doubt cashing in on the fashion before it died.

Aileen Ribeiro, 'Mrs Cornelys and Carlisle House', *History Today*, xxviii, no. 1 (1978), pp. 47–52.

p. 76 Oil on canvas. 1640 × 1540 mm. The Prince de Ligne, Beloeil.

This work is a study made for one of two large-scale paintings commemorating the journey made to England by the Prince, which both hang at Beloeil. In the large-scale version the retinue is even longer, and the canvas is in two sections, the uppermost depicting the Banqueting House balcony full of people overlooking the main scene.

Gillis van Tilborch seems to have specialized in painting celebrations both of high and low life in the Netherlands. His most famous documented English work is the *Tich-borne Dole*, c. 1670 (Mrs John Loudon, Tichborne Park).

Félicien Leuridant, *Une Ambassade du Prince de Ligne en Angleterre 1660* (Brussels, 1923?). *The Diary of John Evelyn*, ed. E.S. de Beer (Oxford, 1955), iii, pp. 256–57. *Pepys's Diary*, i (1970), pp. 237, 247, 260.

p. 77 Oil on canvas. 1397 × 1222 mm. Her Majesty the Queen.

The painting can be dated between 1708, when Tillemans arrived in England, and 1714, when the Queen died, and on costume grounds c. 1708–10.

Millar, *Tudor, Stuart and Early Georgian Pictures in the Royal Collection*, no. 489, p. 167. Robert Raines, 'Peter Tillemans, Life and Work ...', *Walpole Society*, xlvii (1978–80), no. 77, p. 58.

p. 78 Oil on panel. 738 × 992 mm. The Marquis of Salisbury, Hatfield House.

Erna Auerbach and C. Kingsley Adams, *Paintings and Sculpture at Hatfield House* (1971), no. 49, pp. 53–55.

p. 79 Etching. 258 × 178 mm. The Museum of London.

The Four Seasons by Wenceslaus Hollar, introd. J.L. Nevinson, and topographical notes, Ann Saunders (Costume Society, 1979). Pennington, no. 607, p. 98.

p. 81 Oil on canvas. 1041 × 1384 mm. Her Majesty the Queen.

The painting can be dated on costume grounds to the mid 1740s although the presence of two Scotsmen in kilts suggests that the painting was executed prior to 1745. The work has recently been attributed by Elizabeth Einberg, through stylistic comparison with signed works, to Joseph Nicholls, best known for the engravings of City views produced after his paintings in the 1730s.

Millar, *Tudor, Stuart and Early Georgian Pictures in the Royal Collection*, no. 617, pp. 195–96.

p. 83T Pen and ink over pencil with wash. 397 × 302 mm. Trustees of the British Museum.

Binyon, iii, no. 5, p. 36. Raines, *Laroon*, no. 58, p. 133.

p. 83B Engraving. 235 × 325 mm. The Museum of London.

In its ridicule of the extremes of the pannier, it may be compared with Hogarth's *Taste in High Life*, commissioned in 1742 by Mary Edwards (1704–43) to retaliate against those who mocked her old-fashioned dress; after her death the work was engraved against Hogarth's express wish and was published in May 1746 (*B.M. Satires*, no. 2563).

B.M. Satires, no. 2774.

p. 85T Oil on canvas. 1195 × 1448 mm. The Frick Collection, New York.

Waterhouse, *Gainsborough*, p. 33, no. 987, p. 120.

p. 85C Pen and watercolour over pencil. 483 × 749 mm. Trustees of the Victoria & Albert Museum.

The work was engraved by R. Pollard with

aquatint by F. Jukes and published by J.R. Smith on 28 June 1785.

David E. Coke, 'Vauxhall Gardens', *Rococo*, pp. 74-98, no. F23, p. 91.

p. 85B Pen and ink and watercolour over pencil. 383 × 642 mm. Trustees of the Victoria & Albert Museum.

The work was engraved by F.D. Soiron and published by T. Gaugain in January 1793 and is indeed an English version of Philibert-Louis Debucourt's famous aquatint, *La Promenade Publique*, published in Paris in 1792.

Martin Hardie, *Water-Colour Painting in Britain* (1966), i, p. 181.

pp. 86–87 Pen and ink and wash. 162 × 515 mm. Trustees of the British Museum.

Ramberg first appears to have made drawings at the annual exhibition of the Royal Academy in 1784, for there are dated delineations of three walls of the great room at Somerset House (British Museum Department of Prints and Drawings, 1904 1-1-1/3). In contrast, the present work is a compositional drawing for the figures in the print executed by Pietro Antonio Martini (1739–97) and published by A.C. De Poggi on 1 July 1787. That the print was popular is suggested by the fact that another engraving was published by De Poggi, *Portraits of Their Majestys and the Royal Family Viewing the Exhibition at the Royal Academy, 1789*, but based on a Ramberg drawing of the Royal Family dated 1787 (Christie's, 9 July 1985, lot 50). Thus although there is less of a crush in the latter work, on dating and stylistic grounds it is difficult to support the notion that Ramberg's intention was more satiric in the former work, as George maintains. Simply, the royal presence was the selling point of both prints.

B.M. Satires, no. 7219. Sidney Hutchinson, *The History of the Royal Academy* (1968), pp. 66–67.

p. 87B Oil on canvas. 710 × 900 mm. Trustees of the Victoria & Albert Museum.

Several other versions of this painting exist; one sold at Sotheby's, 7 October 1985, lot 69.

p. 88L Pen and ink and wash. 227 × 347 mm. Trustees of the British Museum.

Gillray used Faro as the basis for a number of political prints and although there is no finished etching precisely corresponding to the present work, *Knave Wins All. Modern Hospitality* would appear to be the closest.

Binyon, ii, no. 7, p. 221.

p. 88R Pen and ink and watercolour. 308 × 435 mm. Metropolitan Museum of Art.

John Hayes, *Rowlandson's Watercolours* (1972), p. 55, no. 53.

p. 89 Pen and watercolour over pencil. 308 mm diameter. The Museum of London.

John Hayes, *A Catalogue of Watercolour Drawings by Thomas Rowlandson in the London Museum* (1960), no. 3, p. 11.

p. 90L Pen and ink and watercolour. 232 × 178 mm. Tom Girtin Collection.

p. 90R Woodcut and watercolour. 254 × 227mm. The Museum of London.

The image comes from the de luxe edition of *London Types*, an album of thirteen woodcuts by Nicholson with quatorzains by W.E. Henley, published by William Heinemann in 1898. Library and popular editions, reproduced by lithography, were published at the same time.

p. 91 Watercolour and bodycolour over pencil. 141 × 248 mm. Trustees of the Victoria & Albert Museum.

p. 92 Mechanical reproduction. 230 × 348 mm.

The work was published by Heinemann.

p. 93 Oil on canvas. 765 × 640 mm. Geffrye Museum.

p. 95 Pen and ink and watercolour. 355 × 239 mm. Guildhall Library, Corporation of London.

This drawing comes from a series of fifteen sheets, twelve of which are double-sided and depict figures of aldermen, each with his coat of arms and resting his left hand on a frame intended to receive the arms of his successors in that ward. Apart from small differences in clothing and colouring, they all resemble one another. Together with other manuscripts, now in the British Library and the Society of Antiquaries, the Guildhall Library drawings could once have belonged to Sir Thomas Holme, Clarenceux King of Arms, 1476-94. The name Simon Eyre was used by Thomas Dekker for the protagonist in *The Shoemaker's Holiday*, (1600), although the plot relates to the career of Sir John Spencer.

Catalogue of an Exhibition of Heraldry, College of Arms, 1951, no. 20, p. 17, Anthony Richard Wagner, *A Catalogue of the English Mediaeval Rolls of Arms* (Harleian Society Publications, c, Oxford, 1950), pp. 92–97.

p. 96 Oil on panel. 1219 × 610 mm. Lamport Hall Preservation Trust.

The painting provides the sitter with more of a context than most sixteenth-century merchants' portraits. However, his two surviving account books afford the rarest insight into the business world of Elizabethan London, with its complex trade and credit transactions.

John Isham Mercer and Merchant Adventurer, ed. and introd. G.D. Ramsay (Northamptonshire Record Society, 1962). Brian Dietz, 'Antwerp and London: The Structure and Balance of Trade in the 1560s', *Wealth and Power in Tudor England*, eds. E.W. Ives, R.J. Knecht and J.J. Scarisbrick (London, 1978), p. 191.

p. 97 Oil on panel. 654 × 508 mm. The Worshipful Company of Mercers.

Duckett was also a subscriber to Sir Martin Frobisher's north-west voyages and was one of the commissioners for winding up that enterprise.

T.S. Willan, *The Muscovy Merchants of 1555* (Manchester, 1953), pp. 92–93.

p. 98L Oil and tempera on panel. 375 × 333 mm. Staatliche Museum Preussischer Kulturbesitz Gemaldegalerie, West Berlin.

Rowlands, *Holbein*, pp. 81–85, no. 38, p. 137.

p. 98R Oil on panel. 1800 × 170 mm. Gresham Committee, Mercers' Hall. Strong, *National Portrait Gallery Tudor & Jacobean Portraits*, no. 352, p. 130.

p. 100L Etching, vi state. 85 × 60 mm. The Museum of London.

Pennington, pp. 295–97, nos 1893, p. 305.

p. 100R Pen and ink and watercolour. 314 × 208 mm. British Library Add. MS. 28330.f.30.

p. 101L Etching, iii state. 290 × 391 mm. The Museum of London.

Hollar depicted the inner court of the Royal Exchange on two occasions. The smaller print (Pennington, no. 907) contains a spattering of people taking a leisurely stroll and a man chasing some small boys with a stick. The present print was first issued in 1644 with a small cartouche above the title cartouche containing a Latin dedication by Hollar to the then Lord Mayor, Sir John Wollaston. In this state, it is replaced by the arms of England. Under the title are ten lines of Latin verse signed H. Pechamus which translated, clearly express a chauvinist intent.

Pennington, no. 1036, p. 182.

p. 101R Etching and engraving. 250 × 352 mm. The Museum of London.

B.M. Satires, no. 3653. Herbert H. Atherton, *Political Prints in the Age of Hogarth* (1974) pp. 46, 173. *Rococo*, C24, p. 49.

p. 102 Pen and ink and wash with touches of white. 396 × 533 mm. Trustees of the British Museum.

The presence of ladies in the background and two sightseers in the left foreground, peering up at the statues of monarchs which had been donated by the livery companies, provides some corroborative evidence that the Royal Exchange was by this date on the decline as a business centre and had become more of a tourist attraction. The work was engraved by Bartolozzi and published by Chapman in 1788.

Binyon, i, no. 1, p. 207.

p. 103 Mezzotint. 507 × 355 mm. Guildhall Library, Corporation of London.

Although Fielder (spelt Feilder consistently in the Grocers' Company records) was an assiduous attender of meetings, there is no evidence in the Grocers' Company records as to how he served the Company from, presumably, around 1734. He was neither Clerk nor Beadle. As an artist who began life in a counting house in the City and was based in Spitalfields, Chamberlin was possibly prepared to look more favourably on such a commission than other artists. The painting has not been traced.

p. 104 Pen and ink on vellum. 489 × 356 mm. The Bank of England.

The scroll below, issuing on either side of the arms of the City of London, is inscribed, 'Merchant Adventurors in the famous City of London Trading in all parts of the World'.

Down each side of the central design are the arms of the Directors of the Bank, with the arms of Sir John Houblon, Governor, and Michael Godfrey, Deputy Governor, singly at the head.

An Historical Catalogue of Engravings, Drawings and Paintings in the Bank of England (1928), no. 297, p. 67.

p. 105L Pen and ink and watercolour. 413 × 600 mm. The Bank of England.

A related sketch of Stock Jobbers, executed on the back of an envelope, is in the collection of the Museum of London.

Bank of England Historical Catalogue, no. 164, p. 32. Hayes, *Thomas Rowlandson in the London Museum*, no. 13, p. 15.

p. 105R Pen and ink and watercolour. 311 × 248 mm. Guildhall Art Gallery, Corporation of London.

p. 106 Watercolour over pencil. 470 × 435 mm. Trustees of the Victoria & Albert Museum.

On the table there are a number of finished pieces decorated with well-known patterns, including a marbled plate commemorating the death of Nelson (an example was acquired by the Victoria and Albert Museum in 1984). The standing figure (who is possibly the artist) holds a dividing plate for the easier transfer and centering of patterns. The curious headgear worn by the figure immediately behind him might have been an ad hoc method of limiting the double reflection from the window and his glasses. The purpose served by the geometric pattern on the wall remains a mystery; perhaps it represents some form of professional calculation like the figures chalked on the wall of Hill's carpenter's shop (p. 123T).

Geoffrey A. Godden, *British Pottery and Porcelain 1780–1850* (1963), pp. 73–74.

p. 108L Pen and ink. 75 × 183 mm. Guildhall Records Office, Corporation of London.

After the book had appeared in printed form, the editions of 1600–71 by John Powell, clerk of the markets to the court of James I, included a series of small woodcuts with appropriate mottoes heading the tables and depicted stages in the making of bread. The increasing complexity of the market mechanism resulted in constant wrangles by the eighteenth century and the Assize was abolished in London in 1822.

p. 108R Pen and ink. Large folio 425 × 280 mm. Guildhall Library, Corporation of London.

C.R.H. Cooper, 'The Archives of the City of London Livery Companies and Related Organisations', *Archives*, xvi (1984), pp. 323–53.

p. 111 Oil on canvas. 711 × 965 mm. The Worshipful Company of Clockmakers.

The Vulliamy family of clock- and watchmakers was founded by Justin Vulliamy who came to London from Switzerland in 1704 to study the trade under Benjamin Grey; he inherited his master's business at 68 Pall Mall by the time-honoured method of marrying his daughter and in 1742 first obtained the royal warrant which was to be retained by the family for 112 years.

Sophie in London 1786, trans. and introd. Clare Williams (1933), pp. 100–02.

p. 113T Red chalk. 235 × 304 mm. Trustees of the British Museum.

The paper is either French or Dutch, so the drawing cannot be identified as an English subject with certainty.

Paul Hulton, *Watteau Drawings in the British Museum* (British Museum exhibition catalogue, 1980) no. 54, p. 30. *Rococo*, no. C1, p. 42.

p. 113B Oil on canvas. 812 × 134 mm. National Portrait Gallery.

Brian Allen, 'Carl Marcus Tuscher: A German Artist in London', *Apollo*, cxxii (1985), pp. 32–35. *Handel. A Celebration of his Life and Times 1685–1759* (National Portrait Gallery exhibition catalogue, 1985), ed. Jacob Simon, no. 162, pp. 187–88.

p. 114L Woodcut. 155 × 95 mm. The Worshipful Company of Goldsmiths.

A schematic engraving by A. and I. Kirk of a goldsmith's workshop in 1741 showing nineteen craftsmen using different tools and skills is in the Ashmolean Museum, Oxford; it was evidently made during the brothers' apprenticeship.

Susan Hare, *Touching Gold & Silver. 500 Years of Hallmarks* (Goldsmiths' Hall exhibition catalogue, 1978) no. G, p. 127.

London Silver 1680 to 1780 (Museum of London exhibition catalogue, 1982–83) pp. 48–49.

p. 114R Engraving. 253 × 208 mm. Senate House Library, University of London.

The series of about twenty, devoted to different trades, commenced in the first number and petered out in 1751. Thereafter, the work was more strictly scientific, architectural and botanical in its bias. Charles Grignion sometimes signed the engraved portraits which appeared in the publication. Whoever the artists were, they certainly had pride in their work for the description appended to the *Art of Etching and Engraving* (vol. iii, 1748, p. 180) emphasizes its status.

Universal Magazine, ii (1848), p. 8.

p. 115 Engraving. 250 × 592 mm. City of Westminster Libraries.

The German book collector and connoisseur, Zacharias Conrad von Uffenbach visited Godfrey's laboratory in 1710: 'we bought from him a supply of English salt, etc. and saw his incomparably handsome laboratorium, which is both neatly and lavishly appointed, being also provided with all manner of curious stoves.'

Survey of London vol xxxvi. The Parish of St Paul Covent Garden (1970), pp. 215–18. *London in 1710 from the Travels of Zacharias Conrad von Uffenbach* trans. and ed. W.H. Quarrell and Margaret Mare (1934), pp. 148–49.

p. 117T Pen and ink and wash over black chalk or lead. 275 × 353 mm. Trustees of the British Museum.

Campbell's London Tradesman, published the same year as *Industry and Idleness*, ended with advice on 'how to behave during his Apprenticeship, in order to acquire his Business, obtain the Good-Will of his Master, and avoid the many Temptations to which Youth are liable in this great City.'

Oppé, *Hogarth's Drawings*, p. 41. Paulson, *Hogarth's Graphic Works*, no. 168, pp. 194–95. *Rococo*, no. N1, p. 223.

p. 117B Pencil, red chalk, pen and ink wash. 207 × 296 mm. Her Majesty the Queen.

Although Quirijn van Brekelenkam made tailors' shops something of a speciality in his art and, indeed, they were frequently the subject of seventeenth-century Dutch paintings, Boitard's drawing has more in common with the illustrations to the *Universal Magazine* trade series and the finest trade cards that were being produced around this time. The work was engraved in reverse by George Bickham Junior (who probably drew the border) and published with the title *The Merchant Taylors* in 1749.

Oppé, *English Drawings in the Royal Collection*, no. 71, p. 28. *Rococo*, no. N2, p. 223.

p. 119 Oil on canvas. 1594 × 1352 mm. Trustees of the Victoria & Albert Museum.

Richard Kingzett, 'A Catalogue of Works by Samuel Scott', *Walpole Society*, xlviii (1980–82), nos. G1, G2, pp. 41–42.

p. 120L Watercolour and bodycolour. 381 × 555 mm. National Maritime Museum.

To the right of the clamp on the bench, there is a spherical case shot or shrapnel shell (named after its inventor General Shrapnell of the Royal Artillery) the shell of which was made of thin iron and fixed to a wooden base. The description is derived from the notes on artillery made by a number of cadets at the Royal Military Academy in the early nineteenth century.

p. 120R Watercolour and bodycolour. 557 × 759 mm. National Maritime Museum.

p. 121L Watercolour and pencil. 281 × 396 mm. Private Collection.

This drawing comes from a collection of fifty, which are probably the work of Pieter Verbruggen who was with his father Jan joint master of the Royal Brass Foundry at Woolwich between 1770 and 1781 and sole master after his father's death in 1781 until he himself died in 1786. The young Verbruggen was a pupil and friend of Paul Sandby, who was based nearby as drawing master at the Royal Military Academy and the drawings have a strong stylish connection with Sandby's work, as well as that of another pupil Michael Angelo Rooker.

Melvin H. Jackson and Charles de Beer, *Eighteenth Century Gunfounding*, (Newton Abbot, 1973), no. 9, p. 88.

p. 121R Watercolour and pencil. 301 × 413 mm. Private Collection.

Jackson and de Beer, no. 39, p. 126.

p. 122 Pencil, pen and ink and watercolour. 376 × 302 mm. Trustees of the British Museum.

Sybil Rosenfeld, 'A Georgian Scene-Painter at Work', *British Museum Quarterly*, xxxiv (1969), nos. 1–2, pp. 33–36. Sybil Rosenfeld, *Georgian Scenery Painters and Scene Painting* (Cambridge, 1981), pp. 10–11. Patrick Conner, *Michael Angelo Rooker 1746–1801* (1984), pp. 133–37.

p. 123T Oil on canvas. 470 × 689 mm. Trustees of the Tate Gallery.

The painting was probably that exhibited at the Royal Academy in 1813. Hill also exhibited *A Carpenter's Yard, Enfield* in 1820.

Jack Warans, 'Inside Two "Carpenters' Shops"', *Tate Gallery Illustrated Biennial Report 1982–84*, pp. 22–25. *The Tate Gallery Illustrated Catalogue of Acquisitions 1982–84*, pp. 30–32.

p. 123B Oil on panel. 520 × 710 mm. Sotheby's, 22 July 1986, lot 138.

p. 124 Etching. 192 × 112 mm. The Museum of London.

Smith, *The Cries of London*, pl. XVII, pp. 55–56.

p. 125 Pencil, pen and ink and watercolour. 170 × 251 mm. Museum of London.

A pencil inscription on the back of this work identifies the location as D'Almaine's Pianoforte Manufactory, which was in Upper Chilton Street. There is another drawing of the exterior by Shepherd which shows that it was organized round a courtyard; the wood was stored on the ground level and there were two factory floors above, with large workshop windows on two sides. The presence of two figures who appear to be the owners in both works and Shepherd's more usual delineations of 'Metropolitan Improvements' suggest that the factory was custom-built and something of a show place for the time.

p. 126 Oil on panel. 508 × 400 mm. Trustees of the Victoria & Albert Museum.

The housekeeper's barely subordinate role may perhaps be attributed to the fact that Sheepshanks was a bachelor but wished his housekeeper to appear, by way of light female relief; he was renowned for his liberality.

Heleniak, *Mulready*, pp. 173–74, no. 133, p. 210. Pointon, *Mulready*, no. 67, p. 94.

p. 128 Red chalk over pencil. 260 × 200 mm. Trustees of the British Museum.

The inscription on the first flyleaf, 'Charles Beale/3rd Book 1680', is in the artist's hand, so the drawings were made when he was twenty years of age. Their subject matter and the exceptional quality of the draughtsmanship suggest Dutch rather than English precedents, possibly the outcome of Beale having access to Lely's studio.

Elizabeth Walsh, 'Charles Beale 3rd Book. 1680', *Connoisseur*, cxlix (1962), pp. 248–52. Elizabeth Walsh and Richard Jeffree, *The Excellent Mrs Mary Beale* (Geffrye Museum exhibition catalogue, 1975), no. 61, pp. 54–55.

p. 129 Bodycolour. 147 × 220 mm. Trustees of the British Museum.

The subject relates to an engraving, in which the composition is reversed, the first state of which is lettered, 'Paris Cher [sic for Chez] Monsi(eur) Trolaria' and dates from the early eighteenth century.

Manuscript catalogue for volume II of *British Museum Catalogue of British Drawings*.

p. 130 Oil on canvas. 990 × 1035 mm. Trustees of the Victoria & Albert Museum.

The work was described in the *Ambulator* (1774) as 'The Wapping Landlady and the Tars who are just come ashore'. From the engraving made after the work by Benoist and published by Thomas Bowles on 4 April 1743, it seems that the setting was a Thames-side tavern. The principal focus of attention was a sailor dancing a jig or hornpipe in the centre, to the music of a violin player seated left. Another sailor stood watching also on the left, and behind him two maidservants, one pouring a drink for the other at the bar.

Laurence Gowing, 'Hogarth, Hayman and the Vauxhall Decorations', *Burlington Magazine*, xcv (1953), pp. 4–19. *Francis Hayman R.A.* (The Iveagh Bequest, Kenwood exhibition catalogue, 1960), no. 24, p. 21.

p. 133L Oil on canvas. 762 × 630 mm. Herbert Art Gallery, Coventry.

When the work was exhibited at the Society of Artists in 1769, it proved immensely popular; Walpole thought it 'admirable' and stated that it was taken from 'Nature'. It was engraved in mezzotint by Richard Earlom and published in 1774; a colour version was issued in 1780.

Webster, *Zoffany*, no. 45, p. 44.

p. 133R Oil on canvas. 705 × 622 mm. Holburne of Menstrie Museum, Bath.

Rococo, no. 33, p. 233.

p. 134T Pen and ink and watercolour. 184 × 109 mm. Yale Center for British Art, Paul Mellon Collection.

p. 134B Pen and Indian ink wash. 463 × 318 mm. City of Birmingham Museum and Art Gallery.

Lacking the carefully worked-out detail of a Pre-Raphaelite compositional drawing, the study was obviously executed on the spot at the St James's exhibiting society established in opposition to the Royal Academy.

Deborah Cherry, 'The Hogarth Club: 1858–61', *Burlington Magazine*, cxxii (1980), pp. 237–44.

p. 135L Pen and watercolour over pencil. 235 × 353 mm. Yale Center for British Art, Paul Mellon Collection.

M. Dorothy George, 'The Early History of Registry Offices', *Economic Journal*, i Supplement (1929), iv, pp. 570–79. J. Jean Hecht, *The Domestic Servant Class in Eighteenth-Century England* (1956), pp. 26–33.

p. 135R Watercolour over pencil. 216 × 310 mm. Yale Center for British Art, Paul Mellon Collection.

p. 136TL Wood engraving. 132 × 180 mm.

Punch xxv (1854) p. 44.

p. 136TR Pen and ink. 285 × 189 mm. Visitors of the Ashmolean Museum, Oxford.

Mrs Mounter was Gilman's landlady at 47 Maple Street, off Tottenham Court Road, from 1914 to 1917. She is the subject of five paintings and four known drawings by the artist.

Harold Gilman 1876–1919 (Arts Council of Great Britain exhibition catalogue 1981/82), no. 68, p. 76.

p. 136BL Charcoal. 377 × 380 mm. The Museum of London

Belcher Rediscovered, introd. Richard Adams (Langton Gallery exhibition catalogue, 1986), no. 60.

p. 137L Pencil and watercolour. 385 × 280 mm. National Museum of Wales.

Paul Hills, *David Jones* (Tate Gallery exhibition catalogue, 1981), no. 34, p. 82.

p. 137R Etching. 259 × 187 mm.

Jules Vallès, *La Rue à Londres* (Paris, 1884), p. 100.

p. 138 Pencil, pen and ink and watercolour. 214 × 371 mm. Trustees of the British Museum.

p. 141 Oil on canvas. 1006 × 1251 mm. The Bank of England.

Bank of England Historical Catalogue, no. 363, p. 76.

p. 142 Oil on canvas. 760 × 1245 mm. The Marquis of Tavistock and the Trustees of the Bedford Estates.

There are two other versions of the composition, one dated 1737 in the Tate Gallery and the other in the Guildhall Art Gallery, but with different figures.

p. 143 Oil on canvas. 1337 × 1895 mm. The Museum of London.

Hayes, *London Museum Paintings*, no. 30, p. 60. *Survey of London*, xxxvi, p. 132.

p. 144T Oil on canvas. 553 × 1075 mm. The Museum of London.

The Berlin-born artist chose the market subject to form a pair with a painting of Cremorne Gardens in the early evening, also in the Museum of London. The theme and the curved top to the canvas recall the wood engraved illustrations by William M'Connell for George Augustus Sala, *Twice Round the Clock* (first published in a weekly magazine, *The Welcome Guest* in 1858 and in book form the following year).

Hayes, *London Museum Paintings*, no. 67, pp. 126–27.

p. 144B Oil on canvas. 850 × 1360 mm. The Marquis of Tavistock and the Trustees of the Bedford Estates.

From the technique it would appear that John Frederick Lewis (1805–76) helped his father to complete the painting.

Survey of London, xxxvi, p. 136.

p. 146 Etching and drypoint, iii state. 172 × 205 mm. The Museum of London.

Anderson's other London market scenes include *Smithfield Market* (1911) and *Fruit Porters, Lower Thames Street* (1912), but he is probably best known today for the notable series of line engravings he executed in the 1930s, illustrating rural crafts which were in danger of dying out.

Malcolm C. Salaman, 'Etchings and Engravings of Stanley Anderson, R.E.', *Studio*, xci (1926), pp. 262–63. Martin Hardie, 'The Etchings and Engravings of Stanley Anderson', *Print Collector's Quarterly*, xx (1933), no. 91, p. 245.

p. 147TL Pen and ink and watercolour. 152 × 222 mm. Trustees of the British Museum.

Binyon, iii, no. 43. p. 253.

147TR Oil on canvas. 635 × 527 mm. Trustees of the National Gallery.

Lawrence Gowing *Hogarth* (Tate Gallery exhibition catalogue, 1971–72), no. 129, p. 53. Paulson, *Hogarth. His Life, Art, and Times*, ii, pp. 246–47.

p. 147B Engraving. 470 × 580 mm. The Museum of London.

Subtitled 'The Wonders of the Deep often attempted and never perform'd but by Arnold Vanhaecken 1736', this work pertains to a set of prints representing fish. The verse below the print refers to the Roman origins of Billingsgate and the present low level of the language.

B.M. Satires, no. 2284. 'Vertue III', *Walpole Society*, xxii, p. 71.

p. 148 Etching and drypoint. 275 × 355 mm. The Museum of London.

This print was etched directly from nature for inclusion in a book on the artist published by E. F. d'Alignion and Paul Turpin.

William Gaunt, *The Etchings of Frank Brangwyn R.A.* (1926), pl. 268.

p. 150 Pen and ink and watercolour. 280 × 436 mm. Guildhall Library, Corporation of London.

The work was engraved by Bluck and published by Ackermann on 1 January 1811.

p. 151L Oil on canvas. 785 × 1220 mm. Trustees of the Tate Gallery.

The work was probably first exhibited in the Third Camden Town Group exhibition at the Carfax Gallery in 1912 with the title *The Horse Mart*; it was shown in the same gallery the following year and at Brighton in 1913–14. Its title was changed to *A Sale at the Barbican* when it was exhibited with the Cumberland Market Group in 1915.

Wendy Baron, *The Camden Town Group* (1979), pp. 300–01, 363.

p. 151R Etching with aquatint. 493 × 605 mm. The Museum of London.

No painting of the subject has been traced.

p. 152T Oil on canvas. 965 × 1180 mm. Private Collection.

p. 152B Oil on canvas. 706 × 906 mm. The Museum of London.

Hayes, *London Museum Paintings*, no. 52, pp. 100–02.

p. 153L Oil on canvas. 1006 × 758 mm. Sheffield City Art Galleries.

Anna Robins, 'Feuds and Factions at the New English Art Club', *The New English Art Club Centenary Exhibition* (Christie's exhibition catalogue, 1986), p. 12, no. 84, p. 84.

p. 153TR Lithograph, ii state (unique). 378 × 562 mm. The Museum of London.

Roberto Sanesi, *The Graphic Work of Ceri Richards* (Milan, 1973), nos 21–24, pp. 54–59.

p. 153CR Lithograph. 460 × 615 mm. The Museum of London.

The series covered Billingsgate, Borough Market, Covent Garden vegetable and flower markets, Leadenhall Market and Smithfield and was published by the Curwen Press.

p. 153BR Pencil and watercolour squared for transfer. 343 × 470 mm. Private Collection.

The present work is a study for the large painting now in the Harris Art Gallery, Preston.

William Roberts, A.R.A., A Retrospective Exhibition (Arts Council catalogue, 1965), no. 102. *William Roberts, R.A.*, (Parkin Gallery exhibition catalogue, 1976), no. 59; (Maclean Gallery exhibition catalogue, 1980) no. 26.

p. 154 Oil on canvas. 1435 × 1181 mm. Trustees of the Tate Gallery.

Wood, *Victorian Panorama*, p. 150.

p. 156T Watercolour and bodycolour. 130 × 380 mm. Edinburgh University Library. MS La. III.283, f.471ᵛ.

Compare with Hogenberg's print after Hoefnagel of *Nonsuch* (Hind, i, no. 8, p. 72) in which the water-carrier is shown as a young boy standing beside a conduit fountain. The process of piping water to all London houses took time and money: even the Lauron *Cries*, first published in the 1680s, included a water-bearer carrying his load in two tubs suspended from a yoke, like a milkmaid, and Mayhew records that they were still at work in Highgate and Hampstead in the middle of the nineteenth century.

Nevinson, 'Illustrations of Costume in the *Alba Amicorum*', pp. 171–72. Nevinson, 'The Dress of the Citizens of London 1540–1640', p. 277.

p. 156B Engraving. 254 × 182 mm. Trustees of the British Museum.

Corbett and Norton, iii, no. 80, p. 366. Wilson, 'Street Cries', no. 1, p. 108. Beall, no. E2, p. 117.

p. 157 Engravings. Each approx. 100 × 80 mm. Trustees of the British Museum.

There are small variations in the letters used in the two states. Twenty-two of the silver counters based on the designs are now in the Museum of London and two in the Department of Coins and Medals in the British Museum.

Corbett and Norton, iii, no. 83, p. 368. Wilson, 'Street Cries', no. 3, pp. 108–09. Beall, no. E5, pp. 220–21. *Catalogue of the Pepys Library*, iii, i, nos. 424–25, p. 31.

p. 158 Pen and grey wash over pencil. 330 × 280 mm. The Duke of Marlborough.

Individual studies for some of the figures are known to exist independently; Sotheby's sold a pair, 10 July 1986, lot 43.

Raines, *Laroon*, pp. 13–39, 95–99. *Catalogue of the Pepys Library*, iii, i, nos 426–39, p. 34. Beall, no. E10, pp. 126–30. Sean Shesgreen, 'The Editions, Imitations and the Influence of Marcellus Lauron's Cryes of the City of London', *Studies in Bibliography*, xxxv (1982), pp. 258–71.

p. 159 Oil on canvas. 1250 × 990 mm. The Museum of London.

The painting contains the only known post-Fire depiction of the Little Conduit, where it was intended to construct a magnificent obelisk upon a pedestal, but owing mainly to lack of funds, it was never completed. The view is taken from the west end of Cheapside, with St Mary-le-Bow prominent in the background.

p. 160L Pen and ink and watercolour. 192 × 145 mm. The Museum of London.

p. 160R Pen and ink and watercolour. 201 × 151 mm. The Museum of London.

Beall, no. E15, pp. 134–35.

p. 162L Oil on canvas. 355 × 280 mm. Private Collection.

In the engraved version, Plate 12 of the series, executed by Vendramini and published by Colnaghi on 1 May 1796, the woman on the right was omitted and the identifiable background of St Martin-in-the-Fields replaced by a receding colonnade.

Webster, *Wheatley*, p. 84, no. E123, pp. 182–82. Beall, no. E21, pp. 137–38.

p. 162R Stipple engraving, ii state. 416 × 327 mm. The Museum of London.

Webster, *Wheatley*, no. E98 ii, p. 174.

p. 163L Pen and watercolour over pencil. 280 × 204 mm. The Museum of London.

The drawing is a preparatory study for the third in the series of Cries of London published by Ackermann in 1799.

Hayes, *Thomas Rowlandson in the London Museum*, no. 10, p. 14.

p. 163R Etching. 115 × 68 mm. The Museum of London.

Adams, no. 126, pp. 290–94. Beall, no. E.44, pp. 166–68.

p. 164 Pen and ink and watercolour. 100 × 70 mm. Trustees of the Victoria & Albert Museum.

The series was probably commissioned by Richard Phillips, a City bookseller who achieved the rare distinction of being imprisoned for selling Paine's *The Rights of Man* in 1797 and being elected Sheriff of the City of London ten years later. His publication of *Modern London* in 1804 is more in keeping with the latter, established part of his career. The work was an outsize guide book embellished with some fifty-four engravings, thirty-one of which were after Craig's Cries.

Adams, no. 89, pp. 192–94. Beall, no. E26, pp. 144–46.

p. 165 Oil on canvas. 355 × 455 mm. Stiftung Oskar Reinhardt, Winterthur.

A second, later version of this work is in a private collection in Geneva.

Franz Zelger, *Schweizer Maler des 18 und 19 Jahrunderts* (Stiftung Oskar Reinhardt, Winterthur exhibition catalogue, 1977), no. 9, pp. 31–32. C.F. Hardy, 'J.L. Agasse, The Life and Work of Jacques Laurent Agasse Part II', *Connoisseur*, xlvii (1917), p. 9.

p. 166T Etching. 191 × 114 mm. The Museum of London.

Cries of London, pp. 48–49, 65–66. Beall, no. E49, pp. 170–72.

p. 166B Wood engraving after a daguerreotype. 187 × 118 mm. The Museum of London.

At least some of Beard's daguerreotypes were transferred to the woodblock by H.G. Hine, who added the backgrounds, and engraved by Edward Whymper. Mayhew, *London Labour and the London Poor* (1861–62), vol. i, 345, 365–70. H. and A. Gernsheim, *The History of Photography* (1955), pp. 90–112, 187, 243, 340.

p. 167TL Oil on canvas. 600 × 897 mm. The Museum of London.

From the costume and style of painting, it was executed around 1855, a false date being added later by the artist, possibly to enable him to qualify for an exhibition.

Hayes, *London Museum Paintings*, no. 58, p. 112.

p. 167TR Oil on canvas. 813 × 663 mm. Trustees of the Tate Gallery.

The *Pall Mall Gazette* commented on the work in its review of the Third Camden Town Group exhibition held at the Carfax Gallery in 1912, where it was first shown: '"Piccadilly Circus", both in its crude tones and jumbled composition, happily suggests the noise and confusion of that busy thoroughfare.'

Baron, *The Camden Town Group*, no. 124, p. 311.

p. 167BR Wood engraving. 127 × 199 mm. *Punch*, lviii (1870), Almanack.

p. 168 Pencil. 231 × 138 mm. Trustees of the British Museum.

p. 170T Watercolour. 130 × 380 mm. Edinburgh University Library. MS La. III. 283, f494ᵛ.

J.N. Nevinson, 'Illustrations of Costume in the *Alba Amicorum*', p. 172.

p. 170B Oil on panel. 559 × 559 mm. Yale Center for British Art, Paul Mellon Collection.

Gowing, *Hogarth*, nos. 9–10, p. 14.

p. 171 Oil on copper. 692 × 1073 mm. Private Collection.

The painting was one of two exhibited by Garrard at the Royal Academy in 1796, depicting aspects of Whitbread's business activities. The second, *The Lime-Works at Purfleet*, similarly underlined Whitbread's moral and social concerns, drawing attention to the workforce and the means by which a good employer's responsibilities towards them could be carried out.

Deuchar, *Whitbread*, no. 6, pp. 39–40.

p. 172 Pen and ink. 133 × 114 mm. Trustees of the British Museum.

Binyon, iv, no. 8 (a), p. 24.

p. 173T Watercolour over pencil, heightened with gouache. 635 × 997 mm. The Museum of London.

The identity of the artist is something of a mystery. The work may be dated to around 1810, on stylistic grounds, by costume and because, according to the London trade directories, Findlater and Ellis were only joined by Pugh in that year. The artist appears to have been trained in the topographical tradition of Thomas Malton. A small study of the lighters and Westminster Abbey by the same hand passed through Sotheby's, 14 May 1985, lot 128, bearing the signature P. de Wint.

p. 173B Watercolour. 260 × 369 mm. The Museum of London.

The artist lived in St Petersburg from 1784 to 1801 recording Russian life and although on his return to England he exhibited principally history paintings and landscapes, he seems to have executed a number of attractive genre watercolours of street traders and at least one other of labourers, a cart and team at a gravel pit (Victoria and Albert Museum).

p. 174L Pen and ink. 144 × 200 mm. Whitworth Art Gallery, University of Manchester.

p. 174R Oil on canvas. 711 × 1067 mm. Trustees of the Tate Gallery.

Kensington Gravel Pits was a small village in the district which is now known as Notting Hill at the junction of Bayswater Road and Kensington Church Street. The actual gravel pits were south of the village, adjoining Kensington Gardens.

Stephen Pasmore, 'When Gravel was Dug in Kensington', *Country Life*, clvii (1975), pp. 1335–36. Crouan, *Linnell*, no. 22, pp. 8–9.

p. 175 Watercolour over pencil. 394 × 384 mm. Trustees of the Victoria & Albert Museum.

p. 177T Watercolour over pencil with scratching-out. 250 × 443 mm. Trustees of the British Museum.

F.S. Schwarzbach, 'Scharf', p. 102. Lindsay Stainton, *British Landscape Watercolours 1600–1860* (British Museum exhibition catalogue, 1985), no. 148c, pp. 65–66.

p. 177C Pencil. 196 × 463 mm. Trustees of the British Museum.

p. 177B Pencil, pen and ink and watercolour. 236 × 379 mm. Trustees of the British Museum.

p. 178 Pen and wash over pencil with white heightening. 250 × 430 mm. National Railway Museum, York.

A Series of Lithographed Drawings on the London and Birmingham Railway was first published in four parts by Bourne himself jointly with Ackermann, starting in September 1838 and being completed in July 1839; each part cost a guinea. Soon afterwards the parts were combined in a single volume with the title shortened to *Drawings of the London and Birmingham Railway*. The work was favourably received by the press and a bound volume of the subscription list reveals

a number of illustrious purchasers.

Francis G. Klingender, *Art and the Industrial Revolution*, ed. and revised by Arthur Elton (1968), p. 155, fig. 84. *The Navvies Build*, (Coach House Gallery, Coalbrookdale, Ironbridge Gorge Museum Trust exhibition catalogue, 1980), nos. 41–43.

p. 179 Pencil, pen and ink and grey wash. 270 × 326 mm. Ironbridge Gorge Museum: Elton Collection.

Klingender, p. 155, fig. 82. *The Navvies Build* no. 20. *Train Spotting Images of the Railway in Art* (Nottingham Castle Museum, exhibition catalogue, 1985), pp. 13–14, no. 13.

p. 180 Oil on canvas, arched top. 684 × 990 mm. Birmingham Museum and Art Gallery.

E.D.H. Johnson, 'The Making of Ford Madox Brown's Work', *Victorian Artists and The City*, pp. 142–51. *The Pre-Raphaelites*, no. 88, pp. 163–65.

p. 181 Pastel. 571 × 812 mm. The Mitchell Wolfson Jr College of Documentary and Propaganda Arts, Miami-Dade Community College, Miami, Florida.

The frieze of decorative panels was removed from its setting at Lloyd's Register in 1973 and destroyed.

Herbert Furst, *The Decorative Art of Frank Brangwyn* (Oxford, 1924), pp. 90–94. Vincent Galloway, *The Oil and Mural Paintings of Sir Frank Brangwyn* (Leigh on Sea, 1962), p. 71. The Fine Art Society catalogue, spring 1985, no. 5. *Styles of Empire Great Britain 1877–1947* (The Mitchell Wolfson Jr Collection of Decorative and Propaganda Arts, Miami-Dade Community College, Miami, Florida exhibition catalogue, 1985), no. 71, p. 24.

p. 182 Etching. 636 × 757 mm. The Museum of London.

Gaunt, *Brangwyn Etchings*, no. 38, p. 1904.

p. 183L Watercolour and gouache. 539 × 798 mm. The Museum of London.

p. 183R Charcoal. 510 × 765 mm. The Museum of London.

p. 184 Watercolour and gouache. 360 × 260 mm. Private Collection.

The work probably comes from the set of finished drawings which were bound together for presentation to potential publishers of *London: A Pilgrimage*. Later the album was dismantled and most of the drawings distributed to friends.

Jerrold, *London: A Pilgrimage*, p. 145. Samuel F. Clapp, *Gustave Doré 1832–1883* (Hazlitt, Gooden & Fox exhibition catalogue, 1983), no. 18, pp. 43–44. *Gustave Doré 1832–1883* (Musées de Strasbourg exhibition catalogue, 1983), no. 74, p. 110.

p. 186 Black chalk and stump, heightened with white. 249 × 194 mm. Visitors of the Ashmolean Museum, Oxford.

According to Smith, the model 'was a lad, well known as a beggar by those who walked

St James's Street' (*Vagabondiana*, p. vi).

Hayes, *The Drawings of Thomas Gainsborough*, nos 827, 830–35 (the present sheet no. 832), pp. 301–02. David Blayney Brown, *Catalogue of the Collection of Drawings (in the Ashmolean Museum, Oxford), iv, Early English Drawings* (Oxford, 1982), no. 687, p. 314.

p. 187 Red chalk and pencil. 419 × 305 mm. Pierpont Morgan Library.

A.P. Oppé, *The Drawings of William Hogarth* (1948), no. 77, p. 48. Paulson, *Hogarth's Graphic Works*, i, no. 186, pp. 209–11. George, *London Life in the Eighteenth Century*, pp. 41–56.

p. 188 Etching. 189 × 120 mm. The Museum of London.

Smith, pp. 23–24. Simon Houfe, 'Poor Jack. The Mendicant Sailors of London', *Country Life* clxv (1979), pp. 1381–84.

p. 189L Lithograph, ii state. 315 × 374 mm. Trustees of the British Museum.

Géricault, Tout l'Oeuvre Gravé et Pièces en Rapport (Musée des Beaux Arts, Rouen exhibition catalogue, 1981–82), no. 27. Eitner *Géricault* pp. 213, 228–30.

p. 189R Lithograph, ii state. 314 × 233 mm. Trustees of the British Museum.

A pen and wash study in the Ecole Nationale Supérieure des Beaux-Arts, Paris suggests that the figure was based on direct observation, although the finished design recalls Chardin's *Blind Man of Quinze Vingts*, exhibited at the Salon in 1753 (Henry de Rothschild Collection, destroyed in World War II) and which Géricault might have known through engravings.

Géricault Oeuvre Gravé, no. 26. Philippe Grunchec, *Master Drawings by Géricault* (International Exhibitions Foundation exhibition catalogue, 1985–86), no. 94. Eitner, *Géricault*, pp. 208, 228–30.

p. 191 Wood engraving. 180 × 238 mm. *Pictorial Times*, viii (1846), p. 225.

p. 192 Wood engraving. 179 × 248 mm. *Punch*, v (1843), p. 23.

p. 193 Oil on canvas. 635 × 762 mm. The Forbes Magazine Collection, New York.

The present work is a replica with small variations of the painting first exhibited at the Royal Academy in 1844.

Christopher Forbes, *The Royal Academy (1837–1901) Revisited* (Forbes Magazine Collection exhibition catalogue, New York, 1975), no. 57, p. 124. Wood, *Victorian Panorama*, pp. 127–28.

p. 195L Wood engraving. 161 × 175 mm. *Poor Man's Guardian*, no. 3, 20 November 1847.

p. 195R Lithograph. 362 × 265 mm. Trustees of the Victoria & Albert Museum.

J. and E. de Goncourt, *Gavarni L'Homme et l'Oeuvre* (Paris, 1873), pp. 285–92. J. Armelhaut and E. Bocher, *L'Oeuvre de Gavarni* (Paris, 1873), nos 1239–56, pp. 331–34. H. Béraldi, *Graveurs du XIXe siècle*, vii, (Paris,

1888), nos 249–66, pp. 73–75. Paul André Lemoisne, *Gavarni* (Paris, 1928), ii, pp. 56–82.

p. 197 Oil on canvas. 1371 × 2437 mm. Royal Holloway College.

Chapel, *Victorian Taste*, no. 22, pp. 83–87.

p. 199 Wood engraving. 224 × 297 mm. *The Graphic*, vi (1872), p. 605.

p. 200 Pencil and wash. 408 × 322 mm. Rouen, Musée des Beaux-Arts.

The figure on the left might be Ings, who went to the scaffold wearing trousers and his old butcher's jacket – determined he said 'that Jack Ketch would have no coat of his'. The first of the men to be hooded was Thistlewood, the centre figure.

Portrait engravings were included in George Theodore Wilkinson, *An Authentic History of the Cato-Street Conspiracy* (1820). Eitner, *Géricault*, pp. 54–55.

p. 202 Pen and ink and bodycolour with gold leaf on vellum. 269 × 170 mm. Inner Temple Library Misc. MSS. 188.

Horner suggests that the style of illumination indicates a provenance of the Abbey of St Edmundsbury, Suffolk. From the Selby-Lowndes provenance, it was possibly once owned by William Fleetwood, Recorder of London at the time of Queen Elizabeth.

G.R. Horner, 'Observations on Four Illuminations . . .', *Archaeologia*, xxxix, part 2 (1865), pp. 357–72.

p. 203TL Oil on vellum. 711 × 711 mm. Trustees of the Goodwood Collections.

The work was engraved by Vertue, who dated it to around 1585.

p. 203TR Oil on canvas. 756 × 635 mm. National Portrait Gallery.

Walpole refers to the work as representing 'the time of Lord Chancellor Macclesfield', in which case he should be the middle figure beneath the royal arms, between Sir Philip Yorke (Solicitor General and afterwards Lord Chancellor Hardwicke) and Sir Thomas Pengelly (King's Prime Sergeant, afterwards Chief Baron of the Exchequer). A larger version of the painting, with many more figures, is in a private collection in the United States.

John Kerslake, *National Portrait Gallery Early Georgian Portraits* (1971) i, no. 798, p. 330.

p. 203B Engraving with pen and wash. 262 × 310 mm. The Museum of London. The work appears to be a preliminary design for the engraving *The First Day of Term* which, according to the letters, was drawn by Gravelot but 'invt. et sculp.' by C. Mosley and published in 1738/9. Certainly Mosley did not invent the figures which are by Gravelot. The character having to be restrained in the foreground from punching the gentleman paying court to the lady was not included in the published engraving. Both the engraved architectural setting and the figures were extensively reworked before a final proof

was pulled, illustrating Gravelot's known methods; this sheet suggests that a rough proof of the setting helped the artist gauge the correct perspective.

p. 204T Pen and wash. 180 × 110 mm. Trustees of the British Museum.

The drawing was engraved by J. Record and appeared in the *Tyburn Chronicle*, iv, p. 100. It comes from a group of sixteen for the *Tyburn Chronicle* and *Newgate Calendar* in the British Museum; others are in the Castle Museum, Nottingham and in private collections.

Binyon, iv, pp. 301–03. Hans Hammelmann and T.S.R. Boase, *Book Illustrators in Eighteenth-Century England* (1975), pp. 90, 94–95.

p. 204B Pen and ink and watercolour. 140 × 380 mm. Trustees of the British Museum.

The inscription is dated 3 June 1793.

Binyon, ii, p. 258.

p. 205T Oil on canvas. 470 × 368 mm. National Gallery of Scotland, Edinburgh.

The three-quarter-length portrait print Hogarth executed, in the manner of Thornhill's Jack Sheppard, emphasizes Malcolm's hardness of feature. The painting is more homely, her squat toughness contrasting with the robust refinement of the engraving, and on the table Hogarth places the rosary beads she would as an Irish Catholic have had with her for solace.

Paulson, *Hogarth's Graphic Works*, i, no. 129, pp. 152–53. Paulson, *Hogarth: His Life and Times*, i, pp. 307–12.

p. 205BL Etching. 250 × 190 mm. The Museum of London.

Among Dance's sitters, on his return from an eleven-year sojourn in Italy, was Sir Robert Kite, Lord Mayor of London in 1766–67 and, at the time he was portrayed by Dance, a member of the committee for rebuilding Newgate Gaol.

p. 205BR Pen and ink over pencil with wash and white heightening. 410 × 275 mm. The Museum of London.

A related drawing is in the National Portrait Gallery, though less certainly attributable to the artist. The present work forms the basis of a mezzotint by George White, which idealizes the sitter and further emphasizes his youth.

Kerslake, *Early Georgian Portraits*, i, no. 4313, pp. 248–49.

p. 206 Pencil and brown wash. 236 × 273 mm. Pepys Library, Magdalene College, Cambridge.

Catalogue of the Pepys Library, iii, i, no. 316C, p. 26.

p. 207 Wood engraving. 248 × 179 mm. *Punch*, xvii (1849), p. 117.

p. 208 Engraving. 135 × 70 mm. Guildhall Library, Corporation of London.

p. 209 Oil on canvas. 510 × 675 mm. National Portrait Gallery.

There is an oil sketch of the Committee taking evidence (Fitzwilliam Museum, Cambridge) in a private chamber where the attention is focused on a dramatic confrontation between Bambridge and a standing prisoner. The painting together with a version of the *Beggar's Opera* were purchased by Hogarth's friend, John Huggins, who might have enjoyed the ironic satisfaction of owning a painting of his previous place of employment, in which all the blame for cruelty and mismanagement was firmly laid at the feet of his successor.

Kerslake, *Early Georgian Portraits*, i, no. 926, pp. 330–38. Paulson, *Hogarth: His Life, Art and Times*, i, pp. 196–202.

p. 210L Watercolour and gouache. 317 × 232 mm. The Museum of London.

p. 210R Oil on canvas. 174 × 181 mm. Syndics of the Fitzwilliam Museum, Cambridge.

Paulson, *Hogarth's Graphic Works*, i, no. 205, pp. 238–39. Paulson, *Hogarth: His Life, Art and Times*, ii, pp. 286–91.

p. 211 Aquatint. 236 × 287 mm.

Microcosm of London, ii, p. 16.

p. 213T Oil on canvas. 1448 × 1854 mm. Her Majesty the Queen.

Haydon compiled a sketchbook comprising portrait drawings of the heads of the leading characters depicted, with biographical notes, now in the Royal Library, Windsor. In March 1828, he began to paint the sequel, *Chairing the Member* (Tate Gallery), in which a number of characters reappear and the artist depicts himself looking out of a prison window.

Oliver Millar, *Later Georgian Pictures in the Collection of Her Majesty the Queen* (1969), no. 829, pp. 48–49.

p. 213B Oil on canvas. 1523 × 2107 mm. Royal Holloway College.

Chapel, *Victorian Taste*, no. 29, 96–98.

p. 214 Wood engraving after a photograph by Herbert Watkins. 127 × 195 mm. The Museum of London.

Henry Mayhew and John Binney, *The Criminal Prisons of London and Scenes of Prison Life* (1862) pp. 306–07.

p. 215T Wood engraving. 240 × 190 mm. *London: A Pilgrimage*, p. 136.

For the use of the image by Vincent van Gogh see *English Influences on Vincent van Gogh* (Fine Art Department, University of Nottingham and Arts Council of Great Britain exhibition catalogue, 1974–75), pp. 8, 41, no. 88, pp. 54–55.

p. 215B Oil on canvas. 711 × 914 mm. Baroda Museum, India.

Frith, ii, pp. 141–52.

p. 216 Oil on canvas. 470 × 406 mm. Private Collection.

Wood, *Victorian Panorama*, p. 68.

p. 218 Oil on canvas. 927 × 1257 mm. Trustees of the Victoria & Albert Museum.

Pepys, who was one of the Governors, seems to have been instrumental in proposing the scheme in 1677, but Verrio did not receive the commission until 1681 and there were further delays brought about by the rebuilding of the Hall and the death of the King, so that the face of James II was substituted. Verrio received the final instalment of payment in 1687/8. The immense completed canvas is more static in design, with long lines of figures – the governors, the black-robed masters, the children in blue and Beefeaters in red – assembled on either side of this central design. The entire painting was repositioned in the hall on the west wall in 1762 and in 1902, was removed to Horsham where it still hangs in the dining room.

Croft-Murray, *Decorative Painting*, i, pp. 56–57, no. 17, pp. 238–39.

p. 221 Engraving. 226 × 178 mm. Guildhall Library.

Lord Romney is in the chair, Hanway to his right.

James Stephen Taylor, *Jonas Hanway, Founder of the Marine Society: Charity and Policy in Eighteenth-Century Britain* (1985), pp. xi–xiii, 69–73.

p. 222L Pen and ink. 228 × 197 mm. Thomas Coram Foundation for Children. A description of the breakfast and the uniform was published in the *Gentleman's Magazine*, xvii (1747), pp. 284–85, with an engraving after the sketch for part of the frontispiece, by T. Jefferys.

McClure, *Coram's Children* (1981) pp. 192–94. Cunnington and Lucas, pp. 178–80.

p. 222R Engraving. 400 × 448 mm. Thomas Coram Foundation for Children.

An exterior view showing the women with their babies queuing up at the gates for entry, entitled *A Perspective View of the Foundling Hospital, with Emblematic Figures*, engraved by Grignion and Rooker after Wale, was published on 24 April 1749.

McClure, pp. 76–78.

p. 223 Watercolour. 403 × 527 mm. William Salt Library, Stafford. On loan to the Thomas Coram Foundation.

The work was engraved by Sanders, dedicated to Sir Charles Whitworth, Vice President of the Society of Arts and Treasurer of the Hospital, and published on 7 January 1774.

Nicolson, *Treasures of the Foundling Hospital*, pp. 33–34, 39–49.

p. 224TR Oil on canvas. 1606 × 1556 mm. Trustees of the National Gallery.

Paulson, *Hogarth: His Life, Art, and Times* i, 458–59. Gowing, *Hogarth*, no. 112, p. 47.

p. 224L Pen and ink and watercolour. 188 × 105 mm. Trustees of the British Museum.

The same boy appears to be the model for the figure running barefoot in front of the sedan chair men in Boitard's print *The Covent Garden Morning Frolic*, published by Robert Sayer in 1747. *B.M. Satires*, no. 2877.

p. 224BR Pen and ink. 103 × 87 mm. Whitworth Art Gallery, University of Manchester.

See William Blake 'The Chimney Sweeper' in *Songs of Innocence* (1789) and *Songs of Experience* (1794). In 'The Streets Morning' in *Sketches by Boz* (1836) Dickens observed: 'three or four schoolboys on a stolen bathing expedition rattle merrily over the pavement, their boisterous mirth contrasting forcibly with the demeanour of the little sweep …'

Pointon, 'Urban Narrative in the Early Art of William Mulready', *Victorian Artists and the City*, p. 132. Heleniak, *Mulready*, p. 108.

p. 225 Pen and ink and watercolour. 165 × 230 mm. The Museum of London.

The present work is a study for the engraved heading to *The Little Chimney Sweep. A Favourite Ballad, Founded on Fact*. 'Written by Mr Upton, and set to Music by Mr W.T. Parke', published on 12 April 1808 by Laurie and Whittle. The elder Cruikshank's son, (Isaac) Robert Cruikshank (1789–1856) illustrated the pamphlet written by James Montgomery, *The Chimney-Sweeper's Friend and Climbing Boys' Album*, published in Sheffield in 1824, which advocated the total prohibition of child sweeps.

B.M. Satires, no. 11197, pp. 737–38.

p. 226 Engraving. 106 × 69 mm. Guildhall Library, Corporation of London.

Taylor, *Hanway*, pp. 118–27, 169–70.

p. 227TR Watercolour and bodycolour. 493 × 335 mm. The Museum of London.

According to Dickens in his essay 'The Streets Morning' from *Sketches by Boz* (1836) the Act only added to the child's burden: 'the little sweep, who, having knocked and rung till his arm aches, and being interdicted by a merciful legislature from endangering his lungs by calling out, sits patiently down on the door-step until the housemaid may happen to awake.'

p. 227BL Pen and ink. 144 × 200 mm. Whitworth Art Gallery, University of Manchester.

Pointon, 'Urban Narrative in the Early Art of William Mulready', p. 132. Pointon, *Mulready*, no. 138, p. 159.

p. 229T Oil on canvas. 762 × 1016 mm. Thomas Coram Foundation for Children.

On the walls are a number of paintings still in the Hospital collection, notably Hogarth's *The March to Finchley*, a tapestry copy of Guido Reni's *Salome* and part of a work attributed to Lanfranco on the right, *Elijah Raising the Son of the Widow of Zarephath*.

Nicolson, *Treasures of the Foundling Hospital*, no. 53, pp. 72–73. Wood, *Victorian Panorama*, p. 71.

p. 229B Oil on canvas. 599 × 899 mm. Birmingham Museum and Art Gallery.

In 1848, Ashley described the intake of the Ragged Schools to the House of Commons as comprising: 'street-sweepers, vendors of lucifer-matches, oranges, cigars, tapes, and ballads; they hold horses, run on errands, job for "dealers in marine stores"; such is the euphonous term for "receivers of stolen goods", a body of large influence in this metropolis, without whose agency juvenile crime would be much embarrassed in its operations.' (6 June 1848, *Hansard*, 3rd ser, xcix, 432)

p. 230 Pen and ink over pencil, watercolour

and gouache. 443 × 372 mm. Private Collection.

The composition was used for an illustration in *London: A Pilgrimage*, p. 134, for *Les Porteurs de Bière* in Louis Enault, *Londres* (Paris, 1876) p. 377 and for an etching entitled *Haquet de Brasseur à Londres*, dated 1872.

Clapp, *Gustave Doré*, no. 31, p. 48. *Gustave Doré* (Strasbourg exhibition catalogue), no. 110, p. 132.

p. 231L Pencil. 192 × 150 mm. London Borough of Camden, Local History Collection.

Kate Greenaway evidently attended the annual Charity Children Service at St Paul's on 7 June 1877, for a printed sheet of psalms and anthems with slight pencil sketches of bodices and hats in the margin marks the occasion. For the article published in *Saint Nicholas* in 1879, she depicted a beadle, the girls standing, kneeling in prayer, hiding their faces with their aprons and in procession.

p. 231R Mechanical reproduction. 269 × 210 mm.

Phil May's Gutter-Snipes, (1896).

p. 232 Watercolour and bodycolour. 610 × 457 mm. Trustees of the Victoria & Albert Museum.

p. 234L Pen and ink with traces of bodycolour. 204 × 147 mm. The Worshipful Company of Mercers.

This miniature decorates the first page of the earliest copy in English of the ordinances of the almshouse founded by the will of Whittington, who died on 21 December 1424. The dedication verse at the end of the manuscript names the wardens of the Mercers' Company who served in 1442–43, thus probably dating the manuscript. Alexander believes the miniature to be the work of William Abell, a limner who possibly was also responsible for the illumination of the Cartulary of St Bartholomew, and for a number of other works connected with the City. Stylistically it is conservative, linear and dependent on the conventions of heraldry rather than the burgeoning Renaissance styles of Italy and the Netherlands.

Jean Imray, *The Charity of Richard Whittington. A History of the Trust Administered by the Mercers' Company 1424–1966* (1966), appendix 1, pp. 107–18. Jonathan Alexander, 'William Abell "Lynmour" and 15th-century English Illumination', *Kunsthistorisches Forschungen Otto Pächt*, zu Ehren Ed. A. Rosenauer and G. Weber (Salzburg, 1972), pp. 166–72.

p. 234R Oil on panel. 1083 × 3124 mm. The Worshipful Company of Barbers.

The cartoon for the finished work is owned by the Royal College of Surgeons.

Roy C. Strong, 'Holbein's Cartoon for the Barber Surgeons' Group Re-discovered – A Preliminary Report', *Burlington Magazine*, cv (1963), pp. 4–14. Rowlands, *Holbein*, p. 118, no. 78, pp. 148–49.

p. 235L Oil on paper. 286 × 381 mm. Glasgow University Library.

The present work forms the frontispiece to MS Hunter 364, a late-sixteenth-century manuscript that bears the conventional title, 'Master John Banister's Anatomical Table.' Anatomy demonstrations usually took place four times a year at the Barber-Surgeons' Company; three lectures were given on each occasion – the visceral, muscular and osteological. When the Court of Examiners was set up in 1555, a detailed procedure was ordained and great care was taken to ensure that the anatomy was conducted in a seemly manner. Fine rods and candles were provided for the lecturer, two pairs of sleeves, two aprons, as well as clean knives and probes for the dissectors. In this scene, Banister appears to be wearing the clean sleeves, but not an apron.

G. Wolf-Heidegger and A.M. Cetto, *Die Anatomische Sektion in Bildicher Darstellung* (Basel and New York, 1967), pp. 302–03. Jessie Dobson and R. Milnes Walker, *Barbers and Barber-Surgeons of London* (Oxford, 1979), pp. 39–46. 139.

p. 235R Oil on canvas. 1275 × 1165 mm. The Worshipful Company of Barbers.

The Company commissioned the work on 27 February 1650 and paid 'Greenburye', the artist, £9 10s for the picture in 1651. The setting is the Company's anatomy theatre with its distinctive niches for skeletons and figures; completed by Inigo Jones in 1637, the work must constitute the first interior view. Another portrait of Scarburgh attributed to Jean Demetrius *c*.1660?, which depicts him with a folio open at a Vesalian plate and a view of Rome in the background is in the collection of the Royal College of Physicians.

Piper, *Royal College of Physicians Portraits*, pp. 376–79. Sidney Young, *Annals of the Barber-Surgeons of London* (1890) p. 407.

p. 236 Oil on canvas. 797 × 605 mm. Wellcome Institute for the History of Medicine.

p. 237 Woodcut. 470 × 304 mm. The Museum of London.

Walter G. Bell, *The Great Plague in London in 1665* (1924), pp. 103–04.

p. 239L Etching and engraving. 175 × 278 mm. Wellcome Institute for the History

of Medicine.

p. 239R Pencil and grey wash over red chalk. 219 × 298 mm. The Pierpont Morgan Library, New York.

The drawing was probably in the collection of Horace Walpole, described as 'an original sketch by Hogarth of a Surgeon operating on the ulcered leg of a woman'. Attempts have been made to connect it with the *Harlot's Progress* but other drawings for that series are larger in size and the present work is executed with a freedom of draughtsmanship which would seem to suggest a later date. A pencil version of the subject, also in the Pierpont Morgan Library (B1975.4.1255. Oppé, no. 64) is incised and reddened on the verso for transfer, clearly indicating that it was nevertheless intended for publication as an engraving.

Oppé, *The Drawings of William Hogarth*, no. 65, p. 44.

p. 240 Engraving. 269 × 370 mm. Wellcome Institute for the History of Medicine.

The engraving was published by Robert Sayer and John Smith 1 September 1768.

B.M. Satires, no. 4174.

p. 242 Oil on panel. 1580 × 970 mm. The Wellington Museum, Trustees of the Victoria & Albert Museum.

Kauffmann, *Wellington Museum Paintings*, no. 194, pp. 150–52. Lindsay Errington, *Tribute to Wilkie* (National Gallery of Scotland, Edinburgh exhibition catalogue, 1985), pp. 64–65. David Blayney Brown, *Sir David Wilkie. Drawings and Sketches in the Ashmolean Museum* (Morton Morris & Company/ Ashmolean Museum Oxford exhibition catalogue, 1985), nos. 11–23.

p. 243 Oil on canvas. 1105 × 1987 mm. Walker Art Gallery, Liverpool.

Graphic, xv (1877), pp. 324–25. *Illustrated London News*, lxxii (1878), p. 435.

p. 244 Oil on canvas. 1600 × 1143 mm. The Toledo Museum of Art, Gift of Edward Libbey.

Michael Wentworth, *James Tissot* (Oxford, 1984), p. 117.

p. 246L Watercolour. 130 × 190 mm. Edinburgh University Library. MS La.III.283, f. 254ᵛ.

Nevinson, 'Sketches of 17th-Century London', pp. 1256–57.

p. 246R Pen and ink and wash. 217 × 317 mm. The Provost and Fellows of Eton College.

p. 247 Pen and ink. 127 × 180 mm. Syndics of the Fitzwilliam Museum, Cambridge.

p. 248 Watercolour. 141 × 234 mm. Trustees of the British Museum.

Notes on the Colour Plates

I Watercolour. 578 × 1333 mm. Society of Antiquaries of London.

It is one of several watercolours after Tudor paintings commissioned from Grimm by the Society of Antiquaries between 1779 and 1791. Some allowance must be made for the transcription and the difficulties the artist must have experienced in recording accurately a work that had already suffered from two hundred years of dirt and smoke. This presumably explains the mysterious appearance of a Neo-classical pediment bottom left.

Hyde, *Gilded Scenes*, no. 1, p. 37.

II Oil on copper. 477 × 630 mm. Yale Center for British Art, Paul Mellon Collection.

There is a larger version of the work, measuring 800 × 1040 mm and signed P. Angelles 1726, which was evidently done for Mr Walker, Commissioner of the Customs. A painting of the market by Angelis with the central interest focused on three elegantly dressed women, possibly a lady with her housekeeper and maid, buying vegetables, is in the collection of the Marquis of Tavistock and the Trustees of the Bedford Estates. A small study on panel for the young woman trader in the background left of the preceding work is also in the Mellon Collection.

J. H Plumb, *The Pursuit of Happiness* (Yale Center for British Art, New Haven exhibition catalogue, 1977), no. 106, p. 53.

III Oil on canvas, 1078 × 1756 mm. The Museum of London.

Hayes, *London Museum Paintings*, no. 56, pp. 108–10.

IV Oil on canvas, 622 × 749 mm. Trustees of the Tate Gallery.

One of Hogarth's servants was identified by name as Ben Ives in Samuel Ireland's biography of the artist.

Paulson, *Hogarth: His Life, Art and Times*, ii, pp. 244–46. Gowing, *Hogarth*, no. 197, p. 78.

V Oil on canvas. 940 × 737 mm. Private Coll.

There are two known versions of the work which was engraved by John Raphael Smith with the title *The Pretty Maid Buying a Love Song* and by J. Walker and Francis Bartolozzi as *The Young Maid and Old Sailor* (1785).

Sacheverell Sitwell, *Narrative Pictures* (1937), p. 50. *Henry Walton* (Castle Museum, Norwich exhibition catalogue, 1963), no. 11, p. 12.

VI Oil on canvas, 895 × 692 mm. Her Majesty the Queen.

There are several grounds for doubting the identification of the craftsman as John Cuff.

Firstly, Cuff's main contributions to the development of scientific instruments were mechanical (improved forms of microscope stands) rather than optical, while the painting shows a purely optical workbench with no hint of the hardware. Secondly, the microscopes supplied to the royal collection were made in the 1740s, thirty years before the painting, by which time they would have become obsolete. Thirdly, in 1750 Cuff was declared bankrupt and although he continued to trade, ten years later he was reported as being in a bad way with no shop and no money; his last payment to the Spectacle-Makers' Company was made in 1768. Either he was granted a pension by George III and the present work was in some measure commemorative, painted at royal command, or it represents another maker. A candidate suggested by John R. Millburn is Edward Scarlett the Younger, who was born in 1700; was Optician to George II from 1743 and at least one of his microscopes was in George III's collection.

Millar, *Later Georgian Pictures in the Royal Collection*, no. 1209, p. 152. Webster, *Zoffany*, no. 71, pp. 55–56.

VII Pen and ink and watercolour. 353 × 537 mm. Trustees of the Victoria & Albert Museum.

Hardie, *Water-Colour Painting*, i, p. 117 (as by John Collet).

VIII Pen and watercolour. 356 × 445 mm. Her Majesty the Queen.

Oppé, *English Drawings in the Royal Collection*, no. 194, p. 45.

IX Pen and ink and watercolour with white heightening. 413 × 508 mm. The Museum of London.

The by-election brought about by Lord Hood's appointment as First Lord of the Admiralty was expected by the government to result in his re-election unopposed, instead of which he was defeated by the Foxite candidate, Lord John Townshend.

B.M. Satires, no. 7356. Ralph Edwards, 'The Watercolour Drawings of Robert Dighton', *Apollo*, xiv (1931), pp. 98–102.

X Watercolour over pencil with ink. 218 × 372 mm. Trustees of the British Museum.

Stainton, *British Landscape Watercolours*, no. 148, pp. 65–66.

XI Watercolour over black chalk. 217 × 278 mm. Trustees of the British Museum.

Eitner, *Géricault*, p. 255. *Master Drawings and Watercolours in the British Museum*, ed. John Rowlands (British Museum exhibition catalogue, 1984), no. 135, p. 142.

XII Pencil, pen and ink, watercolour. 381 × 244 mm. Courtauld Institute Galleries (Spooner Collection).

The William Spooner Bequest (Courtauld Institute Galleries exhibition catalogue, 1968), no. 81. Witt, *Hunt*, no. 324, p. 173.

XIII Watercolour heightened with white. 488 × 317 mm. Private Collection.

The present work is one of a number of individual studies Hunt made of street traders, including the *Vegetable Seller*, a *Radish Stall* (Manchester City Art Gallery) and earlier representations of flower girls.

Witt, *Hunt*, no. 507, p. 190.

XIV Oil on canvas. 686 × 1245 mm. The Worshipful Company of Fishmongers.

The work was probably inspired by the description and illustration of the same subject which appeared in Sala's *Twice Round the Clock*. When it was exhibited at the Royal Academy in 1861, it drew a lukewarm response, being criticized generally for its simplistic composition and the triviality of its subject matter.

Allwood, *Hicks*, no. 23, pp. 27–28.

XV See note to the illustration on p. 59.

XVI Oil on canvas. 448 × 419 mm. Trustees of the Tate Gallery.

Wood, *Victorian Panorama*, pp. 216–17.

XVII Oil on canvas. 1873 × 2724 mm. Guildhall Art Gallery, Corporation of London.

Logsdail was inspired to paint the subject by watching the procession of 1887, following a six-year sojourn in Italy. He went to enormous pains to achieve authenticity. He was given permission to visit the mayoral stables in Fore Street and had the coach drawn out and horses harnessed for him. The coachman and footmen went in their liveries to the artist's studio in Primrose Hill to model for him. The Corporation mace was made available. Other figures were based on professional models and artist friends.

Works of Art of the Corporation of London, p. 160.

XVIII Watercolour and bodycolour. 402 × 720 mm. The Museum of London.

The work was painted the same year as Manet's *A Bar at the Folies-Bergère*, with which it makes a fascinating comparison. An undated oil painting of the subject by the artist is in a private collection.

Wood, *Victorian Panorama*, p. 18.

XIX Watercolour. 350 × 250 mm. The Museum of London.

As a young man Goodwin had worked as an assistant to Ford Madox Brown (1821–93) and Arthur Hughes (1832–1915). With its richly orchestrated colours and intense, stippled brushstroke, the present work exhibits the artist's Pre-Raphaelite antecedents. But the domestic subject-matter – unusual for the artist who is normally associated with landscapes – has more in common with the illustrations Hughes and other artists were designing for the literary magazines of the 1860s and 1870s.

XX Pencil, pen and ink, wax crayon watercolour. 480 × 428 mm. The Museum of London.

The work derives from a study on page 25 of Moore's second shelter sketchbook.

Alan G. Wilkinson, *The Drawings of Henry Moore* (Tate Gallery exhibition catalogue, 1977–78), pp. 28–36, no. 158.

Select Bibliography

All books published in London, unless otherwise stated.

ABBEY J.R. *Scenery of Great Britain and Ireland in Aquatint and Lithography 1770–1860* (1952)

ADAMS Bernard *London Illustrated 1604–1851* (1983)

ALLWOOD Rosamond *George Elgar Hicks* (Geffrye Museum exhibition catalogue, 1983)

ALTICK Richard *The Shows of London* (1978)

ANGLO Sydney, introd. *The Great Tournament Roll of Westminster* (Oxford, 1968)

ANGLO Sydney *Spectacle, Pageantry and Early Tudor Policy* (Oxford, 1969)

BANK OF ENGLAND *An Historical Catalogue of Engravings, Drawings and Paintings in the Bank of England* (1928)

BARON Wendy *The Camden Town Group* (1979)

BEALL Karen F. *Kaufrufe und Strassenhändler. Cries and Itinerant Trades. A Bibliography* (Hamburg, 1975)

BEIER A.L. and FINLAY Roger, eds. *London 1500–1700* (1986)

BINYON Lawrence *British Museum Catalogue of Drawings by British Artists* (1898–1907)

BREWER John and STYLES John, eds. *An Ungovernable People* (1980)

BYRD Max *London Transformed* (New Haven, 1978)

CHAPEL Jeannie *Victorian Taste: The Complete Catalogue of Paintings at the Royal Holloway College* (1982)

CLAPP Samuel F. *Gustave Doré 1832–1883* (Hazlitt, Gooden and Fox exhibition catalogue, 1983)

CONNOR Patricia and LAMBOURNE Lionel *Derby Day 200* (Royal Academy of Arts exhibition catalogue, 1979)

CORBETT Margery and NORTON Michael *Engraving in England in the Sixteenth and Seventeenth Centuries*, iii (Cambridge, 1964)

CROFT-MURRAY Edward *Decorative Painting in England*, i (1962)

CROFT-MURRAY Edward and HULTON Paul *British Museum Catalogue of British Drawings*, i (1960)

CUNNINGTON Phillis and LUCAS Catherine *Charity Costumes* (1978)

DORÉ Gustave and BLANCHARD Jerrold *London: A Pilgrimage* (1872)

DYOS H.J. and WOLFF Michael, eds. *The Victorian City* (1973)

EGERTON Judy *George Stubbs 1724–1806* (Tate Gallery exhibition catalogue, 1984–85)

EITNER Lorenz E.A. *Géricault His Life and Work* (1982)

FINBERG Hilda F. 'Pictures of Covent Garden in the Duke of Bedford's Collection', *Country Life*, 1 (1921)

FOISTER Susan 'Paintings and Other Works of Art in Sixteenth-century English Inventories', *Burlington Magazine*, cxxiii (1981)

FOX Celina 'The Development of Social Reportage in English Periodical Illustration during the 1840s and 1850s', *Past and Present*, no. 74 (Oxford, 1977)

FRITH W.P. *My Autobiography and Reminiscences* (1888)

GAUNT W. *The Etchings of Frank Brangwyn. A Catalogue Raisonné* (1926)

GEORGE M. Dorothy *London Life in the Eighteenth Century* (Peregrine edn, 1966)

GERSON H., GOODISON J.W., SUTTON Denys *Fitzwilliam Museum Catalogue of Paintings* (Cambridge, 1960)

GOWING Lawrence *Hogarth* (Tate Gallery exhibition catalogue, 1971–72)

HARDIE Martin *Water-Colour Painting in Britain* (1966–68)

HARRIS John *The Artist and the Country House* (1979)

HAY Douglas, *et al. Albion's Fatal Tree: Crime and Society in Eighteenth-century England* (1975)

HAYES John *A Catalogue of Watercolour Drawings by Thomas Rowlandson in the London Museum* (1960)

HAYES John *Catalogue of the Oil Paintings in the London Museum* (1970)

HAYES John *The Drawings of Thomas Gainsborough* (1970)

HAYES John *Rowlandson's Watercolours* (1972)

HELENIAK Kathryn Moore *William Mulready* (1980)

HIND A.M. *Engraving in England in the Sixteenth and Seventeenth Centuries*, i and ii (Cambridge, 1952–55)

HINDLEY Charles *History of the Cries of London* (1881)

HYDE Ralph *Gilded Scenes and Shining Prospects. Panoramic Views of British Towns 1575–1900* (Yale Center for British Art, New Haven exhibition catalogue, 1985)

INGAMELLS John and RAINES Robert 'A Catalogue of the Paintings, Drawings and Etchings of Philip Mercier', *The Walpole Society*, xlvi (1976–78)

IVEAGH BEQUEST, KENWOOD *The French Taste in English Painting during the First Half of the Eighteenth Century* (exhibition catalogue, 1968)

JACKSON-STOPS Gervase, ed. *The Treasure Houses of Britain* (National Gallery of Art, Washington D.C. exhibition catalogue, 1985–86)

JONES Gareth Stedman *Outcast London* (Oxford, 1971)

KAUFFMANN C.M. *Catalogue of Paintings in the Wellington Museum* (1982)

KERSLAKE John *National Portrait Gallery: Early Georgian Portraits* (1977)

KINGZETT Richard 'A Catalogue of Works by Samuel Scott', *Walpole Society*, xlviii (1980–82)

KNIGHT Vivien, comp. *The Works of Art of the Corporation of London* (Cambridge, 1986)

LARWOOD Jacob *The Story of London Parks* (1877)

LEFANU William *A Catalogue of the Portraits and other Paintings, Drawings and Sculpture in the Royal College of Surgeons of England* (1960)

MAXTED Ian *The London Book Trades 1775–1800* (Folkestone, 1977)

MAYHEW Henry *London Labour and the London Poor* (1861–62 edn)

MILLAR Oliver *Tudor, Stuart and Early Georgian Pictures in the Collection of Her Majesty the Queen* (1963)

MILLAR Oliver *Late Georgian Pictures in the Collection of Her Majesty the Queen* (1969)

MILLAR Oliver *Van Dyck in England* (National Portrait Gallery exhibition catalogue, 1982–83)

MORRIS Linda and RADFORD Robert *The Story of AIA Artists International Association 1933–53* (Museum of Modern Art, Oxford, exhibition catalogue, 1983)

MURDOCH Tessa, comp. *The Quiet Conquest. The Huguenots 1685 to 1985* (Museum of London exhibition catalogue, 1985)

MURRAY Peter *Dulwich Picture Gallery, a Catalogue* (1980)

NADEL Ira Bruce and SCHWARZBACH F.S., eds. *Victorian Artists and the City* (1980)

NEVINSON J.L. 'Sketches of 17th-Century London, A Student's Album', *Country Life*, cxlii (1967)

NEVINSON J.L. 'Illustrations of Costume in the Alba Amicorum', *Archaeologia*, cvi (1975)

NEVINSON John 'The Dress of the Citizens of London 1540–1640', *Collectanea Londiniensa*, (London and Middlesex Archaeological Society, special paper no. 2 1978)

NICOLSON Benedict *The Treasures of the Foundling Hospital* (Oxford, 1972)

OPPÉ A.P. *The Drawings of Paul and Thomas Sandby in the Collection of His Majesty the King at Windsor Castle* (1947)

OPPÉ A.P. *The Drawings of William Hogarth* (1948)

OPPÉ A.P. *English Drawings, Stuart and Georgian Periods, in the Collection of His Majesty the King* (1950)

PAULSON Ronald *Hogarth's Graphic Works* (1970 edn)

PAULSON Ronald *Hogarth: His Life, Art and Times* (1971)

PENNINGTON Richard *A Descriptive catalogue of the Etched Work of Wenceslaus Hollar 1607–1677* (Cambridge, 1982)

PENNY Nicholas, ed. *Reynolds* (Royal Academy of Arts exhibition catalogue, 1986)

PIPER David *Catalogue of the Seventeenth-century Portraits in the National Portrait Gallery 1625–1714* (Cambridge, 1963)

PIPER David *Royal College of Physicians Catalogue of London Portraits*, ed. Gordon Wolstenholme (1964)

POINTON Marcia *The Bonington Circle* (Brighton, 1985)

POINTON Marcia *Mulready* (Victoria and Albert Museum exhibition catalogue, 1986)

POSNER Donald *Annibale Carracci* (1971)

RAINES Robert *Marcellus Laroon* (1966)

ROSENFELD Sybil *The Theatres of the London Fairs in the 18th Century* (Cambridge, 1960)

ROWLANDS John *Holbein* (Oxford, 1985)

SHARPE J.A. *Crime and the Law in English Satirical Prints 1600–1832* (Cambridge, 1986)

SHAW James Byam *Paintings by Old Masters at Christ Church Oxford* (1967)

SMITH John Thomas *Vagabondiana* (1817)

SMITH John Thomas *The Cries of London*, ed. J.B. Nichols (1839)

SNODIN Michael, ed. *Rococo. Art and Design in Hogarth's England* (Victoria and Albert Museum exhibition catalogue, 1984)

STAINTON Lindsay *British Landscape Watercolours 1600–1860* (British Museum exhibition catalogue, 1983)

STEPHENS F.G. and GEORGE M.D. *British Museum Catalogue of Political and Personal Satires* (1870–1954)

STEVENSON Sara and THOMSON Duncan *John Michael Wright. The King's Painter* (Scottish National Portrait Gallery, Edinburgh exhibition catalogue, 1982)

STEWART Bertram *The Library and Picture Collection of the Port of London Authority* (1955)

STONE Lawrence and STONE Jean C. Fawtier *An Open Elite? England 1540–1880* (Oxford, 1984)

STRASBOURG MUSÉES *Gustave Doré 1832–1883* (exhibition catalogue, 1983)

STRONG Roy *National Portrait Gallery Tudor & Jacobean Portraits* (1969)

STRONG Roy *Artists of the Tudor Court* (Victoria and Albert Museum exhibition catalogue, 1983)

SYKES Christopher Simon *Life in the Great London Houses* (1979)

TATE GALLERY *The Pre-Raphaelites* (exhibition catalogue, 1984)

TAYLOR James Stephen *Jonas Hanway, Founder of the Marine Society: Charity and Policy in Eighteenth-Century Britain* (1985)

THOMPSON E.P. and YEO Eileen *The Unknown Mayhew* (1971)

WALKER Richard *National Portrait Gallery Regency Portraits* (1985)

WATERHOUSE Ellis *Gainsborough* (1958)

WEBSTER Mary *Francis Wheatley* (1970)

WEBSTER Mary *Johan Zoffany 1733–1810* (National Portrait Gallery exhibition catalogue, 1976)

WHITLEY William T. *Artists and their Friends in England 1700–99* (1928)

WITT John *William Henry Hunt* (1982)

WOOD Christopher *Victorian Panorama* (1976)

Index

Page numbers in *italic* refer to illustrations, roman numerals refer to colour plates.

Abell, William 9, *234*
Académie Royale des Sciences 114
Ackermann's *Repository* 29
Addison, Joseph 159, 161
Adelphi 172, 173, 196, XI
Aertsen, Pieter 108, 140
Agasse, Jacques Laurent 144, 149, *151*, 164, *165*, 172
Ahmed iben Ahmed, Quadran-Nasir 245
Ainsworth, Harrison 202
alba amicorum 16, 156, 169
Albert, Prince 31, 32, 91, 149
Aldridge's 151
Alexandra, Princess of Wales, later Queen Alexandra 22
Alleyn, Edward 219
Alsop, George 241
Anderson, Stanley 145, *146*
Angelis, Peter 76, 130, 140, 141, 146, II
Anne, Queen 76, 129, 220
Antwerp 94, 96, 98, 99, 101, 109, 140, 186
Archer, Thomas 139
Arlington Street 92
Arris, Edward 234, *235*
Art-Union 192, 193
Artists' International Association 73, 183
Arundel, Alathea, Countess of 75
Arundel, Thomas Howard, 2nd Earl of 64, 75
Assize of Bread 108
Athenaeum 148
Atkinson, John Augustus 172, *173*, *246*, 247
Augusta, Princess 21
Ayscough, James 116

Badcock, William 114
Bagley, John 120
Baker Street 30
Balmerino, Arthur Elphinstone, 6th Baron 66
Bambridge, Thomas *209*
Banister, John 234, *235*
Bank of England 56, 104, *105*
Banks, Sir Joseph 246
Banqueting House 16, 20, 65, *76*, 79, 80, 169
Barber-Surgeons' Hall 235, 236
Barber-Surgeons' Company 99, 233, 234, 239
Barbers' Company 233
Barbican 151
Barlow, Francis 65
Barnardo, Dr 228
Barnes Railway Bridge 51
Bartholomew Fair 25, 26, *27*, *28*
Bastien-Lepage, Jules 155, 166
Bathurst, Henry 210
Baudelaire, Charles 56–58, 91

Bawden, Edward 150, *153*
Baxter, Thomas *106*, 121
Beale, Charles 127, *128*
Bear Quay *119*
Beard, Richard *166*, 195, 228
Bedford House 139
Bedford, Francis Russell, 4th Earl of 139
Bedford, William Russell, 5th Earl and 1st Duke of 139
Bedford, Wriothesley Russell, 2nd Duke of 139
Bedlam *see* Bethlem
Belcher, George *136*, 137
Belgrave Square *91*
Bell, John 239
Bermondsey 23, 77, 78
Bethlem Hospital 233, 236, 238
Bethnal Green 190, 196
Beuckelaer, Joachim 108, 140
Bevan, Robert *151*
Bickham, George, Junior 82
Billingsgate 146, *147*, 148, XIV
Bird, John 110
Blackfriars 20
Blackfriars Bridge 61, 176, 189
Blackwall Yard 119
Blaikley, Alexander 227, *229*
Blake, William 225
Board of Trade 105
Boitard, Louis Philippe 54, *55*, *83*, *101*, 102, 112, *117*, *134*, 202, 223, *224*, 248
Boleyn, Anne 99
Bomberg, David 52
Bond Street 127, 135
Bond, Alderman William 95
Bond, Captain Martin 95
Bonington, Richard Parkes 56, 90
Bonner's Fields 72
Borough Street 26
Boruwlaski, Joseph 246
Bosse, Abraham 79
Boswell, James 11
Bourguignon, Hubert François 82, 131, 133, 201, *203*
Bourne, John Cooke *178*, *179*
Bow Street 209
Bowles, John 81, 143, 237
Bowles, Thomas 82
Boydell's Shakespeare Gallery 71, 86
Boydell, John 70, 171
Boydell, Josiah 171
Boys, Thomas Shotter *8*, 56, 90
Brandoin, Michel Vincent 'Charles' 88
Brangwyn, Frank *148*, 149, *181*, *182*
Brentford 121, 123, 183
Bridewell 130, 209, 217, 223, *224*, 233, 245
Bridget Holmes 241
British Museum 31, 178, 248
British Workman 125
Britton, John 178
Broad Street *70*
Brockley, Kent 137
Brook Green Fair 26
Brookes, George 121
Brown, Ford Madox 58, *180*
Brown, John 196
Browne, Hablot K. 198
Brownlow, Emma 228, *229*
Brownlow, John 228, 229
Brownrigg, Elizabeth 202, *205*
Buckingham House 80
Buckingham, George Grenville, 1st Marquis of 71
Builder 196
Buling, Hans 238
Bullwinckle, J. 116
Bunbury, Henry 84

Bunning, J.B. 148
Burghley, Lord 203
Burnet, John 242
Burton, James 175

Caledonian Market 149, 151, *152*
Caledonian Road 152
Callot, Jacques 79, 186, 188
Camden Town 178, 183
Campbell, Robert 124
Canaletto, Antonio 21, 82, 143
Canning, Elizabeth 202
Cannon Street Station 181, 182
Canonbury 96
Carlevaris, Luca *18*, 19
Carlisle House, Soho Square *74*, 86
Carlton House 84
Carlyle, Thomas 180, 190
Caroline of Ansbach 236
Caroline of Brunswick 89
Carpenters' Company 107
Carracci, Annibale 9, 109, 157, 160
Carter, Benjamin 121
Carter, John 121
Castell, Robert 209
Catherine of Aragon 14
Catherine of Braganza 18
Cato Street Conspirators 201
Chamberlain's Wharf *171*
Chamberlin, Mason 102, *103*
Chambre, John 234
Chapman, J. *102*
Chardin, Jean Simeon 132, 133, 162
Charing Cross 54, 161, 209
Charles I 76, 78, 88, 127, 212, 219
Charles II *16*, 25, 29, *76*, 79, 110, *218*, 235
Charles, Young Pretender 69
Charlotte, Queen 164
Charterhouse 219
Chatelain, Jean Baptiste 82
Chatham 119
Chaucer, Geoffrey 94, 100
Cheapside 21, 155, I
Cheapside Conduit 159
Chelsea 33, 95
Cheselden, William 235, *236*
Chevalier, Hippolyte 195, 196
Chippendale, Thomas 114
Christ Church, Oxford 127
Christ's Hospital 56, 110, 217–19, 231, 233, 241, 245
Cibber, Caius Gabriel 238
Cipriani, Giovanni Battista *221*
Clapham Common 70
Clarenceux King of Arms 95
Clee, Robert 116
Cleveley, John, the Elder 118
Cleveley, Robert 33
Clien, Francis 139
Clifford, Mary 205
Closterman, John Baptist 127
Clothes Exchange 166
Clothworkers' Company 96
Coal Exchange 105
Cochin, C.N. 116
Cochrane, Charles 194
Coldbath Fields 210, 214
Cole, Benjamin 116
Collet, John 12, 29, *30*, 54, *55*, *143*, 159, 219, 247
Colnaghi, Paul 163
Columbani, Placido 115
Combe, William 105, 220, 240
Common Council, City of London 158, 159
Compton *see* Northampton
Conway, William 166
Cooper, Samuel 139

Coopers' Company 108
Copenhagen Fields 149, 150
Corn Exchange 105
Cornelys, Mrs Theresa 75, 86
Court of Chancery 201, *203*
Court of Common Pleas 201, 203, 210
Court of Exchequer 201
Court of Excise 105
Court of King's Bench 201, *202*, 203
Court of Wards and Liveries 201, *203*
Courtauld, Augustin 112
Covent Garden 54, 60, 71, 139–42, 144–46, 169, 247, II
Covent Garden Market *138*, *142*, *143*, *146*, 175
Crachami, Carolina 246
Craig, William Marshall 124, 144, 146, 163, *164*
Cranbrook, Kent 226
Cranmer, Charles 29
Crawhall, Joseph 90
Crespin, Paul 112
Cromwell, Elizabeth 79
Cromwell, Oliver 79
Crooke, Dr Hilkiah 236
Crosby Place 95, 96
Crosby, Sir John 95
Cruikshank, George 32, 33, 135, 176, 194
Cruikshank, Isaac 225
Crunden, John 115
Cuff, John 111
Cumberland Hay Market 151
Cumberland, William Augustus, Duke of 127
Custom House 101, 105, 119, 148
Cyders Cellars, Maiden Lane 207

Dance, George, the Elder 205
Dance, George, the Younger 213
Dance, Nathaniel 202, *205*
Danckerts, Hendrik 80
Dandridge, Bartholomew 82
Darly, Matthew 114
Dayes, Edward *85*, 86
Defoe, Daniel 94, 139, 202
Dekker, Thomas 14
Delamotte, W.A. 240
Derby Day *31*, 32, 59
Deserpz, François 100
Devonshire House 88
Devonshire, Georgiana, Duchess of 88, IX
Dicey, William and Cluer 116
Dickens, Charles 56, 58, 190, 194, 222, 225
Dighton, Robert 12, 54, 71, *105*, 134, 239, IX
Dinteville, Jean de 245
Dollond, John 110, 111
Doré, Gustave *10*, 33, *51*, 61, 91, 165, *184*, 197, 198, *215*, 228, *230*
Doyle, Richard *31*, 32
Drapers' Company 95
Droeshout, Martin 236
Du Maurier, George *136*, 166, *167*, 198
Duckett, Sir Lionel 97
Dudley, Sir Henry Bate 84
Dugdale, Thomas Cantrell 93
Dulwich College 219
Duncan, Sir William 240
Dunstall, John 237
Dupont, Gainsborough 104, 170

East India Company 103, 119
East India House 104, 105
Eastcheap 108

Eckstein, Johannes 28, VIII
Edgware Road 202
Edmonton Statute Fair 26
Edward I 13
Edward III 98
Edward IV 26, 75, 98, 233
Edward VI 14, 16, 217, 233, I
Edward, Prince of Wales, later
    Edward VII 22
Edwards, Edward 155, 163
Egan and Salmon 204
Egan, Pierce 174
Egley, William Maw 57, 58, XVI
Egyptian Hall 30
Elizabeth I 14, 96, 97, 101, 219
Elliot, Katherine 127
Epsom 50
Errero, Nicolo 19, 245
Esselens, Jacob 80
Essex Buildings 25
Eton 219
Euston 178, 179
Evelyn, John 76
Exchange Alley 105, 139
Exeter Change 28, VIII
Eyre, Simon 95

Faber, John, Junior 132, 133
Farringdon Road 56, 142
Fauntleroy, Henry 212
Fawkes, Guy 64
Fawkes, Isaac 27
Ferneley, Anne 99
Ferrers, Benjamin 201, 203
Festival of Britain 152
Fielder, Thomas 102, 103
Fildes, Luke 197, 198, 199, 212
Finchley 69
Fishmongers' Company 15
Fishmongers' Hall 22
Flaxman, John 189
Fleet Prison 208, 209, 210
Fleet River 149
Fleet Sewer 177
Fleet Street 56, 61
Fontaine, Peter de la 116
Fortnum, William 129
Forty Hill, Enfield 121, 123
Foundling Hospital 221, 222, 225,
    228, 237, 238
Fowler, Charles 139, 145
Fox, Charles James 71
Foxe, John 64
Frederick Prince of Wales 21, 81, 113
Freke, John 239
Frith, William Powell 12, 31, 32, 59,
    60, 206, 214, 215, XV
Fry, Elizabeth 211, 212
Furneaux, Captain 246

Gainsborough, Thomas 85, 111, 132,
    170, 186, 221, 226, 236
Gardner, Alan, 1st Baron 71
Garrard, George 169, 170, 171, 172
Gavarni see Chevalier
George I 19
George III 21, 121, 246
George, Prince of Wales, later George
    IV 21, 84, 89, 212
Gerbier, Sir Balthazar 18
Géricault, Theodore 30, 56, 172, 174,
    189, 190, 196, 200, 211, XI
Gertler, Mark 152
Gibbon, Edward 86
Gibson, Charles Dana 91
Gilbert, John 198
Gill, Susan 128
Gillray, James 33, 88, 89, 135, 163

Gilman, Harold 136, 137
Ginner, Charles 151, 166, 167
Girtin, Dr T.G. 90
Gisborne, Thomas 75
Gisze, Georg 98, 110
Godfrey, Ambrose (Godfrey
    Hanckwitz) 115
Godwin, George 241
Golden Phoenix Laboratory 115
Goldsmith Street, Gough Square 107,
    121
Goldsmiths' Company 15
Goodwin, Albert 134, XIX
Gower Street 175
Grace Church 108
Graham, George 110, 111
Grant, Sir Archibald 209
Graphic 58, 181, 183, 197, 198, 212,
    214, 228, 242, 243
Gravelot see Bourguignon
Graves, Henry 217, 227
Gray's Inn Lane 185, 196, 198
Great Exhibition 32
Great Fire 9, 65, 94, 104, 142, 150,
    219
Great Plague 236
Greaves, Walter 33, 50
Green Park 81
Green, Valentine 103
Greenaway, Kate 231
Greenbury, Richard 234, 235
Greenwich 119
Greenwich Hospital 237, 241
Greenwich Pensioners 232, 242
Gregory IX decretals 107
Gresham, Sir Thomas 98, 99, 101
Greuze, Jean Baptiste 134, 161, 162,
    210
Griffier, Jan the Elder 23
Griffier, Jan the Younger 24
Grignion, Charles 82
Grimm, Samuel Hieronymous 14, 26,
    I
Grisoni, Giuseppe 87
Grocers' Company 95, 102
Grosvenor Gate 90
Grosvenor Square 196
Gunpowder Plot 64
Guy's Hospital 236
Guy, Thomas 236
Guys, Constantin 57, 90
Gwynn, John 81

Hall, Clifford 151, 152
Hamilton, John 202, 204
Hammersmith 183
Hammersmith Bridge 33, 50
Hampstead 180
Hampstead Road 178, 179
Handel, George Frederick 113
Hanover Square 219
Hansa Steelyard 97–99, 245
Hanway, Jonas 220, 225, 226
Harding, Fisher 118
Hardy, Frederick Daniel 226
Harman, Thomas 188
Harris, John 115
Harrison, Stephen 14
Harrow 183
Hartmann, Carl 247, 248
Harvey, William 235
Haydon, Benjamin Robert 29, 212,
    213
Hayman, Francis 29, 130, 131, 133,
    161, 221
Haymarket 60, 61, 124
Haytley, Edward 222
Hazlitt, William 190
Heath, James 70

Heath, William 135
Heere, Lucas de 100
Heidegger, Count John James 86
Heins, John Theodore 236
Henning, Archibald 207
Henry II 233
Henry VI 95, 201
Henry VII 233
Henry VIII 13, 14, 76, 79, 96, 98, 99,
    201, 219, 233, 234
Henshall, John Henry XVIII
Herkomer, Hubert 242, 243
Hibbert, George 104
Hickey, Thomas 103
Hickey, William 75
Hicks, George Elgar 60, 148, XIV
Highgate Archway 176
Highmore, Joseph 131, 133, 221
Hill, John 121, 123
Hindley, Charles 155
Hine, Henry Robert 227
Hinton, John 115
Hippodrome 52
Hiseland, William 241
Hodges, William 246
Hoefnagel, Joris 23, 77, 78, 155
Hog Lane, Soho 247
Hogarth Club 134
Hogarth, William 7–9, 11, 12, 20, 21,
    26, 27, 29, 33, 54, 66, 68, 88, 102,
    103, 117, 118, 127–31, 139, 142,
    143, 147, 152, 159, 170, 183, 187,
    189, 193, 202, 205, 208, 209, 210,
    214, 221, 222, 224, 237, 238, 239,
    241, 247, IV
Hogenberg, Francis 99, 100, 155
Holbein, Hans 7–8, 97, 98, 99, 110,
    112, 233, 234, 245
Holl, Frank 212, 213, 214
Hollar, Wenceslaus 16, 18, 64, 65, 79,
    100, 101, 131, 140, 248
Holloway Prison 214
Holman, Francis 119
Holmes, Bridget 127
Home, Robert 110
Hondius, Abraham 24, III
Hone, Nathaniel 186
Hone, William 30
Hood, Thomas 193
Hooghe, Romeyn de 18, 19
Horse Guards 81
Horseferry 23
Horsley, John Callcott 226
Hoskins, John 139
Houghton, Arthur Boyd 58, 199
Houndsditch 116
House of Lords 76
House, Sam 71
Houses of Parliament 192
Howard, John 210
Hugh Alley 108, 149
Hughes, Nathan 72, 73
Huguenots 247.
Hullmandel, C. 189
Hummums 145
Hungerford Market 176
Hunt, Charles 167
Hunt, William Henry 144, 165, 219,
    XII, XIII
Hunt, William Holman 22, 134
Hunter, Dr John 235, 246
Hunter, Dr William 235, 240
Hyde Park 32, 70, 72, 81, 86, 88–90

Illustrated London News 50, 57, 59,
    72, 92, 191, 212, 213, 243
Illustrated Times 196, 197
Inns of Court 201
Ireland, Jane 169

Isham, John 96
Islington 149, 199

Jack-in-the-Green 30
James I 14, 16, 79, 95, 233
James II 127, 158, 235
James Street 144, 145
Janssen, Nicholas 219
Jarman, Edward 104
Jeffreys, George, 1st Baron Jeffreys 66
Jennings, Nicholas 188
Jerrold, Blanchard 33, 59, 91, 185
Johnson, Gerard 96
Johnson, Thomas 114
Jonathan's Coffee House 105
Jones, David 137
Jones, Horace 148, 150, 151
Jones, Inigo 97, 139, 235
Jonson, Ben 25
Judd, Sir Andrew 95
Judge and Jury Society 207
Jullienne, Jean de 84
June, John 21, 240

Keene, Charles 57
Kennington Common 72
Kennington, Eric 152
Kensington Gardens 89, 231
Kensington Gravel Pits 174, 175, 226
Kensington Palace 76
Kentish Town 183
Kilmarnock, William Boyd, 4th Earl
    of 66
King Sreet 139
King's Bench Prison 208, 210, 211,
    212
King's Cross 151
King's Road 242
King's Theatre, Haymarket 61, 87,
    121
King, Tom 143
Kip, Johannes 80
Kip, William 14
Kirgate, Thomas 114
Kneller, Sir Godfrey 245
Knight, Charles 191
Knyff, Jacob 80
Knyff, Leonard 80
Kratzer, Nicholas 110

Laborde, Chas 62, 91
Laguerre, Louis 114
Lajoue, Jacques de 116
Lamb, Charles 190, 217, 225
Lambeth 220
Lambeth Asylum 222
Lambeth Palace 192
Lami, Eugène 56, 91
Lamoral, Claude, Prince de Ligne 16,
    19, 76, 245
Lancaster, Sir James 103
Lançon, Auguste André 134, 137
Laroon, Marcellus 83
Latymer, Edward 219
Laud, William, Archbishop of
    Canterbury 64
Laune, Gideon de 234
Laurens, M. 104
Lauron, Marcellus 20, 110, 158, 202,
    206
Lavery, Sir John 92
Law Courts 22
Lawrence, Sir Thomas 104
Leadenhall 95, 150
Leadenhall Chapel 151
Leadenhall Street 104, 116, 248
Leathersellers' Company 95

Lee and Harper 27
Leech, John 31, 57, 58, 135, *136*, *192*, 198, *207*, 228
Leigh, Roger 95
Lely, Sir Peter 118, 139
Leman, John 15
Levin, Phoebus *144*, 145
Lewis, Frederick Christian *144*, 145, *151*
Lewis, George Robert *151*
Liber de Assisa Panis 108
Lime Street 96
Lincoln Court, Drury Lane 196
Lincoln's Inn Fields 131, 176
Linnell, John 114, *174*, 175
Liotard, Jean Etienne 132
Little Britain 116
Little Tower Hill 124
Lloyd's Register of Shipping 181, 182
Lock, Matthias 114
Loggan, David 18
Logsdail, William 22, *154*, 166, XVII
Londina Illustrata 33, 151
London Bridge 22, 24, 61, 102, 103, 171, 176, 247, III
London Hospital 236
London and Birmingham Railway 178
London Underground XX
Loutherbourg, Philip James de *102*
Lovat, Simon Fraser, 12th Baron 66
Low, David *92*
Ludgate Circus *56*, 61
Ludgate Hill 56

M'Connell, William 60
MacDuff, William *216*, 227
MacGregor, John 227
Madame Tussaud's 30, 167
Maiden Lane 115, 178
Malcolm, Sarah 202, *205*
Mall 80, *81*, *83*, *85*, 131
Malton, Thomas 103, *143*
Manning, George and Maria 206, 207
Mansfield, William Murray, 1st Earl of 70
Mansion House 69, 142
Maple Street 137
Marie de Médicis 16
Marine Society 221
Marks, Barnett Samuel 228
Marlow, William 169
Mary Tudor 13
Mary II 235
Massiot, Gabriel 120, 121
Massys, Quentin 97, 98
Maurer, John 82, 201
May Day *30*
May Fair 26
May, 'Phil' 228, *231*
Mayhew, Henry 59, 125, 135, 164–66, 194–96, 198, 228, 241
McQueen, William 121
Meadows, Kenny 198
Meard Street, Soho 112
Mendelbuch 108
Mendoza, Daniel 174
Mercers' Company 20, 104, 219
Mercers' Hall 104
Merchant Adventurer 96
Merchant Taylors' Company 96, 219
Mercier, Dorothy 116
Mercier, Philip 7–8, 131–33, 161
Merlin, John Joseph 111
Microcosm of London 26, 33, 104, 105, 124, 150, 201, 210, 211, 218, 220, 240
Middlesex Hospital 236
Middlesex Music Hall 52, *53*
Middleton, Sir Hugh 156

Millbank Prison 214, 215
Milton, Thomas 115
Mint 124
Misaubin, Dr Jean 238
Mohammed Ohadu 245
Money Brothers 103
Montagu House 70
Monument 171
Moore, Henry 73, XX
Moorfields 120, 238
Mor, Antonis 99
Morgan, Matt 197
Morland, Henry Robert 7–8, 132, *133*, 161
Morley, Harry 151, *152*
Morning Chronicle 125, 194
Mornington Crescent 178
Mortier, David 80
Mortlake 33
Mortlake Fair 26
Moser, George Michael 112
Mother Needham 129
Mounter, Mrs *136*, 137
Mowbray, John 103
Moxon, Joseph 124
Muller, Johan Sebastian 82
Mulready, Augustus 165, 226
Mulready, William *126*, 127, 172, *174*, 175, 206, *224*, 225, 226, *227*
Munday, Anthony 15
Mytens, Daniel 75

Nash, John 176
National Gallery 31, 245
Nebot, Balthasar 26, 140, *142*, 221
Nevinson, Richard Wynne 61, *63*, 152
New English Art Club 152
New Road (Marylebone Road) 68
Newgate Prison *69*, 70, 202, 204, 207, 210, 211, 212
Newgate Street 149, 150, 217
Newman Street 165
Nicholson, Renton 207
Nicholson, Thomas Henry *50*
Nicholson, William *90*, 166
Nine Elms 145
Nivelon, F. 82
Nixon, John 26, *28*
Nonsuch Palace 155
Norfolk, Charles Howard, 11th Duke of 71
Northampton, Lord William Compton, later 1st Earl of 96
Northcote, James 171
Northumberland, Hugh Smithson, later Percy, 1st Duke of 236

O'Neill, George Bernard 226
Oakley, Octavius *232*, 243
Oates, Titus 65, 66, *67*
Offley, Sir Thomas 96
Ogier, Louisa Perino 112
Ogilby, John 18
Old Bedford Music Hall, Camden Town 52
Old Street, Westminster 227
Olesthorpe, James *209*
Omai 246
Orford, Edward Russell, 1st Earl of 139
Orwell, George 206
Oteswick, John de 95
Overton, Henry 81, 237
Overton, I. 157
Owen, Samuel 148
Oxford Street *63*, 202
Oxford and Cambridge Boat Race 33, *50*, *51*

Paddington Station 59, XV
Page, John 220
Painter-Stainers' Company 97, 109, 118
Pall Mall 86, 116, 127, 186, 227
Pamela 131, 132, 161
Pantheon, Oxford Street 86
Park Village VI
Paternoster Row 20
Patton, S.F. *83*
Peake, Robert 14
Pedlar's Way 152
Peel, Sir Robert 214
Penlez Riots 55
Pentonville 178, 214
Pepys, Samuel 16, 20, 218
Peter Pan 231
Pett, Peter 118
Pett, Phineas 118
Philip II 15, 99
Philips, Charles 235
Phiz *see* Browne, Hablot K.
Piccadilly 30, 54, *93*, 248
Pictorial Times 191, 196
Pinchbeck, Christopher 27
Pine, Robert Edge 236
Pisani, Cclvisi 19, 245
Pitt, Moses 208
Place, Francis 69
Plint, Thomas E. 181
Pool of London 119
Poor Man's Guardian 194
Popish plot 65
Port of London 181
Portal, Abraham 112
Potkyn, John 109
Potter, Israel 166
Primrose Hill 178
Pugin, Augustus Charles 26, 145, 149, *150*, 176, 201, *211*, 222, 223, 240
Punch 31, 57, 58, 72, 125, 135, 136, 192, 193, 241
Punch and Judy 28
Putney 33
Pyle, Richard 21
Pyne, William Henry 149, 164, 172

Ragged School Union 217, 227
Ragged School, Westminster 229
Rahere 25, 240
Ramberg, Johann 33, *52*, *61*, *86*, 88
Ramsden, Jesse 110, 111
Ramsgate 59
Ranelagh Gardens 86
Redgrave, Richard *193*
Regent Canal 178, 179
Regent Street 60
Regent's Park 30
Rejlander, Oscar 228
Reynolds, Sir Joshua 86, 186, 226, 236, 246, 248
Ricci, Marco 81
Rich, Sir William 209
Richard I 12
Richard II 12, 13
Richards, Ceri 152, *153*
Richardson, Jonathan 118
Richardson, Samuel 131
Richmond 33
Rigaud, John Francis 103
Riley, John 127, 241
Ring, Hyde Park 89
Ritz Hotel 92
Roberts, William *52*, *153*
Robinson, George 121, *123*
Rock, Dr Richard 238
Rodwell and Martin 189
Roland, Madame 84
Romney, George 170

Rooker, Edward 82, 176
Rooker, Michael Angelo 121, *122*
Rosamund's Pond 79, 81
Rossetti, Dante Gabriel 61
Rothenstein, William 152, *153*
Rotten Row 88, 89, *90*, 169
Roubaix, Marquis de 76
Rowe, Clifford 73, *183*
Rowlandson, Thomas 12, 26, 33, *69*, 85, 88, 89, *105*, 134, *135*, 145, 146, *147*, 149, *150*, *163*, 164, 201, *211*, 222, 240
Royal Academy of Arts 30, *86*, 192, 235
Royal Artillery 120
Royal Brass Foundry, Woolwich 120, *121*
Royal College of Physicians 233–35, 238, 239
Royal College of Surgeons 176, 235
Royal Exchange *101*, 104, 105, 181
Royal Hospital, Chelsea 241, 242
Royal Laboratory, Woolwich *120*
Royal Military Academy 120
Royal Society 25, 111, 115
Royal Zoological Society Gardens 30, *31*
Rules, King's Bench Prison *211*
Ruskin, John 31, 32
Russell Square 175
Russell, Lord Robert 139
Russia Company 94, 103
Rysbrack, John Michael 221

Sacheverell, Henry Rev. 66
Sadler's Wells 54
St Albans 66
St Andrew Undershaft 96
Saint-Aubin, Gabriel de 84
St Bartholomew's Hospital 233, 238, 239
St Bartholomew's Priory, Smithfield 107
St George the Martyr, Southwark 26, 27
St George's Hospital 236
St George, Bloomsbury 187
St Giles parish 175, 187, 190, 219, 223
St Helen Bishopsgate 95
St James's Palace 19, 70, 83
St James's Park 70, *79*, *81*, 82, 85, 86, 90, 196, 246
St James's Street 186, 209
St John's College, Oxford 96
St John's Wood 151
St Magnus the Martyr 171
St Margaret Street, Westminster 29
St Martin Outwich 95
St Martin's Lane Academy 114
St Martin-in-the-Fields 155, 176
St Mary Magdalen 79
St Mary-le-Bow 21
St Nicholas Shambles 108
St Olave, Southwark 146, III
St Pancras 175, 183
St Paul's Cathedral 20, 31, 56, 61, 78, 104, 107, 181, 182, 189, 217, 219, 220, 231, I
St Paul, Covent Garden 54, 145, 170, II
St Saviour, Southwark III
St Sepulchre, Holborn 211
St Thomas's Hospital 217, 233, 236, 237
Sala, George Augustus 60
Sandby, Paul 70, 120, 121, 127, 134, 159, *160*, 166, *172*, VII
Sandby, Thomas 127
Sanders, John 222, 223

Sandys, Frederick 198
Saussure, Cesar de 82
Sayer, Robert 81
Scarburgh, Charles 234, *235*
Scharf, George 55, *57, 138*, 145, *168*, 176, *177*, 247, *248*, X
Schiavonetti, L. *162*
Schnebbelie, Robert Blemmell 33
Schomberg House 84
Scott, Samuel 118, *119*, 139, 143, 170, 201
Scott, William Bell 181
Selous, Henry Courtney 32
Selve, Georges de, Bishop of Lavour 245
Serre, Puget de la 79
Shaftesbury, Anthony Ashley Cooper, 1st Earl of 65
Shaftesbury, Anthony Ashley Cooper, 7th Earl of 217, 227
Shakespeare, William 25
Shambles 149
Sheepshanks, John *126*, 127
Shelton, William 219
Shepherd, Thomas Hosmer 124, 149
Sheppard, Jack 202, *205*, 215
Shoeblack Brigade 227
Sickert, Walter Richard 33, 52, *53*, 183
Sidall, Richard 116
Skinners' Company 182
Sly, S. *191*
Smirke, Sir Robert 124
Smith, Albert 196
Smith, Fabian 103
Smith, John Raphael *74*, 88
Smith, John Thomas *124*, 159, 165, 166, *188*, 189, 190, 195, 247, 248
Smith, Sydney 225
Smithfield 25, *28*, 64, 149, *150, 151, 153*, 169, *204*, 238
Smollett, Tobias 128
Society for Promoting Christian Knowledge 124
Society for the Propagation of Christian Knowledge 219
Society of Apothecaries 233
Soho 113
Soho Square 164, 176
Somerset House 75
Sophie v. la Roche 111
South Sea House 105
Southampton Court 115
Southill, Bedfordshire 170
Southwark 189
Southwark Fair 26, 33
Spencer, Sir John 96
Spengler, Lorenz 112
Sphere 92
Spitalfields 164

Stadler, J.C. *211*
Stampa, George Loraine 228
Stampe, Jacob 116
Staper, Alderman Richard 95
Steele, Richard 54, 56, 129, 145, 149
Stock Exchange 105
Stocks Market 20, 104, *141*, 142
Stone, Henry 218
Stone, Nicholas 219
Stoop, Dirck *17*, 18
Stow, John 94, 95, 155, 217
Strafford, Thomas Wentworth, 1st Earl of 64, *65*
Strand 54, 172, X
Strawberry Hill 114
Strype, John 26, 142
Stuart, Jack 189
Stubbs, George 128, 169, 170, 172
Sutton, Nichols 143
Sutton, Thomas 219
Swakeleys, Middlesex 112
Swift, Jonathan 149

Tattersall's *151*
Taylor, Jane 116
Taylor, Sir Robert 21
Tempest, Pierce 158
Temple Bar 70
Temple Stairs 24
Teresia, Maria 246
Thake, Joseph 189
Thames 11, 18, 23, 24, 25, 78, 118, 119, 156, 172, 176, 192, 241, III
Thames Street 61
Thistlewood, Arthur 201
Thomas, William Luson 197, 198
Thomson, W. 212
Thornhill, James 139, 142, 202, *205*, 215
Thorp, John Thomas *210*, 211
Threadneedle Street 105
Thurtell, John 206
Tijou, Jean 114
Tillemans, Peter 76, 77, 141
Times (The) 191
Tissot, John James 231, *244*, 248
Tomahawk 197
Tomlinson, Charles 124
Tooke, John Horne 71
Torrington, George, 4th Viscount 170
Tottenham Court Road 68, 121, 125, 176, *177*, 248
Tower Hill 238
Tower of London 11, 16, 31, 78, 102, 124
Townsend, Lord John IX
Trafalgar Square 73
Treasury 105
Trevelyan, Sir Walter 181

Trinity House 104
Tschudi, Burkat 112, *113*
Tuscher, Carl Marcus 112, *113*
Twickenham 172
Tyburn *68*, 202, 204, 205, *206*, 211
Tyers, Jonathan 131
Tyler, Wat 15, 64

Universal Magazine 114, 115

Valles, Jules 134
Van Aken, Joseph *141*, 142, 146
Van Brekelenkam, Quirijn 118
Van Dyck, Sir Anthony 76, 97
Van Leemput, Remigius 139
Van Meer, Michel *16*, 169, 246
Van Tilborch, Gillis 76
Vanbrugh, Sir John 120
Vanderbank, John 236
Vanhaecken, Arnold 146, *147*
Varley, Cornelius 172
Varley, John 172
Vauxhall Gardens 29, *85*, 86, 192
Vecellio, Cesare 100
Veil, Sir Thomas de 209
Venables, Elizabeth 127
Verbruggen, Jan 121
Verbruggen, Pieter *121*
Vernon, John 96
Verrio, Antonio 110, *218*
Victoria, Queen 31, 32, 91
Villette, John 202
Villiers Street X
Vintners' Company 58
Vizetelly, Henry 196
Vulliamy, Benjamin *111*
Vyner, Sir Robert 112

Wale, Samuel 82, 202, *204*, 221, *222*, 228, 237
Walker, Andrew 227
Wallington Hall, Northumberland 181
Walpole, Horace 84, 111, 114
Walton, Henry 7–8, 134, 161–63, 165, V
Walworth, Sir William 15, 64
Wapping 130, 131, 172, 173
War Artists' Advisory Committee 73
Ward, Henrietta 212
Ward, Ned 20
Wardour Street 71
Warwick Lane 239, 240
Watkins, Herbert 214
Watteau, Jean Antoine 84, 112, *113*, 116, 131
Webster, John 14
Webster, Thomas 226

Wellington, Duke of 241
West India Dock Company 104
West, Benjamin 175
West, Rebecca 92
West, Tommy 227
Westminster 219
Westminster Abbey 31, 81
Westminster Bridge 171
Westminster Hall 66, 155, 192, 201, 203
Westminster Hospital 236
Westminster Workhouse 243
Wheatley, Francis 7–8, *70*, 88, 155, *162*, 163, 164, 166, 189, 210, 247
Wheeley, James 116
Whistler, James 33, 148, 153
Whitbread Brewery 169
Whitbread, Samuel I 170
Whitbread, Samuel II 170
White, Robert 156
White, Sir Thomas 96
Whitechapel 196
Whitechapel Art Gallery 73
Whitefriars Glass Factory 121
Whitehall 16, 20, 76, 169, 233
Whitehall Palace 80
Whittington, Richard 233, *234*
Wild, Jonathan 225
Wilhelmina Caroline, Princess of Wales 80
Wilkes, John IX
Wilkie, David 31, 189, 212, *242*
Wilkinson, Robert 151, 166
Willes, Sir John *210*
William III 18, 19, 241
Wills, James 221
Wilson, Richard 139, 221
Wimbourne House 92
Wimbourne, Sir Ivor Churchill Guest, 3rd Baronet and 1st Viscount 92
Windmill Street 116
Woodward, George 134, *135*
Woolwich 118, 119
Worcester, Edward Somerset 4th Earl 14
Wordsworth, William 25
Wormwood Scrubs, Hammersmith 182
Wright, John Michael 112, 201
Wyatt, James 86
Wyck, Jan 24, 80
Wyck, Thomas 80

York, Frederick, Duke of 84

Zoffany, Johan 7–8, 111, *133*, 134, 162, 186, 235, 247, VI